HUMAN SACRIFICE IN ANCIENT GREECE

HUMAN SACRIFICE IN ANCIENT GREECE

Dennis D. Hughes

London and New York

First published 1991
by Routledge
11 New Fetter Lane, London EC4P 4EE

Simultaneously published in the USA and Canada
by Routledge
a division of Routledge, Chapman and Hall, Inc.
29 West 35th Street, New York, NY 10001

Printed in Great Britain by T.J. Press (Padstow) Ltd, Padstow, Cornwall

British Library Cataloguing in Publication Data
Hughes, Dennis D.
Human sacrifice in ancient Greece.
1. Rituals. Human sacrifices, history
I. Title
291.34

Library of Congress Cataloging in Publication Data
Hughes, Dennis D.
Human sacrifice in ancient Greece/Dennis D. Hughes.
p. cm.
Revision of the author's thesis (Ph.D.)—The Ohio State University, 1986.
Includes bibliographical references.
1. Human sacrifice—Greece. 2. Greece—Religion. I. Title.
BL795.H83H84 1991
393—dc20 90–46761

ISBN 0–415–03483–3

For Lisa

Contents

Preface

Three quarters of a century have now passed since the appearance of Friedrich Schwenn's *Die Menschenopfer bei den Griechen und Römern*, which has remained since its publication the standard work on the ritual killing of humans in ancient Greece and Italy. But much has happened in seventy-five years: the majority of the archaeological material was discovered after 1915; several relevant papyri have been published, including a fragment of a commentary on Callimachus which shows that the 'scapegoats' at Abdera were not killed and another which restores the divine recipient of a human sacrifice allegedly performed in Attica to his proper home in Lesbos; and Schwenn overlooked quite a few ancient texts available to him. Also, since 1915 numerous scholarly books and articles have appeared which have a bearing on nearly every aspect of this broad topic. Indeed in recent years there has been quite a renaissance in the study of Greek myth and ritual, on both sides of the Atlantic. An up-to-date, comprehensive study of the evidence has long been overdue.

But just as a comprehensive study is long overdue, so too is it now, I believe, beyond the capabilities of any one individual, unless that person be not only a philologist (with expertise in a wide range of literature, from Homer to the Byzantine period) and historian of Greek religion, but also a physical anthropologist; a social anthropologist, perhaps; an archaeologist certainly (with specialities in Minoan religion and Mycenaean burial customs); and a scholar of the early Greek language preserved in the Linear B script. *Non omnia possumus omnes.* My aims, therefore, have been limited: to collect, organize, and present the evidence in order to make it available to classicists, archaeologists, students of Greek religion, and other interested readers; and then to evaluate, in so far as is possible, the evidence for the ritual killing of human beings in ancient Greece. The emphasis throughout is on the *actuality* of the human sacrifices; accordingly, I have omitted several related topics, such as 'symbolic human sacrifices' (e.g. hair offerings, and figurines sometimes thought to be 'shabtis' substituted for wives or servants in the grave) and human sacrifice as a subject of vase painting. Other topics (e.g. human sacrifice as a dramatic and literary theme) I treat only very briefly. And the bibliography, large as it is, is far from exhaustive.

Chronological limits, for the literary sources, have not proven practical. The earliest text discussed is the *Iliad*, the latest some passages of Johannes Tzetzes (twelfth century), although I mention briefly some even later writers. In fact a good number of the sources are 'late', and although all derive their information from earlier writers, many of these earlier writers are, if not anonymous, undatable; and they themselves most often referred to human sacrifices practised in a still earlier period – the mythical past, I suspect, but in any case a past without even approximate chronological bounds. In fact, for the written evidence, only in a few cases do dates enter into the discussion at all.

The archaeological evidence, on the other hand, is (with reasonable accuracy) datable. But here I have largely allowed the importance of existing finds to govern my chronological limits. With a few minor exceptions I discuss nothing earlier than the Middle Bronze Age; for Cyprus, I begin with the period after the Greek presence had been firmly established on the island. I include finds from Minoan Crete, not only because of the importance (and notoriety) of two discoveries recently made there, but also because of the interaction between the Minoan and Mycenaean cultures and the documented survival of elements of their religions after the close of the Bronze Age. As a rule I discuss only archaeological finds which have been thought by the excavators themselves to represent ritual killings, although I describe some mass burials and cases of altered human bones in an appendix (A), if only to emphasize the difficulty of recovering the circumstances which lie behind the unusual disposition of human skeletal remains. Also relegated to an appendix (B) is a Linear B inscription, thought by some scholars to record an offering of human sacrifices: I find this interpretation improbable, but no conclusive interpretation of the tablet will be possible so long as much of the text cannot be read with certainty or anything approaching consensus among specialists.

My discussion of the archaeological material is subject to another, more serious limitation. I am perhaps going out on a limb in discussing this evidence at all, for my acquaintance with the material is only secondhand, through the publications of the excavators. Several of the finds have appeared only in preliminary reports, and even some of the final publications are very brief. I have attempted to be fair and accurate in my descriptions, and where I raise doubts about the excavators' interpretations I hope to have based my arguments closely on their publications, which I encourage readers to consult. Of course only the excavators (and others with firsthand access to the finds) have the knowledge necessary to come to fully informed conclusions, but these conclusions are not necessarily infallible as a consequence. Indeed it is in the belief that these 'human sacrifices' should not pass unquestioned into scholarly literature as fact – a process which seems already to have begun – that I have stuck out my neck (to use a more appropriate metaphor) and pointed to what I consider uncertainties or weaknesses in the excavators' arguments.

Some smaller points. Translations of Greek and Latin texts are my own. For the sake of convenience (and because the value of the information does not depend upon the identities of the authors) I refer to both the shorter and longer Servian commentaries simply as 'Servius'. For the spellings of most Greek personal names I use traditional English forms, i.e. for the most part those derived through Latin. But for some place names, for the names of festivals and rites, and for divine epithets I employ spellings closer to the Greek: Knossos, not Cno(s)sus (or Gno(s)sus), and Zeus Lykaios, not Lycaeus (so also for a few personal names: Istros, not Ister; Aias, not Ajax; Aineias, not Aeneas). The result is a certain amount of inconsistency (and occasional unhappy combinations such as Dionysus Aigobolos), but inconsistency is in almost any system unavoidable. A more significant matter is that where English translations of non-English books and articles are available, I cite the page numbers of the translations only. I realize that this will cause no little inconvenience for readers on the continent, who cannot be expected to possess English translations in their libraries; nor are the translations always of the highest quality. But for the sake of consistency, economy, and my own convenience I refer to such works in their English versions only.

This book began life as a doctoral dissertation ('Human Sacrifice in Ancient Greece: the Literary and Archaeological Evidence', The Ohio State University, 1986), written under the direction of Stephen V. Tracy, who has been a teacher, friend, and much needed gadfly, now for many years. My research was supported initially by a Presidential Fellowship from Ohio State, and carried out largely while I was an associate member of the American School of Classical Studies at Athens, where I benefited from conversations with numerous members of the School and the scholarly community in Athens, too many to acknowledge individually here. During the final year of writing of my thesis (and again on several occasions more recently), through the permission of B. M. W. Knox and Zeph Stewart I used the admirable library of the Center for Hellenic Studies in Washington, DC. And the thesis could not have been completed without the financial and moral support of my mother, Dr Josephine N. Hughes, and my godfather, R. P. Holubowicz, and I take this opportunity to thank them both again. In 1988–90 my revisions and additional research have been generously supported by Grinnell College. The librarian of the college, Christopher McKee, and the staff of Burling Library were also very helpful; and preparation of the script on computer would not have been possible without the expert assistance of Angie Johnson. I also thank K. Dowden, J. Bremmer, and W. Rösler for sending me as yet unpublished material. Finally, I owe particular thanks to those who have read my manuscript at various stages: S. V. Tracy, J. W. Allison, P. W. Sciulli, and the late J. W. Vaughn; and, more recently, J. Bremmer, R. Parker, R. Stoneman, E. Mease, and L. Hughes. All had helpful comments, criticisms, and suggestions, and this is certainly a better book because of them. But of course for all faults, errors, and omissions I am alone responsible:

Sunt bona, sunt quaedam mediocria, sunt mala plura
quae legis hic: aliter non fit . . . liber.

Grinnell, Iowa
May 1990

Abbreviations

Abbreviations of the names of ancient authors and works are largely from N. G. L. Hammond and H. H. Scullard (eds), *The Oxford Classical Dictionary* (2nd edn: Oxford, 1970), ix–xxii, but in a few cases, these failing, I have used *LSJ*, xvi–xli, and P. G. W. Glare (ed.), *Oxford Latin Dictionary* (Oxford, 1982), ix–xxi. Modern editions of ancient texts, cited by the editor's name only, are listed under this name in the Bibliography.

AR	(*Journal of Hellenic Studies*) *Archaeological Reports*.
BCH	*Bulletin de correspondance hellénique*.
Cook, *Zeus*	Cook, A. B., *Zeus. A Study in Ancient Religion*, 3 vols in 5, Cambridge, 1914–40.
Ergon	*Τὸ Ἔργον τῆς Ἀρχαιολογικῆς Ἑταιρείας*.
Farnell, *CGS*	Farnell, L. R., *The Cults of the Greek States*, 5 vols, Oxford, 1896–1909.
FGrHist	Jacoby, F. (ed.), *Die Fragmente der griechischen Historiker*, 3 parts, Berlin and Leipzig, 1923–58.
FHG	Müller, K. (ed.), *Fragmenta Historicorum Graecorum*, 5 vols, Paris, 1841–70.
IG	*Inscriptiones Graecae*, Berlin, 1873– .
LSJ	Liddell, H. G., Scott, R., and Jones, H. S., *A Greek–English Lexicon*, 9th edn: Oxford, 1940.
LSJ Suppl.	Barber, E. A., *Greek–English Lexicon. A Supplement*, Oxford, 1968.
Nilsson, *GGR*	Nilsson, M. P., *Geschichte der griechischen*

	Religion, 2 vols, Handbuch der Altertumswissenschaft 5.2, 3rd edn: Munich, 1967–74.
Parke-Wormell	Parke, H. W., and Wormell, D. E. W., *The Delphic Oracle*, 2 vols, Oxford, 1956.
POxy.	*The Oxyrhynchus Papyri*, London, 1898– .
SCE 1–3	Gjerstad, E., Lindros, J., Sjoqvist, E., and Westholm, A., *The Swedish Cyprus Expedition. Finds and Results of the Excavations in Cyprus 1927–1931*, 3 vols, Stockholm, 1934–7.
SCE 4.2	Gjerstad, E., *The Swedish Cyprus Expedition*, vol. 4, part 2, *The Cypro-Geometric, Cypro-Archaic and Cypro-Classical Periods*, Stockholm, 1948.

1

Sacrifice and ritual killing: terminology and types

'Human sacrifice in ancient Greece' does not accurately describe the scope of the material covered in this study, which includes a variety of ritual killings, not all of which are properly termed 'human sacrifices'. I have chosen (and retained) the present title, not only because 'The ritual killing of human beings in ancient Greece' would be a rather inelegant title, but also because its terminology possibly would be unfamiliar to many readers, while 'human sacrifice' is a term commonly used and understood by everyone. But it is the validity of this common use and broad application of the term which is questionable, and in this study I shall follow, with some modification, a distinction, frequently drawn by specialists in ancient religion, between ritual killing of humans (or ritual murder) and human sacrifice. According to this distinction, which 'goes well beyond the purely terminological plane',[1] human sacrifices form a subset of 'ritual killings of humans', but not all ritual killings are properly called 'human sacrifices'. In this brief introductory chapter I shall discuss this and other distinctions of terminology and outline the various types of ritual killings to be treated in the chapters which follow.

A ritual act, in the words of Walter Burkert, is an 'action redirected for demonstration', a 'spontaneous reaction artificially exaggerated for purposes of demonstration'; or, in a fuller definition by the same scholar, ritual is 'a programme of demonstrative acts to be performed in a set sequence and often at a set place and time'.[2] The chief characteristics of ritual, therefore, are its demonstrative or communicative function, exaggeration and repetition for demonstrative effect, and the adherence to an unvarying, prescribed set of actions. Burkert's definition of ritual, however, serves only to describe the *form* assumed by countless kinds of human behaviour, and in any given case it remains for the religious historian or anthropologist to identify and elucidate the underlying behaviour (i.e. the unritualized behaviour upon which the ritual act is modelled) and its causes, the thing which is communicated by the ritual act, and its social function: for ritual action is always social action, even if directed only towards a limited social group; and generally rituals may be seen to perform a stabilizing and integrating function in society, defining roles within the group and promoting group solidarity.[3] The beliefs of the participants (in the case of ancient religion, most frequently in the form of myths associated with rituals) must also be taken into account, although in many cases the expressed purpose of a ritual may conceal rather than elucidate its fundamental nature.

Burkert's conception of ritual action is grounded in biological studies of animal behaviour, for demonstrative behaviour of the sort we term ritual can be observed even in animals. Under Burkert's definition, the term 'ritual' embraces basic communicative acts such as laughter and gestures (waving, clapping, handshakes) up to the complex religious performances normally associated with the word. And, if I understand him correctly, for Burkert all ritual action is grounded in very basic and originally instinctive or pragmatic behaviour (often of an aggressive character), which has been redirected or rechannelled for communicative function. Thus it is action which is primary, and ideas and belief are always secondary and play no significant role in the generation of ritual.[4] And I would agree that many if not most ritual actions may be explained as demonstrative forms of basic human responses. Funeral customs provide several good examples, such as weeping and lamentation, natural responses of grief but which in many cultures become formal, stylized, and obligatory elements of a public funeral, indeed sometimes placed in the charge of professional keeners.[5] But I am not convinced that all 'demonstrative acts performed in a set sequence and at a set place and time' can be traced to, or reduced to, such basic spontaneous reactions. To be sure, in many cases the expressed beliefs of the participants do not adequately account for the ritual behaviour, and the meaning and function of the rites must be sought elsewhere. But in some cases it would seem that rituals owe their existence to certain basic beliefs, such as belief in superhuman beings or in life after death. Some funerary customs, e.g. the provision of the dead with food, possessions, and pets, seem best explained as originating in a belief in the continuation of human needs beyond death, although one may in turn derive belief in an afterlife from our inability to face the reality of death.[6] The question of the role of belief in the origin and development of ritual also touches on the vexed question of the relationship between ritual and myth. Most often Greek myths directly associated with rituals were invented (or pre-existing myths adopted) to account for the origin of the rituals: they are 'aetiological myths', which ground ritual action in significant events set in the mythical past. Rituals in turn were viewed as imitations or commemorations of mythical events, which raises the possibility that in some cases ritual actions were in fact conscious re-enactments of myth. More complex interplay – where ritual re-enacts myths which themselves are patterned on earlier ritual – is also possible. But both in specific cases and in general the relationship between ritual action and myth remains a matter of some controversy.[7]

The formal definition of rituals as demonstrative acts performed in a prescribed manner and on set occasions is unaffected by questions of the role of belief in their formation and continuation; and, the question of meaning aside, in most cases it is easy enough to tell the difference between ritual and everyday, pragmatic, non-ritual activity. Thus a ritual killing (whether of an animal or a human victim) is a killing performed in a particular situation or on a particular occasion (a religious ceremony, a funeral, before battle, etc.) in a prescribed, stereotyped manner, with a communicative function of some kind. Ritual killings of human beings are to be clearly distinguished from non-ritual killings, such as murder and killing in battle. Other kinds of killing, e.g. vengeance killing and execution, may or may not be ritual acts; both often involve some ritual elements.[8]

But not every ritual killing is a sacrifice. Religious historians often draw a distinction 'between properly called human sacrifices – those offered to some superhuman recipient – and other rites which may require the killing of human beings without belonging to the cult of superhuman beings'.[9] While I acknowledge the utility of this distinction (and its validity from a phenomenological point of view), nevertheless I shall, in this respect deferring to common usage, extend my use of the word 'sacrifice' to include not only offerings made to gods and heroes but also certain types of ritual killing performed at funerals, during oaths and purification rites, and before battle. For not all animals ritually slain by the Greeks were offered to superhuman recipients, and it is common practice to refer (whether properly or no) to all forms of ritual killing of *animals* as 'sacrifices', but usually with qualifications such as 'funerary sacrifices', 'sacrifices before battle', 'oath sacrifices', etc. And this brings us to another, equally important distinction, which to a great degree mirrors the conceptions and usage of the Greeks. The slaying of human beings in the same circumstances, in the same manner, and with the same ritual purposes as the customary slaying of animals, I designate as 'human sacrifice'. In terms of vocabulary, human sacrifices are those ritual killings for which the Greeks employ words usually reserved for the sacred slaughter of animals, chiefly *thuein*, *sphazein*, and their compounds. That such words would convey to the Greek ear a sense 'to kill ritually like an animal' is indicated by similes used by Aeschylus and Euripides of the sacrifice of Iphigeneia, who is hoisted above the altar 'like a she-goat' (Aesch. *Ag.* 232) and sacrificed 'like a calf' (Eur. *IT* 359), and by Hecuba's impassioned response to the proposed sacrifice of her daughter (Eur. *Hec.* 260–1), when she asks Odysseus what has compelled the Greeks to perform a human sacrifice (ἀνθρωποσφάγειν) on Achilles' grave, where rather it is proper to sacrifice cattle (βουθυτεῖν).

The following are the chief categories of ritual killing of animals in Greek custom, together with some of the terms frequently associated with them:[10] (1) the 'Olympian sacrifice' (θυσία, θύειν) – after elaborate preliminaries, the victim was slaughtered, and its bones (particularly the pelvis with the tail), gall bladder, and fat were burned on the altar as an offering to the gods, but the remainder of the animal was consumed by the worshippers; one thinks first and foremost of large public sacrifices offered in the major festivals of the Greek cities, but *thusiai* were also performed on lesser occasions such as family sacrifices to Zeus Ktesios, weddings, and the introduction of children, ephebes, and brides to the phratry; the Classical *thusia* closely resembles the earlier Homeric sacrifice (ῥέζειν, ἔρδειν, ἱερεύειν, σφάζειν), where the thighbones wrapped in fat, together with small pieces of flesh taken from the whole animal, were burned for the god;[11] (2) sacrifices offered to heroes (ἐναγίζειν, ἐναγισμοί, ἐναγίσματα; ἐντέμνειν) – the victims were not consumed, but deposited in *bothroi* or burned entire (ὁλοκαυτεῖν); (3) offerings to the dead, 'funerary sacrifices' (again ἐναγίζειν, but also frequently σφάζειν and its compounds), where the victims were burned whole or abandoned at the grave;[12] (4) unconsumed and wholly burnt offerings (ὁλοκαυτώματα) performed in the cult of deities, chiefly chthonic deities;[13] (5) sacrifices performed before battle or before crossing rivers or other frontiers on the march (σφάγια, σφαγιάζεσθαι) – the victims slain before an encounter were not eaten, nor were they as a rule offered to a specific deity;[14] (6) oath sacrifices (τόμια; ὅρκιον/ὅρκια τέμνειν), where the participants swore an oath around a slain (and apparently dismembered) animal, often holding or standing on the entrails, or dipping the hands in the blood – the remains were not consumed but disposed of;[15] in addition (7) animals were employed for various purification ceremonies (καθαρμοί), e.g. at Athens, where a pig was slain and then dragged around the Pnyx, and in Boeotia, where the people were purified by passing between the halves of a severed dog.[16] It should also be noted that in 'Olympian' and military sacrifices the slaughtered animals were employed for divination, and that vegetable offerings ('sacrifices' of fruits, grain, etc.) were frequently offered to the gods, heroes, and the dead: several of the same terms (particularly *thuein*) are used for these offerings as for blood sacrifices, and some ancient writers saw a historical relationship between the two.[17]

In the above categorization – admittedly a simplification of a complicated and imperfectly known picture – I distinguish between types of animal sacrifice largely on the basis of the occasion of killing and what was done with the animals after they were slain. The method of killing was usually cutting the throat (although larger animals were first felled by an axe-blow),[18] but the procedures surrounding the slaughter could differ markedly between the various types, as, of course, from location to location and from cult to cult. The distinctions are also mirrored in the sacrificial vocabulary. Discussions of ancient sacrifice have often been marred by a failure to take into account these significant differences in occasion, treatment of the slaughtered victim, and vocabulary; and the use of the word 'sacrifice' for all forms of ritual animal slaughter, while convenient, tends to obscure these differences. And although the use of various sacrificial terms was not always consistent and although it would be hazardous to draw far-reaching conclusions on the basis of vocabulary alone, the distinctions reflected in the language cannot be ignored in any theoretical approach to Greek sacrifice and its origins, even if some or all of these distinctions will eventually break down under the weight of a general theory.[19]

Among the various kinds of blood sacrifice, the most important distinction is between sacrifices where the victims were consumed by the worshippers (1 above), and 'destructive' sacrifices where the victims were not eaten but burned entire or simply slaughtered and abandoned (2–7). This fundamental distinction was the starting point of Karl Meuli's theory of the origin of Greek sacrifice, set out in his important and influential essay 'Griechische Opferbräuche'.[20] In the Olympian sacrifice the worshippers consumed most of the victim, offering to the gods only the bones and other inedible parts, an anomaly which aroused the puzzlement, indignation, or laughter of the ancients themselves.[21] Another curious feature was the need to obtain the victim's 'assent' for the sacrifice; and in some rituals, such as the Athenian Bouphonia, the participants absolved themselves from responsibility for the killing by fixing the blame on one individual or even on the sacrificial instrument.[22] Meuli dubbed such evasive procedures 'Unschuldskomödie', 'comedy of innocence', and he derived the 'Olympian' sacrifice from practices of Paleolithic hunters (paralleled also in the customs of some modern hunting cultures, known from ethnography), who, wishing to avoid responsibility for the killing and fearing that the animal species might cease to offer itself as prey, would reconstruct animals killed in the hunt from their bones. The special treatment of the bones and other remains of slain animals was taken over and maintained by Neolithic herdsmen, and the practice gradually evolved into the sacrifice of Archaic and Classical Greece, where the practice of 'reconstructing' the slain prey from the bones was now (and long had been) construed as an offering to the gods.

Meuli's theory marks a great improvement over many earlier theories of the origin of sacrifice, in that he took into account and attempted to explain a number of puzzling features of Greek sacrificial practice and in that he derived these features from amply documented practices of hunting cultures, rather than simply assigning the origin of sacrifice to a remote and undefined period in the past. Meuli's theory is open to question on a number of fronts: not all the alleged cases of 'reconstructed' animals from the Paleolithic period have been accepted, and the continuity of practice from the Paleolithic through the Neolithic period into the Bronze Age and Archaic Greece of course cannot be demonstrated; and there have been other criticisms.[23] Nevertheless, Meuli successfully showed that the Greeks shared with hunting cultures the anxiety and fear aroused by the killing of animals, and even if the Homeric and Classical sacrifice did not derive ultimately from Paleolithic hunting practices, it is fair to speak of a parallel phenomenon, for many notable features of the Greek ritual seem to be concerned more with reverence for the animal victim and awe before the act of slaughter than with offering a suitable gift to the gods (cf. Pl. *Euthphr.* 14C: τὸ θύειν δωρεῖσθαί ἐστι τοῖς θεοῖς). Also, Meuli's theory is grounded in a basic and continuous human need, the need for food, and the implication for our study is that, if the Olympian sacrifice derived from man's use of wild and then domestic animals for sustenance, human sacrifice played little or no role in its origin or evolution.

Meuli was concerned primarily with sacrifices of the Olympian type, and his summary treatment of other forms of sacrifice was in my opinion less successful. Especially relevant to this study are funerary sacrifices, which Meuli derived from man's violent and destructive impulses in the face of death, which are given ritual expression at the funeral. The killing of animal and human victims, the destruction of property, and various mourning customs such as the tearing of hair and the scratching of cheeks should all be attributed to grief and its concomitant aggressive, destructive urges. In Meuli's opinion customs of supplying the dead with concubines and servitors also originated in the destructive rage of the mourner, and the belief that these women and servants were meant to give pleasure and minister to the deceased he discounted as secondary reinterpretation.[24] Although the origin of funerary sacrifices – the killing and abandoning of animal victims at the grave – remains obscure, in my opinion the practice cannot easily be connected with customs of killing servants to serve their masters after death or with the practice of killing wives at the funerals of their husbands, for both of these customs would seem to be grounded in beliefs in the continuation of life after death. Also, such practices, documented for many peoples both in literary sources and by archaeological finds, seem to have been largely confined to the funerals of royal or wealthy persons, and thus I am not certain that they can be attributed to general human impulses. Belief in an afterlife, cultural factors such as the status of women and servants and slaves, and wealth and the exercise of power by individuals or a class of individuals will all have played a large if not determinative role in the origin of these funerary customs.[25]

There are several circumstances in which human beings might be ritually slain where it was not common, or even conceivable, to kill animals: the slaying or suicide of wives or concubines on their husbands' graves ('suttee'); the killing of slaves to accompany or serve their masters after death; and vengeance killing or execution carried out during funerals. Indeed there are many possible occasions for the ritual slaying of human victims, and it would be erroneous and misleading to group all forms of ritual killing of humans together under the term 'human sacrifice'.

Herodotus took a keen interest in sacrificial practices and collected many unusual customs of both Greek and non-Greek peoples, including a great variety of ritual killings; his choice of vocabulary is often instructive. In a frequently cited passage (2.44.5) he distinguishes between 'Olympian' sacrifices and hero-sacrifices, writing that, in view of Heracles' divinity, the best course is followed by those who both sacrifice (θύουσι) to him as an immortal and offer hero-sacrifices to him as a hero (ὡς ἥρωι ἐναγίζουσι), although the distinction is not always observed by later writers or even by Herodotus himself.[26] For human sacrifices Herodotus most often employs the general term *thuein*. The Tauri sacrifice shipwrecked sailors to 'the Virgin' and impale the heads on stakes before her temple (4.103.1–2). The Scythians, in an elaborate and gruesome ceremony, sacrifice one of every 100 prisoners of war to Ares (4.62.3–4).[27] The Massegetae kill their elderly along with animal victims, and the flesh is boiled and consumed by relatives (1.216.2–3). And among the Greeks themselves, the eldest son of the family descended from Athamas is sacrificed after an elaborate series of ritual trials (7.197). Occasionally Herodotus employs other sacrificial terms: while in Egypt Menelaus made 'blood victims' of two Egyptian children (ἔντομά σφεα ἐποίησε)[28] to obtain favourable winds (2.119.3), and the Persians slaughtered a Greek sailor over the ship's prow during a skirmish off Skiathos (7.180: ἔσφαξαν and σφαγιασθέντι).

On the other hand, Herodotus describes several ritual killings which he does not appear to have regarded as 'sacrificial', i.e. as equivalent or comparable to Greek animal sacrifices. The Egyptians, he asserts, practise no human sacrifice whatsoever (2.45.1–2), but at Papremis they perform a ritual during which a group of men armed with clubs attempts to wheel an image of 'Ares' (Set) into the temple, while another armed band opposes them; and many men, Herodotus asserts, are killed in the conflict, although the Egyptians themselves deny this (2.63.3). If men were in fact killed during the ceremony, we would certainly call this a ritual killing of some kind (or at least a ritual combat resulting in death), but not a 'sacrifice'. Every five years the Getae perform a bizarre rite in which a man is sent as a messenger to the god Salmoxis: the messenger, entrusted with a communication to the god, is tossed onto upturned spears; but in his detailed account Herodotus does not characterize the practice as a 'sacrifice' (4.94.2–3). And the Scythians strangle a concubine and several servants of a deceased king and bury them with him, and after a year's time another fifty servants are strangled, impaled on stakes, and placed upon dead horses around the tomb (4.71.4–72).

In another passage where Herodotus describes a case of 'suttee' he will use, it is true, a 'sacrificial' term, *sphazein*: among a certain Thracian tribe the wives of a dead chieftain vie for the honour of being buried with their lord, and the one selected is slain (σφάζεται) over the grave by her closest relatives (5.5). But the primary sense of *sphazein* is 'to kill by cutting the throat'; the word and its compounds are most often found in sacrificial contexts (so always in Homer), but by the fifth century the term could also be applied to particularly brutal but non-sacrificial killings of human beings, much as our 'butcher'.[29] At Hdt. 5.5 the word may simply indicate the method of killing, without any sacrificial connotations: the Thracians cut the woman's throat, while the Scythians kill their king's concubines and servants by strangling them (ἀποπνίξαντες: 4.71.4). So at Hdt. 5.25 the participles σφάξας and ἀποκτείνας are parallel and refer to the same (evidently non-sacrificial) act. Of course in any given case the method of killing will have a lot to do with the choice of vocabulary, but the method of killing is important in itself and, like other elements of ritual, fixed and invariable. It was a Persian custom, for example, to bury people alive: when the Persian army crosses the Strymon River at a place called 'Nine Ways', they bury nine boys and nine girls alive, and Xerxes' aging wife Amestris buries fourteen boys alive in the hope that the

Underworld god will accept this gift instead of herself (7.114.1–2). We might be inclined to view these acts as 'sacrificial', but in both cases the historian simply uses the verb 'to bury' (*katorussein*), perhaps avoiding sacrificial terms because the custom is so unlike any practice of the Greeks. And even where Herodotus employs sacrificial terminology he will take pains to describe the procedure when it differs markedly from Greek practice, such as Scythian animal sacrifices, where the victim is strangled in a noose and boiled rather than roasted (4.60–1). Interestingly, he also notes that the Scythians do not sacrifice their human victims in the same manner as their animals (4.62.3), an observation which seems to imply an expectation that similar procedures would be followed in both human and animal sacrifices.

Just as there are special, technical words for the various types of sacred slaughter of animals, so also are there terms used of the non-sacrificial killing of human beings, whether we ourselves would view these killings as 'ritual killings' or not. Again Herodotus' usage is instructive. At 9.119.1, he reports that the Apsinthian Thracians sacrificed (ἔθυσαν) Oeobazus, while his companions 'they killed in another way' (ἄλλῳ τρόπῳ ἐφόνευσαν), thus clearly distinguishing between sacrificial and non-sacrificial (and apparently non-ritual) killing. Similarly, at 3.99 he writes that if any man among the Padaei falls sick, his companions kill him (κτείνουσι), and having killed him feast on him (ἀποκτείναντες κατευωχέονται). The women do the same with their ailing friends; but those rare persons who survive to old age they sacrifice and feast on (θύσαντες κατευωχέονται). The contrast seems deliberate. Among the words seldom or never applied to the sacrificial slaying of animals are: *phoneuein* ('murder'),[30] *apokteinein* and *anairein* ('kill'), and *thanatoun* ('put to death, execute'), as, of course, specific words for types of execution (e.g. *anaskolopizein* and *apotumpanizein*) or for stoning to death (*kataleuein*). There are also several words for 'kill' which are neutral and used both of the sacred slaughter of animals and of non-sacrificial killings of humans, such as *pephnein*, *apokteinein*, *kteinein*, and *katakteinein* in Homer. Nevertheless, the choice of words is often a significant indicator of a speaker's conception of a killing, and the Greek vocabulary, much richer in this area (as in others) than our own, reflects a complex cultural attitude towards the taking of life, both human and animal.

This chapter has hardly been meant as a contribution to the

theory of sacrifice, but merely as an introduction for the benefit of readers unfamiliar with Greek sacrificial terms and practices, and as a justification of my occasional use of the Greek vocabulary to differentiate between various kinds of killing (especially between sacrificial and non-sacrificial killing) and of my division of a diverse body of material into chapters and sections. Under the heading 'Funerary ritual killing' (chapter 3) I group together several distinct types of ritual killing: the killing of servants at their masters' funerals, 'suttee', vengeance killing or execution carried out at the graves of murdered men, and 'funerary sacrifices' (the last represented certainly in Greek literature, of a human victim, only by the sacrifice of Polyxena). In the chapter on human sacrifices proper (chapter 4), few distinctions can be made among the various killings. Sacrifices before battle form a separate category (pp. 107–15); only rarely are people said to be slain for use in purification rites;[31] and there is only one case where a human victim is used in what appears to be an oath sacrifice (p. 136). In a few instances human sacrifices are offered in the cult of heroes, and in two cases (in the cults of Artemis and Diomedes: pp. 121–2 and 125–7) it is specified that the victim was burned in a holocaust. In myths and the historical sources *thuein* and related words are often used to describe human sacrifices. But while in most cases the sacrifices are offered to Olympian gods, it is usually assumed that human sacrifices did not as a rule involve consumption (cf. Aesch. *Ag.* 150, where Iphigeneia's sacrifice is a sacrifice 'not to be eaten', and Porph. *Abst.* 2.53.3). Only in the case of sacrifices in the cult of Zeus Lykaios (pp. 96–107) is it specified that the victims were eaten, although this was certainly thought (as it has been thought by some modern scholars) for some human sacrifices reported for the cult of Dionysus. But in most cases few details are given, and the question of consumption is not addressed by ancient writers; and for us the question becomes largely moot if the alleged human sacrifices are not historical.

To *pharmakos* rituals I devote a separate chapter (5). Scholars frequently refer to these rituals as 'human sacrifices', but among the ancient writers who claim that pharmakoi were killed, only the very latest (twelfth century and later) use *thuein* of the killing. The ritual was a purification ceremony and thus at least loosely related to purifications employing animal victims (and there is naturally some shared vocabulary). But again, the question of the relationship between these rites and *katharmoi* involving animals becomes largely superfluous if, as I shall argue, the pharmakoi were not killed. Similarly, I treat the 'Locrian maiden tribute' in a separate chapter (6): the maidens were pursued by the men of Ilion and reportedly killed if captured; but the ritual bears little similarity to sacrificial rites, despite characterizations of the ritual as a *sacrificium* or *thusia* by late authors and despite some modern 'sacrificial' interpretations.

I begin now with the archaeological evidence. The two recent discoveries from Crete represent, in the opinions of the excavators, human sacrifices performed in the cult of deities (the latter also involving consumption of the victims). But the great majority of the evidence, however it is to be interpreted, comes from funerary contexts.

2

Archaeological evidence

MINOAN CRETE

Anemospilia

In 1979 a Middle Minoan (II/IIIA) site at Anemospilia, located on the lower northern slopes of Mt Juktas and about 3 km N–NW of Archanes, was excavated under the direction of Y. Sakellarakis and E. Sapouna-Sakellaraki.[1] The excavation is of great significance not only for the unique architectural plan of the building and for the richness of the finds, but also because four human skeletons – said to be the first discovered in Minoan Crete outside of a burial context[2] – were found in the building. Three of the skeletons apparently were the remains of persons who perished when the building collapsed or in the subsequent fire. But the unusual position of the fourth skeleton has led the excavators to suggest that it belonged to a young man who was sacrificed just moments before the destruction of the building.

The building, surrounded by a peribolos and identified by the excavators as a temple or shrine, appears to have been destroyed by the same earthquake which brought an end to the first palaces in around 1700 BC. The excavated structure consists of three narrow, non-connecting chambers (the east, central, and west rooms) which open to the north onto a corridor or 'prothalamos'. Across the corridor to the north are three doorways corresponding to the three entrances to the rooms, and there is a fourth, wider entrance at the east end of the hall.[3] On the surface layer above the corridor was found part of a large pair of horns of consecration, one of the surface finds which led to the recognition that an important Minoan site lay beneath. The corridor contained a large amount of pottery, both on the floor and in the destruction layer – at least 155 pots, probably many more, with the greatest concentration in the west part of the hall. Before the door to the central room was found the first of the four skeletons, badly burned and poorly preserved, with the head to the north and lower limbs near the door of the central room. In this doorway were found most of the fragments of a bucket-shaped vase decorated with a relief of a bull, and other fragments were found in the hallway, near and among the bones of the skeleton. Because of its decoration and because of its similarity in shape to a vessel pictured in the sacrificial scene on the Agia Triada sarcophagus, the excavators have concluded that the vase had served to collect the blood of sacrificed bulls.[4]

The east room also contained a large amount of pottery, the majority of which had stood originally on a stone stepped bench which runs along the back (south) wall of the room. Among the finds in the central room were nine storage jars, seven of which stood along the east wall, but also a number of smaller vessels. Also found in the central room were two life-size clay feet, which in the excavators' opinion had supported a wooden cult statue.[5] The west room contained little pottery, either in the destruction layer or on the floor, when compared with the other rooms of the building. In the north part of the room near the doorway was a low platform made of loose medium-size stones joined with clay cement, measuring 0.63 by 0.76 metres. The platform was oriented N–S (with the long side on the N–S axis), but with a distinct deviation from the axis of the building. Three skeletons were found in the west room. In the southwest corner was the skeleton of a woman, *c.* 28 years old, 1.54 m tall, lying face down with legs apart and the hands near the face. The skeleton had suffered severe fractures, apparently from the fall of debris during the destruction. A second skeleton, found lying on its back parallel to the west wall of the room, belonged to a male of about 38 years, 1.78 m in height. The right leg was straight, the left bent at a right angle at the knee. The arms were bent with the hands at the level of the sternum. On the little finger of the left hand was a silver and iron ring, and on his left wrist the man had worn an agate seal with a representation of a man rowing a boat, the prow having the form of a bird's head which looks backwards towards the human figure.[6] The third skeleton found in the west room lay on its right side on top of the stone platform in the north part of the room. The skeleton was of a young man of about 18 years, 1.65 m in height. The hands were at chest level; the left leg was bent backwards so that the heel nearly touched the thigh.[7] It is also reported that the bones of the lower (right) side of the skeleton were blackened, while the bones of the upper (left) side were white, a difference in coloration attributed to the absence of blood in the left half of the body at the time of burning. Resting on the skeleton at the abdominal region was a large bronze blade, 0.40 m long and weighing 633 grams, decorated with an incised representation of a fabulous boarlike beast.[8]

The excavators of these remarkable finds have suggested that the skeleton which lay upon the 'altarlike construction' belonged to a victim of human sacrifice and that the woman and the man – possibly a priest – whose skeletons were also found in the west room had performed the sacrifice, the purpose of which had been to avert the impending earthquake which was soon to destroy the building. The instrument of the sacrifice was the bronze blade which was found lying on the young man's skeleton.[9] This interpretation depends largely on the following factors: (1) the identification of the excavated structure as a temple (*naos*); (2) the identification of the low platform in the west room as an altar; (3) the identification of the bronze blade as a sacrificial knife and the significance of its location on top of the 'victim's' body; (4) the significance of the position of the young man's skeleton (on the platform, with one leg bent sharply back); and (5) the significance of the difference in coloration (and degree of burning) between the upper and lower sides of the skeleton.

That the building served some function connected with cult is indicated by a number of the finds: rhytons, portable altars or offering tables, the bull vase, the horns of consecration, and possibly the clay feet.[10] But that the building should be called a 'temple' or 'shrine' is less certain, as the excavated structure has (so far as I am aware) no exact architectural parallel, and as it is clear that there was more to the building than has been excavated.[11] In any case, it does not seem likely that the west room was normally used for bull sacrifices, as the excavators suggest, for it is difficult to imagine a bull being persuaded to negotiate the narrow corridor (containing at least 155 pots, with especial concentration at the west end!) and then to pass through what appears to be a very narrow doorway into the west room.[12]

Both common sense and the available iconographic evidence point to the conclusion that 'das Stieropfer hat wahrscheinlich unter freiem Himmel stattgefunden'.[13] It is also highly uncertain if the very low platform of irregular stones should be termed an 'altarlike structure', much less an 'altar'.[14] Although various fixed stone structures have been identified as sacrificial altars, our most secure evidence comes from artistic representations, which show that the altars employed for the sacrifice of large animals were large movable platforms supported by legs. And as no such altar has survived it has been concluded that Minoan sacrificial altars were made of wood.[15]

The location of the bronze blade on top of the young man's skeleton would certainly appear to strengthen the excavators' case. Yet it is quite possible that this is due to sheer coincidence. Much of the material found within the building had fallen from above, whether from shelves, the walls, the roof, or an upper story.[16] And whether the blade was dropped by a priest who had just killed the young man on the platform, or if rather it fell by chance onto the body during the collapse of the building, is not something which can be determined by archaeology. Furthermore, it is very doubtful that this large (0.40 m) blade belonged to a sacrificial knife, as is suggested by the excavators.[17] By accepted classification, it is a spearhead, the two vertical slots (located about two-thirds of the length of the blade from its tip) serving to attach the blade to the shaft of the spear.[18] The blade could easily have belonged to a spear which had stood against one of the walls or in a corner and which fell towards the centre of the room during the destruction.

The significance of the position of the 'victim's' skeleton is crucial for the excavators' interpretation. It was found lying on the platform (it is unclear whether totally or partially), with one of the legs bent backward so that the heel nearly touched the thigh. From this it was concluded that the young man's legs had been bound.[19] But it is unclear in what position the other leg was found,[20] and there is no indication that the hands were bound: one would be happier with the excavators' interpretation if the skeleton's hands had been found together behind the back, or even crossed in front of the body. Is it possible that the young man simply tripped and fell, landing (or curling up) in this somewhat contorted position during the collapse of the building? Only the publication of a more detailed description can answer this question satisfactorily.

It is also reported that the bones on the left side of the young man's skeleton were white in colour, while those on the right side were black, and anthropologists who studied the skeleton concluded from this difference that the youth had died from loss of blood before his body was burned.[21] But this conclusion appears to be groundless. It is true that such difference in colour indicates different degrees of burning – 'white bone' must mean either (a) unburned bone, or (b) calcined bone which was burned at a higher temperature and for a longer period of time than scorched, 'smoked', incompletely burned bone.[22] As it is also reported that the bones of the left side of the skeleton from Anemospilia showed signs of greater burning than those of the right side,[23] it appears that the white colour of the exposed, left side of the skeleton was due to calcination of the bone during the fire. Uneven burning of a skeleton may be caused by any number of factors, such as the proximity of flammable material to one part of the body, or, conversely, the protection of part of the body from the full intensity of the fire – such as the protection afforded by direct contact with the ground. Another factor which markedly affects the way bones burn is the presence or absence of muscle on the bone, but there is no evidence that the presence or lack of *blood* in a corpse burned at a high temperature will have any appreciable effect on the degree of burning or the resultant coloration of the bones. Thus there does not appear to be anything unusual or unexpected in the pattern of burning found on the young man's skeleton.[24]

The excavation of the building at Anemospilia has been published only in preliminary reports, and this means two things: first, that the excavators' interpretation of the finds is to be regarded as preliminary and therefore subject to revision or change, but also perhaps to be supported by further evidence and argument; and second, that we ourselves should not, and cannot, form a final opinion of the interpretation put forward in this preliminary form. The more detailed description of the evidence, the drawings and photographs which we can expect from a final publication may well answer some of the questions and dispel some of the doubts which I have raised here concerning the excavators' explanation of this extraordinary discovery.

Cannibalism at Knossos?

In 1979, 1980, and 1981 the basement rooms of a Late Minoan IB house, located west of the Stratigraphical Museum at Knossos, were excavated by the British School under the direction of Peter Warren.[25] The building, which consists of six basement rooms bordering on a courtyard to the north, was destroyed at the end of LM IB (*c.* 1450 BC), and its basement was subsequently built over in LM II. In the floor deposit of the largest room, the 'Cult Room Basement', were found fragments of at least thirty-seven vessels, some stone 'tools', beads, and two sealstones. The deposit which had fallen from the first floor included seventy-nine loomweights and at least thirty-seven vessels also, including four pithoi. In one of these had been stored a set of twelve 'cup rhytons', among them a cup decorated with a gorgoneion and figure-of-eight shields alternating with squills. Most important for our purposes is the largest of the pithoi, which was found broken and scattered through the fill. Associated with the main concentration of its fragments were burnt earth, a large amount of edible snails, some shells, and three human bones, a phalanx, a fragment of a sternum, and a cervical vertebra with knife-cut marks. Intermingled with the fragments of the pithos was a jug containing six phalanges (none with cut marks) from a human foot.[26]

To the west of the Cult Room Basement was a smaller room (1.76 × 1.08 m), the 'Room of the Children's Bones'. The room contained three main layers of fill: (1) above the original plaster floor, a layer of grey, clayey soil, containing in its lower level some sherds and animal bones and in its upper level numerous conical cups and fragments of other pottery; (2) a level of soft, black, carbonized earth; and (3) a layer of light brown, unburnt soil, containing a variety of pots and, at its bottom, the black remains of two burnt beams. Found in the second level were 371 human bones and bone fragments, with the greatest concentration in the western third of the room.[27] In the same layer were also found the scapula and two articulated cervical vertebrae of a sheep, one with cut marks. It is now reported that a total of 251 animal bones, both burnt and unburnt and belonging to cattle, sheep, goats, pigs, and dogs, were found in the room, although it is not clear how many came from the second layer. Nineteen of the animal bones had cut marks.[28] But all of the human bones, although they lay in the deposit of black carbonized earth, were unburnt, which suggests that the bones were *in situ* when the burnt ceiling collapsed and fell over them.[29]

From the human skull fragments found in the Room of the Children's Bones it was possible to piece together two skulls, belonging to children aged approximately 8 (skull A) and 12 (skull B) years. A third individual is represented by a skull fragment (C) which did not belong to A or B and which had been 'carefully cut as part of a circle', possibly presenting evidence of trephination. And the number of leg bones recovered indicates that the room held the remains of at least four individuals, all children.[30]

Of the 371 bones and bone fragments found in the room, 79 were observed to have fine cut marks, often far from the end of the bone, a fact which suggested to the excavator and to L. R. Binford that the purpose of the cutting had been the removal of flesh rather than the dismemberment of the bodies.[31] Four bones show deeper marks, apparently made from a chopping action, but otherwise the marks appear to have been made by cutting or sawing with a fine blade.[32] Finally, 'the apparent absence of longitudinal scraping marks confirms that the aim was not to clean the bones of every trace of flesh'.[33] Rather, it would seem that only pieces of flesh had been removed from the bones.

In addition to the human bones found in the Room of the Children's Bones and those associated with the pithos and jug, a few bones (phalanx, incisor, vertebra, and skull fragment, none with cut marks) were found high in the destruction fill in the Cult Room Basement; and at the east end of the North Court were found a right malar bone and a fragment of a limb bone, both with cut marks. In the destruction fill of the Room of the Frescoes (in the northeast part of the house) there were seven more bones, two with cut marks; and a drain just outside the north wall of this room contained along with pottery fragments more bones and bone fragments, twenty-seven in all, with no cut marks reported. Most of the bones from the drain have been identified as belonging to children, and none is certainly an adult's (this also seems to be the case with the bones from the Cult Room Basement and the Room of the Frescoes). It is uncertain if any of these bones belonged to any of the children found in the Room of the Children's Bones. In all, fifty-one children's bones were found elsewhere in the house, eight with knife-cut marks.[34]

Several other human bones were found in the North Court, at the north end of the Corridor (which runs N–S between the Cult

Room Basement and the Room of the Frescoes), and in LM I–II levels outside of the house to the north of the Room of the Frescoes (one of these a child's clavicle with cut marks). The majority of these bones belong to adults, not children, but none of the adult bones showed any cut marks. All of these bones are said to be from less pure contexts and therefore cannot be dated with certainty to the time of the house's destruction.[35]

Warren has suggested that the children's bones present evidence for 'human sacrifice and possibly ritual consumption'. Among other possible explanations, Warren rejects survival cannibalism, alimentary cannibalism, preparation for secondary burial, and 'ordinary murder'. In support of his interpretation he stresses the nature and location of the marks (both indicating that the aim was the removal of flesh), the cult context in which the bones were found, the presence of the bones of a sheep which apparently had been slaughtered, and the apparent good health of the children at the time of death, a 'necessary condition for ancient sacrifice'.[36] Warren acknowledges that it is impossible to *prove* that the flesh was consumed after its removal, but he feels that the presence of a few human bones (one with cut marks) together with burnt earth, snails (said to be edible), and shells associated with a pithos may indicate that the flesh of the children had been cooked. Warren originally suggested that the cooking had been done in the pithos but now feels that the large size of the vessel (93 cm high) renders this unlikely.[37]

The bones from Knossos are not the only human bones on which cut or chop marks have been observed in the past few years in Greece. This can hardly be sheer coincidence, but must rather be the result of cleaning and careful examination of excavated bones (along with a growing regard for their importance) in recent years; and it is probable that the presence of cut marks on human bones went unnoticed in the past. Among the recent cases, the most remarkable report comes from an Early Helladic cemetery at Manika near Chalkis, where the *majority* of the bones studied had various cut marks and holes. The excavator, who at first proposed human sacrifice or ritual cannibalism as an explanation, now suggests that the cut marks were made during preparation for burial. The location of many of the marks suggests that they resulted from the cutting of tendons, perhaps in order to force the corpse into a contracted position for burial. The apparently very high percentage of bones with cut marks may suggest preparation for primary burial, although secondary burial in ossuaries was also practised at the site.[38]

The possibility that cut marks represent a stage of preparation for burial or reburial should also be considered for the children's bones from Knossos.[39] Both the condition in which the children's bones were found and the distribution of the cut marks may indicate some kind of secondary burial custom. It is reported that the bones were 'largely disarticulated' and found 'scattered over the whole level', not the bones of 'skeletons fallen *in situ*, but a jumbled, disarticulated heap'.[40] And although it was once thought that whole bodies had been placed in the room, it is now more plausibly concluded that partial skeletons and disarticulated bones were placed or thrown into the room.[41] Also, by no means all of the bones of the two children were recovered; in particular, hand and foot bones, wrist and ankle bones, and the epiphyses of the limb bones are poorly represented.[42] It therefore seems possible that skeletons, rather than bodies of recently dead children, had been removed from elsewhere and placed in the basement after the flesh had partially or largely decomposed. This would account both for the scattered, disturbed state of the bones and for the apparent absence of many of them, for frequent handling or moving of skeletal remains commonly results in partial disarticulation and in underrepresentation of the smaller bones.[43] Everything in the published reports is consistent with a hypothesis that the skeletons were already largely devoid of flesh at the time they were moved into the room.

The distribution of cut marks on the bones may also favour this interpretation. As can be seen from a drawing of a reconstructed skeleton and from a chart of the bones recovered from the Room of the Children's Bones, the marks tend to cluster on certain bones and for the most part only in certain areas of the bone (often, it appears, at points of muscle attachment). Of seventy-nine bones with cut marks, over one third (twenty-seven) are ribs; and all four scapulae, all six clavicles, and all three ulnae recovered from the room had cut marks (the two clavicles and the ulna found in other locations also were cut). In all, only 21.3 per cent of the bones and bone fragments from the Room of the Children's Bones had cut marks at all, although calculated against the minimum number of bones possibly represented the percentage is significantly higher (35.7 per cent). Of children's bones found elsewhere in the house the percentage is still lower: eight of fifty-one bones (16 per cent). On the basis of the information now available, it seems possible that this uneven distribution may represent an effort to remove soft tissue from the bones *only where such tissue remained* – i.e. from skeletons of children who had been dead for some time, perhaps several years.[44]

Also, the location of many of the cut marks – on skull fragments, mandibles, clavicles, and other areas of seemingly little culinary appeal – does not support the suggestion that the marks were made in an effort to obtain meat for consumption. In fact, flaying or skinning is now proposed to account for some of the marks, although no reason is suggested for this operation.[45] But a single explanation for all of the marks on the human bones, which are largely consistent in appearance, would be preferable methodologically. Furthermore, it is now reported that some of the marks – one on the inner surface of the right petrous temporal bone of skull B and others on the inner surfaces of ribs – could only have been made by cutting *from within* the skull and the chest; it is suggested that the former resulted from an effort to remove the brain and that the latter were made by cutting from the front of the skeleton, after the lungs and heart had been removed from the thoracic cavity.[46] But of course these marks could also have been made when the brain and other organs had largely decomposed. And cut marks found on the jaws and around the eyes and ears may also represent an attempt to clean the skulls of decayed tissue.

In favour of Warren's interpretation is the presence of animal bones, some with cut marks, together with the human skeletons in the Room of the Children's Bones; and possibly further study of the marks on the animal bones will establish a clear link between the human and animal remains. But until then it cannot be assumed that the animals were killed or cut at the same time, in the same way, or for the same reasons, especially as both burnt and unburnt animal bones were found, while none of the human bones was burnt. From the presence of an ovicaprid vertebra with cut marks Warren concludes that the animal was sacrificed along with the children.[47] But while two of the children were placed in the room with their skeletons at least partially intact, this does not seem to have been the case with the sheep or any other of the animals. It therefore seems possible that the animal bones were not connected directly with the children and represent the remains of (ordinary) meals taken within the house. Alternatively, if the children had been moved to the house from their tombs long after death, some of the animal bones could be the remains of funerary meals or sacrifices performed not in the house but at the grave.[48] And if the cut marks on the human bones did in fact result from defleshing before reburial, then it is possible that the sheep's vertebra was also cut during this process, when the animal bones would have been indistinguishable from the human bones with which they were mixed. Finally, there appear to be several fine marks close together on the ovicaprid vertebra,[49] similar to those found on the children's skeletons but not what we would expect from the single stroke needed to sever the jugular in the act of sacrifice.

A serious objection to this suggestion, of course, is that the bones were found not in a funerary context but in the basement of a building. Furthermore, although secondary burial was commonly practised in Crete in the Bronze Age, I am not aware of any evidence for the removal of flesh or intentional disarticulation before reburial.[50] But the removal of flesh from bones is a common feature of secondary burial in other cultures (including modern Greeks and, it now appears, some Early Helladic peoples), and at present the practice cannot be ruled out for the Late Minoan I period.[51] It also cannot be ruled out that preparation for reburial took place outside of the cemetery. And if the house at Knossos was indeed a place where cult activities were performed, it is conceivable that one such activity was 'undertaking': preparation for burial, primary or secondary, may well have been a sacred activity in Crete in the Bronze Age.[52]

This suggestion cannot at present be supported by any parallel, but this is equally true of Warren's interpretation of the bones: there is no other evidence for ritual cannibalism in Crete in the Bronze Age. Neither explanation is entirely satisfactory, and perhaps other possibilities should be considered. Many features of the excavation are puzzling: the presence of a few human bones in a pithos and a collection of foot phalanges in a jug; the scattering of human remains throughout and even outside the house; the presence of adult bones, without cut marks; and the apparent fact that human skeletons or dismembered bodies were simply abandoned (for how long cannot be determined) in the basement. Even if 'the killing of children, flaying, and removal of flesh and organs' constituted a 'central function' of the building,[53] we would expect the practitioners of these ghoulish arts to dispose of the remains more tidily, if their base of operations were to remain habitable (thoroughly cleaned skeletons, awaiting transport to a place of reburial, would perhaps be less objectionable). And it seems possible that the pithos had been employed – not for cooking or refuse – but in order to transport skeletons to the house from their original resting place.[54]

It is hoped that more conclusive results will be achieved by further examination of the cut marks and comparison with other marks of known cause, perhaps along the lines of a recent re-examination of the Krapina Neanderthal remains (where, incidentally, several factors point to secondary burial rather than cannibalism).[55] In the meantime it is worth noting that allegations of cannibalism have been viewed with increasing scepticism in recent years. Best known (and most controversial) is the recent work of W. Arens, who in the course of a study of the subject was unable to find solid, firsthand evidence of cannibalism as a customary, accepted practice in *any* society, past or present.[56] Arens does not deny that such practices have ever existed, but he argues that convincing proof is wanting and that certainly the practice is by no means as widespread as has been commonly held by anthropologists; and further that archaeologists have all too readily followed the anthropologists' assumption of a widespread custom when confronted with broken, cut, or disturbed human bones. Similar criticisms and cautions have been voiced by others.[57] Such cautions certainly do not mean that alimentary or ritual cannibalism should no longer be entertained as an explanation for cut or broken bones; but cannibalism should not be considered certain, or even probable, without strong supporting evidence and without a thorough exploration of alternatives.

Other?

Before the eventful summer of 1979, there had been very little reason to suspect that the Minoans practised human sacrifice in any form.[58] In 1967 and 1968 an Early Minoan II settlement was excavated at Myrtos under the direction of Peter Warren. Room 89, the 'Room of the Hearth and Skull', contained a hearth, on each side of which were two small, low benches. Warren suggested that the room may have had 'a special and possibly ritual character', a view he supported by the presence in the room of fragments of a human skull, probably of an adult male in his twenties or thirties. No other bones were found in the room, and thus the skull fragments do not seem to represent remains of a burial or of a person who had failed to escape from the room at the time of its destruction. Warren concluded that the skull had been 'deliberately situated near the tripartite structure with the central hearth' and that 'thus the possibility of ancestor worship . . . or even human sacrifice cannot be ruled out'.[59]

In one of his publications of the children's bones from Knossos, Warren writes:

> That child sacrifice was not totally unknown in Bronze Age Crete is suggested by a scene on a Late Minoan I ring impression recently published from Khania. It depicts a large seated female figure, probably a goddess, before whom stands a child in a skirt, most probably a girl. Over the child is what looks very much like a hilted sword, one poised for the kill.

Although Warren provides no reference, there can be little doubt that he refers here to a ring impression published by Papapostolou in 1977.[60] But Warren's description is misleading. First of all, the smaller figure does not appear to be 'standing' before the goddess. The legs are bent sharply inward at the knees, a position which suggests to Papapostolou that the figure is dancing; that she is leaping also seems possible – in either case hardly an appropriate activity for a sacrificial victim. Also, the object which Warren interprets as a sword is by no means certainly a sword; it does not even seem to be pointed at the end, and Papapostolou suggests that it is a mallet.[61] Finally, and most importantly, the object does not seem to be 'over the child' or 'poised for the kill'. Rather, it touches, and appears to extend upward from, the smaller figure's upraised hand: it is fairly clear that she is meant to be holding or waving the object in her hand. The smaller figure thus seems to be engaged in some sort of ritual performance, dancing and holding a long object in one hand, before the seated, and presumably divine, figure.

This is not the first time that it has been suggested that a Minoan seal represents a human sacrifice. On a sealstone in the British Museum three male figures are depicted: one of them holds what is apparently a sword behind his back while grasping with his other hand the head of the central figure; to the left is a third figure in a 'sitting' position, possibly meant to indicate that he is dead. Of this scene Furtwängler wrote: 'Menschenopfer? Schlachten von Gefangenen?' But there is little merit to the suggestion that a human sacrifice is depicted on the gem. As the central figure is helmeted, the context seems to be military rather than religious, and the gem may represent, as Furtwängler alternatively suggested, an execution of captives. But probably it is simply a combat scene.[62]

It is very unlikely that either of these two seals represents a human sacrifice. But before we leave Crete behind us it is worth noting that most of our knowledge of Minoan religion in general, and Minoan sacrifice in particular, is based upon artistic representations. We have several scenes of animal sacrifice,[63] but no similar representations with human victims bound upon altars. The iconographic record (if we exclude the two dubious instances above) is at present conspicuously silent on the matter of human sacrifice in Crete in the Bronze Age.

THE LATE BRONZE AGE ARGOLID

Tholos Tombs

In 1926 Axel Persson excavated a tholos tomb near the village of Dendra in the Argolid. Four pits had been dug in the floor of the tomb.[64] A large pit before the entrance, pit IV, contained a 'mixture of charcoal and earth, containing small gold mountings, bronze fragments, bits of burnt ivory, beads of faience and semi-precious stones, etc. etc., but no bones'. A smaller pit to the rear of the tomb (pit II) contained 'unburnt bones of human beings and animals, including the well-preserved skull of a dog', some faience beads, pieces of gold and bronze, and fragments of a large stirrup jar.[65] Fragments of the same vase were also found in pits IV and I, on the floor of the tomb, and in the dromos.[66] Pit III, near the south wall of the tomb, contained the skeleton of a young woman – the 'Princess' – adorned with a gold necklace and girdle. A long narrow pit on the opposite side of the tomb (I) contained two skeletons, of a man and a woman. A great variety of precious objects was found with the burials, including a silver and gold cup with an inlaid design of bulls' heads, which rested between the breast and arm of the 'Queen', and a large gold cup decorated *en repoussé* with octopuses, dolphins, and 'argonauts', which lay on the breast of the 'King'. Also found with the King were a silver goblet decorated with deer and hounds and a gold and silver cup decorated with figures of bulls. Four bronze swords lay at either side of the King, and at his feet was a heap of weapons – a sword, spearheads, knives, and two lead horns.[67] In addition to the three burials in pits I and III, the remains of at least three other skeletons were found scattered on the floor and in the upper layers of pits I and IV. Also on the floor were numerous fragments of gold, ivory, and bronze, gold and faience beads, etc.[68]

Persson maintained that the smaller 'sacrificial pit' (II) contained the 'remains of a servant and a dog who had to accompany their master in death', comparing the killing of dogs and captives at the funeral of Patroclus in the *Iliad* (23.173–6). Persson also suggested that 'possibly the remains of the three skeletons, displaced by the tomb robbers, which were found on the chamber floor and in the upper layers of the pits, should be interpreted in the same way'. Furthermore, in Persson's opinion the King and Queen had been buried at the same time, and he suggested that the dual burial might represent a case of 'suttee', the slaying or suicide of a wife at her husband's funeral. Persson compared Indian and Thracian customs and the Greek legends of Evadne, Laodameia, and Polyxena in support of his interpretation, admitting, however, that 'a convincing proof . . . naturally cannot be produced' in the case of the dual burial in the Dendra tholos.[69]

In a detailed re-examination of the evidence from the Dendra tholos, Mylonas argued that pit II, which contained human bones and the bones of a dog, is best explained as a refuse pit into which some of the remains of previous burials had been swept, a practice paralleled in the chamber tombs:

> If indeed the shaft was a sacrificial pit and if the skeletal remains in it belonged to persons and dogs sacrificed at the burial of the King, then at least the most easily identifiable bones of 'the servant' would have been found in the pit and mentioned, as the head of the dog was mentioned.[70]

I note in addition that the human skeletal remains in pit II appear to have been insufficient to permit study by Fürst and that three dog's teeth were found on the floor directly above the pit.[71] If these teeth belonged to the skull in the pit (as seems quite probable), then the dog had been long dead before the skull was placed in the shaft. It therefore seems probable that the human and canine bones represented the remains of earlier burials made on the tomb's floor. A burial period prior to the burials of the King and Queen is also suggested by the presence of fragments of a stirrup jar not only in pit II, but also in the King and Queen's pit (I), pit IV, on the floor, and in the dromos. Similarly, fragments of a jug with a beaked spout and a triple handle were found on the floor, in the dromos, and in pits I and IV. In Persson's fanciful reconstruction the stirrup jar was shattered during the final services for the royal couple, but this is highly improbable: rather, the jar must have belonged to a burial made prior to the digging of pits I, II, and IV. Also indicative of an earlier burial period are the numerous small finds scattered over the floor and in pits I and IV, clearly the remains of clothing and other ornaments from previous burials made on the floor of the tomb.[72]

Persson reported that three skulls and other bones belonging to at least three individuals were found on the floor and in the upper layers of the pits. The skeletons may have been disturbed by tomb robbers, as Persson suggested,[73] but this suggestion does not satisfactorily account for the presence of human bones in the upper layers of the pits: these at least are best explained as remains of burials made before pits I and IV were dug. Apparently Persson felt that the bones found in the upper layers of pits I and IV had sifted down into the fill. But it seems more likely that material on the floor, including human bones – which would have lain beneath substantial piles of dirt created when the pits were dug – ended up in the top of the fill when the pits were refilled, while the earth taken from the tops of the piles remained relatively pure and free of finds (although it is curious that the articulated bones were placed back over pits I and IV, rather than swept to the side of the tomb, into the dromos, or into pit II). Alternatively, the bones found on the floor might represent burials made later than the digging of pits I and IV. But no evidence provided by Persson indicates that the burials represented by these scattered skeletal remains were necessarily contemporaneous with any of the burials in the pits.

Less successful was Mylonas's attempt to show that the King and Queen were not buried simultaneously, although it is true that Persson 'failed to point out clear evidence on which his conclusions were based'. Mylonas argued that the weapons found in a disorderly pile at the King's feet had been pushed aside in order to accommodate the later burial of the Queen – which is possible, but hardly certain. He also tried to separate the two burials by his suggested dates for some of the grave gifts of the King and Queen. Persson dated the King's gold cup with the marine decoration to *c.* 1500 BC, on stylistic grounds, and felt that it and two other of the King's cups were imports of Cretan manufacture. He then dated the Queen's cup with the inlaid bulls' heads to *c.* 1400. In Persson's view the Cretan cups had come to the mainland, by trade or military action, in the late fifteenth century, and the burial of the King and Queen took place at some time during the first half of the fourteenth century BC. Mylonas wished to bring forward Persson's dates for the King's precious grave goods to a time closer to 1400. Of the Queen's inlaid cup he wrote only that whereas Persson dated it to *c.* 1400, 'it seems to us that it belongs to much later times'; and from the supposed discrepancy in date he concluded that the burial of the Queen was later than the burial of the King.[74]

Objects of precious metal are notoriously hard to date, and the vessels found with the King and Queen cannot possibly be dated with enough precision to determine whether the two were buried simultaneously or not. But the stirrup jar, fragments of which were found on the floor, in pits I, II, and IV, and in the dromos (and which in my opinion belonged to a burial previous to that of the King and Queen), was dated by Furumark to Mycenaean (= Late Helladic) IIIA1. In terms of absolute chronology, this places its manufacture (approximately) in the period 1390–1370/60.[75] The Queen's cup with the inlaid bulls' heads may now be assigned, from its close similarity to a Late Cypriot IIA cup from Enkomi, to this period also.[76] The King's cup with the marine decoration has been dated to anywhere from the sixteenth to the fourteenth century, but Hurwit has argued for its mainland manufacture, favouring a date of *c.* 1400–1375.[77] To all appearances, the King and Queen were buried at some time in the first half of the fourteenth century, just as Persson, despite the greater span of time covered by his dating of the various objects from the tomb, long ago suggested.[78]

But were the King and Queen buried on the same day? Persson's expressed reasons for maintaining this were the presence of fragments of the stirrup jar and the jug with the beaked spout near both skeletons at the bottom of pit I and the fact that common burial gifts – a steatite lamp, a gold necklace, and a decorated ostrich egg – were found in the middle of the pit between the King and Queen.[79] The presence of sherds of the same two vases at both ends of pit I at least seems to indicate that the pit was dug at a single time and not extended to accommodate a second burial.[80] But nothing in Persson's publication precludes the possibility that the pit was left open, or reopened, for a subsequent burial. In this case the unusually long (*c.* 5 m) pit would have been dug with a view to the eventual accommodation of two burials, presumably of man and wife. But whether the King and Queen were interred simultaneously or not, the use of a single long pit for two burials is exceptional: the usual practice, when people were buried under the floor in tholos tombs, was to bury them separately, and pits were not normally reused for subsequent burials.[81] Given the unusual nature of the dual burial from Dendra it is perhaps more probable that Persson was correct in considering it simultaneous. The possibility of 'suttee' cannot be excluded and will be discussed further below. But it is also possible that the dual burial was occasioned by the simultaneous death of a man and wife from disease, accident, or violence. Such a simultaneous death might well have caused a departure from normal burial practices, particularly in the case of an important and wealthy couple, whether royal or not.

Much less can be said about the other case where 'human sacrifice' has been offered as an explanation of burials within a Mycenaean tholos tomb. In the late 1960s a tholos tomb at Kazarma, located about 14 km from Nauplion on the Nauplion–Epidaurus road, was excavated under the supervision of Spyridon Marinatos and published in preliminary reports by E. Protonotariou-Deïlaki.[82] The tomb, which is of approximately the same size as the Dendra tholos, is dated by pottery finds to LH I/early LH II (late sixteenth to early fifteenth century). It was reopened in LH IIIC (twelfth or early eleventh century), when a small calf was sacrificed on a pile of stones near the entrance. There were three pits in the tomb, each containing a single burial.[83] Above these in the centre of the tomb were traces of a large fire, on the outer edges of which were found an abundance of animal bones and two human skeletons. The skeletons were without funeral gifts and are reported to have been found 'in a kneeling position'.[84] Deïlaki suggested that the skeletons belonged to slaves sacrificed on the stone pile just inside the entrance of the tomb.[85] It is difficult to evaluate this suggestion on the basis of the brief descriptions given in the preliminary reports. The precise location of the skeletons is not stated, nor is the reason why it is thought that the two persons were slain on the stone platform. Only a puzzling reference to the unusual position of the skeletons might indicate that they did not represent ordinary burials made on the tomb floor.

Chamber Tombs

Not infrequently skeletons or scattered human bones have been found in the fill or on the floor of the dromoi of Mycenaean chamber tombs. These are usually interpreted as the remains of earlier interments which had been swept unceremoniously from the tomb's chamber to make room for new occupants or had been given a more careful secondary burial (sometimes in a pit or niche) in the dromos.[86] Other skeletons have been shown to represent burials made in the dromos at some time later (and in some cases much later) than the final use of the chamber.[87] But in the following four cases it has been suggested that skeletons found in the dromoi near the tombs' entrances belonged to servants or slaves slain at the funerals of their masters.

(i) Mycenae, Lower City, Tomb 15. In 1887 and 1888 Tsountas excavated fifty-two chamber tombs in the vicinity of Mycenae and reported that human bones were often found in the dromoi. In the dromos of Tomb 15 Tsountas found six skeletons buried one over the other, at different depths, in the stone fill before the triangle above the door. With the skeletons were some undecorated potsherds and some animal bones. In Tsountas's opinion the six burials were most probably made simultaneously when the dromos was filled in for the final time. If they had been made at six different times, he argued, and if the dromos had been cleared for the purpose, the earlier burials would not have escaped disturbance. Also, if only part of the dromos had been dug out to make new burials, it would have been difficult to estimate each time the depth of the burial below; and no signs of repeated digging were observed. Tsountas concluded that the six skeletons were the skeletons of slaves or prisoners of war, slain when the last burial was made in the chamber.[88] But from his description it also seems possible that the skeletons represent a multiple burial made in the dromos at some time after the final use of the tomb.

(ii) Argos, Necropolis of Deiras, Tomb VI. In the early twentieth century Vollgraff excavated nine chamber tombs at Argos. Vollgraff reported that human bones were found before the entrance to Tomb VI at the level of the top of the door, buried under a pile of stones. 'Le sacrifice humain', he continued, 'accompli lors de la fermeture définitive du tombeau, nous était déjà connu par les fouilles de Mycènes', with reference to Tomb 15 of the lower city excavated by Tsountas.[89] The burial in the dromos of Tomb VI may have been made during the final closing of the tomb, but it seems unlikely that it was made on the occasion of the final burial in the chamber, for although the tomb was unplundered, no trace of a final burial was found. Vollgraff seems to have thought that the skeleton had totally disintegrated, but the fact that all of the vases in the chamber had been shattered may suggest that the tomb was re-entered at some time after the final burial and then resealed. At this time the chamber may have also been cleared of skeletons and, for reasons unknown, not reused for burial.[90]

(iii) Mycenae, 'Third Kilometre Cemetery', Tomb 505. In the dromos of Tomb 505 Wace found the remains of at least fifteen human skeletons. One of these (no. II), the skeleton of a child tucked into a hollow in the dromos wall, was probably a secondary burial. Only two skeletons, nos XIV and XV, were found *in situ*, lying side by side 6.80 m above the floor, with their heads against the dromos wall: these burials in Wace's opinion were made after the tomb had suffered damage and been abandoned. In the stone fill before the top of the stomion were 'a number of skulls and quantities of other human bones . . . the remains of at least 6 skeletons', IV–IX. These skulls and bones, along with the remains of six other skeletons (I, III, and X–XIII) found in the dromos 'seemed to represent *disiecta membra* thrown out of their original resting place'.[91] Nevertheless, in a general discussion of burial customs at Mycenae, Wace wrote that 'there was no evidence in these tombs except perhaps the skeletons lying in the dromos of Tomb 505 before the entrance to the chamber, for or against the view that the Mycenaeans practised human sacrifice', and elsewhere he referred vaguely to 'the special circumstances which seem to have governed the cases of the skeletons found in front of the door of Tomb 505'.[92]

Although the vagueness of these allusions has led to some

confusion over which skeletons Wace meant,[93] there can be little doubt that he was referring to skeletons IV–IX: for these, together with skeleton I (which Wace clearly considered the remains of a burial removed from the chamber) were the only skeletons found before the door.[94] But it is difficult to understand now why Wace, who at one point interpreted these skulls and other skeletal remains as mere *disiecta membra*, should have suggested at another that they might represent 'human sacrifices'. Besides the fact that these skeletons were reportedly not *in situ*, there is another serious objection to this suggestion: the chamber of Tomb 505 had been thoroughly cleared out and, apparently because a fault in the rock had resulted in serious structural damage, was not reused.[95] It seems likely that most of the skeletal remains were placed in the dromos during this wholesale clearance, and it is possible that the two *in situ* burials (XIV and XV) were made at this time also. In any case, the clearing of the chamber renders it impossible to establish a definite link between any of the skeletons in the dromos and the final burial in the tomb.

(iv) 'Prosymna' (the Argive Heraeum), Tomb VII. At *c.* 2 m above floor level, there was a fill of large stones which extended 2 m into the dromos from the door of Prosymna Tomb VII. On top of the stones lay a skeleton, partially covered by a large limestone slab, which leaned against the wall of the dromos. There were no funeral gifts, but potsherds in the surrounding earth dated the burial to LH III, the period when the tomb was chiefly in use. Of this burial Blegen wrote:

> Its curious position directly upon the mass of stone fill, blocking approach to the door of the tomb, leads one to wonder if some close connection is not to be recognized between these remains and the remains interred within the chamber of the tomb. Was this perhaps a slave or servitor, the victim of sacrifice or self-destruction, who was laid to rest as the faithful guardian before the door of his master's sepulchre?[96]

The floor of Tomb VII was completely covered by a thin layer of ash and carbonized matter. Blegen entertained three possible explanations for this – cremation on a pyre within the tomb, fumigation of the tomb, or 'burnt offerings and sacrifices in a cult of the dead'; and he seemed to incline to the last. Blegen noted similar ash-layers in other tombs in the cemetery, which he interpreted as remains of fires lit for purposes of fumigation. But he was uncomfortable with this interpretation in the case of Tomb VII, for there was 'no trace whatsoever of the subsequent burial for which the chamber was *ex hypothesi* fumigated'.[97] That the final burial in the tomb was a cremation, however, seems highly unlikely: a thin (1 to 2 cm) layer of ashes covering the entire area of the chamber would not appear to be the remains of a funeral pyre. Thus it seems that a connection between the skeleton which lay before the top of the door and 'the remains interred within the chamber' cannot be demonstrated, for, once again, these latter are wanting.

In three of the four cases the suggestion that burials in the dromos represent human sacrifices or servants slain at their masters' funerals is open to serious question, since there were no traces of burials within the chamber to which the dromos burials might be claimed to be ancillary. While Tomb 505 at Mycenae seems to have been abandoned because of structural damage, it remains a mystery why no final burials were found in Prosymna Tomb VII and Argos Tomb VI. A mystery: and yet it is a curious fact that quite often no final *in situ* burial is found in unplundered Mycenaean chamber tombs.[98] One might wonder if Prosymna Tomb VII was opened with the intention of burying a body, but when the chamber was for some reason deemed unsuitable the burial was made instead on a pile of stones in the dromos. Something similar may have happened with Tomb VI at Argos; or this burial may have been made at some time after the tomb had been closed for good. Dromoi were sometimes employed for burials when the chamber was no longer in use, and Frödin and Persson wrote of skeletons found in dromoi at Asine that 'these "doorkeepers" . . . must not be looked upon as sacrificed slaves, as has previously been suggested', with apparent reference to some or all of the cases discussed here.[99]

Of these four cases, the burial (apparently simultaneous) of six persons above the door of Tomb 15 of the lower city of Mycenae merits the most serious consideration and may represent some sort of funerary ritual killing, as Tsountas suggested. But it also may simply have been a multiple burial unconnected with any burial in the chamber. Clearly Tsountas's suggestion exerted an influence on other archaeologists confronted with puzzling dromos burials of their own; but it is worth noting that later in life Tsountas himself came to question his belief that the Mycenaeans practised 'human sacrifice', feeling that he may have been influenced by his interpretation, since shown to be mistaken, of skeletons found in Grave Circle A at Mycenae.[100]

CYPRUS

With the exception of a dubious instance from the Late Bronze Age,[101] the evidence for ritual killing at funerals in Cyprus belongs to a time after Greek-speaking settlers had firmly and widely established their presence on the island. Indeed it is often suggested that the colonists brought the custom of 'human sacrifice' with them from the mainland.[102] Of nine alleged 'slave burials', eight date to the Cypro-Geometric and Cypro-Archaic periods, from the mid-eleventh into the sixth century BC. There is a final, very questionable instance from Cypro-Classic II (*c.* 400–325 BC).[103]

(i) Lapithos, Necropolis at Kastros, Tomb 412. No skeletal remains were preserved in the chamber, possibly because the roof and one wall of the tomb had collapsed. Pottery in the chamber dates the tomb's use to late Cypro-Geometric I. The dromos had an unusual, irregular shape: apparently one wall of the dromos was hollowed out near its entrance in order to accommodate a burial; a short extension (2.40 m), not in line with the original dromos, was then made to lead to the new burial. The burial consisted of three well-preserved skeletons: two of these lay together, one (no. I) on its left, the other (II) on its right side, both in contracted position. A third skeleton (III) lay face down over skeleton no. II, with a single jug placed between their skulls. The fill of the dromos consisted of 'intact layers of homogeneous *chavara*', which indicates that the entire dromos was cleared when the triple burial was made. 'Probably', Gjerstad concluded, 'it is a burial of slaves killed at the funeral of the deceased buried in the chamber.'[104]

One of many curious aspects of this burial is the alteration of the dromos. At the least this alteration suggests that the tomb was opened more than once: for why should the dromos of a newly made tomb be changed on the occasion of its first use, even if slaves were in fact slain during the funeral? And we might well ask why such an alteration should have been made at any time. To me it appears that the intention was to create another, if rather crude, tomb: a wall of the dromos was hollowed out, a sort of enclosure was made with stones, and a new 'dromos' was dug without regard for the orientation of the original. I wonder if there may have been some connection between this and the collapse of the roof and one wall of the chamber: was the tomb seen to be unsafe for further use, and a makeshift tomb constructed at the entrance of the dromos? If so, the skeletons might represent a simultaneous triple burial, or conceivably one or more of the skeletons had been removed from the ruined chamber to the new grave in the dromos.[105] The dromos of Tomb 428 of the same cemetery had been similarly hollowed out near its entrance and used for a (single) burial, but in this case pottery found with the burial dates it to a time after the final use of the chamber. Also, a Cypro-Geometric III burial was made on a pile of stones in the dromos of Tomb 407, whose chamber was in use only in Cypro-Geometric I. And sizeable niches were cut in the walls of the dromoi of Tombs 408 (for a single burial) and 410 (containing six vases but no skeletal remains): in each case the niche postdates the final use of the tomb. Like Tomb 412, Tombs 407, 408, and 410 had all suffered serious damage to their chambers.[106]

It is possible that Gjerstad was correct in viewing the burial in the dromos of Tomb 412 as a 'slave burial': that it was a multiple burial, that only a single grave gift (regrettably not described or illustrated) was accorded the deceased, and the manner in which the bodies were carelessly heaped together might all be seen to point to this conclusion. And yet the creation of a sort of crude tomb for the burial – something we do not encounter in any of the other alleged cases of 'slave burial' but which is paralleled by a post-burial in the dromos of Lapithos Tomb 428 – suggests that the triple burial might be connected just as easily with the unsuitability of the chamber for use as with the final burial in the tomb itself.

(ii) Lapithos, Necropolis at Kastros, Tomb 417. The chamber contained two burials, apparently of a man and a woman, which date to early Cypro-Geometric I.[107] Remains of a third skeleton were also found, a skull outside the door in the dromos and fragments of bone beneath the door packing:

The body was therefore buried there when the door was

> closed, and probably represents a slave burial, the door-keeper of the deceased who was killed at the funeral in order to watch the door of the tomb, and serve them in the life to come, as he had done previously.[108]

It also seems possible that the third skeleton represents an earlier burial which had been pushed aside to make room for a new burial, when pottery was also moved to a corner of the tomb, although it does not seem to have been the custom at Lapithos to sweep earlier interments into the dromos.[109] And Gjerstad clearly considered the skeleton to be *in situ*, although he did not provide explicit evidence for this.

(iii) Lapithos, Necropolis at Kastros, Tomb 420. In the chamber there were three burials, all dating to early Cypro-Geometric I.[110] Also, a niche had been cut in the wall of the dromos near the tomb's entrance for the burial of a child, enclosed by three stone slabs. In the middle of the dromos two skeletons were found lying on their backs with their heads towards the entrance of the dromos. There were no funeral gifts, and the dromos fill consisted of intact layers of chavara. Again Gjerstad concluded that 'probably, they represent burials of slaves killed at the funeral of the deceased, buried in the tomb-chamber'.[111] As with Tomb 412, the homogeneity of the filling indicates that the dromos was cleared when the burial was made in the dromos. But here also portions of the roof and one of the walls of the chamber had caved in, and again we might ask if the tomb was opened and deemed unfit for use. The total absence of funeral gifts with the dromos burials may support Gjerstad's interpretation but also renders it impossible to date the burials relative to the interments made in the chamber.

(iv) Lapithos, Necropolis at Kastros, Tomb 422. There were two burial periods in the chamber of Tomb 422. Of the first, assigned to early Cypro-Geometric I, only scattered skeletal material and some pottery remained. This level was covered over with a layer of chavara, upon which lay a well-preserved skeleton of the later Cypro-Geometric III period, identified as the skeleton of a warrior from a piece of an iron pike lying at its side. The fill of the dromos consisted of a lower layer of chavara mixed with potsherds from the first burial period, a layer of homogeneous chavara, and a top layer of dark sandy earth. Between the top

layer and the second chavara filling three skeletons were found, lying one over the other near the entrance of the dromos. The uppermost skeleton was covered with two stone slabs, with a third smaller slab placed over its neck. Of this uppermost skeleton 'the shoulder-blades were on top of the ribs, the processes of the spinal column were turned up, the hands were tied to each other and the feet were crossed'. It was concluded that the body had been laid face down, bound hand and foot, in the dromos. Beneath it were the skull and scattered bones of a second skeleton ('from the position of the bones it seems that the body had been placed there in a mutilated condition'), and on the bottom a damaged skeleton lay in outstretched position with the head towards the entrance of the dromos (and in a direction opposite to that of the topmost skeleton). Next to the lowermost burial were an amphora and a jug.[112] Also found in the dromos were two rectangular blocks of poros stone, each with a rectangular hole cut in its middle. Cuttings in the rock edge of the dromos suggest that the larger of the blocks had originally lain across the dromos. Gjerstad, who discussed only the larger block, interpreted it as a sacrificial table upon which the three persons whose remains were found in the dromos were immolated, whereupon 'their blood poured down in the hole to satisfy the spirit of the deceased, buried in the tomb'.[113]

As the uppermost skeleton had clearly been bound, we have in Tomb 422 good evidence of some sort of killing, and arguably a ritual killing. The killing may have been carried out on the unusual blocks: at least it is probable that they functioned together and played some role in the funeral, although it is curious that there were two blocks (when we might expect either one or three); and the difference in size may indicate that their functions were not identical. It also seems likely that the three persons were slain in connection with the burial of the person whose skeleton lay in the chamber, although this burial is itself rather mysterious. Burials in the Lapithos cemetery were usually accompanied by substantial amounts of pottery, but with the exception of an iron pike the 'warrior' had no grave gifts. Also, the upper part of his skeleton had been moved slightly from its original position.[114] Both facts suggest that the tomb was entered again at some time after the 'warrior's' burial; and if such was the case, then the connection between his burial and the material in the dromos would seem to be severed. But as portions of the wall and roof of the chamber had collapsed, it is also possible that the 'warrior's' skeleton was disturbed by the fall of rock or that the tomb was entered not through the dromos but through Tomb 425 or Tomb 426, with which Tomb 422 communicated after its collapse.[115]

(v) Lapithos, 'Prostemenos', Tomb P. 74. This tomb was excavated by the expedition of the University Museum (University of Pennsylvania) in 1931 under the direction of Virginia Grace and published in 1965 by A. Pieridou. Four burials were found in the chamber, belonging to two burial periods (early Cypro-Geometric I and Cypro-Geometric II). Partially beneath the blocking wall of the door, on a platform of earth, was another burial:

> The skeleton was placed with the head towards the entrance, with the arms extended and drawn very near to the body at the elbows and the legs close together at the knees. A single jug was placed over the left upper arm of the skeleton. Miss Grace thought, that this uncommon position of the skeleton indicated a sacrifice rather than a last burial.[116]

Pieridou invites us to compare Tomb 422 of the Kastros cemetery, but of course the closest parallel is the burial beneath the door packing of Tomb 417, although the bodies were placed in opposite directions. In the case of Tomb 417, I suggested that the burial may have been a burial displaced from the chamber; but the skeleton in the doorway of Tomb P. 74 was *in situ* and accompanied by a grave gift. Still, it is not certain that the burial in the doorway coincided with the final interment in the chamber. The burial which Pieridou considered the last (without, however, making clear her reasons) had been disturbed.[117] If this 'disarranged' skeleton did in fact represent the last burial made within the chamber, then the burial beneath the door packing could not have been made on the occasion of the final burial; rather, it would seem that the burial in the chamber was disturbed at the time when the actual final burial was made in the doorway.

(vi) Salamis, Tomb 2. Salamis Tomb 2, a built chamber tomb (as opposed to the rock-cut tombs discussed above) had been used for burial in two periods, Cypro-Geometric III/early Cypro-Archaic I and late Cypro-Archaic I.[118] The tomb had been plundered and only fragmentary skeletal remains were found in the chamber. Near the entrance of the tomb were the skeletons of two asses with their bronze trappings and the remains of a chariot.[119] At a

distance of *c.* 2.5 m from the door of the chamber lay a human skeleton with the legs close together and the hands joined 'as if fastened together in front of the body'. There was no evidence of a pit or grave, and there were no funeral gifts. A human skull and other bones were found nearby, these having been 'obviously dispersed by the plow'.[120] Karageorghis concluded that the skeletons represented sacrificed slaves buried when the dromos was refilled with soil at the time of the second burial in the chamber. As with Lapithos Tomb 422, we seem to have convincing evidence of a burial (apparently again a triple burial) made in the dromos at the time of the final use of the chamber: some form of ritual killing seems indicated.[121] And in this case it is certain that the dromos was opened and refilled on the occasion of the last burial, as the asses must have played a role (presumably the transportation of the body) in the funeral; and the asses clearly had been slain (or buried alive). Still, it is strange that while the asses were found on floor level, the human skeleton lay less than a half a metre from the top of the dromos fill.

(vii) Tamassos, Tomb IV.11. Tomb 11 of section IV, one of three 'royal' built tombs excavated at Tamassos by Ohnefalsch-Richter in the last century, was never properly published and has long been completely destroyed. But Masson collected references to the tomb in the various writings of the excavator and reinterpreted the evidence. Tomb 11, dated to the end of the seventh century BC, had a long dromos, in which what Ohnefalsch-Richter had termed 'the earth grave of two warriors' (Grave IV.4) appears to have been located. With this burial were found skeletons of horses buried with their bronze gear, mistakenly thought by Ohnefalsch-Richter to be pieces of armour. Masson interpreted the 'warrior burial' as a burial of sacrificed slaves in the light of the similar discoveries made in the dromos of Salamis Tomb 2.[122] But of course an immediate connection between the horse and human burials can now no longer be established.

(viii) Salamis, 'Cellarka', Tomb 83. The chamber of Tomb 83 (probably early Cypro-Archaic II) of the Archaic and Classical cemetery 'Cellarka' (located *c.* 500 m south of the 'royal' necropolis) had been thoroughly plundered and contained no skeletal remains, but the stratigraphy of the dromos filling indicated two burial periods.[123] Also, several later pit burials had been made in the dromos. But skeleton *h* lay directly on the layer of fill (5)

associated with the first burial period and was covered by the layer (4) associated with the second. The head and lower legs had been displaced by looters' pits, but the remainder of the skeleton was undisturbed: 'This suggests that the skeleton was not thrown out of the chamber, but was buried at the time of the second burial in the dromos, then covered with layer (4).' Karageorghis interpreted this as the skeleton of a sacrificed slave.[124] But this was no ordinary 'slave burial' (if such it was), for fragments of an egg were found with the skeleton, and there was an iron ring on one of its fingers. Also, the surrounding earth was stained a dark brown, and two bronze nails were found near the skeleton's chest: this suggests that the body was buried in a wooden coffin.[125] The stratigraphy of the fill indicates that the dromos was opened at least twice and that skeleton *h* was buried near the tomb's entrance when the dromos was filled in for the final time. But we cannot be absolutely certain that the burial of this skeleton, so unlike any other of the 'slave burials' we have encountered, was connected with the final interment in the chamber.

(ix) Vouni, Necropolis of Korakas, Tomb 10. Tomb 10 was a rectangular shaft cut into the rock in between two chamber tombs (7 and 11), which both date to the Cypro-Classic II period. A skeleton, without funeral gifts, lay on its back, uncomfortably wedged between the sides of the very narrow grave (maximum width at the bottom: 0.25 m). In Westholm's opinion this may have been 'a sacrificial burial of a slave, killed when his master was buried' in either Tomb 7 or Tomb 11.[126] But only the poverty of this burial and the narrow dimensions of the grave might be seen to support this interpretation. A similar shaft grave (Tomb 5) of the same cemetery contained a burial accompanied by a single jug, but the burial apparently was not considered 'sacrificial' by either Westholm or Gjerstad.[127] It is probable that both Tombs 5 and 10 were graves of relatively poor people, but there is no good reason to think that they had been sacrificed or killed in connection with the funerals of their more well-to-do neighbours in the cemetery.

For the most part the Cypriot dromos burials exhibit more differences than points of comparison, and it is doubtful that they all were made under the same circumstances or reflect one and the same custom. Among the differences are the number of skeletons, the presence or absence of grave goods, the location of the burials, and the treatment of the corpses. At first glance the burials in the dromoi of Lapithos Tombs 422 and 412 may seem closely comparable: in each case three skeletons were piled together in the dromos, the uppermost face down. But the similarity ends there, for the binding of one person, the reported mutilation of another, the covering slabs over the bodies, and the mysterious blocks found in the dromos of Tomb 422 render this burial unique and combine to build the most persuasive case for 'foul play' among the Cypriot 'slave burials'. The burials in the doorways of Lapithos Tombs P. 74 and 417 also resemble one another – at least if the latter was in fact *in situ*. Yet in neither case is it certain that the burial was made at the same time as the last burial in the chamber: it is possible that these 'doorway burials' were themselves the final burials, despite what may seem to us a very strange location. All archaeology can tell us is that occasionally the citizens of Geometric Lapithos buried their dead in the doorways of tombs – apparently either because the chamber was considered no longer suitable for burial or because there was something special about the person interred in the doorway.

In the cases of Lapithos Tombs 412 and 420 and Salamis Tomb 83, the homogeneity of the fill indicates that the burials were made when the dromos was cleared and refilled for a final time. But again it is uncertain if the burials were related to any of the burials in the chamber. Structural damage may have rendered Tombs 412 and 420 unusable, necessitating burial in the dromos instead. And the burial in the dromos of Tomb 83 – with a ring, an egg, and a coffin – stands apart from the other dromos burials, and I doubt that this otherwise innocent-looking burial represents the same 'custom' or circumstances as the violent triple burial of Lapithos Tomb 422. The burial in the dromos of Salamis Tomb 2 was clearly connected with the funeral of the last person interred in the chamber, when two asses were killed and left in the dromos; and one of the humans may have been bound. The dual burial in the dromos of Tamassos Tomb IV.11 may also have been contemporary with the horse burials found there, but here the evidence is lost beyond recovery. Finally, the interpretation of the burial in Vouni Tomb 10 as that of a sacrificed slave is without foundation.

ARCHAEOLOGICAL EVIDENCE OF 'SUTTEE'?

In his discussion of the burial of the 'King' and 'Queen' in the Dendra tholos Persson referred to three other dual burials, from Asine, Gonia, and Zygouries.[128] The first was the Middle Helladic grave Asine 52–3, excavated by Persson, which contained the burial of a man of about 40 years and a 30-to-40-year-old woman. Both skeletons were in contracted position, and the woman's skeleton lay partially over that of the man's so that the skulls nearly touched. This unusual arrangement and the fact that the lower skeleton was undisturbed indicates that the two were interred simultaneously, and Persson seems to have considered this a case of 'suttee' also.[129] A MH grave (VII) at Gonia also contained two skeletons, lying close together each on its left side. From the relative size of the skeletons and the presence of three bone hairpins near the skull of the smaller, Blegen concluded that they were skeletons of a man and a woman. The burial seems to have been simultaneous, and 'the two persons interred together were presumably man and wife'.[130] The MH Tomb XXII at Zygouries contained in its lowest layer two skeletons, in a very poor state of preservation, which faced each other. The two had been buried 'almost surely at the same time', but as the burial seems to have been of an adult and a child, I am not certain why Persson cited it in this connection.[131]

In order to evaluate Persson's interpretation of the man-woman burials from Asine and Gonia let us look briefly at the Middle Helladic cemetery at Lerna, which is at once the largest and the best documented. Of 228 graves only 16 contained more than one burial.[132] Some of these multiple burials were consecutive (i.e. represented reuse of the grave), while in eight or nine cases the dual or multiple burials were probably or very possibly simultaneous.[133] Two of these graves contained burials of an adult male and an adult female, and in one case the burial is almost certainly simultaneous. Another grave contained five skeletons, three of adult females, one of an adult male, and one of an infant. And there were also four dual burials of adult males, at least one of which was simultaneous.[134] But the great majority of the Lerna graves contained single interments: of the adult burials, I count thirty-six males, twenty-nine females, and three of undetermined sex. Clearly, therefore, the majority of men in this community did not require their wives to accompany them to the grave. And as other kinds of multiple burial, including burials of two adult males, are also found in the cemetery, it seems probable that all of the simultaneous dual and multiple burials were due to simultaneous death from disease or accident.[135] Death from some sort of violence cannot be excluded, nor can the possibility of suicide from grief be ruled out. But even if the suicide of a wife upon the death of her husband was something deemed highly honourable, but not obligatory, we should expect better representation than we find in the Lerna cemetery.

The figures from other Middle Helladic cemeteries are similar. The dual burial at Asine was one of two dual burials in the 105 graves excavated, and Grave VII at Gonia was the only grave (of seven) which contained more than one skeleton.[136] And of all MH graves, only around 12 per cent held more than one burial.[137] But as in most cases the skeletons did not benefit from anthropological study and as the question of simultaneity was usually not addressed, the publications are of little value here. No doubt the findings would not differ significantly from those from Lerna and would support the conclusion that 'suttee' was not a custom in the Middle Helladic period.[138]

The above observations are fine – as far as they go. But according to Herodotus, among the Scythians it was only at the funerals of kings that concubines (along with servants) were killed (Hdt. 4.71.4), a practice which he explicitly contrasts with the burials of other Scythians (4.73.1). And even if not the prerogative of royalty, the practice of 'suttee' may have been confined to the nobility, to the leaders of a warrior society: we should perhaps be looking for evidence, not of a *Volkssitte*, but of an *Adelssitte*.[139] And yet in the shaft graves in the two grave circles at Mycenae – tombs of a military ruling class *par excellence* – there is no evidence of the custom.[140] Our knowledge of burial practices in the tholos tombs is imperfect, as burials were most often made on the floor; and because the tombs were usually plundered, the skeletal material has not survived. But thus far the only certain dual burial of a man and a woman is that found in pit I of the 'royal' tholos at Dendra. And I know of no evidence of 'suttee' from Mycenaean chamber tombs, although in this case the evidence is obscured by repeated reuse of the tombs.

The suggestion that dual burials represent the practice of 'suttee' has also been made, very tentatively, for a few Middle and Late Minoan burials. A LM II chamber tomb at Knossos contained two skeletons, one in very poor state of preservation, which were identified as the skeletons of a man and a woman on the basis of their grave goods. The 'woman' was buried on the floor, the 'man' on a bench along a wall of the tomb. In the excavators' opinion the two were buried at the same time, and 'it is therefore worth bearing in mind the possibility of a wife or concubine killing herself or being killed on the death of her husband or master'.[141] In another cemetery in the Knossos area, a LM IIIA2 tomb (X) had on its lowest layer two skeletons, tentatively identified from their grave goods as skeletons of a man and a woman, and possibly, but not certainly, interred simultaneously. In the same cemetery a MM II/IIIA tomb (XVIII) contained the remains of at least nine burials; two of these were 'perhaps' of a man and woman, and they seem to have been buried simultaneously, for the skeletons were undisturbed and the arms of the 'woman's' lay over the left knee of the 'man'. With apparent reference to these two cases, S. Hood wrote: 'In cases where a pair of skeletons were found, the possibility cannot be quite excluded that there was only one occasion of burial, and that some form of suttee was practised, although there was no evidence to indicate this.'[142] Hood has also (but again very tentatively) suggested that the Mycenaean settlers of Cyprus practised some form of 'suttee', but here the evidence seems even less compelling.[143]

In order for it to be determined with a reasonable degree of probability that a dual burial represents a case of 'suttee', I recommend the following: (1) the sex (and age) of the two persons should be determined, not merely from the grave goods or the size of the skeletons, but by anthropological study; (2) the simultaneity of the burials should be established or at least shown to be probable;[144] (3) ideally, there should be physical evidence of the violent death of the woman; (4) again ideally, there should be some indication of the special nature – or what has been called the 'ritual character' – of the burial, such as the subordination of the woman's burial to the man's by its position, or a distinction between the two persons regarding the amount of grave gifts or manner of burial;[145] (5) if 'suttee' is to be shown to be a custom, then we should expect a certain frequency of man–woman burials in a given cemetery or in tombs of the same type in the same region and period; we might also expect some uniformity in the manner of burial;[146] (6) on the other hand, if it was only the boon of kings, nobles, or warriors to be accompanied in the afterlife by their wives or concubines, then their burials should be clearly distinguishable from those of ordinary citizens; and even here support from parallels would be desirable. In short, without evidence of violent death, parallels from the same cemetery or period, or some indication of the 'ritual character' or special circumstances of the burial, archaeology is unable to distinguish between cases of 'suttee' and ordinary burials of men and women who happened to die at the same time.

It would not be fitting to close this section without mention of a Protogeometric burial recently excavated at Lefkandi in Euboea, certainly among the most spectacular and important discoveries in the history of Greek archaeology. A shaft, consisting of two compartments, contained in one compartment the burial of three or four horses, and in the other, which was lined with mudbrick coated with plaster, a human skeleton and the remains of a cremation in a bronze amphora. The skeleton was of a woman, lying on her back with her feet together and her hands crossed at the stomach: she had been buried wearing gilt coils in her hair, a gold and faience necklace with a gold pendant, and gold discs over her breasts. Beside her head lay an iron knife with an ivory handle. In the amphora was found a remarkably well-preserved cloth, but it is unclear from the preliminary report what human remains, if any, had survived. On the grounds that the rim of the amphora was decorated with a hunting scene and that beside the amphora were found an iron sword, a spearhead, and a whetstone, it is thought that the amphora held the cremation of an adult male. Above the grave a large apsidal building (10 m wide and at least 45 m long) had been constructed in mudbrick on a socle of rough stones. Upon discovery of the burial which lay beneath the building

> it was . . . clear that the structure was not a temple erected for the worship of one of the Olympian gods but was a heröon in honour of the warrior whose ashes, accompanied by his consort and his horses, were buried at its centre.[147]

Traces of an intense fire and a circle of postholes filled with charred wood – to all appearances the remains of a funeral pyre – were found beneath the clay floor of the heröon, and it seems that the cremation of the presumed warrior was the central event of an elaborate funeral ceremony.[148] But what place did the woman's burial have in the ceremony? That her burial represented some sort of 'suttee' is not expressly suggested by the excavators, although it is surely implied in the sentence quoted above. But if her killing or suicide was motivated by a belief that she would accompany her husband or master in the life to come, then it may seem strange that her body was not cremated along with his on the funeral pyre, as, for example, in the Indian custom. And yet the distinction between modes of burial – even if difficult to explain – would seem to argue against the chance death of a couple from the same cause, and we find the same combination of cremation and inhumation in Celtic and Germanic burials thought to represent cases of 'Witwentotung'.[149] On the basis of the information now available, a fairly strong case could be made that the burial at Lefkandi (which seems to satisfy most of the criteria suggested above)[150] represents some form of the practice also, but of course judgement should be suspended until the appearance of a more detailed publication.

CONCLUSION

The excavators' interpretation of the finds from Anemospilia depends on a number of factors, which may seem compelling in combination. But if the room in which the three skeletons were found was not a place where blood sacrifices were normally performed, if the 'altar' was not an altar, and if the 'sacrificial knife' was in fact a spearhead, then the case for human sacrifice is much weakened and rests largely on the position of the 'victim's' skeleton. In my opinion it has not yet been convincingly demonstrated that the young man was not simply a victim of earthquake rather than of sacrifice; but the possibility that the quake interrupted a violent scene of a non-sacral character should perhaps also be considered. The situation with the children's bones from Knossos is very different: here there is indisputable evidence for the repeated cutting of the bones, and removal of flesh seems the only reasonable explanation. But why flesh was removed and what was done with it afterwards are not questions that archaeology can answer, at least so long as parallels are wanting. To my mind certain features point to some sort of burial preparation rather than to cannibalism, but at present any interpretation is necessarily largely speculative.

The skeletons on the floor of the 'royal' tholos at Dendra could have belonged to persons buried either before or after the burial of the King and Queen; surely the skeletal remains in the small pit in the rear of the tomb came from a previous burial. The two skeletons found on the floor of the Kazarma tholos possibly present better evidence of 'human sacrifice', but it is impossible to judge from the brief publications. Of four alleged instances of 'slave burial' in the dromoi of Mycenaean chamber tombs, only the burial of six individuals one over the other in the dromos of Tomb 15 at Mycenae might reasonably be considered evidence of ritual killing, and even here the interpretation is by no means certain. The case for some form of funerary ritual killing in Cyprus is, at least in two cases (Lapithos Tomb 422 and Salamis Tomb 2), convincing, although the opinion that Greek settlers brought the custom with them from the mainland will be open to question as long as the Mycenaean evidence remains at best equivocal.

Whether the Greeks at any time practised 'suttee' is an open question. Even when the simultaneity of man–woman burials can be established, it is difficult, if not impossible, to distinguish between cases of 'suttee' and burials of men and women who happened to perish at the same time from disease, accident, or violence. Such was the case with the dual burial in the Dendra tholos, as Persson himself acknowledged; but the evidence from the Protogeometric burial at Lefkandi may prove to be more conclusive.

3

Funerary ritual killing in Greek literature and history

THE FUNERAL OF PATROCLUS

It has sometimes been remarked that human sacrifices, which occur fairly frequently in Greek myth and early epic, are noticeably absent from the Homeric poems, an omission attributed to the humane sensibilities of the poet.[1] There is, however, one seeming exception: Achilles' slaughter of twelve Trojan captives before the pyre of Patroclus in the twenty-third book of the *Iliad*.[2] This incident so distressed Plato that he simply denied that Achilles had committed the deed, and the reactions of many modern Homeric scholars have been similar: shock and distaste (reactions sometimes projected back onto the psyche of Homer himself), a quick dismissal, or, more often than not, complete silence.[3] Scholars of Greek religion and funeral practices, on the other hand, have shown great interest in the slaying of the captives, considering it valuable evidence for actual custom among the early Greeks. But the precise nature of the custom has been disputed.

In the eighteenth book of the *Iliad*, after Patroclus' body has been recovered and brought back to camp, Achilles vows to his fallen companion:

> 'But now, Patroclus, since I go after you under the earth,
> I shall not perform your funeral before bringing here
> the armour and head of Hector, your great-hearted slayer.
> And before the pyre I shall slash the throats of twelve
> of the Trojans' splendid sons, enraged at your slaying.'
> (*Il.* 18.333–7)

On the following day Achilles receives his new armour and

returns at long last to battle. At one point he retires from his bloody rampage in the river in order to select the promised twelve Trojans:

> . . . but when his arms had tired from killing,
> alive from the river twelve young men he chose,
> compensation for the dead Patroclus, Menoetius' son.
> He drove them out to shore dazed like fawns
> and bound their hands in back with well-cut straps,
> which they themselves wore on their pliant coats,
> and he gave them to comrades to take to the hollow ships.
> But back he sped, eager to slaughter more.
>
> (21.26–33)

When Achilles has killed Hector and returned to camp, he again calls out to the departed spirit of Patroclus:

> 'Rejoice, o Patroclus, even in Hades' halls,
> for even now I fulfil for you all that I promised before:
> to drag Hector here and give him to dogs to tear at raw
> and before the pyre to slash the throats of twelve
> of the Trojans' splendid sons, enraged at your slaying.'
>
> (23.19–23)

On the following day a huge pyre is built for Patroclus. Sheep and cattle are flayed; Achilles wraps the corpse in their fat and piles the flayed bodies around Patroclus. Then, after leaning amphoras of honey and oil against the bier, Achilles slays four horses and two of his (or Patroclus') nine 'table dogs' and hurls them onto the pyre (23.163–74). The slaughter culminates with the twelve Trojan captives:

> And twelve noble sons of the great-hearted Trojans
> he slew with bronze. And grim deeds he devised in his heart,
> and released the fire's iron might, that it consume all.
> He then groaned aloud and called his dear friend by name:
> 'Rejoice, o Patroclus, even in Hades' halls,
> for even now I fulfil for you all that I promised before:
> twelve noble sons of the great-hearted Trojans
> along with you the fire devours them all. But Priam's son
> Hector
> by no means will I give to fire to feed on, but to dogs.'
>
> (23.175–83)

Finally, on the morning after the funeral Achilles orders his men to quench the smoking pyre with wine and gather up Patroclus' bones:

> '. . . and these are easy to distinguish,
> for he lay in the middle of the pyre, but the others apart
> on the edge were burned, in a jumble, horses and men.'
> (23.240–2)

The slaying of the twelve Trojan warriors at the pyre of Patroclus has been interpreted in three basic (if not always clearly distinct) ways: (1) that the killing was a sacrifice, fully equivalent to animal sacrifices performed for the dead, or in the cult of heroes and chthonic deities;[4] (2) that the Trojan captives were meant to attend Patroclus as servants in the world below;[5] or (3) that the killing was motivated, largely or solely, by anger and revenge.[6] In the first two cases it is assumed that the incident derived from actual custom, but that the poet of the *Iliad* had 'forgotten' or misunderstood the true meaning of an obsolete practice preserved in the epic tradition.

Erwin Rohde argued most eloquently and at greatest length for the sacrificial character of the slaying:

> what else but a sacrifice, i.e. a repast offered in satisfaction of the needs of the person honoured . . . can be intended by this stream of blood about the corpse; this slaughtering and burning of cattle and sheep, horses and dogs, and finally of twelve Trojan prisoners on or at the funeral pyre? . . . The whole procedure gives a picture of primitive sacrificial ritual in honour of the dead and differs in no particular from the ritual of sacrifice to the θεοὶ χθόνιοι.[7]

Rohde found these extravagant funeral proceedings inconsistent with the Homeric conception of the soul's miserable and shadowy existence after death and therefore felt that the description of Achilles' deeds before Patroclus' pyre derived from a time when the ghost of a dead man was considered powerful and dangerous, requiring propitiation, a period, moreover, of 'vigorous worship of the dead'. But the meaning of Achilles' actions, which 'cannot be made to fit in with the ordinary circle of Homeric ideas', was no longer understood by the time of the composition of the *Iliad*.[8]

Crucial to Rohde's interpretation is the assumption that all of the various victims – sheep and cattle, horses and dogs, and

Trojan captives – were equivalent and slain for the same purpose; but this assumption is questionable. Sheep and cattle are also killed at Achilles' funeral (*Od.* 24.64–5) and seem to be the usual victims of funerary sacrifices.[9] But at the funeral of Patroclus the animals are also flayed and their fat wrapped around the corpse, a procedure which suggests a second (and apparently secondary) function – to supply fat to help the body to burn.[10] The dogs and horses, however, are not flayed, and in any case they belong to an entirely different class of animal from sheep and cattle.[11] Homer gives no indication of the reasons for their killing, but the simplest and widely accepted interpretation is that they are to be counted among the possessions of Patroclus. The slaying of horses and dogs may thus be seen as an extension of the practice of providing the dead with weapons and other goods, well known to archaeology, which lies behind the Homeric phrase κτέρεα κτερεΐζειν and the like.[12]

If the slaying of the Trojan captives in fact derived from an actual custom of sacrificing human victims to appease the ghost of the deceased, this original sacrificial character has left no discernible trace in the language of the poem.[13] The word used to describe the killing at *Il.* 18.336 and 23.22, *apodeirotomein* ('cut the throat of'),[14] appears only in these two places in the *Iliad*, although it occurs once in the *Odyssey* (11.35), where Odysseus slays sheep over the bothros to awaken the spirits of the dead. It is used by Hesiod (*Theog.* 280) of the beheading of Medusa. The simple form *deirotomein* is used of the two dogs killed at Patroclus' funeral (*Il.* 23.174), of cattle slaughtered by Hermes in the Homeric Hymn to Hermes (405), but also twice in the *Iliad* (21.89, 21.555) and once in the *Odyssey* (22.349) with human (but non-sacrificial) objects. Thus *deirotomein* and *apodeirotomein* seem to be purely neutral terms, applicable both to human and animal objects and without specifically sacrificial connotations. In this respect they may be contrasted with *sphazein*, which, while equivalent to *(apo)deirotomein* in basic meaning, is used in Homer only of animals killed in the act of sacrifice.[15] And the other expression used to describe the killing of the Trojan captives, χαλκῷ δηϊόων (23.176), is a formula borrowed from the battlefield.[16]

The fact that the Trojan captives were twelve in number might be taken as an indication of the sacrificial nature of the killing, for sacrifices of twelve animal victims occur occasionally both in the

Homeric poems and in later Greek cult.[17] But the number 'twelve' is used sixty times in the two poems, with a great variety of applications: men killed or wounded in battle, the amount of a leader's ships, the number of a person's children, etc.[18] The ransom offered by Agamemnon to Achilles includes twelve horses (*Il.* 9.123, 9.265, 19.244); several items in Priam's ransom for Hector's body are in sets of twelve (24.229–31); and in the *Odyssey* Maron gives Odysseus, among other gifts, twelve amphoras of wine (*Od.* 9.204). Thus 'twelve' is a relatively large number, appropriate to gifts and offers of ransom as well as to offerings to the gods. Homer's fondness for the number may be due in part to its adaptability, in its various forms (δώδεκα, δυώδεκα, δυοκαίδεκα), to the hexameter. But the occasional appearance of the number in sacrificial contexts is not sufficient grounds for attaching sacrificial significance to the slaying of the twelve captives.

More frequently it has been maintained that the slaughter of the captives preserves a memory of a prehistoric custom of killing servants or slaves at their masters' funerals in order that they might serve them in the life to come. It is true that such practices are known from other cultures,[19] but there is no good evidence for Greece of any period. And as with the sacrificial interpretation, there is no indication of the supposed custom in the text of the poem, and again it must be assumed that the poet was unaware of the original sense of an obsolete practice. For if Homer fails to explain why Achilles slew sheep, cattle, dogs, and horses before Patroclus' pyre, he expresses very clearly Achilles' reasons for killing the Trojans. Achilles twice gives anger over Patroclus' death as his motivation (*Il.* 18.337, 23.23), in each case linking his promise to slay the captives to the mutilation of Hector's corpse. And the poet himself refers to the twelve Trojans as a *poinē* of Patroclus (21.28): compensation, requital, or payment for his death, a 'blood-price'.[20]

There is no reason, I might add, to believe that Homer wished to 'downplay' the incident, as has sometimes been alleged. 'That the writer has certain qualms on the subject is indicated by the brevity – not at all like Homer – with which the most shocking part of the story, the slaughter of human beings . . . is hurried over', wrote Rohde, and Murray that the incident 'is crowded into a shame-faced line and a half . . . You could scarcely have a clearer case of a poet recording a fact against his will.'[21] While it is true that only one and a half lines are devoted to the actual killing, the act is mentioned a total of six times in the poem, including 23.181–2, where Achilles addresses Patroclus immediately following the killing, and 23.241–2, surely a gratuitous allusion if Homer truly had not wished to dwell on the episode. As early as the eighteenth book Achilles promises to slay the Trojans (18.336–7), and in the twenty-first seven lines are devoted to their capture (21.26–32). Together with the vengeful mutilation of Hector's corpse (the importance of which has been recognized),[22] the slaughter of the captives is given great prominence in this section of the poem.[23] Furthermore, whatever we ourselves may think of the morality of the killing, there is little justification for the commonly held opinion that the poet meant to condemn Achilles' actions explicitly with the words κακὰ δὲ φρεσὶ μήδετο ἔργα at 23.176.[24]

Homer represents the killing of the Trojans as an act of anger and vengeance for Patroclus' death at the hands of Hector. But that it is precisely comparable to other acts of revenge in the poem, as has sometimes been stated,[25] is clearly not the case, for elsewhere acts of vengeance are carried out on the field of battle: it is rather the killing of Hector which is equivalent to these.[26] But in the case of the twelve Trojans, Achilles promises to kill a specific number of warriors, he captures them alive for the purpose, and on the next day he slaughters them before the pyre during an elaborate funeral ceremony. Surely this is vengeance of a very different order: it is a ritual act, which might be termed 'ritual revenge'. This is true not only in that Achilles' act is incorporated into the ritual sequence of the funeral ceremony; but the killing itself is an 'action redirected for demonstration', 'a spontaneous reaction artificially exaggerated for the purpose of demonstration'.[27] When Patroclus is killed, Achilles' grief is overwhelming, and from this grief stems an uncontrolled violence, directed not only towards Hector and all other Trojans, but even, it seems, towards himself (18.32–4). These are the spontaneous reactions to Patroclus' death: grief, anger, violence, the need for vengeance. Yet in the very midst of his indiscriminate slaughter in the river, Achilles calmly captures twelve Trojan warriors, binds their hands, and turns them over to his fellow soldiers for later execution at the funeral. This cool-headed, premeditated selection not only distinguishes the slaughter of the captives from actions committed in direct emotional response to

Patroclus' death and indicates its essentially ritual character, but also it provides the best argument that the passage is based upon actual practice: the slaying of captives cannot be explained solely in the context of Achilles' psychological state and is thus less likely to have been purely a product of the Homeric imagination.

But what is the purpose of this special, ritualized act of vengeance? From Achilles' perspective, the slaying is clearly perceived to be in Patroclus' interest: 'Now I fulfil for you', says Achilles, twice (23.20 and 23.180). The repeated invocation of Patroclus and the exaction of a 'blood-price' before the pyre – like the stretching of Hector's corpse next to the bier of Patroclus before the funeral (23.25–6) and the later dragging of the corpse around the burial mound (24.15–18) – must have been meant to render the action perceptible to Patroclus' spirit. And yet a funeral is a communal act, and its rituals are directed as much towards the living as the dead, if not more so. Achilles takes his revenge on the battlefield, but his vengeance is recreated and put on display, as it were, during the funeral, thus reinforcing the solidarity of the army after the loss of one of its members. When the act is seen in this light, the funeral seems a natural and suitable occasion for the exaction of vengeance.[28]

Is there any relationship between what I call 'ritual revenge' and funerary sacrifice, the killing of animal victims which are burned whole or abandoned at the grave? Or to sacrifices to heroes, generally thought to have developed from funerary sacrifice? Meuli derived funerary sacrifices from the grief and rage felt upon the death of a loved one: weeping, the tearing of hair and clothing, the destruction of property, and the killing of animals and humans are all expressions, sincere or merely ceremonial, of these natural emotions. And thus in Meuli's view we should understand Achilles' slaughter of men and animals before Patroclus' pyre.[29] But even if Meuli's derivation is correct, I should think that the killing of members of the opposing army after the death of a warrior in battle constitutes a special case; and there is no certain evidence of such 'destructive sacrifices' of human victims in Greece at the funerals of persons who had died non-violently. On the surface there is an undeniable similarity between vengeance carried out at funerals – at least as represented by Homer – and the act of 'funerary sacrifice'. But there are also important differences: the performance of funerary sacrifices is not confined to cases where the deceased died by violence; the element of vengeance is (seemingly) absent; and the victims are animals. One might speculate on possible prehistoric or 'original' relationships between funerary sacrifice and the sort of ritualized vengeance killing found in Homer: the exaction of vengeance even in the case of non-violent death,[30] the development of funerary sacrifice from a custom of avenging murder at the grave, the substitution of animals for human victims, etc. But it is quite possible, and in my view more probable, that the sacrifice of animals and the exaction of vengeance at the tomb were two independent rituals, in origin and in their subsequent development.

Even if 'ritual vengeance' carried out at funerals is distinct in origin and function from other forms of funerary ritual killing, it remains possible that such an act could be 'over-determined', i.e. that it could be viewed by the participants as performing additional functions, beyond the primary purpose of exacting vengeance. It would not be surprising if an act of ritual vengeance should also be considered a kind of sacrifice offered to honour or appease the dead or if it should be accompanied by a belief that those killed would thereafter serve the deceased in the world below.[31] Still, there is no evidence in the text of Homer of such beliefs; the 'over-determination' of Achilles' action has rather been a product of modern times. And scholars have all too readily dismissed the poet's own representation of the slaughter of the Trojans, without adequately addressing the question why Homer should have understood it as he did. At least we should expect his characterization of the act to have been intelligible and acceptable to his audience, and it is plausible that actual ritual practice lay behind the 'blood-price' exacted by Achilles at Patroclus' pyre. This is imaginative literature, of course, and Homer's picture of the funeral proceedings may be highly exaggerated and inaccurate from a historical point of view. Still, it does not seem likely that he would simply invent a ritual detail such as this from thin air.[32] And the existence of such a custom is supported by the sporadic occurrence of similar ritual killings even in the historical period.

FUNERARY RITUAL KILLING IN GREEK HISTORY

According to Justinus, Alexander had the accomplices in the assassination of Philip II killed at his father's tomb: *Prima illi cura paternarum exequiarum fuit, in quibus ante omnia caedis conscios ad tumulum patris occidi iussit* (Just. *Epit.* 11.2.1). Justinus' *Epitome* of Pompeius Trogus may not be our most reliable source for Alexander's history, but I can see no decisive reason to reject his testimony here. Other writers speak of the punishment of conspirators (Plut. *Alex.* 10.4, Diod. Sic. 17.2.1, Arr. *Anab.* 1.25.1), but it is not said how or where. Diodorus, it is true, treats the punishment of the assassins and the burial of Philip as two distinct events, and in that order. But it is possible that the execution took place at the tomb but before the funeral ceremony itself (for so we may read Justinus' sentence, understanding the execution as only the first act in a lengthy process of *exequiae*); or that Diodorus, who disposes of the punishment of the conspirators and Philip's funeral in a single sentence, in the process of abridging his source obscured the relationship between the punishment and the burial.[33] In addition, a papyrus fragment concerning the death of Philip contains, in two successive lines, references to execution by *apotympanismos* (apparently a method of execution whereby criminals were shackled to boards and left to die)[34] and to Philip's corpse; but the fragment, which has defied certain interpretation, may not refer to an execution at the funeral itself.[35] In any case, Justinus' statement is not directly contradicted by any extant account, and, *faute de mieux*, we seem to have a historical example of execution at the tomb, and possibly during the funeral, of a murdered man.

Alexander's campaign against the Cossaeans has also been cited in this connection. According to Plutarch, after the death of Hephaestion Alexander received an oracle from Ammon instructing him to sacrifice to Hephaestion as a hero. He proceeded to hunt down and massacre the Cossaeans, 'and this was called', concludes Plutarch, 'the *enagismos* ['hero-sacrifice'] of Hephaestion' (*Alex.* 72.2–3). It has been suggested that Alexander was imitating Achilles here,[36] but if so, he was imitating Achilles' deeds on the battlefield, not the ritual killing of the twelve Trojans. This surely is not a case of human sacrifice but rather of sacrificial metaphor applied (it is not said by whom) to a military campaign, undertaken to assuage Alexander's grief. In fact, we find the same metaphor in Plutarch's account of the military exploits with which Pyrrhus consoled himself for the loss of his son (*Pyrrh.* 31.1). And Plutarch's version of the events is highly suspect, for he is the only source to connect Alexander's campaign against the Cossaeans with the oracle from Ammon. Indeed Arrian places the campaign well after Hephaestion's death, when Alexander was already recovering from his grief (*Anab.* 7.15.2), but well before the arrival of the oracle enjoining hero-sacrifices to his friend (7.23.6; cf. Diod. Sic. 17.111.4–6 and 115.6).

Another of Achilles' deeds finds a parallel in fourth-century history. According to a number of accounts, all probably deriving ultimately from Aristotle, Simus of Larissa, the tyrant of the mid-fourth century, dragged Eurydamas son of Meidius around the tomb of his (Simus') brother Thrasyllus, whom Eurydamas had murdered.[37] Aristotle will have adduced the contemporary example in defence of Achilles' dragging of Hector's body around the burial mound of Patroclus, an action to which Plato had raised objections (*Resp.* 3, 391B); but Achilles, Aristotle argued, was only following a custom of his native Thessaly. One source states, on the authority of Callimachus, that Simus killed Eurydamas before dragging his body (Schol. Bb Ov. *Ib.* 331), so it is possible that the execution took place at the tomb also. Still, it seems doubtful that this was a Thessalian custom, as is alleged in the sources, rather than an individual act of Simus. Still less credible is the contention that the Homeric description of Achilles' dragging of Hector was based upon Thessalian custom: the reverse, that Simus consciously imitated the passage from the *Iliad*, is much more plausible.[38]

In 182 BC the Achaean general Philopoemen was taken captive and later (it was said) forced to drink poison in his cell at Messene. When Messene fell, the Messenian commander Deinocrates committed suicide, those who had voted for Philopoemen's death were killed immediately, and those who had voted to have him tortured were arrested, to die themselves by torture (Plut. *Phil.* 18.4–21.2). The Achaean army then marched to Megalopolis with Philopoemen's cremated remains, and according to Plutarch a group of Messenian prisoners of unspecified number was stoned to death around the tomb (*Phil.* 21.5). The stoning of the prisoners, though not mentioned in other sources (Livy 39.50.9; Paus. 8.51.8), is historical, for the young Polybius, from whom Plutarch will have derived his information,[39] was present at the funeral (*Phil.* 21.3).

In addition to these historical examples, in Plato's *Laws* the Athenian recommends that a slave who has killed or plotted the death of a free man be taken by the public executioner to within sight of the dead man's tomb to be flogged, the number of stripes being determined by his accuser. If he survives the flogging, he is to be put to death (Pl. *Leg.* 9, 872B–C). Plato's insistence that the slave be brought to a point where he can see the tomb suggests another motive for execution at the grave: to impress upon the killer, as he is executed facing the tomb, the reason for his punishment and the magnitude of his crime.

The killing of conspirators at Philip's tomb was an execution, as were Simus' killing of Eurydamas and Plato's recommended punishment of a slave. The stoning of the Messenian prisoners, on the other hand, was an additional act of retribution, and of the historical cases it is most closely comparable to the slaying of the Trojans in the *Iliad.* But all of the killings may be classed together as acts of vengeance carried out, if not during the funeral itself, then at the tomb of a murdered man. And it may be, as scholars have suggested, that these scattered instances reflect an earlier, more widespread practice. If so, then the custom will have existed in pre-legal society, before legal process and public execution took the place of private vengeance by the clan.[40] But it is possible that the custom was from the beginning a military practice, occasionally adopted also by absolute rulers. For such it was both in the *Iliad* and in the historical period. Finally, it seems possible that Achilles' slaughter of Trojan captives was partly responsible for the survival, or revival, of such customs: this at least is likely in the case of Alexander, who claimed ancestry from Achilles and for whom according to tradition Achilles was something of a role model.[41]

Whatever the prehistory of these practices, there is no justification for considering the execution of Messenian captives a sacrifice to the heroized Philopoemen (as did Rohde), much less a survival, perhaps no longer understood, of a custom of providing the dead with servitors (Schwenn).[42] It was clearly an act of vengeance, even if the reprisal extended well beyond the actual perpetrator, as it had in Homer. And it is worth noting that the authors who reported these ritual killings do not seem to have regarded them as sacrifices of any kind. Had the killing of the Messenians been so regarded, we should have expected a word of protest from that staunch opponent of human sacrifice, Plutarch.[43] But, on the contrary, Plutarch wrote that Philopoemen was buried ὡς εἰκός, ἐνδόξως (*Phil.* 21.5), and he seems to have considered the stoning as the last of a series of acts of vengeance (τιμωρία: *Phil.* 21.1) exacted for Philopoemen's death. Plato surely was not advocating human sacrifice, and I see no essential difference between his suggested manner of execution and the historical cases. As in the *Iliad*, sacrificial vocabulary is lacking in all of the accounts, and, more significantly, the reported means of killing – flogging, stoning, and possibly apotympanismos (? at Philip's tomb) – are all methods of punishment and execution, not of sacrifice.[44]

EVIDENCE OF 'SUTTEE' IN GREEK MYTH?

In Euripides' *Suppliants* (980–1071) Evadne leaps from a cliff onto the pyre of Campaneus, a dramatic suicide which Nilsson called 'precious testimony as to Mycenaean funeral customs'. But the view that this story derives from a prehistoric custom of 'suttee', voiced also by others,[45] is open to a number of objections. For one thing, Evadne's leap appears for the first time in this play and may well have been the invention of Euripides, who was fond of the themes of noble suicide and willing self-sacrifice.[46] Also, suicide from grief in Greek literature is not limited to the suicide of widows: Jocasta slays herself over the bodies of Polynices and Eteocles (Eur. *Phoen.* 1455–9 and 1282), and Haemon commits suicide over the body of Antigone (Soph. *Ant.* 1231–43). And when Plato wrote that many people have gone willingly to Hades to be with their dead boyfriends, wives, and sons, he spoke largely from the point of view of the adult male – and he may not have been thinking solely of mythical examples (*Phd.* 68A).[47] Thus, in real life apparently as on the stage, people – lovers, wives and husbands, mothers and fathers – occasionally took their own lives in grief over the loss of loved ones or in the hope of rejoining them after death.

Nilsson also wrote of Evadne's suicide that 'it is absolutely inconceivable that such a myth was invented under the conditions which we know to have existed in Greece from Homer onward'.[48] But the fact is that such stories continued to be invented, told, and retold throughout antiquity. The earliest known example is the suicide of the wife of Protesilaus, the first of the Greeks to perish at Troy: in the *Cypria* she was called Polydora, but she appears with the more familiar name Laodameia in numerous, and increasingly lurid, later versions.[49] Indeed it is in the Hellenistic period that such stories begin to enjoy their greatest popularity. In the *Argonautica* Cleite hangs herself after the death of Cyzicus (Ap. Rhod. *Argon.* 1.1063–5), and Lycophron has the earliest extant version of Oinone's leap onto the corpse of Paris (*Alex.* 61–8). Hero's leap from her tower to the body of Leander, most familiar from the sixth century poem of Musaeus (338–43), had a Hellenistic model.[50] And, not surprisingly, Parthenius' collection of erotic tales, culled from a variety of Hellenistic sources, contains its share of suicides, including the suicides of grieving men: of Cyanippus, who slays himself at the pyre of Leucone, and of the necrophilic Dimoetes (Parth. *Amat. Narr.* 10.4 and 31.2).[51] In still later antiquity Quintus of Smyrna will imitate the *Suppliants* in his description of Oinone's suicide (Quint. Smyrn. 10.411–89), explicitly comparing her with Evadne at 10.479–81.

Thus, stories of the suicides of wives and lovers could indeed be invented and admired in an age when such suicide was not sanctioned by custom, and rather than preserving 'precious testimony as to Mycenaean funeral customs', their popularity may say more about male attitudes of Classical and Hellenistic times. Suicide from grief – no doubt an occasional reality – provided moving and sensational material for poets and playwrights, but the study of their creations belongs to the history of literature rather than the history of Greek religion and funeral customs. The most that we can say on the basis of the literary evidence is that a culture which showed admiration for the suicide of widows in its literature may at an earlier stage have encouraged such suicide by custom. But simple human motives, adequate to explain the suicides of grieving wives in literature, are not in themselves sufficient to account for the existence of such a custom, which would involve such factors as the social and legal status of women.[52]

The slaying of Polyxena on Achilles' tomb has also been thought to preserve a memory of an early Greek custom of 'suttee',[53] but this again is improbable. The story was told first in the *Ilioupersis*, but almost nothing is known for certain of the motives and circumstances of the killing.[54] The earliest extant versions are found in Euripides. In the *Trojan Women*, Polyxena is slain at Achilles' tomb as a funerary sacrifice.[55] In the fuller treatment in the *Hecuba*, Achilles' ghost appears above his grave to demand Polyxena's sacrifice before he will grant fair winds for the Greeks' journey home, and Polyxena bravely submits to sacrifice by Neoptolemus on Achilles' grave (*Hec.* 1–628). Polyxena is also called an honour or prize (*geras*) for Achilles (41; cf. 94, 114–15, and 309), and her blood a drink-offering to his shade (536–8; cf. 392–3). And Hecuba herself wonders if vengeance may be Achilles' motive for demanding the sacrifice (263–70). Many of the details (including Polyxena's courageous deportment in the face of death) may be Euripidean embellishments, but in want of other evidence it seems likely that the story in the *Ilioupersis* was told essentially as it is here, a human sacrifice demanded by Achilles' ghost and carried out by his son. An influence of the Iphigeneia myth on this version is quite probable (just as the Greeks must sacrifice a virgin to obtain fair winds for their departure for Troy, so too must they sacrifice a virgin on their return), and thus the inspiration for the story might better be traced to the epic tradition than to customs of the Bronze Age.[56] In fact, there was a variant in which Polyxena was not sacrificed but rather buried by Neoptolemus, after dying of wounds inflicted by Odysseus and Diomedes. It is possible that this was the earlier version.[57]

The story of Achilles' love for Polyxena and the representation of the sacrifice as a 'funerary wedding' or 'nuptial sacrifice' seem to date only from Hellenistic times.[58] And still later is the version in which Polyxena, herself in love with Achilles, commits suttee-like suicide over his grave (Philostr. *VA* 4.16 and *Her.* 19.11). Thus arguments for an early Greek custom of suttee or a custom of 'Totenhochzeit' (the 'marriage' of a virgin bride to a man who has died unwed), based as they are on late romantic reworkings of the legend, seem to be without foundation. If anything, the original myth would seem to represent a custom of sacrificing female war-captives over the graves of fallen warriors, but I would agree with Schwenn that no secure conclusions about actual practice can be drawn from the story.[59]

LUCIAN *DE LUCTU* 14

In the *De luctu* (*Περὶ πένθους*), Lucian rails against funeral customs, mourning, and the belief that the dead have any feelings or wants beyond the grave. Among the targets of his attack (inspired by the Cynics' standard criticisms of burial customs)[60] are the practice of placing an obol in the mouth of the deceased (*Luct.* 10), the bathing and dressing of corpses (11), the tearing of hair and clothing (12), and the erection of tombstones (22–3). But at *Luct.* 14 the satirist gives an extreme example of human folly in the treatment of the dead:

> But why am I saying these things? For how many people have slain over their dead both horses and concubines, how many have slain even cupbearers and burned or buried clothing and other ornaments with the dead, as if they could use them there and enjoy them in the world below?

To whose customs was Lucian referring here? Of those few scholars who have mentioned the passage,[61] most have cited it together with Achilles' slaying of Trojan captives in the *Iliad* as evidence for an early Greek custom of providing the dead with servants in the world below.[62] Rohde, however, seems to have believed that Lucian alluded to practices in Greece of his own time, the second century after Christ.[63] More recently, Kurtz and Boardman, in a chapter of *Greek Burial Customs* devoted to funerary rites in the Classical and Hellenistic periods, write as follows:

> There is no clear evidence for human sacrifice, although Lucian's account (*de Luctu* 14) of the way folk killed horses, concubines and cup-boys to serve them in the after life is not specifically referred to heroic antiquity.[64]

Thus it is suggested that while it is probable that Lucian *was* referring to heroic antiquity, it remains possible that he was thinking of later Greece as well.

If Lucian was referring solely to 'heroic antiquity', his source will have been Greek legend. Yet, as we have seen, the material is meagre. Possibly Lucian was thinking of the four horses slain at Patroclus' funeral (*Il.* 23.171–2), but clearly the Trojan captives also slain on this occasion – however their killing has been interpreted by modern scholars – could hardly have been models for Lucian's cupbearers. Likewise, the reference to the killing of concubines could not have been based on the suicides of Evadne and other legendary wives (for they were wives, not concubines, and they took their own lives), although it is worth noting that the verb employed here by Lucian, *epikatasphazein*, was – with the reflexive pronoun – a common term for this sort of suicide in erotic literature.[65] The slaying of Polyxena seems to have been simply a funerary sacrifice in the earliest versions (pp. 61–2), but that her sacrifice could be understood in later antiquity as a means of providing Achilles with female companionship in the world below is indicated by a passage of Dio Chrysostom, which (though appearing in a very different context) bears a marked similarity to Lucian's Cynical argumentation in the *De luctu*. Dio (*Or.* 6.18) puts the following words in the mouth of Diogenes the Cynic: 'And the Achaeans were so foolish as to think that even the dead have need of women and to slay Polyxena on the tomb of Achilles.'

Polyxena and the horses slain before Patroclus' pyre offer two possible models from 'heroic antiquity' for *Luct.* 14. But I know of no legend in which a cupbearer is killed at a funeral. Besides, to all appearances Lucian alludes to *actual* practices here, as he does throughout the diatribe. But there is no good evidence, literary or archaeological, for such customs in Greece of Classical, Hellenistic, or later times. Furthermore, the construction πόσοι . . . οἱ δέ and the plurals 'horses', 'concubines', and 'cupbearers' clearly imply that the killing of horses, concubines, and cupbearers at funerals was a quite common practice. Thus, given the paucity of evidence for such practices in Greece of any period, another possibility should be considered: that Lucian alluded, at least largely, to *non-Greek* customs. It is true that Lucian is concerned primarily with Greek burial practices, but in *Luct.* 21 Lucian will refer also to Persian, Indian, Scythian, and Egyptian customs; and his point will be that although these peoples dispose of their dead in different manners, they all mourn the dead, sharing with the Greeks the same foolish notion that the dead continue to be sentient beyond the grave. And to reach beyond the Greek world for an extreme example of human behaviour is quite in Lucian's manner: in the companion piece to the *De luctu*, for example, Lucian's criticism of Greek animal sacrifice culminates with a mention of the Tauri, who scorn the use of animal victims in favour of human sacrifices to their 'Artemis'; and he will go on to ridicule Assyrian, Phrygian, Lydian, and Egyptian beliefs (*Sacr.* 13–15).

For the killing of concubines, Lucian may have been thinking of the Indian custom of suttee, well known to the Greek world since the expedition of Alexander, and certainly known to Lucian.[66] And Herodotus (5.5) had described a similar custom in Thrace, where there was a fierce competition among the wives of a dead chieftain to be chosen to accompany him in the world beyond. But there is another passage of Herodotus which I believe Lucian certainly had in mind when he wrote *Luct.* 14: at the sumptuous funeral of a Scythian king, a concubine, a cupbearer, a cook, a groom, a servingman, a courier, and horses were all killed to accompany their king after death (Hdt. 4.71.4). All three of Lucian's victims – horses, concubines, and cupbearers – appear here also, and to my knowledge these are the only two places in ancient Greek literature where they do appear together as victims slain at a funeral ceremony.

Lucian, in fact, frequently draws upon Herodotus, and often for ethnographic material.[67] In *Luct.* 21, Herodotus seems to have been a source of his knowledge of Egyptian embalming (Hdt. 2.86–90) and the 'Scythian' custom of eating the dead (1.216.2, actually a practice of the Massegetae). And he appears to have been particularly fascinated with the Scythians and their customs: his description of Scythian oath-taking in *Tox.* 37 was apparently based on Hdt. 4.70, and at the opening of the *Scytha* (1) he jokingly alludes to the 'Scythian' custom of sending messengers to the god Zamolxis (Salmoxis), actually a practice of the Thracian Getae described by the historian (4.94). I do not mean to suggest that Lucian alluded exclusively to Scythian burial customs here. Rather I think that he looked to a number of societies – Indian, Thracian, Scythian, and possibly Greek (at least as represented by Polyxena and the horses slain for Patroclus); and he may have known other examples from other cultures.[68] Indeed the phrasing of the passage suggests that he had more than one people in mind and that the killing of horses and concubines was more common than the practice of killing cupbearers. But Herodotus' description of the Scythian royal funeral was certainly a major inspiration for his statement, and the assumption that he alluded exclusively to Greek customs is surely incorrect: *De luctu* 14 should not be considered valuable evidence for Greek funerary practices of any period.

HOMER AND THE ARCHAEOLOGICAL EVIDENCE

The relationship between 'Homeric' burial practices, preserved chiefly in the lengthy description of Patroclus' funeral in the *Iliad*, and actual practices, represented by archaeological finds, is a complex issue and well beyond the scope of my interests here, which are confined to a single aspect of Patroclus' elaborate funeral ceremony. Also, as in any discussion of Homeric funeral customs, it should be borne in mind that the *Iliad* is poetry: Homer, Andronikos has done well to remind us, is neither historian nor archaeologist.[69] It is true that every element of the Homeric funeral has found some parallel in an archaeological find.[70] But as no one burial containing all of the elements or on anywhere near the scale of Patroclus' funeral has been discovered, it is likely that the Homeric description is a composite of various practices 'remembered' or known from various places and times, whether from the late Bronze Age or a period closer to the poet's own day. And even where there is a similarity between an archaeological find and an element of the Homeric funeral, an actual, historical relationship cannot be taken for granted; this is perhaps nowhere so true as in the area under consideration here. With these cautions in mind, let us look briefly at possible relationships between the slaughter of the Trojan captives and the archaeological evidence for funerary ritual killing described in chapter 2.

Archaeologists have often mentioned the twelve Trojan captives in connection with their discoveries.[71] And yet it has been nearly universally held by these archaeologists that their finds represent a custom of killing servants or slaves that they attend their masters in the afterlife; thus they seem to follow religious historians in assuming that Homer misunderstood the meaning of the practice he described in the poem. But such reasoning is methodologically suspect. If excavated skeletons indeed represent a custom of killing slaves as postmortem attendants of their masters, it would be simpler, and, I think, much sounder to conclude that there is no connection whatsoever between the killing of Trojans (who were prisoners of war, slain, it is expressly stated, for the sake of vengeance) and the archaeological remains. On the other hand, if we wish to explore possible connections between the Homeric incident and archaeology, we should ask whether Homer's representation of Achilles' actions might shed some light on our interpretation of the archaeological finds. If the Homeric description was based upon an actual custom of exacting vengeance at funerals (a custom for which there is later historical evidence also), it is worth considering the possibility that some of the dromos burials represent remains of such a practice as well.

One aspect of the Mycenaean and Cypriot 'slave burials' cannot be overemphasized: their extreme rarity. At Salamis, some 150 tombs have been excavated, but only in the dromoi of two tombs (and these by no means the largest or richest) has any evidence suggesting ritual killing been found. And even if we accept the excavator's interpretation for all of the alleged 'slave burials' from the Kastros cemetery at Lapithos, there were only four cases in twenty-nine tombs, which were frequently reused; and as many as 300 years separate the earliest of these dromos burials from the latest.[72] As for the Bronze Age mainland, in only four instances have dromos burials been interpreted as representing 'human sacrifices', while thousands of chamber tombs have been excavated. Only very infrequently, it seems, were people killed at funerals in these places for any reason, and this infrequency suggests that the killings were prompted by some extraordinary circumstance. Could this extraordinary circumstance have been the murder of the main occupant of the tomb, or his death in battle? Might the skeletons found in the dromoi of these tombs represent, not slaves or servants of the deceased, but rather his killers, or members of a military enemy slain in retaliation for his death?

Also to be considered is the fact that the alleged victims were in most cases treated with very little respect. They were provided with few if any funeral gifts and apparently wore little in the way of clothing; in only one case is jewelry (a ring) reported (Salamis Tomb 83). Two of the Cypriot victims seem to have been bound (Lapithos Tomb 422 and Salamis Tomb 2); a third was reportedly buried 'in a mutilated condition' (Lapithos Tomb 422); and two bodies were thrown unceremoniously face down upon the corpse below (Lapithos Tombs 412 and 422). Also, with the exception of the 'slave burials' found in the Dendra and Kazarma tholoi (and in the one case the interpretation is extremely doubtful, in the other the material is inadequately published), the victims were buried outside of the tomb: they lie, like the Trojan captives, ἄνευθεν, apart (*Il.* 23.241–2). Would this have been the case if the intention had been to provide the deceased with servitors in the afterlife?[73]

The possibility that the dromos burials represent victims of ritual execution or vengeance killing merits serious consideration, at least in some of the cases. The apparent lack of regard shown to the victims, their occasional binding, and their exclusion from the tomb all argue against the common view that these are burials of slaves meant to serve their master after death. And the rarity of such burials suggests that some unusual circumstance lay behind the killings – a rarity, at any rate, which seems difficult to explain if it was in fact the *custom* of wealthy Mycenaeans and their descendants in Cyprus to require the company of slaves in the world below. Furthermore, while there is no good written evidence for a practice of killing servants to attend their masters after death, we do have a few accounts of vengeance killing or execution carried out at the grave. And the remains of such a custom would look, I think, very much like most of the 'slave burials' which have thus far been uncovered. Imagine if a large Hellenistic tomb should be found in the area of Megalopolis with a mass burial of human skeletons (showing fractures on the skulls and other bones) at its entrance: we would probably hear again of 'human sacrifices' or of attendants slain at their master's funeral (though perhaps there would also be some surprise expressed at finding evidence of such practices at so late a date). But if the tomb could be dated to the 180s BC and its occupant identified accordingly as Philopoemen, then we should know the circumstances and the true nature of the ritual killing.

The funeral of Patroclus has been cited by Alexandrescu and Eftimie in connection with their remarkable discoveries at Istria on the Black Sea. Here three Archaic tumuli, built over central pyres, contained peripheral burials of humans and horses. Two skeletons from Tumulus XVII had been bound, and pits dug beneath Tumulus XII held two mass burials, containing between them thirty-five human skeletons, mixed in with the remains of at least eleven dismembered horses (cf. *Il.* 23.242: ἐπιμὶξ ἵπποι τε καὶ ἄνδρες). Although the pottery was almost exclusively Greek and although no separate Greek cemetery has been found, it has been concluded from the manner of burial that the tumuli belonged to the indigenous Thracian population. And chiefly on the grounds of the violent treatment of the bodies, the excavators argue convincingly that the persons found on the edges of these truly Homeric tumuli were not servants slain to attend their masters after death. Rather, they compare the slaughter of the Trojan captives and suggest that these burials may represent cases of vendetta, vengeance killings for the murders of the persons cremated on the central pyres; but they suggest further that these 'sacrifices expiatoires' may not have been restricted to funerals of persons who had themselves died by violence.[74] Certainly these burials differ in character and scale from those under consideration here, but I feel that most of the observations of the Romanian archaeologists hold good for the less spectacular Greek burials as well.

The soil of Cyprus has been particularly rich in yielding parallels to Homeric burial customs, and J. N. Coldstream has argued that the circulation of the epic had a direct influence on Cypriot funerary practices.[75] Coldstream notes the following similarities between the archaeological finds and the funeral of Patroclus: amphorae are often found in the dromoi of tombs at Salamis (cf. *Il.* 23.170), a cattle bone was found in the dromos of Tomb 2, and sheep bones in the dromos of a tomb at Palaiopaphos (cf. 23.166); horse (or donkey) burials are common at Salamis (cf. 23.171);[76] Salamis Tomb 1 contained a cremation, and above the pyre were found 'six unburnt and unbroken pots . . . which had evidently been used for putting out the flames' (cf. 23.250);[77] the remains of the cremation were placed in a bronze cauldron (a step down from the epic gold) with traces of cloth (cf. 23.252–4); a large tumulus was built over Salamis Tomb 3 (cf. 23.255–7); and finally, a human skeleton, apparently bound, and the remains of two others were found in the dromos of Salamis Tomb 2 (cf. 23.175).

Coldstream continues: 'For most of these practices, if taken singly, the hardened sceptic could adduce parallels from pre-Homeric Cyprus or from other lands not too far distant from the Greeks', and he himself provides some examples.[78] Perhaps I am Coldstream's hardened sceptic, but in the area under consideration here four of the nine alleged instances of funerary ritual killing date to Cypro-Geometric I and II, i.e. to pre-Homeric Cyprus.[79] Furthermore, Coldstream's typical Cypriot royal burial is actually made up of features taken from various tombs at Salamis, and in one case from elsewhere (Palaiopaphos) in Cyprus. The '*combination* of so many features' which Coldstream finds so striking does not occur in any single burial.[80] Of the Homeric features, Salamis Tomb 2 offers amphorae, asses, the human skeletons, and a cattle bone (although this seems to belong to the first burial period in the eighth century, not to the period of the 'human sacrifices').[81] But there is no evidence that the deceased from either burial period was cremated;[82] the asses and humans in the dromos were not. Thus, if the burial in Tomb 2 (and other tombs at Salamis show even fewer Homeric features) was influenced by the Homeric description of Patroclus' funeral (or anything like it), the imitation was not very close or thorough, and any influence was slight. It seems possible that descriptions of elaborate heroic burials in epic poetry inspired among these wealthy Cypriots a desire for lavish funeral ceremonies, but certainly none of the material from the royal tombs justifies the conclusion that the 'burials were conducted with strict attention to Mycenaean precedent as described by Homer'.[83]

Homer represents the killing of the twelve Trojan captives as an act of vengeance, and it is possible that some of the archaeological evidence should be interpreted in this way also. It may be that the incident derives from Mycenaean practices, but it is also possible that the poet, or one of his predecessors, knew of a custom of vengeance killing at the tomb from some place in the Greek world of his own time. On the strength of the present evidence I would not go so far as to suggest that this place was Cyprus, although one prominent Homeric scholar has done so.[84] On the other hand, the possibility that the Homeric funeral description exerted a direct influence on Cypriot burial procedure seems, in this respect especially, rather remote.

4

Human sacrifice in Greek myth, cult, and history

INTRODUCTION: MYTH AND HISTORY

In this chapter I am interested principally in the 'historical' human sacrifices, by which I mean sacrifices which were presented as historical, and apparently believed to have been historical, by the authors who reported them, and which also have frequently been accepted as such by modern scholars. But first I shall discuss some myths of human sacrifice, which I have divided into two sections. In the first ('mythical human sacrifices') I treat myths in which specific (and most often named) individuals are sacrificed, usually offering themselves willingly in times of emergency, but also a few other miscellaneous stories of human sacrifice; in the second ('mitigated human sacrifices and animal substitution') I discuss in more detail some aetiological myths which served to account for existing rituals: according to these, earlier human sacrifices (usually repeated sacrifices, with anonymous victims) had been 'mitigated', i.e. replaced by non-fatal rituals or by animal sacrifices.

By distinguishing thus between mythical and historical human sacrifices I begin with the presupposition that the 'myths' of human sacrifice are indeed mythical and not historical. This, of course, is impossible to prove, and many scholars, while rejecting the historicity of individual human sacrifices in myths of my first category, nevertheless have felt that the legends preserve a memory of a practice of human sacrifice in earlier times. Wachsmuth's statement, for example – 'wenn auch kein einzelner Fall Probe hält, bleibt dennoch in der gemeinschaftlichen Quelle dieser mythischen Erzählungen, der aus uralter Zeit fortgepflanzten Sage von dem Brauche, Menschen zu opfern, Grund genug zum

Glauben an denselben' – may be taken as typical not only for his century but for much of our own.[1] Still, not all scholars have agreed with this assessment, e.g. Schwenn, who already in 1915 saw that 'eine alte Opfersitte, die so manche annehmen, lässt sich aus diesen Sagen keineswegs erschliessen'.[2] The difference of opinion is actually part of a much broader disagreement about the function and meaning of myth, but the old view which sees myths primarily as repositories of obsolete cultural practices and beliefs has in this century been called into question by more and more scholars, from a variety of viewpoints.

The myths of 'mitigated' human sacrifices connected with existing cult practices have more often been accepted as factual, but in recent years scholars have tended to reject these also. But this does not mean that these myths are unimportant for the study of Greek religious belief and ritual. If they did not preserve the actual histories of the rituals with which they were associated, they still may be presumed to have had meaning for the societies which created and maintained them. Exactly what this presumed meaning was may in many cases be unclear, and it is likewise uncertain how closely the myths were associated with the practices they served to explain. Did these aitia play an essential role in the beliefs of the worshippers, were they 'cult myths' integrally bound with the rites which they accompanied? Were they the inventions of local *theologoi*, or merely of poets, unconnected with the local cults, or even of later mythographers? Many of the preserved myths of this type appear to be relatively late inventions, some even showing the influence of Hellenistic romance. Still, the pattern exhibited by these myths – transgression, institution of human sacrifice, and its later abolition in favour of animal sacrifices or other rituals – is itself quite ancient (as its presence in the Iphigeneia story shows), and I believe that this type of myth was originally associated closely with cult practices. But the age of the myths does not really concern us: some meaningful function may be assumed for the later myths also, and the persistence of the pattern suggests a continuity of religious thought (or at least of mythopoetic inclinations) from Archaic into Hellenistic times. But of course aetiologies invented only in the Hellenistic age clearly cannot be taken to preserve the actual early histories of cult practices.

Finally, it is not always easy to distinguish the mythical from what is 'presented as historical' or 'believed to have been historical': such a judgement may be largely subjective and made from a modern point of view which does not always reflect that of the ancients, many of whom believed in the actuality of mythical characters and events or at least did not take adequate care to distinguish between the historical and the legendary.[3] The division of the material into mythical and historical is therefore to some extent arbitrary. But my discussion of mythical human sacrifices is largely intended to serve as a preface to the 'historical' human sacrifices, many of which show marked similarities (such as the motifs of mitigation and animal substitution) with their mythic counterparts. Thus my division of the material into mythical and historical is not only somewhat arbitrary but also, as it were, temporary, for I strongly suspect – and in many cases hope to show – that most if not all of the human sacrifices discussed in the historical section belong rather to the realm of myth and pseudo-history.

MYTHICAL HUMAN SACRIFICES

A number of myths tell of noble young maidens who, usually in accordance with an oracle, are sacrificed or voluntarily offer themselves for sacrifice in order to ward off an enemy attack or other calamity from their city. One or more daughters (accounts vary) of Erechtheus were sacrificed during a war with Eleusis, while in another version a daughter of Cecrops, Aglaurus, threw herself from the walls of Athens during the same war.[4] Similarly, when plague and famine beset Athens during the war with King Minos, the daughters of Hyacinthus (sometimes identified with the daughters of Erechtheus) were slain on the tomb of the Cyclops Geraestus.[5] The daughters of Leos were also slain to drive plague or famine from Athens, and a sanctuary, the Leokorion, was constructed in the agora in their honour.[6] And Heracles' daughter Macaria willingly offered herself for sacrifice when Athens was besieged by Eurystheus, and a spring at Marathon was named for her.[7]

Similar sacrifices are known from locales other than Athens. An oracle promises success to Heracles and the Thebans in their campaign against Orchomenos if the noblest citizen among them should die willingly by his own hand; when Antipoenus demurs, his daughters, Androcleia and Alcis, readily volunteer themselves as victims.[8] And another pair of Boeotian maids, the daughters of

Orion (Metioche and Menippe), willingly offer themselves to deliver their city from pestilence.[9] Nor was the theme of virgin sacrifice confined to wars of the heroic past: among the stories from the Messenian Wars (eighth and seventh centuries), whose 'history' was concocted after Messenian independence in 370 and preserved chiefly by Pausanias, is a long and involved tale according to which the Delphic oracle requires the Messenians to sacrifice a virgin to the gods of the Underworld; a series of reversals leads to Aristodemus' murder of his own daughter, and in the end it is decided that the oracle has been fulfilled by her death (Paus. 4.9.3–10).[10] Parthenius (*Amat. Narr.* 35) preserves a very similar story from Hellenistic romance (here the location is Crete and the victim Cydon's daughter Eulime) – so similar in fact that there must be some connection between the two stories. In both tales an oracle is consulted and enjoins the sacrifice of a virgin, to be selected by lot; the allotted victim's lover comes forward to claim that she is with child, and in the end her womb is cut open; but in one case (Parth.) the lover's claim proves true, in the other (Paus.) false. If nothing else the similarity between the two tales indicates how fine was the line in this period between historical writing and romance, and how readily it could be overstepped.

In some cases it is young men, not young women, who are sacrificed. In the *Phoenissae* Creon's son Menoeceus slays himself on the highest tower of Thebes, but the 'myth' may have been invented by Euripides himself.[11] When the Tyndaridae invade Attica, in accordance with an oracle Marathus willingly offers himself for sacrifice before the engagement, thus giving his name to the deme Marathon.[12] And when the Eleans consult the oracle during a prolonged drought, they are instructed to sacrifice a noble boy to Zeus. A youth named Molpis volunteers, rain falls, and the Eleans build a sanctuary of Zeus Ombrios, setting up a statue of Molpis there.[13]

Frequently mentioned together with myths of this type – but differing from them significantly – is the story of the Athenian King Codrus. An oracle had proclaimed to the Peloponnesians that they would be unable to capture Athens if they should kill Codrus. But the Athenians got wind of the oracle, and Codrus, *pro patria non timidus mori*, went out of the beseiged city disguised as a beggar and, having killed one soldier from the Peloponnesian camp, was killed by another, thus saving Athens from destruction.[14] Like the daughters of Erechtheus and other heroines and heroes, Codrus died willingly to save his country, but he was not, strictly speaking, sacrificed, and Burkert has connected the dynamics of this myth with 'scapegoat' rituals, whereby a community sends an animal or human being from its midst in order to bring destruction upon an enemy.[15] But the Codrus myth also shows a close affinity to another Greek story, in which both sacrificial and 'scapegoat' motifs are absent: Temon, a prominent citizen of the Aenianes, dresses as a beggar and goes among the Inachians, who give him a clod of earth in mockery, thus unwittingly fulfilling an oracle to the effect that they would lose all of their land if they shared any part of it (Plut. *Quaest. Graec.* 13, 294A–B). It therefore appears that in the Codrus story the motif of willing self-sacrifice and thematic patterns akin to scapegoat rituals have been grafted onto a more widespread type of folktale, in which disguise as a beggar serves to trick an enemy into the damaging fulfilment of a prophecy.[16]

Most scholars would now agree that these myths of human sacrifice have no historical value. For one thing, the wars (not to mention the plagues, droughts, and famines) during which the sacrifices are performed are themselves mythical (and sometimes interchangeable, as the identification of the Hyacinthides and daughters of Erechtheus shows), as are the oracles which enjoin them.[17] Also, many of the myths served as aetiologies for the names of various places and cult areas (Marathon, the sanctuary of Aglaurus, the Leokorion, the rock of Molpis, the spring Macaria), in which case, it is generally agreed, the thing explained precedes, historically, the explanatory myth. Furthermore, the similarity of the myths (a city is threatened with attack or afflicted by plague or famine; the oracle is consulted, and a human sacrifice ordained; the daughter or son of a king or nobleman comes forward; the city is delivered) does not argue for their historicity: history repeats itself, it is true, but not with such ideal regularity and felicitous outcome. It is clear that new stories of human sacrifice continued to be fashioned upon earlier models, although it is not possible to trace the thread back to a single paradigmatic myth.

The majority of the stories described above are myths in the full sense, in that they have partial reference to things of collective importance to the societies which created and maintained them, even if this reference is only to the name of a person or place.[18] But the origin and function (beyond aetiology) of these myths is uncertain. Although the occasion of the human sacrifice is sometimes plague or famine, a close association with military practices is probable: before war the Athenian army sacrificed at the sanctuary of the Hyacinthides, and Athenian ephebes would swear an oath at the sanctuary of Aglaurus before departing for battle.[19] It is therefore problematic but highly interesting that the victims are most often women, while in ancient Greece war was strictly the domain of males.[20] Burkert sees in such myths a manifestation of the sexual renunciation required of hunters and warriors: 'Man declines to love in order to kill: this is most graphically demonstrated in the ritual slaughter of "the virgin," the potential source both of a happy union and of disruptive conflict within the group.'[21] But I would interpret the myths somewhat differently. The selfless devotion of these legendary victims, particularly poignant in the case of young maidens, served to inspire the army to courage and patriotism in the face of the enemy. But perhaps poignancy is not the principal effect of the stories; rather their value may lie chiefly in the contrast inherent in the sexual 'role reversal', which would pose a direct challenge to the male warrior. This is apparent both in Lycurgus' speech against Leocrates (which preserves a lengthy extract from Euripides' *Erechtheus*, fr. 50 Austin, where the male–female opposition is already implicit) and in the funeral oration attributed to Demosthenes: 'if women dare to do this, indeed men must keep their devotion for the fatherland unsurpassed' (Lycurg. *Leoc.* 101); and (with reference to the daughters of Leos) 'when those women possessed such manliness [ἀνδρείαν], they [the Leontidae] regarded as not right that they prove lesser men than those women' (Dem. 60.29; cf. Cic. *Nat. D.* 3.19, 50, and Diod. Sic. 17.15.2). Thus tales of women who died selflessly to save their country effectively inspired men to be prepared to do the same, although the women in the myths are accorded a sacrificial death rather than a 'manly' death on the battlefield.[22] Still, I should not wish to argue that this was the sole function, or the original function, of these stories, for possibly earlier myths created for other reasons were adopted to serve this inspirational purpose only in the fifth and fourth centuries BC.

There are a few other Greek tales involving human sacrifice which differ, to a greater or lesser extent, from those described above. During a storm on his return voyage from Troy, the Cretan king Idomeneus vows to sacrifice the first thing he shall encounter upon landing. This turns out to be his son: in one version Idomeneus sacrifices him, while in another the intended sacrifice is never carried out (Serv. Verg. *Aen.* 3.121 and 11.264). Similarly, when one of the rulers of Haliartus consults the Delphic oracle about a drought, he is instructed to kill the first person he meets on his journey home. He is met by his son Lophis, whom he dutifully slays on the spot; and from the place where the blood falls water rises up, becoming the Lophis River (Paus. 9.33.4).[23] Thus the same motif employed in the story of Idomeneus' return provides here an aetiology for the river's name, although in this case the killing is not represented as a sacrifice. The folk-motif, familiar from the story of Jephthah's vow in the Old Testament, also appears in an aetiology for the name of the river Maiandros: in return for success in battle Maiandros vows to sacrifice to the Mother of the Gods the first person to greet him on his return. He is met by his son, wife, and daughter, but after leading them to the altar he has second thoughts and throws himself into the Anabainon River, which henceforth is called the Maiandros.[24]

Herodotus tells a story which he claims to have learned from the Egyptian priests, according to which Menelaus, after the Trojan War, finally finds Helen in Egypt. But unable to leave because of adverse winds, Menelaus sacrifices two native children, thus incurring the wrath of the formerly hospitable Egyptians (Hdt. 2.119.3). And just as the Greeks, so also the Trojans encounter unfavourable sailing conditions in their flight from Troy.[25] During a tempest Chaon, one of the companions of Helenus, vows to sacrifice himself should they escape alive; they do, and Chaon becomes the eponymous hero of Chaonia in Epirus (Serv. Verg. *Aen.* 3.335, with an alternate version). A story of human sacrifice is also connected with the foundation of Methymna. An oracle instructs the colonists to offer a maiden to Amphitrite, and the lot falls to a daughter of Smintheus. But in an effort to save her a young man named Enalus grabs her and leaps into the sea; he later appears in Lesbos bearing tales of his marvellous rescue by dolphins.[26]

Finally, a well-known myth tells of a tribute of maidens and young men sent from Athens to feed the Minotaur in Crete in atonement for the murder of Androgeos.[27] This tribute is not, technically speaking, a human sacrifice, although it has often been called one. The myth, although unique in its details, belongs to a large group of stories in which young women and men are offered to appease the wrath of monsters of various kinds. Laomedon must expose his daughter Hesione to a sea-monster sent by Poseidon, but she is saved by Heracles; and in a similar story Perseus rescues (and then marries) the Aethiopian princess Andromeda, who has been tied to a rock as a meal for another Poseidon-sent monster.[28] And Pausanias informs us that the ghost of one of Odysseus' sailors, who had raped a virgin and been stoned to death by the people of Temesa, remained in the land killing young and old alike. Upon instructions from the Delphic oracle the inhabitants built a shrine for the 'Hero' and gave him annually the most beautiful virgin in the city as a bride, until Euthymus, three times an Olympic victor in boxing in the early fifth century, fell in love with the maiden to be offered that year, rescued her, drove out the Hero, and married the girl (Paus. 6.6.7–11).[29] In Thespiae the citizens were required each year to select by lot a young man to be offered to a dragon which was besetting the land; one year Menestratus, the lover of the allotted victim (Cleostratus), devised a breastplate covered with fishhooks and, offering himself in place of Cleostratus, destroyed the monster (Paus. 9.26.7–8). Similarly, a giant beast called Sybaris (or Lamia) ravaged the area of Delphi, killing men and cattle daily. When the Delphians consulted the oracle about leaving the region, the god told them to expose a youth before the monster's cave; a beautiful young man, Alcyoneus, was chosen by lot, but the hero Eurybatus, who happened to pass by while Alcyoneus was being led to his death, fell in love with the youth and, taking his place, killed the monster (Ant. Lib. *Met.* 8).

The absence of sacrificial language in these stories is notable: the young victims are given either as nourishment or as sexual partners to the monsters, and they are exposed rather than killed in the act of sacrifice.[30] And although a certain likeness can be observed between these stories and myths of human sacrifice (both those described above and those to which we shall presently turn), according to a traditional (if no longer fashionable) distinction, they might better be termed folktales than myths.[31] But several of the tales are connected, at least superficially, to cult practices: there was a shrine to the Hero at Temesa (Paus. 6.6.8 and 11; Strabo 6.1.5), the story from Thespiae served as an aetiology for Zeus' epiklesis, the 'Saviour' (Paus. 9.26.8), and the episodes surrounding the Cretan tribute provided aitia for several Attic, Naxian, and Delian rites (Pl. *Phd.* 58A–B; Plut. *Thes.* 17.6,

18, 20.5, 21, 22.3–5, and 23; Hesych. s.v. Δηλιακὸς βωμός). Furthermore, the story of Theseus and the Minotaur (as many other of Theseus' deeds) has been thought to have originated in Attic rituals of initiation of adolescents.[32] Indeed it is possible to see an initiatory origin in all of these tales which involve the exposure and threatened consumption (or devirgination) of young maidens and men, averted only by last-minute rescue by a youthful hero (and which often end in marriage, or, we may presume, homosexual union). Still, there is no need to claim (and no way to demonstrate) that all such stories owed their existence to particular rituals of initiation, for myths and folktales certainly may exhibit 'initiatory patterns' and initiatory motifs independent of any existing rites. But perhaps a closer connection between initiation ritual and myth can be seen in myths involving 'mitigated' human sacrifices of young women and men.

MITIGATED HUMAN SACRIFICES AND ANIMAL SUBSTITUTION

Blood on the altar: initiation rites?

Pausanias tells a story which gives the origin of the *diamastigōsis*, the ritual flogging of Spartan youths on the altar of Artemis Orthia. During a sacrifice to Artemis the participants, representing the four quarters of Sparta, fell to quarrelling and bloodshed. Many were killed on the altar, while others perished from disease. Thereupon an oracle instructed the Spartans to 'stain the altar with human blood', and a custom was instituted of sacrificing human victims chosen by lot. But Lycurgus changed the human sacrifice into the whipping of ephebes, and 'thus the altar is filled with human blood' (Paus. 3.16.9–10; cf. Suda s.v. Λυκοῦργος). Pausanias also reports that the statue of Artemis, which the priestess holds during the scourging, is the image brought by Orestes and Iphigeneia from the land of the Tauri, and he views the custom as a survival, in modified form, of the celebrated Tauric human sacrifices (3.16.7–11).[33]

The human sacrifice – just as the derivation from the Tauric custom – is certainly not historical. In fact, Plutarch (*Arist.* 17.8) provides an alternate account of the origin of the diamastigōsis: in 479 BC, when Pausanias and the Spartans were sacrificing before the battle of Plataea, they were attacked by Lydians, who seized and threw away the sacrificial offerings; but, though unarmed, the Spartans warded off their attackers with sticks and whips. In commemoration, the ephebes are beaten around the altar and a 'procession of the Lydians' follows. The picture is further complicated by the fact that there seem to have been not only two different aetiological myths but also two different rituals. Xenophon (*Lac.* 2.9) describes a rite in which boys try to steal as many cheeses as possible from the altar of Orthia while opposed by others (presumably other boys), who scourge them, a custom to which Plato (*Leg.* 1, 633B) also alludes. The myth involving the attack upon Pausanias clearly should be associated with the ritual described by Xenophon. Plutarch, however, connects this myth with the contemporary ritual of scourging, which elsewhere he reports he has witnessed (*Lyc.* 18.1). One might conclude from this that the ritual described by Xenophon and the diamastigōsis of Roman times were one and the same custom, but for the fact that none of the later sources mentions the theft of cheese or the struggle between two groups. And Xenophon, who reports that the boy caught stealing would be whipped only for a short time, does not seem to have regarded the punishment as especially severe, while later writers emphasize the brutality of the beatings, the shedding of blood, and the length of the ordeal, indeed several of them reporting that the scourging could result in death.[34] Conceivably the two rites were distinct, but contemporaneous, rituals (for different age groups?); but it is safest to conclude that the brutal scourging developed from the earlier form known to Xenophon and Plato and that Plutarch inadvertently associated a myth appropriate to this earlier form with the ritual of his own day. In this case the 'procession of the Lydians' would be a survival from the earlier period – a survival which may explain the currency of a myth attached to an outmoded form of the rite and which may also be an indication that the brutal flagellation did in fact develop from the earlier ritual contest. But the myth of human sacrifice will have been invented only when the ritual had assumed its bloodier form, for which our earliest witness is Cicero.[35] Thus the historical ritual seems to have undergone a development which is the very opposite of the 'mitigation' found in myth.

Although various interpretations of the diamastigōsis have been proposed (including acceptance of a prior stage of human sacrifices), it is beyond any reasonable doubt that the flogging was in origin a ritual of initiation.[36] The Spartan *agōgē* offers the clearest and most extensive evidence for 'rites of passage' for boys and adolescents among the ancient Greeks; the participants in the diamastigōsis were ephebes; and the elements of blood-drawing, mutilation, and trial by physical ordeal have numerous parallels in the initiation rites of other cultures.[37] Furthermore, initiation rites often involve the symbolic killing of the initiate (followed by 'rebirth' and reintegration, with new status, into the community), and Brelich suggested that the Spartan myth of human sacrifice served to reinforce the symbolism of death inherent in the ritual.[38]

Less can be said about another bloody ritual in the cult of Artemis, also associated with human sacrifice, as the only evidence for the ceremony is a brief allusion of Euripides at the close of *Iphigeneia among the Tauri*. Here Athena instructs Orestes and Iphigeneia to bring the image of the Tauric goddess to Attica, where Orestes is to build a temple at Halai to house the statue:

> 'And institute this custom: when the people celebrate,
> as atonement for your sacrifice let them hold a sword
> to a man's neck and cause blood to flow,
> for holiness's sake and that the goddess have due honour.'
> (Eur. *IT* 1458–61)

Athena then instructs Iphigeneia concerning the foundation of Artemis' cult at Brauron (*IT* 1462–7). It is possible that the association of the cult of Artemis Tauropolos with the near sacrifice of Orestes to the Taurian Artemis was the invention of Euripides (rather than a cult myth from Halai). But Halai, like Sparta, claimed to possess the image of Tauric Artemis,[39] and the lines would appear to be senseless if Euripides did not refer to an actual, contemporary ritual which involved the (non-fatal) cutting of a male's neck with a sword. It is a plausible conjecture that this was some kind of initiation rite: the proximity of the temple of Artemis at Halai to her precinct at Brauron, where initiations of Attic girls took place, the association of the two cults by Euripides, and the nature of the ritual may all point to this conclusion.[40] And it is probable that Artemis presided over the initiations of adolescents of both sexes at various places in Greece from an early period.[41]

Animal substitution

More frequently human sacrifices in Greek myth are replaced with animal sacrifices. At Potniae in Boeotia there was a temple of Dionysus Aigobolos, the 'Goatslayer' or 'Goatthrower'. Pausanias preserves an aition for the cult and the epithet of the god:

> For when they were sacrificing to the god, they were led by their drunkenness to the point of violence, so that they even killed the priest of Dionysus. And when they had killed him, immediately a pestilential disease befell them, and an oracle arrived from Delphi instructing them to sacrifice a boy in life's prime to Dionysus. But not many years later they say that the god substituted a goat as victim instead of the boy.
>
> (Paus. 9.8.2)[42]

The similarity of this myth to the aition for the ritual flogging at Sparta is obvious: violence breaks out during a sacrifice, a plague ensues, an oracle ordains the institution of a human sacrifice, and the sacrifice is later altered, although here the god himself assumes the role played by Lycurgus at Sparta. And the myth offers a succinct example of the pattern (transgression, plague, oracle, institution of human sacrifice, abolition of human sacrifice) which we find, though not always with all of these elements, in other aitia of Greek cult practices.

There is in fact a good deal of variation in the way the substitution of animals is effected in myths of this type. In a story from Aristodemus' *Collection of Myths*, an oracle proclaimed that a plague besetting Sparta would cease if a maiden of noble birth should be sacrificed each year. One year the lot fell to Helen, and she was led forth to be sacrificed. But an eagle swooped down, snatched away the sacrificial knife, carried it off to the cattle herds, and dropped it on a heifer; the heifer was substituted for the human victim, 'and henceforth they refrained from virgin killing'.[43] Schwenn suggested that this story was inspired by the myth which accounted for the whipping of Spartan ephebes and invented to provide a female counterpart to the sacrificed boys;[44] and the myth certainly seems late in its extant form. But the mention of a yearly sacrifice and the specification of a *damalis* as the substituted victim may suggest that the myth was originally connected with an existing sacrificial rite, although a late source who names the 'apotropaic gods' as recipients of the sacrifice

(Lydus *Mens.* 4.147) cannot be trusted.

Also unique in its details is the story of Phrixus. In the version of pseudo-Apollodorus, Athamas' second wife Ino plots the death of Phrixus and Helle, Athamas' children by Nephele. Ino induces dearth in Boeotia, prompting Athamas to send messengers to Delphi. On their return, Ino persuades them to report falsely that the dearth will end if Phrixus is sacrificed to Zeus. Athamas leads his son to the altar as bidden, but Nephele sends a golden ram to rescue Phrixus and his sister. Later, in Colchis, Phrixus sacrifices the ram to Zeus Phyxios. Thus, ultimately, an animal is sacrificed in place of a human victim (Apollod. *Bibl.* 1.9.1).[45]

The best-known myth involving the substitution of an animal for a human victim is of course the myth of Iphigeneia. In the *Cypria* Agamemnon kills a deer, Artemis demands the sacrifice of Iphigeneia in compensation, but the goddess herself substitutes a hind in the maiden's place and transports her to the land of the Tauri.[46] In the Hesiodic *Ehoeae* the virgin's name is Iphimede, and her image is substituted and sacrificed on Artemis' altar, while Iphimede herself is immortalized as Artemis of the Crossroads (Hes. fr. 23 Merkelbach-West), a version apparently followed by Steisichorus (fr. 38 Page). The story of Iphigeneia bears a marked similarity to cult myths from Mounychia and Brauron. In the Mounychian version a she-bear is killed, plague follows, and the Athenians are instructed by an oracle to sacrifice a virgin to Artemis; on the condition that his family receive the priesthood in perpetuity, Embarus volunteers his own daughter, but hiding her in the adyton he sacrifices a goat dressed in her clothing. In the Brauronian myth a bear is killed, plague ensues, and in atonement young girls must 'play the bear' before marriage; although the element of human sacrifice is absent (at least in the extant versions), the identification of young girls with animals is a prominent feature of the ritual.[47] These myths were closely associated with maiden initiations practised in the two Attic cults.[48]

The cult legends of Mounychia and Brauron were clearly related to the myth of Iphigeneia, but how they were related to one another historically is a very complex question, which cannot be satisfactorily answered in the present state of our knowledge. But Iphigeneia's association with Brauronian cult is particularly strong: she was said to have founded the cult, she had a herôon in the sanctuary, and there was even a tradition which located the story of Agamemnon and Iphigeneia at Brauron, not Aulis, with a bear rather than a hind as the substituted victim.[49] And Aeschylus appears to have alluded to Brauronian ritual when he described Iphigeneia as clothed in a yellow dress at the time of her sacrifice (Aesch. *Ag.* 239: κρόκου βαφάς), for Attic girls would also be dressed in a yellow garment (κροκωτός) during their stay at Brauron.[50] In light of the significant role that Iphigeneia played at Brauron it is arguable that a myth from the Attic cult of Artemis was borrowed for use in the Trojan Cycle. In the *Iliad* Agamemnon has a living daughter named Iphianassa (*Il.* 9.145 and 287), and Homer does not mention the sacrifice of Iphigeneia. Possibly the similarity of the names suggested the adoption of the Iphigeneia myth into the story of the Trojan War, and the scene of the sacrifice was by the time of the *Cypria* located in Aulis, the traditional (and Homeric: *Il.* 3.303) departure-point of the Greek forces. The variants of the myth found at Brauron and Mounychia, in which Iphigeneia plays no part, would have been necessitated by the appropriation of Iphigeneia by epic as a daughter of Agamemnon, and the story that she was sacrificed by Agamemnon at Brauron would represent a later effort to reclaim her under her new identity. It is difficult to say where the Hesiodic account fits into this hypothetical scheme, for the location is not specified and Agamemnon's daughter has yet a third name, Iphimede.[51] And certainly other reconstructions are possible, including the location of a pre-Homeric ritual and myth at Aulis (for which Dowden has made a strong case recently), although there is no certain evidence for cult activity in Artemis' sanctuary there before the fifth century. But in any case, this myth–ritual complex seems to have been quite widespread.[52]

The existence of cult myths connected with initiation rituals in Attica strongly suggests that the similar story of Iphigeneia also originated in a myth associated with activities in the cult of Artemis and that the animal substitution was an original feature of the story. Thus the commonly held opinion that the sacrifice of Iphigeneia reflects an early practice of human sacrifice and that her rescue and the substitution of an animal represent revisions made at a time when Greek sentiment no longer tolerated the practice is questionable and at best simplistic.[53] The *Cypria*, in which a deer was substituted, is usually dated to before 650, while the earliest extant versions in which Iphigeneia actually dies are Aeschylus' and Pindar's.[54] Solmsen recently sought to bridge this gap by arguing that the actual sacrifice also appeared in the *Ehoeae* (mid-sixth century) and that the passage containing the story of the substituted image and the immortalization of Iphigeneia (fr. 23.21–6 Merkelbach-West) represents a later 'correction' added to the original text.[55] Solmsen noted the curious word order of the passage (where Ἰφιμέδην μὲν σφάξαν (17) is completed by εἴδωλον only in line 21) and cited the parallel of Hom. *Od.* 11.602–4 (on Heracles' image in Hades, generally acknowledged to be an interpolation); and it seems possible that lines 21–6 were indeed added to an earlier text. But even so, this does not necessarily mean that the lines about the image and Iphigeneia's apotheosis were tacked on to a text in which Iphigeneia actually perished on the altar (as Solmsen argued), for they may simply have replaced an earlier, traditional version also containing the rescue. And even if Solmsen was correct, the existence of an early version in which Iphigeneia dies does not necessarily mean that she died in the original version. At present the bulk of evidence points to a conclusion that the rescue of Iphigeneia and the substitution of an animal were essential elements of a myth which originated in Artemis' cult, and that Iphigeneia's role in a myth accompanying the initiations of maidens (in Attica, or as in Attica) predated her entry into literature.

To this category perhaps belongs the 'sophism of the Thessalians', which has been called the 'most naive instance of ritualistic fraud that has come down to us'.[56] A Thessalian named Aratus or Diotimus promised a hecatomb of human victims to Apollo Kataibasios; but he never carried out his promise, and every year the Thessalians would renew the vow but again postpone its fulfilment. Although not expressly stated in the sources, it is possible that the legend and the perpetually postponed human sacrifice were connected with an annual hecatomb of animal victims in the cult of Apollo Kataibasios. Alternatively, the story may be merely a late explanation of the phrase 'Thessalian sophism', which in its earliest attestation (Eur. *Phoen.* 1407–13) refers to a deceptive wrestling manoeuvre used in combat.[57]

Finally, a much discussed sacrifice of a calf to Dionysus Anthroporrhaistes (the 'People-smasher') on Tenedos involved a sort of animal substitution, although no myth of prior human sacrifices is given in our source, Aelian. The Tenedians would treat a pregnant cow as a woman in childbed, and when the calf was born it was dressed in buskins and sacrificed; the person who struck the fatal blow was stoned by the populace and thus driven to the sea (Ael. *NA* 12.34). Given the similarity of this ritual to the myth attached to Artemis' cult at Mounychia, in which a goat was dressed in human clothing in myth (though this may not have been an actual ritual detail), and given the grim epithet of Dionysus on Tenedos, it is surprising that we have no myth of human sacrifice associated with this rite. It is quite possible that there was one; indeed, some modern scholars have sought to remedy this deficiency in the ancient tradition by arguing that an original human sacrifice lay behind this strange ritual.[58] But this explanation is improbable. Far more attractive is Meuli's suggestion that the Tenedian calf sacrifice represents an instance of the 'comedy of innocence', whereby hunters and sacrificers attempt in all manner of ways to deflect from themselves the blame for the killing of their prey, including the reconstruction of the animal from the bones (see pp. 6–7). Thus the calf sacrifice at Tenedos, far from originating in a practice of human sacrifice, may have sprung from anxiety and guilt over the killing of animals. In order that the community release itself from responsibility for the sacrifice, the blame for the 'murder' is placed upon one man, who is driven from the community to the sea (where presumably he will undergo purification). In Meuli's opinion, when guilt for animal killing was no longer felt and the stoning and flight no longer comprehended, the victim came to be viewed as a substitute for the god himself.[59] The closest parallel to the calf sacrifice at Tenedos is the Athenian Bouphonia, to which it is often compared: the sacrifice of an ox to Zeus Polieus was also treated as a murder, and the blame, after a trial, was finally fixed upon the sacrificial axe.[60] And the 'reconstruction' of the ox – the carcass was stuffed with straw and yoked to a plow – presents a striking example of 'comedy of innocence'. But at the Bouphonia the victim was not dressed or treated as a human being, and unquestionably the Bouphonia was from its origin an ox sacrifice. Nevertheless, an original human sacrifice has been posited in this case also.[61]

The festival of Artemis and Dionysus at Patrae

At Patrae, in a combined festival of Dionysus Aisymnetes and Artemis Triklaria, a procession of children would go down at night to the Meilichos River wearing wreaths made of ears of corn. These they laid before the goddess, and after bathing in the river, they donned wreaths of ivy and proceeded to Dionysus' sanctuary (Paus. 7.20.1–2). Pausanias' description of these rites is preceded by a lengthy, elaborate tale which gives the origin of the yearly night-festival. Comaetho, a priestess of Artemis, and her lover Melanippus make love in the sanctuary of the goddess, and as a consequence Artemis visits Patrae with dearth and pestilence. The Delphic oracle is consulted and ordains that the guilty pair be sacrificed and that the sacrifice be repeated annually with the most beautiful maiden and young lad as victims. The human sacrifices cease only when the hero Eurypylus arrives with a chest containing the image of Dionysus (7.19.1–10). But the garlands of corn ears worn by the children are said to be the same as those worn by the sacrificial victims (7.20.1).

The myth follows a pattern which is by now quite familiar, although in this case the violation which prompts the human sacrifice concerns Artemis in her capacity of protectress of chastity. Also, the story of Comaetho and Melanippus owes much to Hellenistic erotic literature and is thus of no great antiquity, at least in the form in which it has come down to us.[62] Another difference is that the story provides an aition not for an animal sacrifice (although certainly sacrifices were performed during the festival; hero-sacrifices to Eurypylus are mentioned in Paus. 7.19.10) or for a ritual involving the shedding of human blood, but for peaceful and harmless rites. On the simplest level, the myth accounts for the association of the cults of Artemis and Dionysus and the participation of young people of both sexes in the festival. The myth also provides an explanation for the name of the river in which the children bathe: after the institution of the human sacrifices the river was called Ameilichos; but after their abolition, the name was changed to Meilichos (7.19.4 and 7.19.9).

Modern interpretations of the myth and ritual have varied greatly. Farnell accepted the human sacrifices as historical, interpreting them as a 'ritual designed to produce crops'. Nilsson, while accepting the role of fertility in the rites, seriously questioned the actuality of the human sacrifices; the bath he interpreted as 'eine Reinungs- und Suhnzeremonie', although he found it strange that this should take place towards the end of the festival. But Herbillon, finding this objection insurmountable, suggested that the bath had taken the place of early human sacrifices, by immersion, to a river goddess Triklaria.[63] More recently, and to my mind more plausibly, Massenzio suggested that the rites performed by the Patraean children were rites of initiation.[64] The participants are *paides* and *parthenoi*. At night they depart from the city (a 'rite of separation'), bathe in the river (a common feature of initiations, Christian baptism the example which comes immediately to mind),[65] and then return, transformed, to be welcomed back by adult members of the community ('rite of incorporation'). The removal of the corn ears and the donning of wreaths of ivy is also symbolic of their altered status. The initiation process is further reinforced by the symbolism of death. In earlier times, it is said, a boy and a girl were sacrificed to Artemis; the sacrifice is symbolically re-enacted by the offering of wreaths of corn to Artemis, for similar wreaths according to tradition were worn by the sacrificial victims. This is not to say that the festival served solely to initiate young people into adulthood and/or the cult of Dionysus Aisymnetes.[66] The initiations were incorporated into a larger festival, in which the whole community participated.[67]

Dionysus and Artemis

The reader will no doubt have noticed that in most of the cases discussed above the recipients of the human sacrifices are Dionysus and Artemis, whose cults are linked together at Patrae. And modern scholars have frequently concluded that these two deities especially were recipients of human sacrifices, at least in prehistoric times. We shall also find a few human sacrifices imputed to Dionysus and Artemis among our 'historical' sources. But before we turn to these, let us look very briefly at some aspects of myth and ritual which contributed to the association of the two gods, both in ancient and modern times, with human sacrifice.

On the level of myth at least, there is no lack of violence associated with Dionysus. Drunkenness leads to murder; struck with madness, men and women slay their own children; those who resist the god are torn to pieces, or meet other violent ends; and Dionysus himself is cut apart by the Titans and consumed.[68] We also hear of *sparagmos* and *omophagia*, the rending and uncooked consumption of animals by maenads, and until quite recently ritual sparagmos and omophagy of animal victims were accepted as fact in the cult of Dionysus. The correspondence between the consumption of raw animal flesh in ritual and the myths which tell of the rending of Dionysus and his human opponents led Dodds and others to conclude that at one time human representatives of the god were slain and eaten in Dionysiac cult.[69] But more recently scholars have shown more caution. 'There is no reliable evidence for actual human sacrifices in any Dionysiac cult', writes M. L. West, and Henrichs has demonstrated that the vivid and gruesome picture of delirious maenadism and ritual omophagy, which we owe to Euripides, vase paintings, and writers of later antiquity, is highly exaggerated.[70] In fact there is no truly reliable evidence for the practice of sparagmos and omophagy of *animals* in Dionysiac ritual.[71] Thus, even in the case of animal sacrifices the reality seems to have been far less sensational than literary and artistic representations would lead us to believe.

From an early period Iphigeneia was associated with the goddess worshipped by the inhabitants of the Chersonese, the Tauri. In the *Cypria* Artemis replaced Iphigeneia on the altar with a hind, transported her to the land of the Tauri, and made her immortal (Procl. *Chr.*, p. 104 Allen). Herodotus reports that the Tauri sacrifice Greeks and shipwrecked sailors to 'the Virgin', who the Tauri themselves say is the daughter of Agamemnon (Hdt. 4.103.1–2). But the identification of the Tauric goddess with Iphigeneia is not particularly apt, as Iphigeneia was the victim, not the recipient, of a human sacrifice. It was this incongruity, perhaps, which led Euripides to make her a priestess of the Tauric goddess, identifying the latter with Artemis (Eur. *IT* 36, 80, etc.). Euripides is also the first to make an explicit connection between the *taurikē gē* and Artemis' epithet Tauropolos (*IT* 1453–7), although the false etymology crops up again in later writers.[72] But presumably the name Tauropolos was chiefly responsible for the association of Artemis and Iphigeneia with the Tauri in the first place.

> In thus transplanting the legend to the land of the Tauri the Greek legend-makers were not merely following the indication given by the similarity between the name of the barbarians, and the epithets of their goddess; it satisfied the scruples of the national conscience, which preferred to think of the human sacrifices hinted at in their own ceremonies, *e.g.* at Brauron, as practised by *barbarians* rather than by their own ancestors.

So wrote England in his commentary on the *IT*, and some fifty years later Platnauer wrote similarly: 'Actually the ritual of Artemis Tauropolos contained traces of much earlier human sacrifice. This false aetiology is a conscious attempt to clear the Greeks by attributing such sacrifices to barbarians.'[73] Although there may be a grain of truth in these statements, it is by no means certain that the Greek rites which 'hinted at' or 'contained traces of' human sacrifices did in fact derive from them. The epiklesis Tauropolos and the existence of bloody initiation rites in Artemis' cult at Halai (and perhaps elsewhere) are sufficient to account for the identification of Artemis with the Tauric goddess. But the identification, first made in the historical period and perfectly understandable, has little bearing on our study of the prehistoric worship of the Greek deity.

The 'mitigation' of human sacrifice

The human sacrifices which are replaced or 'mitigated' in these myths are not historical. The myths were 'aetiological myths', in that one of their functions was to provide 'histories' for existing rites and institutions which had no known histories in the real sense. The persons who perform in these mythical dramas, bringing deliverance from the burden of human sacrifice, are themselves mythical: Lycurgus is at best a semi-legendary figure, Eurypylus a hero from the Trojan War; and at Potniae the god himself declares an end to the human offerings. Furthermore, the fact that most of these myths follow a set pattern of transgression, plague (or other calamity), oracle, human sacrifice, and abolition of human sacrifice in favour of a less severe ritual does not argue for their historical value, particularly as myths involving human sacrifice belong to a much larger category of myths which ground existing institutions in a violation of existing social or religious order.[74]

But what functions did these myths serve in the religious life of the Greeks? Apropos of the goat sacrifices to Dionysus at Potniae Brelich writes:

> the myth affirms that the sacrifice of goats is the substitution for a human sacrifice, an extreme remedy for a crisis provoked by a misdeed. The real cult, like any cult, is a means to maintain order, to prevent it from falling back into

> chaos (which myth concretizes in the catastrophe – the plague – against which the cult itself is said to have been instituted). The cult culminates in the immolation of a goat which the myth presents as a substitution for the human sacrifice; this means that the myth – organically belonging to the cult – has the function of rendering the sacrifice of a goat equivalent to a human sacrifice (fully equivalent, because the god himself institutes it as such).

And in a similar vein, but with broader reference, Henrichs writes:

> In established Greek religion, the myth of human sacrifice and the practice of animal substitution must be seen as two complementary aspects of the same ritual mechanism, by which a divine claim to a human life is settled without actual loss of human life, either by a token shedding of human blood or more often by sacrificing an animal instead of the ideal human victim.

Thus both Brelich and Henrichs emphasize the equivalence of the animal sacrifice with the mythical human sacrifice.[75] The sacrificial animal, then, is in a meaningful sense substituted for the human victim, but the substitution is symbolic rather than historical.

In myth a condition of disorder stands opposed to the order which the cult promotes and maintains. The observance of cult rules and social order, to which the transgression of the myth is opposed, and the performance of sacrifice, whose mythic counterpart is the human sacrifice, insure the well-being of the community, the opposite of which is represented in myth by the powerful symbol of pestilence. But in the myths the human sacrifice performs a dual role: on the one hand, the offering of a human sacrifice releases the community from plague, but on the other, the demand for human sacrifice represents a continuation of the punishment – and hence the condition of abnormality. It is only when the worshippers are released, either immediately or after a period of time, from the burden of human sacrifice that full order is restored. Thus, if it is true in one sense that the animal and human victims are equivalent, in another the value of the animal sacrifice lies precisely in the fact that it is *not* a human sacrifice. It is the cessation of human sacrifices, at a mythical point in time, which marks the full restoration of order and the institution of those rites which are thereafter enacted in the cult.

The use of myths of human sacrifice in rites of initiation presents a special case, but their function here may still be viewed within the broader symbolic context outlined above: in initiation the myths are directed toward the young, but the aim of initiation is, like that of all cult practices, the maintenance of social order and differentiation. In the case of the ritual flogging at Sparta, the physical ordeal and letting of blood are themselves symbolic of the initiates' death, but this symbolism, Brelich argues, is reinforced, or 're-symbolized' through a myth of an original human sacrifice (p. 81). In other rituals plausibly identified as initiation rites, the symbol of human sacrifice functions similarly. This can be seen most clearly in the rites performed at Patrae, where the identification of the initiates with the sacrificial victims of old is reinforced by the wearing of wreaths of corn. But if a symbolic death of the initiates is achieved through this identification, if they 'become' for a moment sacrificial victims, so too does their 'rebirth' begin with the removal of the wreaths. Thus, in both the goat sacrifices at Potniae and the initiations at Patrae the deliverance from human sacrifice is as important as the equivalence of sacrificial animal, or initiate, with the mythical human victim. In the one case the substitution of the animal victim marks the restoration of social order centred around the act of sacrifice; in the other, the initiates' release from their status as sacrificial victims marks the beginning of their adult life in the community.

THE ATHAMANTIDS AT ALOS

The earliest historical description of a human sacrifice in Greece is Herodotus 7.197. According to the historian, Xerxes passed through Alos (or Halos) in 480 BC:

> When Xerxes had arrived at Alos in Achaea the tour guides, wishing to explain everything about the place, told the local story [all about the sanctuary of Zeus Laphystios], how Athamas son of Aeolus, conspiring with Ino, plotted the death of Phrixus, and how afterwards in accordance with an oracle the Achaeans imposed upon the descendants of Athamas the following tasks: ordaining that whoever was the eldest of this family was to be kept out of the *lēïton*, they

> themselves kept watch over the building – the Achaeans call their prytany building the 'lēïton' – but if he should enter, it is not possible for him to go out before he is about to be sacrificed. And in addition to these things they told further how already many of those who were going to be sacrificed in fear went into exile, but with the passage of time they would come back, and if caught they were sent to the prytany building. And they explained how he is sacrificed, covered all over with fillets, and how he is led out in a procession. And the descendants of Cytissorus the son of Phrixus endure these things, because when the Achaeans in accordance with an oracle were making Athamas a purification of the land and were about to sacrifice him, this Cytissorus arrived from Aea in Colchis and rescued him, and in doing so he brought down the wrath of the god upon his descendants. But Xerxes, having heard what went on in the grove, both avoided it himself and commanded the whole army to do the same. And he respected the residence of the descendants of Athamas and the temenos alike.
>
> (Hdt. 7.197)[76]

This passage is difficult and confusing for a number of reasons. The text itself is uncertain in several places, and corruption and interpolation have been suspected.[77] It is also peculiar how Herodotus chooses to frame the description of the ritual performed at Alos with two different myths. He begins with the story of Phrixus' sacrifice, but omits the rescue of Phrixus on the golden ram. Then, following his account of the rites he tells us how Athamas himself was going to be sacrificed but was rescued by his grandson Cytissorus. Both myths are given by Herodotus as aitia for the ritual. It is possible that the two myths were connected in some way: in Sophocles' second *Athamas* it appears that Athamas was required to be sacrificed as a punishment for the attempted sacrifice of their children (Schol. Ar. *Nub.* 257). But Herodotus fails to make the connection clear.

But it is the description of the *aethloi* undergone by Athamas' descendants which perplexes the most. These ordeals are presented by Herodotus in the following sequence (A = the eldest Athamantid):

(a) A is forbidden entry to the lēïton, which is guarded;
(b) A enters, is caught, and kept there until his sacrifice;

(c) many AA, about to be sacrificed (apparently having been caught entering the building), flee in fear;
(d) AA return and are sent to the lēïton;
(e) A is sacrificed.

Although we cannot expect perfect logic from religious ritual, Herodotus' account approaches absurdity. If the eldest Athamantids were forbidden entry into the prytany building, why did they try to enter? It must be that they were obliged by religious duty to do so. But if the building was guarded, how did they enter? Disguised? By stealth? Were the guards inattentive; or did they allow them to enter? And if it was their religious duty to try to enter, why then did they – now apparently shirking their obligation – try to escape? And again, how did so many elude the guards? And if they fled out of fear of being sacrificed (as Herodotus avers), then why in heaven's name did they return? Again, the only answer seems to be that they were under a religious obligation to return and attempt to enter the building for a second time.

The only reasonable solution to these problems is to suppose that we are dealing with a prescribed sequence of actions, a sort of ritual drama which must be enacted, perhaps upon coming of age, by the eldest son of the priestly family at Alos. He must have been allowed to enter the building, or have allowed himself to be caught by the guards trying to do so. He was kept there until the appointed day of sacrifice but was then permitted to 'escape' and go into exile. Later, after an unspecified period of time (χρόνου . . . προϊόντος), he returned and apparently repeated his attempt to enter the prytany building. At this point the 'sacrifice' was carried out. We are also told that the victim was led in a procession, covered from head to toe with woollen bands (στέμμασι πᾶς πυκασθείς). And here myth may shed some light on the ritual. Phrixus is delivered from sacrifice by a golden ram sent by Zeus, which he later sacrifices to Zeus Phyxios (see p. 83): such rescues we have seen in other myths of human sacrifice, and it seems probable that a ram was sacrificed in the place of the human victim, in ritual as in myth.[78] The dressing of the eldest Athamantid in wool establishes the identity of the human and animal victims, the reverse of the situation at Mounychia, where in myth Embarus sacrificed a hind dressed as his daughter, or on Tenedos, where the sacrificial calf wore buskins.

We can be reasonably certain, I think, that the human sacrifice was never carried out.[79] This is suggested first of all by the logical inconsistencies in Herodotus' description of the ritual. Also, twice in this description the victims are said to be *about to be* sacrificed, and we encounter the same use of the verb *mellein* in the myth of Athamas, who, about to be sacrificed, is rescued by his grandson Cytissorus.[80] This correspondence of language suggests that the mythical rescue had its counterpart in ritual, although we can only guess how the rescue was effected. Much remains mysterious about these unusual rites, and I hesitate to speculate further on their nature.[81] But certain features of the ritual sequence – the various ordeals which must be undergone, the seclusion in the prytany building, the myth and the threat of sacrifice, the 'escape' followed by a period of exile – are common elements of 'rites of passage' and together may suggest that the ritual functioned to initiate a young member of the family into the priesthood of Zeus. Or possibly the fifth-century ritual represented a survival of old initiation rites undergone by all young males in the area, but now conserved only in the family which claimed direct descent from Athamas.

It would be interesting to know exactly how Herodotus obtained the information which he relays to us. It is beyond any reasonable doubt that Xerxes' conversation with the guides, which results in his pious avoidance of the sanctuary, is a fiction.[82] It is also reasonably certain that Herodotus never himself saw any part of the ceremonies, for otherwise his account of them would not have been so muddled; and if he had, surely he would have said so. One or both of the myths Herodotus may have known from the Athenian stage. Aeschylus wrote an *Athamas* (fr. 1–4a Radt), and Sophocles wrote a *Phrixus* and two plays entitled *Athamas* (fr. 721–3 and 1–10 Radt). The dates of Sophocles' plays are unknown, but an allusion in the *Clouds* to the preparation of Athamas for sacrifice in Sophocles' second *Athamas* provides 323 as a *terminus ante quem* for the tragedy (Ar. *Nub*. 256–7). In Sophocles' play it was Heracles who rescued Athamas (Schol. Ar. *Nub*. 257), and if Herodotus was familiar with the drama (or the tradition which Sophocles followed), then possibly the alternate version he gives (in which Athamas is rescued by Cytissorus) represents an effort to correct the prevailing tradition with a regional version (ἐπιχώριος λόγος: Hdt. 7.197.1) which he knew from other sources. His statement that Athamas plotted together with Ino against Phrixus (rather than being deceived by his wife) also seems to represent a departure from the traditional story. The information about the ritual itself Herodotus attributes to local guides, whom he places with Xerxes in 480 in his history. Possibly Herodotus himself learned of the ritual from such guides, although we may be justly suspicious of a detail which permits the Persian king to hear of the local custom in a ficticious encounter on the march. It therefore seems possible that Herodotus owed his knowledge only to distant reports about the strange goings-on at Alos. In either case there is a good possibility that the account was dressed up and exaggerated for the historian, and it would be easy for his informants to omit one small detail – the 'rescue' of the human sacrificial victim – in a desire to impress. It is also possible that by the 420s the actual human sacrifice was already reported as a thing of the past – a ritual which had been 'mitigated' but which could safely be represented as still current at the time when Xerxes passed through Alos before Thermopylae. In any case Hdt. 7.197 is very far from being a reliable eyewitness account of the performance of a human sacrifice.

THE CULT OF ZEUS LYKAIOS

To the west of the plain of Megalopolis in Arcadia rises Mt Lykaion, known also in antiquity as Olympus and Hiera Koruphe.[83] On one of the mountain's three crests (the present Ai Lias) was a sanctuary of Zeus Lykaios, where, probably every four years, the festival of the Lykaia was celebrated along with games said to be among the oldest in Greece. A circular earth-and-ash altar forms the summit of Ai Lias, and upon this altar, it was persistently rumoured in antiquity, human sacrifices were performed in the cult of Zeus Lykaios.[84]

Alcman composed hymns to Zeus Lykaios,[85] but the earliest extant references to his cult and festival are found in the epinician odes of Pindar, who mentions briefly the festival of Zeus Lykaios and the Lycaean altar in connection with the Lycaean games (*Ol.* 9.96, *Ol.* 13.107–8, *Nem.* 10.48). Also in the fifth century, the Spartan king Pleistoanax received asylum on the mountain and lived for nineteen years in a house associated with the sanctuary (Thuc. 5.16.3). And at the end of the *Electra* (1273–4) Euripides refers briefly to the Lycaean precinct. But the earliest reference to human sacrifices performed on the mountain belongs to the fourth century BC. In the *Republic* Socrates discusses the evolution of the tyrant from the 'protector':

> 'What then is the beginning of the transformation from protector to tyrant? Is it not clearly when the protector begins to do the same as the man in the story which is told concerning the sanctuary of Zeus Lykaios in Arcadia?'
> 'What story?' he said.
> 'How the man who has tasted of the piece of human entrails – one of these having been cut up along with the entrails of the other victims – it is necessary for this man to be turned into a wolf. Or haven't you heard the story?'
> 'I have.'
>
> (Pl. *Resp.* 8, 565D–E)

It should be noted that while Socrates refers to the above as a story (*muthos*), this does not necessarily mean that he does not believe that human flesh is consumed in the rite. Rather, like several later writers, Socrates (or rather Plato) doubts that the participant who tastes of human flesh is transformed into a wolf.

Also in the fourth century, the author of the pseudo-Platonic *Minos* (315B–C) and Theophrastus (fr. 13.22–6 Pötscher) refer briefly to the sacrifice on Mt Lykaion, both citing it as an example of human sacrifice still practised in Greece in their own day (see pp. 115–16). It is likely that the source for both writers was the passage in the *Republic*, as it will later be for Polybius (8.13.7), who borrows Plato's comparison of the tyrant to the Arcadian wolf-man. Hence these brief references cannot be considered secure evidence that the sacrifices were being performed in the second half of the fourth century, and they add little to our knowledge of the ritual, other than the detail that the sacrifice was performed during the festival of the Lykaia.[86]

Our other information about the cult of Zeus Lykaios comes from a much later period. Pausanias visited the site, and he implied that the human sacrifices continued to be performed in his own time, writing that on the altar 'they sacrifice in secret; I did not wish to inquire further into the details of the sacrifice: let it be as it has been from the beginning' (Paus. 8.38.7). But although he did not expressly mention the human sacrifice, Pausanias was aware that a participant in the ritual was supposed to turn into a wolf:

> For they say that after Lycaon someone would always be turned from a man into a wolf at the sacrifice of Zeus Lykaios, but that he would not become a wolf for all his life. Rather, if while he was a wolf he refrained from human flesh, they say that afterwards in the tenth year he turned back from a wolf into a man. But if he had tasted human flesh he remained a beast forever.
>
> (Paus. 8.2.6)

But Pausanias, like Plato, doubts that this transformation actually took place, although he is willing to grant that Lycaon himself was turned into a wolf (8.2.4–5). Pausanias shows similar scepticism elsewhere when he tells the story of one Damarchus, who was said to have undergone the transformation:

> But concerning the boxer named Damarchus, who was by birth an Arcadian of Parrhasia, except for his victory at Olympia I do not believe the other things said by pretentious men, namely that he was changed from a man to a wolf at the sacrifice of Zeus Lykaios and that ten years later he again became a man. Nor did it seem to me that this was said about him by the Arcadians, for in this case it would also be said in the inscription at Olympia, which runs as follows:
>
> Damarchus son of Dinyttas set up this statue,
> a Parrhasian by birth from Arcadia.
>
> (Paus. 6.8.2)

Pliny and Augustine also tell the story of Damarchus, although in their accounts the name has been corrupted into Demaenetus:

> Euanthes, not at all despised among the writers of Greece, relates that the Arcadians write that someone from the clan of a certain Anthus, chosen by drawing lots among the family, is led to a certain pond in the area, and that after hanging his clothes on an oak, he swims across and goes off into the wild; and that he is turned into a wolf and consorts for nine years with others of the same species. If during this period he has abstained from eating humans, he returns to the same pond, and having swum across it he regains his shape, but with nine years added to his former appearance. And Euanthes [?] adds a still more fabulous detail, that he

> receives again the same clothing. It is a marvel how far Greek credulity can go, for no lie is so outrageous that it lacks a witness. Thus Scopas [?], who wrote a book on *Olympic Victors*, reports that Demaenetus the Parrhasian, at the sacrifice that the Arcadians would make to Lycaean Jove even at that time from a human victim, tasted the entrails of a sacrificed boy and was turned into a wolf. And that when he had been restored to his own form he competed athletically in boxing and returned from Olympia a victor.
>
> (Pliny *HN* 8.34)[87]

> Varro . . . relates other things no less incredible, about that notorious witch Circe . . . and about the Arcadians, who, having been chosen by lot, would swim across a certain pool and there would be transformed into wolves and live with like beasts in the wilds of that region. But if they did not feed on human flesh, after nine years, having swum back across the same pool, they were again transformed into men. In fact he even mentioned by name a certain Demaenetus, who when he had tasted of the sacrifice which the Arcadians were accustomed to make to their Lycaean god from a slaughtered boy, was changed into a wolf, and that in the tenth year, restored to his own form, he trained himself in boxing and won a victory in an Olympic contest.
>
> (August. *De civ. D.* 18.17)

The obvious similarities between the passages suggest that Pliny and Augustine had this information from the same source, namely Varro; but while Augustine cites Varro without naming the latter's sources, Pliny names these without mentioning Varro. Pausanias will have known the story of Damarchus from Greek writers (whom he characterizes as *alazones andres*), among them, perhaps, the author of the *Olympionikai* whose name has been corrupted beyond repair in the manuscripts of the *Naturalis historia*.

Pliny and Augustine conclude their accounts with the story of the boxer transformed into a wolf upon consuming human flesh at the sacrifice. But before this they both state that the 'wolves' were selected by lot; and Pliny adds that they were chosen only from a certain family, the descendants of Anthus. Drawing of lots and the cannibalistic feast: the two methods would seem to be irreconcilable, although they are clearly related in some way.

Various solutions have been proposed, but the simplest is that the two traditions reflect a historical change in the rite. Burkert has plausibly suggested that with the founding of Megalopolis in 371 BC the organization of the Lykaia was transferred to the new Arcadian capital, where Zeus Lykaios was given a sanctuary in the agora. The ritual continued to be celebrated on the mountaintop, but it was 'civilized' at this point and placed in the charge of one family, the descendants of Anthus.[88] Both Hyde and Moretti dated the epigram which Pausanias read on Damarchus' statue base at Olympia to a period 'certainly before Alexander' and placed Damarchus' victory at Olympia in the fifth or early fourth century. Moretti suggested a more specific date of around 400 (Ol. 95).[89] If this dating is approximately correct, then both Damarchus' transformation into a wolf and Plato's brief description of the rites predated the founding of Megalopolis and the presumed changes in 371. It thus seems quite likely that Plato owed his knowledge of the human sacrifices to the circulation of a story that a well-known Olympic victor had participated in the ritual on Mt Lykaion.

Another solution to the problem has been proposed recently by M. Jost. Burkert's suggestion of a historical change is unacceptable to Jost because of Pausanias' statement (8.37.8) that secret sacrifices were still performed on the altar in his day. And noting that the presence of a lake on the peak of Lykaion is unlikely, she suggests that the wolf-transformation of the descendants of Anthus was an independent ritual performed elsewhere in Arcadia, perhaps in the area of Tegea.[90] It is true that the location of the ritual described by Euanthes is not specified by Pliny or Augustine, but it is also true that the two rituals were treated together by Varro, and in the texts there is no indication that they were performed at two different places. Also, a *stagnum* need not be a large body of water, and even if no pond of sufficient size could be found on Lykaion itself, nothing precludes the descent of the chosen participant down the mountainside before his swim and 'transformation'. In fact, Pliny's assertion that the participant was 'led to a certain pond of this region' (*ad stagnum quoddam regionis eius duci*) indicates movement, perhaps over some distance, from the place where the lottery was conducted. Besides, several features of the two rituals are identical (the transformation, the period of nine years, the abstention from human flesh), so that at the very least one form was the doublet of the other, and the problem of the historical relationship and development of the two rites remains. And finally, when Pliny turns from his account of the wolf-transformation of the descendants of Anthus to describe the transformation of Demaenetus, he writes that the future Olympian was turned into a wolf during the sacrifice which 'even at that time' (*etiamtum*) the Arcadians offered from a human victim. This statement seems to indicate a consciousness on the part of Pliny (or Varro) of the incompatibility of the two accounts, and may also be taken to suggest that the two rituals were performed in the same location, but that selection by lottery from among the Anthidae was the later form of the ritual.

Closely associated with the Arcadian rites is the myth of Lycaon, son of Pelasgus and legendary founder of Lycosura and the Lycaean games. The myth has come down to us in several different versions. Pausanias preserves the simplest, that Lycaon sacrificed an infant, pouring its blood on the altar of Zeus Lykaios; and thereupon Lycaon was changed into a wolf (Paus. 8.2.3). In a more detailed account of pseudo-Apollodorus, Zeus comes in disguise to Arcadia in order to put the impiety of Lycaon's fifty sons to the test. The sons kill a child, mix the entrails among the sacrificial victims, and set them before Zeus. But Zeus overturns the table and blasts Lycaon and his sons with the thunderbolt, sparing only the youngest son, Nyctimus (Apollod. *Bibl.* 3.8.1). In other versions Lycaon kills his own son (Nyctimus), his grandson (Arcas), or an unspecified human victim and serves him to his divine visitor.[91] The extant versions of the myth are late, but the story goes back at least to the time of the Hesiodic *Ehoeae* (fr. 163 Merkelbach-West). The myth also bears a striking resemblance to the myth of Tantalus, who serves his own son to divine visitors, and shows some similarity to the story of Thyestes, whose children are served to him by his brother Atreus. Like these stories, the myth of Lycaon was a popular subject in tragedy.[92]

The sanctuary of Zeus Lykaios was a holy precinct, into which entrance was forbidden.[93] According to Polybius, Theopompus wrote that those who entered the *abaton* lost their shadows (Polyb. 16.12.7 = Theopompus, *FGrHist* 115 F 343). Plutarch adds that persons who enter the sanctuary are called 'deer'; if they enter knowingly they are stoned to death by the Arcadians, but if unintentionally they are sent 'to Eleutherae' (*Quaest. Graec.* 39, 300A–D = Architimus, *FGrHist* 315 F 1). According to Pausanias anyone who entered the precinct would die within a year's time; and entrance to the sanctuary at Megalopolis was also forbidden (Paus. 8.38.6 and 8.30.2). And animals who entered the precinct became sterile (Schol. Callim. *Jov.* 12–13). In myth, Lycaon's grandson Arcas pursues his mother Callisto, who has been transformed into a bear, into the forbidden sanctuary, but before the Arcadians can kill them they are rescued by Zeus and transformed into constellations.[94] Pausanias also tells us that there was a spring called Hagno on Mt Lykaion. In time of prolonged drought the priest of Zeus Lykaios would pray to the water of Hagno, offer the customary sacrifices, and touch the surface of the spring with an oak branch. A mist would rise from the water, become a cloud, and attract other clouds to itself. And rain would fall on Arcadia (Paus. 8.38.4).

Not surprisingly, this intriguing collection of ancient passages has given rise to a wealth of modern interpretations. Much of the scholarly discussion once centred on the etymology of 'Lykaios' and the question whether Zeus Lykaios was a 'wolf god' or a 'light god'.[95] For H. D. Müller the god was a chthonic deity, whose symbol was the wolf; the victim of the sacrifice represented Olympian Zeus, whose slaughter and consumption by the worshippers dramatized the triumph of the chthonic Zeus, which in turn represented the triumph, in mid-summer, of the destructive part of the year over the fruitful. Mannhardt also viewed the Lykaia as a mid-summer festival; but for Mannhardt the wolf was the 'corn wolf', and the rites served to encourage the growth of crops and to ward off pestilence and infertility. In the opinion of W. Immerwahr, the wolf was the symbol of exile, Zeus Lykaios was to be identified with Zeus Phyxios (Zeus 'of Banishment'), and the human sacrifice was a propitiatory sacrifice meant to atone for the original crime of the Parrhasian people.[96] Cook, like Mannhardt, viewed the rites as vegetation rites. But for Cook, who argued at length that Zeus Lykaios was a god of light, the original victim was the king responsible for the crops and weather – in short, the 'Slain King' of Sir James Frazer. And Nilsson, emphasizing the ritual performed at the spring Hagno, concluded that the human sacrifice was originally 'ein Wetterzauber'.[97] Still others have envisioned a secret society, a wolf brotherhood, comparing e.g. the leopard-men of Africa.[98]

More recently, Burkert has offered a detailed reconstruction and interpretation of the rites performed on the Arcadian mountaintop. Burkert concludes that the wolf-transformation was in origin a ritual of initiation: the removal of clothing and the swimming across a body of water are typical features of 'rites of passage'; 'sons of bears' and 'wolves' may have designated distinct age-groups (cf. Paus. 4.11.3, where the Arcadian soldiers wear wolf and bear skins); and, noting that in order to compete in the Olympic games Damarchus could not have been much older than sixteen at the time of his 'transformation', Burkert compares the 'wolf's' tenure in the wild to the Spartan Krypteia. And the fact that the rites were celebrated in conjunction with athletic contests may further indicate the role of the festival in the integration of the Arcadian youth into the adult male community.[99]

The reader may begin to feel that initiation has supplanted the Corn Spirits, Year Demons, totems, Dying Gods, and Slain Kings of yesteryear as a convenient but facile and unfounded explanation of some of the more puzzling rituals of the ancients. And no doubt the results of the enthusiastic search in this century for traces of puberty rites in Greek ceremony and myth will need some correction and modification in the future. Yet it is beyond question that ceremonies which we term 'initiations' played a significant role in the education of youth in early Greek society.[100] A common and prominent feature of initiations in many cultures is the symbolic death of the initiate, which sometimes takes the form of a myth in which children are killed or sacrificed: in Pliny *HN* 8.34 and August. *De civ. D.* 18.17 the victim is a *puer*, and in the myth of Lycaon the victim is often a male child, *pais* (although sometimes an infant).[101] Nevertheless, the interpretation of the ritual as an initiatory rite is not without difficulties. It was certainly a very selective one, with apparently only one 'wolf' chosen in each ceremony. But such selectivity is not an uncommon feature of rituals now identified as initiatory; in fact with very few exceptions scholars are compelled to speak of 'survivals' of early initiation rites, for very often the documented rituals of historic times involve only a single participant or a limited number of youths.[102] Thus the Lycaean ritual might be viewed as a survival from a time when all the initiates underwent the 'transformation'; or the 'wolf' might be seen as a special representative of the members of his age-class, all of whom were liable to undergo the change during the sacrifice. It is also uncertain into what group the youths were initiated by means of the ceremony: into the adult male society as a whole, into a restricted 'wolf brotherhood', or into the priesthood of Zeus Lykaios.[103]

There are certain marked resemblances between the Arcadian rites and the Delphic Septerion, which has also been interpreted as an initiation rite in origin. Every eight years a youth of noble family was led along a route known as Dolonia to a wooden hut. Having set fire to the hut and overturned a table set within it, the boy fled without looking back. Then, after a period of 'wanderings and servitude' he was purified at Tempe and returned crowned with laurel to Delphi. The Septerion was performed shortly before the Pythian games.[104] The similarities between the Septerion and the Lycaean ritual are suggestive: the period of exile; the connection with athletic contests; possibly the name of the road, Dolonia (Gernet suggested that the story of Dolon in the *Iliad* preserved traces of a ritual in which a young man was dressed, like Dolon, in a wolfskin);[105] and the overturning of the table. In the myth of Lycaon Zeus overturns the table (*trapeza*) upon discovering the nature of the repast. And while this detail served as a rather lame aition for the name of the town Trapezous, it may also have reflected a detail of the ritual: the participant in the sacrifice who 'discovered' that he had consumed human flesh kicked over the table before fleeing, transformed, into the wilderness.[106]

But the question which concerns us most is whether human victims were actually slain and consumed during the rites performed on Mt Lykaion. It should be noted that these rites are better attested than any other Greek ritual involving the sacrifice of human victims; in fact, with a few negligible exceptions, this is the only 'historical' human sacrifice for which we have more than one authority. We have at least one contemporary reference to the ceremony (Pl. *Resp*. 8, 565D–E); and Plato and Theophrastus must be considered relatively reliable witnesses, especially if we set them beside the scholiasts and lexicographers to whom we owe much of our information about pharmakos rites (chapter 5). On the other hand, the multiple attestation may be deceptive: Plato may have been the sole source for Theophrastus and the author of the *Minos*; Pausanias, Pliny, and Augustine seem to have known of the human sacrifices only in connection with the story of Damarchus; and quite possibly this story was Plato's source of information also.

The reality of the human sacrifices was long ago thrown into question by archaeology. In 1902 the earth altar on Mt Lykaion was excavated by Kourouniotis.[107] Kourouniotis laid six trenches across the altar, which consisted of a mixture of earth, stones, ash, and burnt bones to a depth of 1.50 m before bedrock. Coins and pottery from the fill indicated a period of use from *c.* 600 into the fourth century BC,[108] and thus Pausanias' belief that the sacrifices continued into his own time (8.38.7) would certainly appear to be mistaken. Numerous bones were found in the fill of the altar, mostly of small animals but some of cattle and pigs. No human bones could be discerned. And although it was not stated in the report, the fact that several species of animals were distinguished suggests that the skeletal material was studied by a qualified person. Thus archaeology has failed to confirm the strong literary tradition of human sacrifices on the mountaintop. Perhaps it cannot be said that archaeology has conclusively disproved this tradition, for if the victims were infants, possibly their skeletal remains would not have survived (although many bones of small animals, including birds, were identified); or conceivably the remains of the human victims would be removed for separate burial elsewhere. But the results of the excavations certainly cast a very strong doubt upon the claims that human sacrifices were performed on the altar, and they demonstrate that the usual sacrifices were of animal victims.

In spite of the negative verdict of archaeology, some scholars continue to accept the human sacrifices as historical.[109] But the results of the excavation have caused others to doubt, if not to reject, the tradition that human sacrifices were performed during the festival.[110] And Burkert notes that the inwards of humans and animals would hardly be distinguishable and that those who partook of the communal meal were other than the priests who had prepared it. The power of suggestion, fostered by tradition, would work on the imagination just as well as the reality. Thus in Burkert's view the participants will have believed in earnest that the sacrificial meal contained a portion of human flesh, and this belief will have contributed to the efficacy of the initiation rite.[111]

Of course it is not only the verdict of the excavation which invites suspicion over certain details of the ritual. We ourselves do not believe that participants in the sacrifice actually turned into wolves, and we may wonder further how a particular participant would be aware that he had ingested a piece of human *splanchna*. That the wolf-men remained in the wild for nine full years might also be questioned,[112] and although there is no reason to doubt that entry into the temenos was forbidden, some of the reported consequences are clearly symbolic rather than actual. And the ancients themselves expressed doubt about several aspects of the tradition. Polybius (16.12.7) takes Theopompus to task for claiming that trespassers into the sanctuary lose their shadows; Plato characterizes the report of wolf-transformation as a myth; and Pliny, Augustine, and Pausanias are even more emphatically sceptical. Indeed it does not seem inappropriate to speak of a *tradition* of scepticism concerning the rites on Mt Lykaion; and there may even be faint traces of an ancient controversy over their nature. According to Euanthes it was the Arcadians themselves who wrote of the selection of the werewolf by lottery,[113] while it was a writer on Olympic victors who reported the human sacrifices. Although Pliny and Augustine do not make clear the connection between the two contradictory accounts, the version attributed to the Arcadians may in fact represent an Arcadian reply to reports of human sacrifice centring around the Olympic boxer Damarchus. It does not seem impossible that in early accounts the description of the ritual was coloured with details from the cult myth, and what was a selection by lottery from the beginning was magnified by rumour into a cannibalistic feast like that served up by Lycaon to Zeus. At some point the Arcadians took it upon themselves to set the matter straight. A confusion of ritual and mythic details seems to underlie reports of human sacrifice in other cases (e.g. the rites at Alos discussed above), and this suggestion has the merit of resolving the problem of the two forms of the ritual. But perhaps the truth lies somewhere in a compromise between Burkert's suggestion of a historical change and the suggestion offered here.

Of the history of the cult we may trace only the sketchiest of outlines. Finds from the sanctuary indicate a cult from the seventh century BC,[114] and the myth of Lycaon, closely associated with (if not generated by) the ritual, was attributed to Hesiod (fr. 163 Merkelbach-West). But it is not until the fourth century that we hear of human sacrifice and cannibalism in the cult, and it seems possible that the participation of a famous Olympic victor in the rites in the late fifth or early fourth century was responsible for Plato's – and perhaps a widespread – acquaintance with the sacrifice and wolf-transformation. At some point it seems that the cannibalistic meal, real or feigned (but very probably the latter), was replaced by a lottery conducted within a single family, a change associated by Burkert with the founding of Megalopolis in 371 and the transfer of the official cult to the new city. But it is conceivable that the lottery was a feature of the older ritual as well. Apparently use of the altar was soon discontinued, for the excavation of the altar produced no finds later than the fourth century. At some point in the third century the festival and the games were also discontinued; but they were soon re-established in around 215.[115] In Strabo's time the sanctuary was still 'honoured to a small extent' (Strabo 8.8.2), and there is some archaeological evidence for continued activity in the Roman period. Two late inscriptions (one Augustan, the other second-century) mention the Lycaean games, which have now been combined with the Kaisareia; but it is likely that the games were now held in Megalopolis, for in the mid-second century, when Pausanias visits the site, the Lycaean games (and with them, presumably, the festival) are no longer being held on the mountaintop, and there are no statues on the statue bases (Paus. 8.38.5); the golden eagles are gone from the columns before the altar (8.38.7; cf. 8.30.2); and the sanctuary has every appearance of being totally abandoned.[116] From his description, the site does not seem to have been very much different in the second century than it appears today, and it was apparently only myth and tradition – perhaps with some encouragement from local guides – which led the learned traveller to assert that the Arcadians still sacrificed on the earth-and-ash altar and to hint darkly that human victims were slaughtered and consumed there even in his day (8.38.7).

HUMAN SACRIFICE IN WARTIME

Σφάγια and 'dichotomy' in history and prehistory

In his lengthy list of human sacrifices (see pp. 122–30) Porphyry states that according to Phylarchus it was common practice for all the Greeks to kill human beings before setting out against the enemy (Porph. *Abst.* 2.56.7 = Phylarchus, *FGrHist* 81 F 80). Regrettably, we know nothing of the context of this remarkable statement.[117] But we do know that by Phylarchus' time (third century BC) the customary sacrifices made before battle, *sphagia*, were of animal victims: there is abundant evidence for these sacrifices in the historians, particularly Xenophon.[118] Phylarchus' assertion, therefore, must be referred to the prehistoric period, and it seems not unlikely that he based this statement upon the many sacrifices of human victims – the Hyacinthides, Macaria, Menoeceus, etc. – performed in time of war in Greek myth and on the tragic stage (see pp. 73–6). Possibly Phylarchus went further and connected these mythical human sacrifices with the customary sphagia performed before battle, claiming that at some time animals had been substituted for the human victims of heroic times. Indeed such arguments have been made in modern times. 'Das uralte Opfer vor dem Kampfe, das wie kein anderes Unheil abwehrt, die σφάγια par préférence, ist das Menschenopfer', wrote Eitrem in 1938. But Eitrem based this contention on very shaky foundations: besides the fragment of Phylarchus, he cited the sacrifice of Persian captives before the battle of Salamis (as we shall see, almost certainly not historical), the sacrifice of royal children in myth, and a story of human sacrifice enjoined by an oracle during the First Messenian War (again, unhistorical).[119] None of this can be taken as secure evidence for the practice of human sacrifice, in historic or prehistoric times, although we can readily see from Eitrem's collection of examples how it was possible for Phylarchus to come to the conclusion that he did. And even if human victims were sacrificed before battle in prehistoric times, I am not convinced that the supposed practice had any direct connection with stories of voluntary self-sacrifice of noble youths and maidens in Greek myth (which need not owe their existence to historical reality). And surely Phylarchus' assertion should not be taken in itself as secure evidence, for we have no reason to believe that Phylarchus was any better informed – for the prehistoric period – than we are.

Nilsson suggested that human victims were used in early Greece for a different kind of military ritual. In 182 BC the Macedonian army performed a purification ceremony (*lustratio*), during which a dog was cut in two pieces: the fore part was placed on the right side of the road, the hind part, with the entrails, on the left, and the army marched in between in full armour (Livy 40.6.1–7). The same ritual is described by Curtius (10.9.11–12) for 323 BC (cf. Hesych. s.v. Ξανθικά and Suda s.v. ἐναγίζειν = Polyb. 23.10.17). And according to Plutarch, the Boeotians would perform a public purification (*katharmos*) by passing between the parts of a severed dog (*Quaest. Rom.* 111, 290D). Similar rituals of 'dichotomy' are known from several other, particularly Near Eastern, cultures, including the Hittites and Persians.[120] Nilsson called attention to a similarity between the Boeotian and Macedonian rituals and a story related by 'Apollodorus': when Peleus sacked Iolcus with the help of Jason and the Dioscuri, he killed Acastus' wife Astydameia and, having torn her body limb from limb, led the army through her severed parts into the city (Apollod. *Bibl.* 3.13.7). On the basis of this similarity Nilsson suggested that at one time human beings were used instead of dogs in the Macedonian and Boeotian rites.[121]

It is true that human beings were sometimes employed as victims in the Hittite ritual (so also by the Persians in Herodotus), but the sole evidence for Greece is the myth preserved in 'Apollodorus'. Also, in the myth the dismemberment is an act of punishment, for earlier Astydameia had falsely accused Peleus of making sexual advances (*Bibl.* 3.13.3); thus Astydameia is not slain expressly or solely for use in the purification ceremony. Furthermore, it is possible that this is not the earliest version of the story. In other accounts (including Pindar's) the woman's name is not Astydameia but Hippolyta: both the name and the presence of the 'Potiphar's wife motif' in the story suggest that originally Hippolyta, like Hippolytus, was destroyed by horses.[122] Possibly the source of the variant in 'Apollodorus' (Pherecydes?)[123] combined a brutal death found in the tradition with details of contemporary Macedonian, Boeotian, or Near Eastern purification rites. This seems more likely than the view that this unique (and possibly secondary) version of the myth preserves a memory of 'human sacrifice' in early Greek military practice.

Agesilaus at Aulis and Pelopidas at Leuctra

Plutarch relates two stories of human sacrifices which were enjoined in time of war but never carried out. In 396 BC Agesilaus, while the Greek forces assembled at Geraestus in Euboea, went with some friends to pass the night at Aulis. In his sleep a voice told him that since only he and Agamemnon ever commanded a combined force of all the Greeks and since he was setting out from the same place and against the same enemy, he should make the same sacrifice that Agamemnon made before departing for Troy. But Agesilaus, unwilling to repeat the folly of Agamemnon (or insensitive behaviour: ἀπάθειαν or ἀμαθίαν in the MSS.), instructed his seer to sacrifice a hind. But the seer did not follow correct local procedure (in some unspecified respect), and the Boeotarchs dispatched agents who arrived in time to interrupt the sacrifice and throw the thigh-pieces from the altar. As a result Agesilaus departed on his expedition angry with the Thebans and distressed by the omen of the disrupted sacrifice (Plut. *Ages.* 6.4–6).

In 371 BC, before the battle of Leuctra, Pelopidas dreamt that he saw the daughters of Scedasus weeping at their tombs. Scedasus appeared to Pelopidas and instructed him to sacrifice a virgin with blond hair to his daughters, if he wished to be victorious over the Spartans. According to the legend (known, with variations, from several sources), Scedasus' daughters, the Leuctrides, committed suicide after being raped by Spartan youths; their father then killed himself at their tomb.[124] But Pelopidas is shocked at Scedasus' command, which he finds dreadful and unlawful. When he communicates his dream to his seers and officers, a debate ensues, some citing cases where human sacrifices resulted in military success, while others are opposed to the performance of a human sacrifice (see pp. 117–18). The debate is interrupted when a filly with a bright red mane breaks free from the other horses, bursts into camp, and stops before the debating leaders. The seer Theocritus thereupon declares that the filly is the victim required by the dream. So the horse is led to the tombs of the daughters of Scedasus and duly sacrificed (Plut. *Pel.* 21–2).

As neither of these human sacrifices was actually performed, the two accounts are not of much significance for our study. Still, it might be argued that the stories indicate that human sacrifice was an option still seriously considered in the fourth century and that the two human sacrifices might have been carried out, had it not been for the good sense of Agesilaus or the opportune appearance of a filly. Believe who will, but it is most unlikely that either incident is historical. Two other authors, Xenophon and Pausanias, tell of Agesilaus' visit to Aulis and the disrupted sacrifice, but neither says anything about his dream or the human sacrifice it enjoins (Xen. *Hell.* 3.4.3–4; Paus. 3.9.3–6). Plutarch does not specify why Agesilaus went to Aulis, but Xenophon and Pausanias make it clear that he went in order to invite comparison with Agamemnon: it was a propaganda ploy. Thus it is possible that the story of the dream was created by Agesilaus himself or one of his company.[125] But it may just as easily have been the invention of some historian who wished to carry the comparison of Agesilaus and Agamemnon to its logical extreme. The interruption of the sacrifice by the Thebans, however, seems actually to have occurred: at least it appears in all three sources. But even this incident may have been fabricated after the fact, in order to provide an inauspicious beginning to Agesilaus' disappointing venture in the East (cf. Plut. *Ages.* 6.6 and *Pel.* 21.3).[126]

Similarly, the story of the Leuctrian maidens provided a reason for the defeat of the Spartan army. There must have been a tomb of local heroines in the vicinity, but the story that the girls were raped by Spartans specifically may have been invented either after the fact or on the spot before the historic battle. Again it is not easy to disentangle fact from fiction. Xenophon, our earliest and most reliable source, says merely that the Thebans decorated the maidens' tomb before the battle (*Hell.* 6.4.7). And in Paus. 9.13.6 it is not Pelopidas but Epaminondas who offers a sacrifice (victim unspecified) to the daughters of Scedasus. Diodorus (15.54.1–3) says nothing of the sacrifice, and only Plutarch and the author of the *Amatoriae Narrationes* attributed to him connect the sacrifice with Pelopidas. In the latter account Scedasus also appears to Pelopidas in his sleep, but only to enjoin the sacrifice of a white colt to his daughters ([Plut.] *Amat. Narr.* 3, 774D). Conceivably the victim sacrificed on this occasion was in fact a horse, and the story of the human sacrifice miraculously avoided developed around this kernel of truth; but it is perhaps more likely that *Amat. Narr.* 3 is merely an abbreviated version of the story given in the *Pelopidas*. Whatever the case, Pelopidas' dream and the ensuing debate on human sacrifice are legendary embellishments which should not be mistaken for fact (nor shall I comment on the availability of blond-haired virgins in a military camp), and for my purposes it is sufficient to note that the motif of animal substitution, familiar from myth, remained productive even in the 'history' of the fourth century.

Themistocles at Salamis

At dawn before the battle of Salamis (480 BC) Xerxes seated himself on a golden throne to view from above the battle which was about to commence. Meanwhile, Plutarch tells us, Themistocles performed the sphagia, the customary sacrifices before an engagement:

> But while Themistocles was slaying the sphagia alongside the admiral's trireme, three captives were brought to him, most handsome in appearance to look upon and magnificently dressed in raiment and gold. And they were said to be the children of the King's sister Sandauce and Artayctes. When the seer Euphrantides caught sight of them, since at the very same moment a large and bright flame flashed up from the victims and a sneeze from the right-hand side gave good omen, he clasped Themistocles' hand and bade him offer prayers and consecrate the young men and sacrifice them all to Dionysus Omestes, for in this way salvation and victory together would fall to the Greeks. But while Themistocles was struck with fear at the seer's pronouncement as a great and terrible thing, the many – as usually happens in great contests and difficult situations – hoping for salvation from unreasonable rather than reasonable deeds, together with one voice invoked the god, and having led the captives to the altar they insisted that the sacrifice be carried out as the seer enjoined. This at any rate was said by Phainias of Lesbos, a philosopher not unversed in historical writing.
>
> (Plut. *Them.* 13.2–5 = Phainias fr. 25 Wehrli)

What are we to make of this remarkable story? As Henrichs has pointed out, the description of Greek ritual is accurate enough and couched in traditional vocabulary; the offering of the sphagia and the interpretation of omens by the seer are customary practice. The human sacrifice itself, of course, is highly exceptional, but it could be explained, Henrichs continues, as a 'ritual solution to a communal crisis' resorted to in the highly tense pre-battle atmosphere. And that the prisoners are noble, handsome, and three in number – 'although highly suspicious from a historical view' – are details consistent with Greek cult practice (i.e. animal sacrifice).[127] But there is one detail which immediately throws the historicity of the human sacrifice into question: that the divine recipient of the sacrifice is Dionysus Omestes, the 'Raweater'. Not only is this god a stranger to Athens, but also, as we now know from a fragment of Alcaeus published in 1941, Dionysus Omestes was worshipped on Lesbos, the native island of Alcaeus – and of Plutarch's source Phainias. Thus the fourth-century historian has inserted a deity worshipped in his own homeland into an account of an Athenian sacrifice.[128]

The presence of Dionysus Omestes in the story does not in itself disprove the actuality of the human sacrifice, for it is conceivable that Phainias introduced the Lesbian deity, or merely the epiklesis 'Omestes', into an otherwise factual account. On the other hand, if Phainias had had a reliable description of the incident before him, it would not have been necessary to supply a god alien to Athens as the recipient of the sacrifice. Also, there is no other evidence for a connection between Dionysus and the battle of Salamis, while Artemis, Aias, and Zeus Tropaios all received sacrifices for their role in the great victory.[129]

The strong suspicions raised by the presence of the Lesbian Dionysus are confirmed by an insurmountable difficulty in the account of Phainias. According to Plutarch and, it may safely be assumed, his source Phainias, the sacrifice took place before battle. Where then did the royal victims come from? In his life of Aristeides (9.1–2) Plutarch writes that the three Persian youths had been taken captive on Psyttaleia and sent immediately to Themistocles. Phainias is almost certainly Plutarch's source for this information also.[130] But according to Aeschylus, Herodotus, and others, the capture of Psyttaleia took place *after* the main fighting; and, what is more, all of the Persians on the island were killed (Aesch. *Pers.* 435–71; Hdt. 8.95; Paus. 1.36.2; Aristodemus, *FGrHist* 104 F 1, 4). Thus Phainias, in order to supply the victims for the human sacrifice, was obliged to transfer the taking of Psyttaleia to a time before the battle proper and to contradict reports that all of the Persians perished on the island.

Two very shaky options remain open to anyone who should still wish to maintain that the human sacrifice is historical. One might argue that the sacrifice did in fact take place, but that the victims did not come from Psyttaleia. But where then did they come from? And why then did Phainias find it necessary to bring in Psyttaleia at all, especially as this involved a drastic rewriting of history? Second, one might transfer the sacrifice to a time *after* the battle, as one scholar has done recently.[131] But sphagia were not performed at the end of a battle, but before it began: it is for this very reason that Phainias was obliged to move the capture of Psyttaleia to the beginning of the action. And even if it were possible that the human sacrifice was performed after the battle, Phainias still contradicts the accounts of earlier writers – one of whom was present at the battle[132] – who agree that all of the Persians on the island were slain. The human sacrifice is not historical, as has been recognized by many, but by no means all, of the scholars who have discussed the incident.[133]

It is still possible to make some observations about the development of the story, which may not have been manufactured out of whole cloth. Phainias himself may have betrayed a knowledge that all the Persians on Psyttaleia were killed when he wrote that Aristeides 'killed everybody' (ἀπέκτεινε πάντας), then adding feebly, 'except such distinguished men as were taken alive' (Plut. *Arist.* 9.1). According to Aeschylus many of the Persian nobility were among those killed on Psyttaleia (*Pers.* 441–4), and this may have suggested to Phainias to procure his royal victims from the island. Also, in a story preserved by Diodorus (11.57.1–5), when Themistocles arrived at the Persian court, Xerxes' sister demanded that the death of her sons at Salamis be avenged: Themistocles was tried, but having mastered Persian for the purpose, he successfully defended himself. This anecdote and the story of the human sacrifice are clearly related in some way, and three possibilities suggest themselves. First, Diodorus' source may have been familiar with Phainias' account of the sacrifice, but refrained from any reference to the sacrifice, perhaps in order to protect Themistocles' reputation.[134] But if so, he thoroughly effaced every trace of Phainias' version: the name of Xerxes' sister has been changed (from Sandauce to Mandane), the number of her sons is not mentioned, and reference is made only to the killing (*anairesis*) of her sons 'at the time when Themistocles defeated the Persian fleet around Salamis'. Of course the story of Themistocles' trial is itself of most questionable historicity, but both this anecdote and the story of human sacrifice may contain a grain of truth: that a son or sons of a sister of the Persian King were killed in the battle, perhaps even on Psyttaleia. Thus the actual death of one or more of Xerxes' nephews could have given rise to the two stories, independently – the second possibility. A third possibility (and in my view the most likely) is that Phainias, or his ultimate source, was familiar with the anecdote from the Persian court and used it as the basis of his story: Themistocles was held responsible for the death of Xerxes' nephews, and their death in battle was transformed and magnified into a sacrifice by the author whose fiction was eventually preserved for us by Plutarch.[135]

Who was the original author of the fiction? Was it Phainias? It has been rightly observed that in Phainias' account Themistocles is favourably contrasted with the throng: the general shrinks from so horrendous a deed, but in the end he is compelled by his soldiers to carry out the human sacrifice.[136] But I find it difficult to believe that the story was *invented* for this purpose, for it differs from the similar stories of Agesilaus and Pelopidas (who also were shocked at the very idea of a human sacrifice) in one important respect: at Salamis the sacrifice was carried out. Thus I am inclined to agree with Peter Green, who attributes the story to 'an anonymous Athenian propagandist'. A story first designed to attack Themistocles was later converted artfully by Phainias to illustrate his humanity.[137]

LISTS OF HUMAN SACRIFICES

'List' perhaps is not the best word for the two passages I shall discuss first, from the pseudo-Platonic *Minos* and Theophrastus. But what I mean by the term is a passage in which the author, rather than describing or alluding to a single case of human sacrifice, gives examples of the human sacrifices known to him. Interestingly, the lengths of these passages stand in inverse proportion to their antiquity – interestingly, but not surprisingly, for it is in the Hellenistic Age that local histories, works on religious topics such as Istros' *Collection of Cretan Sacrifices*, and miscellanies such as Monimus' *Collection of Wonders* began to abound.[138] These and many other works of this nature have not survived, and we owe the preservation of fragments referring to human sacrifices to writers of still later antiquity, chiefly the Christian apologist Clement and the Neoplatonist Porphyry of Tyre. Even when these writers do not name their sources, it is probable that their examples of human sacrifice were culled from compilations of cult practices, local legends, 'wondrous things', etc., which appeared chiefly in Hellenistic and Roman times.

In the *Minos*, Socrates' interlocutor presents an argument for the relativity of custom. While among us human sacrifice is not the custom, he says, but rather is considered unholy, the Carthaginians offer human sacrifices to Kronos as something holy and lawful to them: 'And not to say that only barbarian peoples follow customs different from ours, but also those in the Lycaean festival and the descendants of Athamas perform such sacrifices, Greeks though they be' ([Pl.] *Minos* 315B–C). The author of the dialogue probably knew of the sacrifice to Zeus Lykaios from Plato's mention in the *Republic* (8, 565D–E), and of the sacrifice of the descendants of Athamas from the confused description of Herodotus (7.197). He may also have owed something to Pl. *Leg.* 6, 782C, where Plato wrote that human sacrifice was still practised by many peoples, but without providing examples. In any case, these brief allusions add very little to our knowledge of the two rites, nor should the use of the present tense be taken as reliable evidence that either ritual was still performed in the second half of the fourth century.

In this same period Theophrastus (*c.* 370–288/5 BC), whose treatise *Περὶ εὐσεβείας* was drawn upon extensively by Porphyry in the *De abstinentia*, also uses Carthaginian and Arcadian customs as examples of current human sacrifices. In the beginning, wrote Theophrastus, people made sacrifices only from the fruits of the earth. But in time, negligence of piety and scarcity of crops led them to consume human flesh, and they made first offerings of their human victims to the gods:

> And from then up to the present day they perform human sacrifices with the participation of all, not only in Arcadia during the Lykaia and in Carthage to Kronos, but also periodically, in remembrance of the customary usage, they spill the blood of their own kin on the altars, even though the divine law among them bars from the rites, by means of the *perirrhantēria* and the herald's proclamation, anyone responsible for the shedding of blood in peacetime.[139]
>
> (Porph. *Abst.* 2.27.2 = Theophr. fr. 13.22–6 Pötscher)

Although the passage as a whole is of extreme interest for its view of human evolution and the origins of blood sacrifice, we learn as little here about the Lycaean ritual as we did from the *Minos*. And the sentence quoted above is as puzzling as it is brief: the construction 'not only . . . but' leads us to expect the references to Arcadian and Carthaginian human sacrifices to be followed by a third location for what appears to be a description of a third ritual, in which human blood is also shed upon altars; but none is given, and the subject of the verb, ῥαίνουσι ('spill'), is left unexpressed. Among the solutions that have been proposed, the most interesting is that of Bernays, who suggested that Theophrastus referred in the second clause to the ritual performed at Halai, where a man's neck was cut in the service of Artemis (see p. 81), but that Theophrastus intentionally veiled his allusion to these bloody rites because he was a metic in Athens and like Aristotle rendered vulnerable by his Macedonian connections. But the suggestion is perhaps more ingenious than convincing.[140]

From Theophrastus we move forward in time to Plutarch (*c.* AD 46–after 119), who in his life of Pelopidas gives a brief list of human sacrifices performed with beneficial outcome. Before the battle of Leuctra, Pelopidas, instructed in his sleep to sacrifice a maiden to the daughters of Scedasus (see pp. 110–11), relates his dream to his seers and commanders:

> Some of them would not allow the command to be ignored or disobeyed, citing as examples from among the ancients Menoeceus son of Creon and Macaria daughter of Heracles, and from later times Pherecydes the Wise, who was killed by the Lacedaemonians and whose skin in accordance with an oracle was preserved by the kings, and Leonidas, who, following an oracle, in a certain sense sacrificed himself on behalf of Greece, and further those who were slain by Themistocles to Dionysus Omestes before the sea battle at Salamis. For the successes which attended these bear witness. And furthermore, when Agesilaus was leaving on an expedition from the same place and against the same enemy as Agamemnon, the goddess asked for his daughter as a sacrificial victim, and he saw this vision while asleep at Aulis; but he did not give her, but rather in his weakness he brought the expedition to an inglorious and ineffectual end.

Others then offer arguments against carrying out the unlawful and barbarous sacrifice (*Pel.* 21). In this short list Plutarch distinguishes clearly between heroic and historical times with the phrases τῶν μὲν παλαιῶν and τῶν δ' ὕστερον, citing Menoeceus and Macaria as instances from ancient times. As 'historical' examples Plutarch uses two events described elsewhere in his writings, Agesilaus' failure to carry out a human sacrifice at Aulis and the sacrifice of Persian captives by Themistocles (see pp. 109–10 and 111–15), which indicates that the arguments in favour of human sacrifice were Plutarch's own invention, not something he found in his sources for the battle of Leuctra. And Leonidas' courageous stand at Thermopylae is a sacrifice only metaphorically, as Plutarch indicates with the qualification τροπόν τινά.[141]

Plutarch's only other example from 'historical' times is the Spartans' killing of Pherecydes the Wise. It is uncertain whether this killing was an actual sacrifice in Plutarch's source (the context implies this, but the verb is the non-sacrificial *anairein*). This Pherecydes is certainly to be identified with Pherecydes 'the Theologian' of Syros (mid-sixth century BC), who during a visit to Sparta was said to have predicted the defeat of Messenia and intervened on behalf of Lycurgan measures against the accumulation of wealth.[142] Plutarch states that he was killed by the Spartans, but there were several other versions of his death and burial, including his suicide at Delphi and his death from illness on Delos (Diog. Laert. 1.117–22; Diod. Sic. 10.3.4). But what seems to have been the prevailing tradition (also involving the skin!) has him die, in Magnesia, Delos, or an unspecified locale, of *morbus pedicularis* – a tradition, in fact, of which Plutarch himself was aware (Diog. Laert. 1.118 and 120–22; Porph. *VP* 55; Suda s.v. Φερεκύδης Βάβυος Σύριος; Plut. *Sulla* 36.3). Plutarch is the only source to tell of the preservation of Pherecydes' skin; but a quite similar story is known for Epimenides, whose relics (and possibly just his skin) were said to have been buried in the Spartan Ephoreia.[143] And according to the Argives, Epimenides was killed by the Spartans (Paus. 2.21.3). It is thus likely that there has been some confusion or borrowing between the legends surrounding the two sages. And it is perhaps unnecessary to add that these stories about Pherecydes and Epimenides, which belong to a larger class of tales about wise men's sojourns in Sparta,[144] are not historical, and the sacrifice of Pherecydes may safely be consigned to the realm of legend.

It is not surprising that Plutarch's list of human sacrifices is so brief, given his limited rhetorical purposes in the passage. One wonders what sort of list this widely read, if uncritical, writer would have drawn up had his purpose been to recount all the human sacrifices known to him. But the examples selected for *Pelopidas* 21 hardly give us reason to expect much from such a list. And elsewhere when Plutarch writes of human sacrifice (*De superst.* 13, 171B–D), he gives no examples from Greece, but only references to Gallic, Scythian, and Carthaginian customs, and to the burying alive of 'twelve persons' by Xerxes' wife Amestris (apparently a conflation of Hdt. 7.114 and 3.35.5).

In the *Protrepticus*, Clement of Alexandria (*c.* AD 150–*c.* 215) argues that the pagan gods are mere *daimones*, who delight in human slaughter, gladiatorial shows, and war. Further, they have often required of mankind 'savage libations':

> Indeed Aristomenes the Messenian sacrificed 300 men to Zeus of Ithome, thinking that hecatombs of such quantity and quality give favourable omens. Among these was Theopompus the Lacedaemonian king, a noble victim. And the Taurian race, who live along the Tauric peninsula, immediately sacrifice to the Tauric Artemis whatever stranger they catch in their land or those who have been shipwrecked at sea. These sacrifices of yours Euripides presents upon the tragic stage. And Monimus in his collection of *Wonderful Things* recounts that in Pella in Thessaly an Achaean man used to be sacrificed to Peleus and Cheiron. And the Lyctians (these being a people of the Cretans), as Anticleides reveals in the *Homecomings*, used to sacrifice human victims to Zeus; and Dosidas [*sic*] says that the Lesbians offered the same sort of sacrifice to Dionysus. And the Phocaeans – for I shall not pass over them either – would offer a wholly burnt sacrifice of a human to Artemis Tauropolos, as Pythocles relates in the third book of *Concerning Concord*. And Erechtheus of Attica and Marius sacrificed their own daughters, the former to Persephone, as Demaratus says in the first book of the *Subjects of Tragedy*, and Marius to the averting deities, as Dorotheus relates in the third book of his *Italian History*.

Clement concludes by saying that human sacrifice is murder, which does not become a holy act simply because the slaughter is offered to a deity and performed in a sanctuary or 'upon altars rather than in the streets' (*Protr.* 3.42).

Six of Clement's eight examples are from the Greek world. Clement does not set out on the right foot with his first statement, that Aristomenes sacrificed 300 human victims to Zeus Ithometes, an error which has been perpetuated in modern scholarship.[145] Pausanias tells us that from ancient times it was the custom in Messenia for someone who had killed 100 of the enemy in battle to offer a sacrifice called the 'hekatomphonia'; and during the 'Second Messenian War' Aristomenes was said to have performed this sacrifice to Zeus of Ithome three times (Paus. 4.19.3). The story was widely known, but Plutarch doubted that Aristomenes could have killed 300 enemies by himself and attributed the story to Messenian boasting (*Rom.* 25.3; cf. Plut. *Quaest. conv.* 4.1, 660F; Pliny *HN* 11.185; Polyaen. 2.31.2). Thus Clement has misunderstood the well-known story, thinking that Aristomenes had *sacrificed* 300 men, when in fact he was supposed to have performed a special animal sacrifice three times, having thrice reached a total of 100 soldiers killed in combat.[146] And as for Aristomenes' noble 'sacrificial victim' Theopompus, according to Myron of Priene the Spartan king was killed by Aristomenes (in battle) before the end of the First Messenian War (Myron, *FGrHist* 106 F 3; cf. Plut. *Agis* 21.2). But Pausanias rejected Myron's testimony because Tyrtaeus (fr. 5.1–2 West) had spoken of Theopompus as responsible for the capture of Messene, which finally brought the conflict to a close. Pausanias therefore followed Rhianus (*FGrHist* 265 F 42) in assigning Aristomenes exclusively to the second war (4.6.1–5).

Another of Clement's examples – the human sacrifices to Zeus performed by the Lyctians – also arouses suspicion, and here we have a rare opportunity to know something of the context of the fragment. Clement attributes the information about the Lyctian human sacrifices to Anticleides' *Nostoi* (*Homecomings*), and thus these human sacrifices must have been connected in some way with Anticleides' account of the return of the Lyctian king Idomeneus from Troy (Anticleides, *FGrHist* 140 F 7). Anticleides will have recounted the story of Idomeneus' vow to sacrifice the first thing he encountered upon arrival in Crete (see pp. 76–7). Thus, given the legendary context of the fragment of Anticleides, it is very possible that the human sacrifices were themselves legendary.[147] Perhaps Anticleides wrote that the Lyctians, having banished Idomeneus, were themselves obliged to perform human sacrifices in order to rid themselves of plague. Or Clement, in asserting that the Lyctians used to perform human sacrifices to Zeus, may simply have been generalizing from the single human sacrifice performed in the legend by Idomeneus. It is also possible that these alleged human sacrifices were connected with secret sacrifices said by Agathocles to be performed on Mt Dikte, probably in the cult of Zeus. It would not be surprising if sacrifices performed in secret should give rise to rumours of human sacrifice.[148]

Less can be said about Clement's other examples of human sacrifice, because of the brevity of the references. Clement asserts that at Pella an Achaean would be sacrificed to Peleus and

Cheiron. Clement's source, Monimus (*FHG* 4 fr. 1), is otherwise unknown, but the very title of his work, *Collection of Wonders*, hardly argues for the historical accuracy of the information. Although Clement uses the present infinitive here (καταθύεσθαι), it seems possible that Clement or his source generalized from an individual (and mythical?) incident; that the object of the verb is singular (Ἀχαιὸν ἄνθρωπον) might suggest this.

Dosiades' assertion that the Lesbians offered human sacrifices to Dionysus (Dosiades, *FHG* 4 fr. 5) should perhaps be taken more seriously, for this must be Dionysus Omestes, whom we have already met as the recipient of a human sacrifice in the unlikely locale of Attica (pp. 111–15) and to whom one very late source maintains human sacrifices were offered. But the statement of Apostolius (18.59: τούτῳ γὰρ ζῶντας ἀνθρώπους ἔθυον οἱ πάλαι) must be regarded with caution: Lesbos is not mentioned, and it is thus possible that Apostolius' assertion (despite the imperfect tense) was based solely on the alleged human sacrifice performed before the battle of Salamis. It is clear that there was a strong *tradition* of human sacrifice in the cult of Lesbian Dionysus (hence the choice of Omestes as the recipient of the fictional sacrifice at Salamis), but that this tradition was based upon fact is questionable: there were probably aetiological myths to account for the savage epithet of the god, and it is likely that these or other myths attached to the cult of Omestes lie behind the assertion of Dosiades.[149] In fact, we now possess the remains of one such myth in a mutilated papyrus fragment of a commentary on Alcaeus; the passage is largely unintelligible, but 'Omestes' appears clearly in a story which seems to involve a human sacrifice.[150]

That the Phocaeans sacrificed human victims in a holocaust to Artemis Tauropolos is also open to question, but again proof one way or the other is not possible. Although Clement's attribution of this statement to Pythocles' *Concerning Concord* (Pythocles, *FGrHist* 833 F 2) has been questioned, the human sacrifice itself has often been accepted as historical.[151] We have already met with Artemis Tauropolos at Halai on the Attic coast, where her worship was associated by Euripides with the Tauric goddess and the human sacrifices reportedly performed on the Tauric peninsula (p. 81). This association seems to have been prompted largely by the epiklesis of Artemis at Halai, which historically had no connection with the Tauri or their goddess (pp. 89–90). And

I suspect that the allegation of human sacrifices in the cult of Tauropolos at Phocaea also stemmed from this association, although at Halai the association was apparently based not only on the epiklesis but also on a bloody ritual practised there. Possibly similar rites were performed in the Phocaean cult also. But that Clement specifies that the sacrifice was a holocaust may suggest that his source was a myth according to which a holocaust of animals was said to have originally consisted of human victims (cf. the extravagant sacrifice performed for Artemis Laphria at Patrae, where wild animals were thrown alive onto a burning altar: Paus. 7.18.11–13). That the assertion derives from a myth of this sort is more likely than the possibility that it was grounded in actual human sacrifices, for which we have no evidence beyond the brief reference of Clement.

Clement's final example of a Greek human sacrifice, the sacrifice of the daughter of Erechtheus (Demaratus, *FGrHist* 42 F 4), is mythical and need not detain us. And the passage taken as a whole does not inspire confidence. Although Clement does cite his sources, some of the citations appear to be false,[152] and as he seems to have known of some of the human sacrifices only through intermediate sources, the possibility of error is increased. He makes no distinction between mythical and historical human sacrifices, and he was clearly indifferent to the nature of his sources, citing *inter alia* a play of Euripides, a work on tragic subjects, the *Nostoi* of Anticleides, and Monimus' *Collection of Wonders* as his authorities. And he blunders badly in his understanding of Aristomenes' military exploits and the nature of the hekatomphonia. It is conceivable that the human sacrifices performed in Pella, Lesbos, and Phocaea were historical, for the brevity of the references does not admit of proof or disproof. But it is also possible – and in my opinion much more likely – that myth and rumour, rather than fact, lay behind the traditions of human sacrifice in these three places. At any rate, Clement, who is both uncritical and biased, should not be considered a reliable authority without additional confirmation.

The lengthiest and most interesting list of human sacrifices in the ancient world is that of Porphyry (third century after Christ), who argued against the consumption of meat in his treatise *De abstinentia* (*Περὶ ἀποχῆς ἐμψυχῶν*). I have already discussed Porphyry's quotation of Theophrastus, who had cited Carthaginian and Arcadian rituals as examples of human sacrifices still practised in his own time, above (pp. 116–17). Later in the second book, Porphyry argues that simply because animals are sacrificed and used for divination, this does not mean that their flesh is to be eaten. He continues:

> Indeed history has handed down the memory not only of those instances recorded by Theophrastus, but also of many more cases of the ancients sacrificing even human beings; and in no way because of this are human beings also to be eaten. And to show that we do not state these things lightly but that history is full of such examples, it is sufficient to cite the following cases. For also on Rhodes on the sixth day of the month Metageitnion a human being used to be sacrificed to Kronos. Now this custom, having lasted a long time, was altered, for they would keep one of those condemned to death by the people until the time of the Kronia, and during the festival they would lead the man outside the gates opposite the seat of Aristoboule, where, having given him wine to drink, they would slay him. And in the city now called Salamis, but formerly known as Coronis, in the month known among the Cypriots as Aphrodisios, a human being used to be sacrificed to Agraulus, the daughter of Cecrops and the nymph Agraulis. The custom persisted until the time of Diomedes: then it underwent a change, so that the person was now sacrificed to Diomedes. And the temple of Athena and that of Agraulus and Diomedes are within one precinct. The one who was slain, led by the ephebes, would run three times around the altar, whereupon the priest would strike him on the throat with a spear, and so would he burn him entirely on the pyre which had been heaped up. But Diphilus the king of Cyprus, who was born around the time of Seleucus the Theologian, abolished this rite, changing the custom into an ox sacrifice. And the *daimōn* accepted the ox instead of the human being: thus is the sacrifice of equal value. And in Hieropolis in Egypt, Amosis, as Manetho testifies in his book *Concerning Ancient Customs and Piety*, also abolished the custom of killing a human victim. The victims were sacrificed to Hera and were tested, just as unblemished calves are sought out and marked. Three victims were sacrificed each day, but Amosis ordered that an equal number of wax figures be placed in

their stead. And they used to sacrifice a human being to Dionysus Omadios, tearing him apart, both on Chios and on Tenedos, as Euelpis of Carystus says. Moreover, Apollodorus says that the Lacedaemonians would sacrifice a human being to Ares.

The Phoenicians, in the great misfortune of war or plague or drought, would sacrifice someone of their most beloved, whom they selected by vote, to Kronos: the *Phoenician History* is full of such sacrifices, which Sanchouniathon composed in the Phoenician tongue but which was translated into Greek in eight books by Philo of Byblos. And Istros in his *Collection of Cretan Sacrifices* says that in ancient times the Kouretes sacrificed children to Kronos. But that human sacrifices were abolished nearly among all peoples is reported by Pallas, who made the best collection of the facts concerning the mysteries of Mithras in the time of the emperor Hadrian. For also in Laodicea in Syria a virgin was sacrificed each year to Athena, but now a deer is sacrificed. Indeed the Carthaginians in Libya used to perform the same sacrifice, which was stopped by Iphicrates. And the Doumetani of Arabia every year would sacrifice a child, whom they buried under the altar which they used as a cult image. And Phylarchus relates that all of the Greeks in general would kill a human being before setting out against the enemy. And I needn't mention the Thracians and Scythians, and that the Athenians killed the daughter of Erechtheus and Praxithea. But even in our own day, who is not aware that in the Great City a human being is slaughtered in the festival of Zeus Latiarios? And certainly human flesh is not for this reason to be eaten, simply because through some necessity a human being is employed for sacrifice.

(Porph. *Abst.* 2.53.3–56.10)

Of Porphyry's sixteen examples of human sacrifice, half belong to the Greek world. That he describes the rites practised on Rhodes and Cyprus in particular detail suggests that these descriptions had a factual basis, even if the 'histories' of the two rituals are largely mythical. In Rhodes a condemned man was executed every year on a specific day during the Kronia. It was said that this custom had originally been a human sacrifice, but that after a long time it had been altered to the execution of a criminal. It is thus implied that the killing was not considered or performed as a sacrifice any longer. The idea that this execution was originally a sacrifice to Kronos may have arisen from the fact that the execution was carried out during Kronos' annual festival, together, perhaps, with the reputation for human sacrifices which the Greek deity had acquired through an association with the Phoenician Baal.[153] Whether or not this execution had any close connection with the cult of Aristoboule ('Best in Counsel') is difficult to say, as it is stated merely that the condemned prisoner was led out of the gates which were opposite her statue or temple (*hedos*).

The Rhodian ritual was interpreted by Deubner as a pharmakos ('scapegoat') ritual, but his interpretation was based upon slight and superficial similarities.[154] On Leucas a condemned man was kept in order to be used in a sort of 'scapegoat' ritual; yet he was not executed but (at least if he survived a precipitous fall into the sea) allowed to escape over the borders (see pp. 160–2). At Abdera the pharmakos was led out of a specific gate of the city, but neither was he a criminal nor was he killed during the ceremony (pp. 156–7). And in Greece not only pharmakoi but also criminals condemned to death were led out of specific, 'unlucky' gates of the city.[155] Also, the detail that the condemned man in Rhodes was slain opposite the seat of Aristobouie has an interesting parallel in Attica: at Melite there was a sanctuary of Artemis Aristoboule, built by Themistocles, in the area where in Plutarch's day the bodies of executed criminals were thrown out (Plut. *Them.* 22.1–2); thus the connection between Artemis Aristoboule and execution may have been widespread.[156]

The killing of a condemned man on Rhodes seems to have been primarily an execution. The fact that the execution was performed during a religious festival and was at least superficially connected with the cults of Aristoboule and Kronos suggests that the execution may have served some religious function, the nature of which now escapes us. But the claim that the execution derived from an original human sacrifice – where presumably the victim was not a criminal and where correct sacrificial procedure was followed – may be no more than a mythological aetiology such as those I have discussed above.

The sacrifice at Salamis in Cyprus is said to have undergone two changes. The first, by which the human sacrifice was transferred from the cult of Aglaurus to the cult of Diomedes upon the arrival in Cyprus of the latter, is of course mythical, serving to explain the fact that Aglaurus and Diomedes shared the same temple. The second change – the abolition of the human sacrifice and the institution of an ox sacrifice in its place – appears at first sight to have been historical, for it is dated to the reign of a Cypriot king, Diphilus. But unfortunately nothing whatsoever is known of Diphilus or the time of his rule. That he was said to have been born during the lifetime of Seleucus the Theologian is of no help, for this Seleucus is equally unknown. There seem to be no grounds for identifying him with Seleucus of Alexandria, the contemporary and (to his rue) dinner guest of Tiberius (*FGrHist* 341 T 2; *FGrHist* 634), with the grammarian from Emesa of the same name (*FGrHist* 780), or with any other known Seleucus; certainly he was not any of the Seleucid kings. In fact it was during the lifetime of the first known Seleucus, Seleucus I Nicator (Syrian king, 312–281 BC), that the Cypriot kingships were suppressed by Ptolemy; thus if our Seleucus was a contemporary of an actual king in Cyprus, he must have lived earlier than the late fourth century. But as long as Diphilus and Seleucus remain unknown, it is best to conclude that they are legendary, not historical, figures.[157] And of course the substitution of an animal for a human victim at Salamis conforms to the familiar mythological pattern, with Diphilus assuming the role played by Lycurgus at Sparta and Eurypylus at Patrae.

Schwenn discussed the human sacrifices at Salamis in his chapter on 'Menschenopfer im Totenkult', accepting them as historical and interpreting them as burnt offerings for the hero Diomedes. Schwenn pointed to a similarity between this rite and the funeral rites for Patroclus in the *Iliad*: the victim is led three times around the altar just as Hector's corpse was dragged three times around Patroclus' burial mound (*Il.* 24.14–18). Also, the fact that the sacrificial instrument was a spear suggested to Schwenn that 'vielleicht hat man damit andeuten wollen, dass der Geopferte eigentlich als Kriegsgefangener galt'.[158] But if the animal substitution was mythical, as I strongly suspect it was, then it is possible to reconstruct the ritual as it was in its 'final stage' of development, using the details of its 'earlier' form to complete our picture. In a yearly festival an ox is sacrificed in the cult of Diomedes and burned, like the supposed former human victim, in a holocaust. The ephebes participate in the ritual. Possibly the ox is led three times around the altar, or possibly (as an imitation of the original human sacrifice) a human being must run around the altar. The ox is then slain (with a spear?), and possibly a human being is cut on the neck with a spear, in a manner analogous to the ritual cutting performed at Halai (p. 81). In any case, in the ritual the identity of the sacrificial ox and a human participant – who we can safely assume is himself an ephebe – is established.

It is fairly clear, I think, that we are dealing, not with an original human sacrifice, but with an original rite of initiation. The participation of ephebes, the myth of a former human sacrifice, and the use of a spear (λόγχη) – not the usual sacrificial implement, but appropriate to an initiation into the military or the adult hunting community – all point to this as the most satisfactory interpretation.[159] The ephebes were told that 'once upon a time' they themselves were the sacrificial victims, and perhaps one of them was actually treated as such in the ritual and chased around the altar of Diomedes before an ox was slain in his place. But if it was the ox which was led around the altar by the ephebes, then there is an interesting early parallel in a bull sacrifice in the cult of Poseidon Helikonios, known from a Homeric simile, in which *kouroi* drag a bull around the altar of the god (*Il.* 20.403–5).

After a detailed description of the Egyptian sacrifices to 'Hera', Porphyry cites an otherwise unknown Euelpis of Carystus (*FHG* 4 fr. 1) as his source for the information that on Chios and Tenedos human sacrifices were offered to Dionysus. For Chios, it is very possible that the assertion was based on the epiklesis Omadios, comparable to Omestes on Lesbos, together with myths associated with the cult of Dionysus on the island. Aelian (*VH* 3.42) mentions the 'Bacchic sting' which afflicted the women of Chios, in a passage where he also tells the story of the daughters of Minyas, who rent apart (διεσπάσαντο) a young boy like a fawn. It is not difficult to imagine how the Chian version of the myth could have led Euelpis to report that on Chios they sacrificed to Dionysus, rending apart (διασπῶντες) a human being.[160] As for Tenedos, it is probable that Euelpis' reference was not to Dionysus Omadios but to Anthroporrhaistes, and I have already discussed the sacrifice – of a calf treated like a human infant and dressed in buskins – performed in his cult on Tenedos and described by Aelian (*NA* 12.34). As I noted above, Aelian provides no myth to account for this unusual rite, but it is possible that there was a myth of human sacrifice associated with the calf sacrifice (pp. 85–6). Euelpis, then, may have known of such a myth, or (like some modern scholars) he may simply have made his own deduction about the origin of the Tenedian calf sacrifices.[161]

The statement of Apollodorus of Athens (second century BC) that the Spartans used to sacrifice men to Ares (Apollodorus, *FGrHist* 244 F 125) may also have been based upon myth. Schwenn suggested that this must have been a reference to sacrifices made during war, but we know that the sacrifices performed by the Spartans during war were, in the historical period, animal sacrifices: their pre-battle sphagia were offered to Artemis Agrotera, but after a victory they would sacrifice either an ox or a cock to Ares (depending on how the victory was won); and the Spartan ephebes sacrificed dogs to Ares-Enyalios.[162] Thus it appears that Apollodorus was speaking (or speculating) about the prehistoric period (cf. his etymology of Enyalios in *FGrHist* 244 F 124 and his discussion of dog sacrifices to Ares in 244 F 126). Likewise, Phylarchus' surprising assertion (*FGrHist* 81 F 80) that all of the Greeks killed human victims before battle, discussed above, must have been a reference to prehistoric, i.e. mythical, times (pp. 107–8).

That Istros in the third century BC referred the Cretan human sacrifices to Kronos to ancient times (τὸ παλαιόν) is an unmistakable signal that this is not an allusion to actual cult practice, but rather to the mythical Kouretes (Istros, *FGrHist* 334 F 48). And it has often been suggested that the assertion that the Kouretes sacrificed children to Kronos merely represents a learned reinterpretation of the dance of the armed Kouretes, frequently depicted in art, around the child Zeus.[163] The Kouretes, of course, are actually protecting Zeus; that the human sacrifice was said to have been offered to Kronos may be connected with the story of Kronos' swallowing of his children and his attempts to kill Zeus, a myth which has been interpreted in modern times as retaining a memory of human sacrifices to Kronos.[164] But it is in my view more likely that Istros preserved a genuine myth connected with animal sacrifices and initiation ceremonies in Archaic Cretan cult. The associations of the mythical Kouretes with Cretan rituals involving kouroi are well known, and the myth of the Kouretes' dance around the infant Zeus (whose story as a whole shows marked initiatory features) was probably connected to actual 'war dances' performed by bands of young Cretan soldiers, of whom the Kouretes 'of old' are the mythical projections.[165]

Porphyry's quotation of Pallas, who had written that human sacrifices were abolished nearly among all peoples, is problematic:

> Καταλυθῆναι δὲ τὰς ἀνθρωποθυσίας σχεδὸν τὰς παρὰ πᾶσί φησι Πάλλας ὁ ἄριστα περὶ τῶν τοῦ Μίθρα συναγαγὼν μυστήριων ἐφ' Ἁδριανοῦ τοῦ αὐτοκράτορος.
>
> (*Abst.* 2.56.3)

In my translation I have placed the phrase 'in the time of the emperor Hadrian' as if it depends upon συναγαγών and dates the time of the composition of Pallas' work on Mithraism; and certainly the word order suggests this.[166] But it is also possible that the phrase depends upon καταλυθῆναι and dates the abolition of human sacrifices.[167] The latter interpretation may at first sight seem the more plausible: the Romans had issued edicts against human sacrifice before, and Lactantius, in a passage discussed below, mentions a Cypriot human sacrifice 'which has recently been abolished under Hadrian's reign' (Lactant. *Div. Inst.* 1.21: see pp. 133–4). Still, if Hadrian had actually issued a ban against human sacrifice in the empire, we should expect ὑφ' Ἁδριανοῦ instead of ἐφ' Ἁδριανοῦ.[168] And it seems unlikely that Porphyry and Lactantius themselves believed that the Romans had banned human sacrifice from the empire, for both writers cite as a contemporary example the supposed human sacrifices offered to Jupiter Latiaris in Rome (*Abst.* 2.56.9; *Div. Inst.* 1.21.3).[169] Furthermore, of the two examples which Porphyry, probably still following Pallas, adduces in support of Pallas' general assertion, in the first the substitution of a deer for a human victim at Laodicea would seem to be mythical (and not a historical change under Hadrian's rule), and in the second Iphicrates is said to have put an end to human sacrifice at Carthage.[170] And even if these examples were not taken from Pallas, it certainly seems that Porphyry himself understood Pallas to mean that human sacrifices were abolished at various times and various places, and not during the reign of or by edict of Hadrian.

It is noteworthy how many of the human sacrifices in Porphyry's list are said to have been 'mitigated' or abolished (Rhodes, Salamis, Hieropolis, Carthage, Laodicea, and Pallas' general statement); indeed the passage is as much about the mitigation of human sacrifice as it is about human sacrifice *per se*. And it is curious that Porphyry, who cites many sources in this passage, fails to reveal his source for his first two examples, which he describes in exceptional detail. That his source was the same for both the Rhodian and Cypriot human sacrifices is suggested by the length of the accounts, by the fact that dates are given for both rituals, and by the location of the islands in the eastern Mediterranean.[171] In fact all of the abolished human sacrifices and several others for which no abolition is reported (Chios, Tenedos, Phoenicia, Arabia) are located in the eastern Mediterranean, the Near East, or northern Africa. It seems possible that Porphyry had a single source for many of these examples, and an obvious candidate is Pallas, who we know wrote about the abolition of human sacrifice 'nearly among all peoples' and who (himself possibly from the Near East) was probably responsible for the Syrian and Carthaginian examples which follow this general statement.[172]

Like Clement, Porphyry selects as his final example of Greek human sacrifice the sacrifice of the daughter of Erechtheus. But on the whole Porphyry's discussion is more impressive, learned, and at least in some cases more reliable than Clement's. Still, as is the case with Clement, the less detailed the descriptions are, the less easy it is to judge the reliability of the information. Porphyry usually cites his sources (though some he may have known only secondhand through intermediate sources), but it is still very uncertain if Euelpis, Apollodorus, Istros, and Phylarchus had any solid grounds for their assertions, which appear divorced from their contexts in the list of Porphyry. In two cases the detail of the descriptions vouches for their essential accuracy, but the rituals performed on Rhodes and Cyprus may have been an execution and an initiation ceremony respectively, and their 'histories' mythical aetiologies no different from the myths of human sacrifice which were attached to the flogging of youths at Sparta and other rites and sacrifices from various places in Greece.

THE AGRIONIA AT ORCHOMENOS

Plutarch is our source for yet another violent ritual, which has been called 'clearly a mitigated form of human sacrifice'.[173] In his thirty-eighth *Greek Question* Plutarch asks, 'Who among the Boeotians are the Psoloeis and who are the Oleiai?' The answer is that the daughters of Minyas were driven by madness to desire human flesh and drew lots to determine whose child they would consume; the lot fell to Leucippe, and they tore her son Hippasus to pieces. For this they were called the 'Destructive Ones' (?), while their husbands, because of the dark clothes they donned in their grief, were called 'Sooty' (*Quaest. Graec.* 38, 299E).[174] Plutarch continues:

> And to the present day the Orchomenians call by this name the women descended from this family. And there takes place every other year during the Agrionia a flight and pursuit of these women by the priest of Dionysus holding a sword. And he is permitted to kill anyone he catches, and in our own time Zoilus the priest did so. But no good came of this for them; rather, Zoilus became ill from a sore which befell him, and, after suffering for a long time from the putrefaction, he died. And the Orchomenians met with public damage suits and fines, and they transferred the priesthood from the family, selecting the best man from among them.
>
> (*Quaest. Graec.* 38, 299F-300A)

There seems to be no good reason for questioning the essential veracity of this account, for Plutarch asserts that the events took place in his own lifetime (ἐφ' ἡμῶν).[175] Thus we seem to have a certain example of a ritual killing of a human being in Greece in the first or early second century after Christ.

Less certain, however, is the nature of the ritual performed at Orchomenos. It is surely incorrect to speak here of a human sacrifice, even in mitigated form. Plutarch does not say that it was permitted to 'sacrifice' the woman, but merely to kill her (*aneilein*), and with a sword, not a sacrificial *machaira*. It was rather the daughters and female descendants of Minyas, not the priest, who played the role of sacrificers, in the myth and probably in the ritual.[176] Certainly some act must have preceded this ritual of flight and pursuit, and it is likely that this was a re-enactment of the sparagmos and consumption of Hippassus: other passages of Plutarch suggest that the women may have rent ivy in place of the mythical human victim.[177] In any case, it is for the mythical crime, re-enacted in ritual, that the women must flee before the sword. The parallel from Dionysiac ritual which immediately springs to mind is the stoning and flight of the sacrificant at the calf sacrifice in Tenedos (pp. 85–6). But perhaps a closer parallel is a ritual performed in Tegea, during which the priestess of Artemis pursued a man, 'just as Artemis pursued Leimon' (Paus. 8.53.3). And although in the myth Artemis killed Leimon, we can be reasonably certain that no such thing happened in the festival of Apollo at Tegea.[178]

There is good reason to believe that ritual killing was not a regular feature of the Agrionia at Orchomenos either. Plutarch states that if the priest catches one of the women he is permitted to kill her (ἔξεστι), yet he appears to know only of the case of Zoilus. Therefore, given that the Agrionia were held every other year, perhaps from great antiquity, the priests of Dionysus would seem on the whole to have been very slow of foot or inept with the sword. But surely this was a mock pursuit, and the women were meant to get away. That Zoilus did in fact kill one of the women should be attributed to accident (in what may have been a fairly dangerous performance), or possibly to the heat of the moment or the religious zeal of this particular priest.[179] But the clearest indication that the priest was not supposed to catch and kill any of the women is the fact that the extraordinary step was taken of removing the hereditary priesthood from Zoilus and his family.[180]

The ritual performed at Orchomenos may have been a case of ritual re-enactment of myth. And yet the myth may ultimately have been grounded in early ritual: myths of the pursuit of maenads are at least as old as the *Iliad*, where Lycurgus pursues the nurses of Dionysus with an ox-goad (Hom. *Il.* 6.130–40). Perhaps this and similar myths were originally based on ancient rituals of pursuit and flight in Dionysiac cult, the significance of which is now obscure. For Meuli, the ritual at Orchomenos was an instance of 'comedy of innocence': like the priest of Dionysus on Tenedos, the women are pursued for perpetrating the 'murder' of a sacrificial victim, an animal in reality but a human being on the level of myth. More recently, Graf and Dowden have emphasized the sexual conflict in this myth–ritual complex and view the ritual described by Plutarch as an *Ausnahmeritual*, a rite in which societal norms and relationships are temporarily turned on end: in their frenzy the women predominate, tearing apart a male victim; but the pursuit of the women by the men (and their death in myth) marks a reassertion of male dominance and a restoration of normality. In addition, it should be noted that sparagmos and omophagy, which appear in most myths of this type, also represent a clear (if only symbolic) departure from the norm, i.e. from usual Greek sacrificial practice, a fairly orderly procedure which involves both the use of a knife and the cooking of victims before consumption.[181] And of course the consumption of a human victim is highly exceptional as well.

MISCELLANEOUS

Like Clement, Lactantius (*c.* AD 240–*c.* 320) has a lengthy discussion of pagan human sacrifices, but only his first example belongs to the Greek world:

> In Salamis of Cyprus Teucer sacrificed a human victim to Jove. And this sacrifice he handed down to posterity, and it was recently abolished during the reign of Hadrian.
>
> (Lactant. *Div. Inst.* 1.21)[182]

This is the sole reference we possess to this human sacrifice, for I can see no good reason to identify it with the human sacrifices for Diomedes at Salamis described by Porphyry.[183] We do have a brief reference to a Cypriot Zeus Eilapinastes and Splanchnotomos (the 'Feaster' and 'Entrail-cutter'), and it is possible that this god and Lactantius' Jove are to be identified.[184] Lactantius' statement is also the only reference, so far as I am aware, to a human sacrifice performed by Teucer, the legendary colonizer of Salamis, and the sacrifice is, of course, mythical. And Lactantius in his brief notice leaps quickly from the time of the colonization of Cyprus to the abolition of the human sacrifices under Hadrian. This last piece of information will be for some confirmation that the human sacrifice was historical and lasted into the second century, but I am not certain that Lactantius can be considered a reliable witness. The only human sacrifice of which he is certainly aware is mythical; he gives no details of the ritual, cites no source, and does not seem to have been well informed about the sacrifice. And if the Zeus to whom he referred was indeed Splanchnotomos (an epithet which refers to sacrificial practices, as does Eilapinastes) we might imagine an animal sacrifice to which a myth of cannibalistic child sacrifice was attached, similar to the myth of Lycaon. Indeed it is quite possible that an epithet alone could give rise to rumours of human sacrifice, even without the support of an accompanying myth: the names Anthroporrhaistes, Omadios, and Omestes, which Dionysus wore in the eastern Mediterranean, have a particularly savage ring, and Splanchnotomos is no less gruesome. And although it is possible to read in these names memories of 'primitive' human sacrifices, other explanations are perhaps more likely.[185] But nothing can be said for certain on the basis of the brief assertion of the Christian apologist.

It is possible that the epiklesis of the hero Palaemon (Melicertes) on Tenedos contributed to the story of human sacrifices in his cult. In the *Alexandra* (229) Lycophron calls Palaemon Brephoktonos ('Infant-slayer'), and from a scholion on the verse we learn that Palaemon was worshipped on Tenedos and that there 'they also used to sacrifice infants to him' (Schol. Lycoph. *Alex.* 229). These human sacrifices have been accepted as factual in the past,[186] but we now have a fuller account in the *Diegeseis* on Callimachus' *Aetia*, in which the mythical character of the human sacrifices is clear. After Ino drowns herself with Melicertes in her arms, the child's body washes up on Tenedos. The Tenedians build an altar, on which in times of great danger a woman must sacrifice her own infant, whereupon she is immediately blinded; 'but this custom was later abolished, when the descendants of Orestes colonized Lesbos' (Callim. fr. 91 Pfeiffer). Thus we have yet another human sacrifice abolished already in the heroic past; and it is possible that the myth served as an aition for an existing ritual of some kind. Or possibly the story was invented merely to account for the name Brephoktonos, which by a curious transference Palaemon, who in myth is himself killed as an infant, assumes in Tenedian cult. The epithet may have had some connection with initiations and mysteries such as we find in Palaemon's cult centre at Isthmia.[187]

In Tzetzes' commentary on Lycophron we find an account of a human sacrifice performed at Tanagra: 'among the Boeotians White Hermes is honoured; for when the people of Tanagra were being attacked by Eretrians they sacrificed a boy and a girl in accordance with an oracle, and as a consequence they set up a statue of White Hermes' (Tzetz. Schol. Lycoph. *Alex.* 679). This is the sole reference to this human sacrifice (it is not found in the older scholia); and Tzetzes' note and the old scholia provide the only evidence for a Hermes Leukos at Tanagra.[188] But Pausanias (9.22.1–2) informs us that Hermes had two sanctuaries in Tanagra, under the names Hermes Kriophoros ('Ram-bearer') and Promachos ('Champion'). It is interesting that the aetiology for the latter epiklesis involves Hermes' direct participation in the war between Tanagra and Eretria, and possibly White Hermes and Hermes Promachos should therefore be identified. It is unclear how the aition preserved by Tzetzes was meant to account for the god's epiklesis at Tanagra, but in any case the myth, which conforms to the familiar sequence of war-oracle-human sacrifice-victory, should not be considered historical.

Stephanus of Byzantium glosses Lemnos as follows: 'From the so-called Great Goddess, whom they call Lemnos, and to her they say also maidens were sacrificed.' The information apparently (but not certainly) goes back to Hecataeus (Steph. Byz. s.v. Λῆμνος = Hecataeus, *FGrHist* 1 F 138a). Once again it is difficult to evaluate so brief a statement, but it is likely that the gloss has some connection with Athenian legends surrounding the colonization of Lemnos. According to Herodotus, a group of Pelasgians, having been expelled from Attica, settled in Lemnos; later they returned, and out of vengeance they seized some Athenian women who were holding the festival of Artemis at Brauron and took them back with them to Lemnos (Hdt. 6.137–138.1 and 4.145.2). This story had clearly been invented in order to justify the subjugation of Lemnos by Miltiades in the last decade of the sixth century, but Herodotus seems to have been the first to connect the rape of the Athenian women with the expulsion of the Pelasgi who had been hired to construct the wall around the acropolis. In other sources the colonizers of Lemnos are Tyrsenians, and according to one the image of Artemis was taken from Brauron along with the women.[189] Now, the Lemnian Great Goddess was Bendis, the Thracian goddess whose cult was introduced into Athens in around 430 BC; she was closely associated with and often identified with Artemis.[190] Aristophanes' *Lemnian Women* involved both Bendis and the maidens who 'play the bear' at Brauron – and hence to all appearances the story of the rape at Brauron. The play also concerned a more celebrated tale, the story of the Lemnian women who murdered all the men of the island save King Thoas, who was spared by his daughter Hypsipyle; in some sources this Thoas is identified with the king of the Tauri, who presides over the sacrifice of strangers to Artemis, with Iphigeneia as her priestess.[191] I strongly suspect that the human sacrifices to the Lemnian Great Goddess figured somewhere in this complex of associations and that the maiden sacrifices were in some way related to myths of the Iphigeneia type and/or to the

Tauric human sacrifices. In any case, these certainly are not Greek human sacrifices at all, but rather human sacrifices imputed by Athenian writers to the legendary Tyrsenian colonizers of Lemnos. Whether anything in the worship or mythology of Bendis inspired connections with Brauronian Artemis or the religion of the Tauri is difficult to say, but the human sacrifices to the Great Goddess may be – rather than valuable evidence for Lemnian cult practice – merely a remnant of a myth which by chance has not survived.[192]

A final instance, from Hellenistic history: in the third century BC a certain Apollodorus plotted revolution in Cassandreia. Diodorus (22.5.1) reports that in order to secure the loyalty of his fellow conspirators Apollodorus invited a young friend to a sacrifice and, having sacrificed the unsuspecting boy, served to his men the boy's inwards and wine mixed with his blood. If this represents a third-century story (rather than a later invention), then it is our earliest example of a large class of similar accusations, remarkably consistent in detail, levelled against 'outsiders', both political revolutionaries (e.g. Catiline) and members of various religious groups, most notably the Jews and early Christians.[193] But such allegations differ in character from most of the material discussed in this chapter (an exception perhaps is Clement, whose uncritical attack on the pagan religions was undertaken in much the same spirit) and, belonging largely to the Roman world, fall outside the scope of this study.

CONCLUSION

Such, then, is the written evidence for the practice of human sacrifice in ancient Greece. And if one should draw up a list of those places where human sacrifices were said to have been performed, it would not be unimpressive: human victims felt the sacrificial knife at Alos, on Mt Lykaion in Arcadia, in Messenia, Pella, Tanagra, Phocaea, in Athens herself; on the islands of Crete, Cyprus, Rhodes, Lesbos, Chios, and Tenedos. If we expand our list to include those sacrifices I have classified (from the outset) as mythical, we add Sparta, Thebes, Potniae, Orchomenos, Patrae, and Aulis. And as recipients of these human sacrifices we find Zeus, Kronos, Artemis, Ares, Dionysus, Hermes, and the heroes Peleus and Cheiron, Palaemon, and Diomedes.

And yet closer and more cautious examination of the individual cases begins to raise suspicions and yields a different picture. Our earliest historical account of human sacrifices is also one of our most detailed: but Herodotus' confused description of the rites at Alos does not hold up well under the scrutiny of logic and common sense. At the battle of Salamis Themistocles sacrifices three Persian princes: but Aeschylus and Herodotus know nothing of the incident, the victims are slain before the battle but procured after it, and the sacrifice is offered to a deity whose home is Lesbos, not Attica. The cannibalistic banquets on Mt Lykaion are attested in several sources, and three writers of the fourth century refer to these rites as still current in their day; but when we turn to archaeology for confirmation, the earth of the mountaintop remains obstinately silent.

But perhaps archaeology's negative verdict should not surprise us. All that our texts can tell us is that some of the Greeks *believed* that human sacrifices were performed on Mt Lykaion, at Alos, and elsewhere. But did they *know*? Joseph Fontenrose's words, though written in a different connection, are not out of place here:

> We hardly appreciate the great difference between his [Herodotus'] time and ours in the reporting of events, the preservation of records, the means of communication, the general state of knowledge. The Greeks had almost none of our facilities in communications and records: there was nothing of what we call media; there was little in the way of archives. We scarcely realize how much they depended on oral reports and how ready men were to believe what they were told.

This last point is put somewhat less gently by a Roman writer of the first century: *mirum est quo procedat Graeca credulitas.*[194]

For more than half of the 'historical' human sacrifices we are indebted to two writers, one Christian, the other pagan, of late antiquity. And while Clement and Porphyry often cite sources from earlier times, they have also severed small fragments from their contexts, or reduced information to brief paraphrase. Imagine if some writer of later antiquity had only Pausanias as his source for the practice of human sacrifice among the Greeks:

> They used to sacrifice human victims to Artemis at Sparta, and at Patrae to Artemis Triklaria. And were not children slain for Dionysus at Potniae and virgins offered yearly to

> the Hero of Temesa? And the Messenians and Thebans – for I shall not pass over these either – shed the blood of maidens in time of war,

he could write, in perfect sincerity. Yet restore these excerpts to their places in the text of Pausanias (3.16.9–10; 7.19–20.2; 9.8.2; 6.6.7–12; 4.9.3–10; 9.17.1), and we apprehend their true nature. Would it be any different should the Egyptian sands yield up those texts of Phylarchus, Istros, Apollodorus, Monimus, Dosiades, Pythocles, and Euelpis which chance has denied to us?

5

The pharmakos and related rites

INTRODUCTION

The ritual expulsion of pharmakoi was, under various forms, a custom common to a number of Greek cities.[1] In Ionia and Athens the rite was performed during the Apolline festival of the Thargelia. The ritual is also attested for the Ionian colony of Abdera, probably as a part of the Thargelia also, and similar rites are known for the Phocaean colony Massilia, for the island of Leucas, and for Chaeronea in Boeotia. The essential element of the ritual was the expulsion from the community of one or two persons called (at least in Ionia, Athens, and Abdera) 'pharmakoi', with the expressed purpose of purifying the city. In the different cities the pharmakoi were variously dressed and decorated, paraded about the city, whipped with fig branches and squills, cursed, and pelted with stones. In the end they were driven across the city's borders; according to some sources, they were killed.

Interpretations of these rituals have varied greatly. For Mannhardt the pharmakos originally represented the vegetation spirit (*Wachstumsgeist*), who through whipping with magical plants and other means was at once freed from harmful influences and invested with procreative powers for the coming year. Similarly, Frazer saw the pharmakos as a representative of the 'god of vegetation', who was slain, annually or on the occasion of drought or famine, that he might be born afresh with renewed powers. But Deubner, denying any connection with fertility rites, emphasized instead the kathartic function of the ritual: the pharmakos was a 'scapegoat', who, laden with all the impurities which had accumulated during the year, removed these in his person from the community.[2] More recently, Burkert views the expulsion of the pharmakos as a ritual reflex of communal instincts of self-preservation, which during crises find an outlet in aggression against one member of the community.[3]

Numerous parallels for the Greek ritual have been adduced by scholars from other cultures: the 'scapegoat' of the Old Testament, Hittite rites, and a strikingly similar custom from modern-day Tibet, to name a few.[4] Also, within Greece itself the ritual has been seen to have far-reaching application: the stories of Thersites, Aesop, Codrus, Pentheus, and Oedipus, and the institution of ostracism have all been viewed in the light of pharmakos rituals.[5]

In Ionia and Athens pharmakoi were expelled during the spring, pre-harvest festival of the Thargelia. The Athenian festival, about which we are better informed, was held on the sixth and seventh days of the month Thargelion. On the first day a ram was sacrificed to Demeter Chloe, and the city was purified by means of two pharmakoi. On the second day the *thargēlos*, a pot filled with seeds of various kinds, was offered to Apollo. Choral competitions were also held; and the *eiresiōnē*, a branch hung with wool, fruit, cakes, and oil-flasks, was carried from door to door during the festival.[6] As the Thargelia were held at a time when the crops were grown but not yet fully ripe, it is not surprising that the festival would also involve purification, intended to prevent harm to the young fruit and thus to insure an abundant harvest.[7] And yet, in the historical period at least, this purification does not seem to have been primarily agricultural, for the phrase 'to cleanse the city' appears in our earliest source, Hipponax, and often thereafter.[8] The expulsion of pharmakoi was thought, it seems, to effect the cleansing of the polis from all defilements, which might bring crop failure, drought, or famine, but which also posed the more direct threat to humans of pestilence.

In fact, the association of the ritual with disease and the purification necessary for its prevention is well documented and arguably quite ancient. According to Helladius (in Phot. *Bibl.* 279, vol. 8: 182 Henry) the Athenian ritual was 'a means of averting pestilential diseases', and although several etymologies of 'pharmakos' have been proposed, the most plausible explanation (despite the occasional presence of a long alpha in the second syllable) is that the word is simply the masculine form of *pharmakon* ('drug, medicine'). The association of the rite with Apollo, therefore, may stem from the god's connections with purification and with disease and its prevention and cure.[9] It thus seems possible that the pharmakos ritual was not originally a rustic ceremony connected with vegetation and fertility (as it has most often been regarded) and that the incorporation of the rite into a largely agricultural festival was a secondary development in its history.

But let us leave aside speculation on the meaning and origin of this strange custom and allow the ancient sources to speak for themselves. As with the evidence for human sacrifice, I shall concentrate on the reliability of the sources and the question whether or not the pharmakoi were killed during the ritual – a point on which the disagreement among ancient writers has continued into modern times.

IONIA

Johannes Tzetzes, the Byzantine scholar of the twelfth century, provides us with six fragments of the Ionian poet Hipponax (sixth century BC) relevant to the pharmakos:

5 to cleanse the city and be struck with fig branches
6 striking him [?] in winter and thrashing him [?]
with fig branches and squills like a pharmakos
7 and it is necessary to make him into [?] a pharmakos
8 and in the hand to furnish [fut. inf.] dried figs and cake
and cheese, such as pharmakoi eat
9 for they have long awaited them gaping,
holding fig branches, as they hold for pharmakoi
10 (that?) he be dried out with hunger; and on his member,
led a pharmakos, may he seven times be thrashed.

(Tzetz. *Chil.* 5.745–58 = Hippon. fr. 5–10 West)[10]

From these fragments we learn that in Ionia[11] the pharmakos was fed figs, cakes, and cheese, that he was whipped (apparently on the penis)[12] with fig branches and squills, and that the function of the ritual was 'to cleanse the city', a phrase which will recur often in later sources. That is about all. But Tzetzes, in the passage which preserves these fragments, tells us much more:

The pharmakos, the *katharma*, in ancient times was as follows:
if misfortune laid hold of a city through divine wrath,

whether famine or plague or any other ill,
the most ugly man of all they would lead as to a sacrifice,
for the cleansing and cure of the ailing city.
And, having set up the sacrifice at the suitable place
and having given in his hand cheese, cake, and dried figs,
and having whipped him seven times on the penis
with squills, wild figs, and other wild plants,
in the end on a pyre they would burn him on wild wood,
and into the sea they would scatter the ash to the winds,
for the cleansing, as I said, of the ailing city,
as also Lycophron mentions somewhere, of the Locrian maids,
saying something like this – I don't know the verses exactly:

'When burning the limbs with barren branches
Hephaestus throws out to the sea the ashes
of her who perished from Traron's peaks.'
But Hipponax explains the whole custom best.

(*Chil.* 5.728–45)

Hipponax fragments 5–10 then follow. Unfortunately these fragments, despite Tzetzes' assertion, by no means explain the custom fully, and it is uncertain from what source Tzetzes obtained the additional information not found in the quotations, namely that the pharmakos was burned on a pyre, that his ashes were scattered into the sea, and that he was killed when a city was afflicted with famine, plague, or other misfortune.[13]

While it is true (as we shall see) that Tzetzes was not the first to claim that pharmakoi were killed, he is the first and only ancient writer to assert that they were burned on pyres and that their ashes were scattered into the sea. What was his source for these striking details? That it was Hipponax himself[14] is unlikely: if it had been, surely Tzetzes (not one to conceal his learning) would have provided quotations of Hipponax to substantiate his statements. But he did not, and this led Gebhard to suggest in his dissertation on pharmakos rituals that Tzetzes merely transferred the details of the burning on wild wood and the scattering of the ashes into the sea from Lycophron's account of the burning of the Locrian maidens, from which he quotes (with two changes) three verses in order to illustrate the treatment of the pharmakos (*Alex.* 1157–9). It is an attractive suggestion,[15] but scholars have objected, perhaps with some justification, that Tzetzes cited the burning of the Locrian maidens only as a parallel: the analogy would not have occurred to Tzetzes without some initial point of comparison between the maidens and pharmakoi. And under the weight of criticism Gebhard himself soon altered his opinion.[16]

The solution to the problem may lie in the identification of the words 'pharmakos' and 'katharma' made by Tzetzes and a few earlier writers.[17] We know that certain abominations, such as monstrous births, were burned on the wood of wild trees.[18] Also, certain kinds of waste, called *oxuthumia*, were burned at the crossroads, and oxuthumia are sometimes identified with katharmata, a word used to designate various sorts of purifications and waste from purifications and sacrifices.[19] Closest to Tzetzes' account of the pharmakos ritual is a passage of Lucian's *Alexander*, where the charlatan priest of Asclepius is said to have burned one of Epicurus' works on fig wood in the middle of the agora and then cast the ashes into the sea (*Alex.* 47). The details of the burning and casting of the ashes into the sea were clearly based upon actual ritual practices. It therefore seems possible that Tzetzes' description was founded on a knowledge of a method of destroying and disposing of certain kinds of (non-human) pollutions and waste matter. The identification of 'pharmakoi' and 'katharmata' (for which I find no good evidence in early sources – the two words at any rate are hardly synonyms)[20] may have led Tzetzes to transfer a means of disposing of the latter to his description of the final treatment of the former. This supposed burning of the pharmakos in turn suggested to his versatile mind a comparison with the Locrian maidens.

Tzetzes' assertion that the 'sacrifice' was performed in time of plague or famine also has no foundation in any extant fragment of Hipponax. But we know from a fragment of the poet (fr. 104.47–9 West) that the Ionian ritual was regularly enacted during the Thargelia. It is possible that the expulsion of pharmakoi was both an annual rite and an exceptional measure taken during plague and other misfortune,[21] but one wishes that there were evidence for this from a source earlier and more reliable than Tzetzes. In any case, Tzetzes seems to have been unaware that the ritual was performed annually during a religious festival, and his statement about plague and famine may have been his own contribution to pharmakos lore: possibly he was influenced by myths of human sacrifices performed under such circumstances (see pp. 73–6) or by an aetiological myth for the pharmakos ritual such as the Athenian story which traces the custom to the plague resulting from the murder of Androgeos (pp. 152–3).

From the few fragments of Hipponax which have come down to us it is evident that the pharmakos was a frequent character in his poems. Verses 3–4 of fragment 92 (West),

> καί μοι τὸν ὄρχιν τῆς φαλ[
> κ]ṛάδηι συνηλοίησεν ὥσπ̣[ερ φαρμακῶι

(with the probable restoration of φαρμακῶι), refer to the custom of striking the pharmakos on the genitals with fig branches.[22] And from two glosses of Hesychius (Hesych. s.vv. κραδησίτης and κραδίης νόμος; cf. [Plut.] *De musica* 8, 1133F–1134A; Hippon. fr. 152 and 153 West) we learn an epithet of the pharmakos (*kradisitēs*) and that the 'fig tune' was played on the aulos to accompany the departure of the pharmakoi, who were whipped with fig branches and fig leaves; Hipponax seems to have chided his fellow poet Mimnermus for composing such tunes. It is important to note that Hesychius mentions only that the pharmakoi were 'sent out' (τοῖς ἐκπεμπομένοις φαρμακοῖς): the detail, and quite possibly the verb also, will have derived from a poem of Hipponax. Thus, in sixth-century Ionia the pharmakoi were escorted out of the city in a procession or parade accompanied by music. Not a word is said about their being killed.

Verses 47–9 of fragment 104 (West),

> ὁ δ' ἐξολισθὼν ἱκέτευε τὴν κράμβην
> τὴν ἑπτάφυλλον, ἣν θύεσκε Πανδώρηι
> Ταργηλίοισιν ἔγκυθρον πρὸ φαρμακοῦ,

where a quotation from Athenaeus (9, 370B) supplements a lengthy papyrus fragment, present a number of textual difficulties, and the exact meaning is obscure.[23] Nevertheless, largely because of the occurrence within the space of two lines of a word for 'sacrifice' and the word 'pharmakos', the fragment has often been viewed as evidence that the Ionian pharmakos was sacrificed during the Thargelia.[24] According to this interpretation, the person mentioned in the poem used to sacrifice a cabbage in a pot (or possibly a cake) instead of a pharmakos, the usual sacrificial victim. This does not seem to make a great deal of sense (if the pharmakoi were indeed sacrificed in Ionian ritual, under what circumstances would someone substitute a cabbage? Or if people would sacrifice a cabbage at the same time as the sacrifice of the pharmakos, why then would they be said to do so 'in place of' the pharmakos?). And even if the Ionian pharmakoi were killed I am not convinced that *thueskein* could be properly applied to the killing, usually thought to have been effected by stoning; in fact, before Tzetzes none of the sources who state that the pharmakos was killed uses *thuein* or any other sacrificial term for the slaying.[25] But it is not only possible but preferable to construe the lines differently: πρό, as Deubner pointed out, may mean not only 'instead of' but also 'before' or 'on behalf of'.[26] The fragment may refer to a private custom performed at the time of the public pharmakos ceremony,[27] and it does not seem unlikely that members of the community would make a small offering *on behalf of* a pharmakos. But little can be said with assurance about the sense of the fragment.

Such, then, are the lines of Hipponax which refer directly to the pharmakos. But Tzetzes' assertion that the pharmakos was killed has inspired a diligent search for references to the practice in other fragments of the poet. In most of these fragments there are clear references to killing or death, but that any of the fragments contains an allusion to pharmakos rituals is doubtful. Fragment 128 (West) is quoted in Ath. 15, 698C, as an instance of Hipponactean parody of epic hexameters:

> Sing for me, Muse, Eurymedon's son, the sea-Charybdis,
> the knife-in-the-belly, who eats not nicely,
> sing, that he by a pebble [. . .] suffer an evil fate,
> by popular will, along the shore of the barren sea.

Masson and other scholars have argued that lines 3–4 refer to the slaying of the pharmakos.[28] But I can see little merit to the suggestion. Hipponax wishes death upon an enemy, a death by stoning, if indeed this is the meaning of ψηφῖδι ('pebble') in line 3. Parallels in Callimachus suggest rather that the word refers to a pebble cast in voting and that κακῇ should be supplied in the lacuna, yielding a sense 'by an adverse vote'. Also – unless this is a case of extreme comic understatement – a pebble would not seem to be a fatal missile.[29] But, for the sake of argument, let us assume that the reference is to stoning. It is true that stoning played a role in the pharmakos ritual at the Ionian colonies Abdera and Massilia (although not, as we shall see, stoning to death: pp. 156–60) and that a certain Pharmakos was stoned to death in a myth which probably belongs in Ionia (p. 153). But references to stoning as a form of mob justice are quite common in Greek literature, myth, and history, and not all victims of stoning are pharmakoi: in the *Acharnians*, for example, the chorus threatens to stone Dicaeopolis to death for making a private peace with Sparta (Ar. *Ach.* 280–346). Thus, if fr. 128 does refer to death by stoning – a penalty in reality reserved for heinous offences such as sacrilege[30] – then the poet comically characterizes his enemy's gluttony as a crime worthy of such punishment.

Similarly, scholars[31] have seen an allusion to the pharmakos in fragment 37 (West): '(s)he was bidding them [?] pelt and stone Hipponax'. But here again I can see no good reason to see this as a reference to pharmakos rituals. It is true that we find the verb *ballein* also in fragments 5 and 6, but in fr. 5 (and probably in fr. 6) the reference is to striking or pelting the pharmakos with fig leaves. And even if fr. 37 does allude to the ritual, as *leuein* does not in itself mean 'stone to death' (this would be *kataleuein*), the fragment cannot be used to support the view that pharmakoi were killed. But it seems more likely that here Hipponax merely represents some enemy as urging on the crowd to mob violence against him, without allusion to the ritual stoning of pharmakoi.

A reference to pharmakos rituals has also been detected in Hippon. fr. 118E (West), a papyrus fragment of a commentary on Hipponax.[32] These are the first five preserved lines (lines 2–6):

> ạṷ̓τοὺς ἐπὶ χρόνο[ν] ẹω . . [
> σ]ῶμα ψύχηται· νῦν δ̣[ὲ ἐ]π̣ὶ ἄμμον θα-
> λα]σσίαν ἐ̣[κ]βάλλουσι. τρ[ιτα]ῖον ἐκ κήρυ-
> κο]ς, ἀσμẹ[ν . . .]έ μιν· πρ[ὸς] αὐτὰ τὰ ἀνδρ̣[ ]
>]. [ἥν]ẹγκεν αὐ[τὸ]ν τριταῖον

> them for [. . .] time . . . [the]
> body may grow cold; but as it is, onto the sand of
> the sea they throw [it?] out. The third day from
> the herald [?], and happy . . . him; towards the [. . .] themselves
> . . . brought him the third day . . .

In the remainder, of which only ends of lines are preserved, something happens near the sea (lines 15–16), 'they throw out' is repeated (17), and there is mention of a father (18), a corpse (20), a bone (21), someone (the grammarian?) named Aristophanes (22–3), and a common burial ground (πολυανδρεῖον: 23–4).[33]

It should be borne in mind that fr. 118E is a commentary, although it appears that a trimeter (τρ[ιτα]ῖον ἐκ κήρυκος, ἀσμε[ν. . .]έ μιν) and a few other isolated words from the poem of Hipponax are imbedded in the commentary.[34] Only minimal sense can be made of the passage, but it appears that the commentator is explaining, rather repetitively, the phrase τριταῖον ἐκ κήρυκος and discussing the disposal of a body cast out onto the beach on the third day after death. Apparently the procedure found in Hipponax is being contrasted with more usual methods of burial.[35] But I can see nothing whatsoever in the preserved text to suggest that this is the body of a pharmakos. Nor is the information contained in the fragment consistent with Tzetzes' description, in which to all appearances the pharmakos is cremated immediately (*Chil.* 5.737). And Tzetzes' account, true or false, was the chief reason for suspecting that the Ionian pharmakoi were killed in the first place.

Certainly the conclusion that the poem concerned the disposal of a dead pharmakos cannot be justified merely by the reference to a corpse in the fragment.[36] But according to Tzetzes the ashes of the pharmakos were strewn in the sea after the 'sacrifice' (*Chil.* 5.738), and from this Masson concluded that the Ionian pharmakos was killed on the shore. Masson noted that the seashore is mentioned both in the epic parody (fr. 128.4) and in the commentary (fr. 118E.3–4 and 15–16).[37] Yet it is difficult to reconcile the information contained in the two fragments, for in fr. 128 Hipponax wishes his enemy killed *on* the shore, while in 118E it appears that someone brought (line 6) a body, three days after death, *to* the shore, where it is thrown out (lines 4 and 17) onto the sand. And it is more difficult still to bring these two fragments into agreement with the information provided by Tzetzes, who said only that the ashes of the pharmakos were scattered into the sea (*Chil.* 5.738). Furthermore, in other places in his writings, overlooked by Masson and other scholars, Tzetzes tells us that the ashes were scattered, not into the sea, but 'almost over the whole city' (Tzetz. *Chil.* 8.908), 'in the whole city' (Tzetz. Schol. Ar. *Plut.* 454b), and, simply, 'everywhere' (Tzetz. Schol. Ar. *Ran.* 733a). As Koster has written of these Tzetzean variations, 'vides, quam mobilis ingenii homo noster fuerit'.[38] To argue that in these last three cases Tzetzes was thinking of the Attic or some other pharmakos ritual (and not the Ionian, ostensibly described in connection with the fragments of Hipponax) would mean giving far too much credit to this most unreliable scholar.

And where, according to Tzetzes, was the pharmakos killed? At the suitable place (εἰς τόπον . . . τὸν πρόσφορον), he says, rather vaguely, in the *Chiliades* (5.733). But elsewhere he is more specific: the pyre was set up in the middle of the agora (Schol. Ar. *Plut.* 454b). A *topos prosphoros*, to be sure, but hardly a credible detail! If nothing else it is certain that the Ionian pharmakoi were expelled from the city, as in other locations.[39] Although highly implausible, this detail is reminiscent of the passage of Lucian where Alexander burned a book of Epicurus in the agora and threw the ashes into the sea (*Alex.* 47): this he did 'as if burning Epicurus himself', by which of course Lucian meant to suggest the relish with which Alexander destroyed the offending tome. But it is not impossible that the words could be taken to mean that human beings, not books, were customarily burned in the marketplace. And Tzetzes was familiar with Lucian.[40] But whatever the origin of this detail, clearly to Tzetzes' mind the pharmakos was not killed on the shore; nor does he ever say that he was stoned to death. In fact, he nowhere says expressly how the pharmakos was killed, although it seems to me implicit in all his descriptions that the pharmakos was burned alive (Tzetz. *Chil.* 5.737 and 8.906, Schol. Ar. *Plut.* 454b, Schol. Ar. *Ran.* 733a). Hence references to the seashore, to corpses, or to stoning in Hipponax cannot be reconciled with the information given by Tzetzes. On the other hand, in the few extant fragments of Hipponax with explicit references to pharmakoi, there are no references to pyres, to the scattering of ashes, or to their being killed by any means.

Tzetzes appears to have transferred a method of disposing of various non-human 'pollutions' to the pharmakos ritual; the use of the word 'katharma' both for such waste matter and (in later writers) for the pharmakos may have suggested to Tzetzes that this was the method of disposing of the human 'scapegoats' also. Acquaintance with Lucian *Alex.* 47 or some similar comic passage may also have played a role. Of course the starting-point of these imaginative flights must have been a belief that pharmakoi were killed. But this belief does not seem to have derived from Hipponax or specifically Ionian information. I have discussed the passage of the *Chiliades* as if it were a description of an Ionian ritual, but in fact there is no good reason to refer this information

– other than what comes directly from Hipponax – to Asia Minor: Tzetzes does not mention a location, and elsewhere he shows himself to be indifferent to geographical detail. In fact, when later he writes of the pharmakos – now ostensibly the Athenian pharmakos – in a scholion on Aristophanes, he will repeat the same details from Hipponax which he used in the *Chiliades* (Tzetz. Schol. Ar. *Plut.* 454b). It is thus probable that he had no particular city or region in mind when he composed his account in the *Chiliades*, and his belief that the pharmakoi were killed very probably derived from a tradition connected, not with Hipponax, but with Aristophanes and the Athenian form of the ritual.[41]

ATHENS

The earliest references to pharmakoi in Athens are found in Old Comedy, where 'pharmakos', like 'katharma', is used as a term of abuse.[42] Only slightly more informative is a passage of Aristophanes' *Frogs*, in which the chorus complains that good men, like the good old coinage, are now passed over in favour of the basest newcomers, 'whom in former days the city would not have used lightly even as pharmakoi' (*Ran.* 732–3). Nothing is said about the treatment of pharmakoi here; but it is implied that they were particularly despised, and we learn that the city of Athens did in fact 'use' them. But it is a passage of the *Knights* which has drawn the most attention in the scholarship. The chorus addresses Demos:

> Thus I see you do well,
> and there is, as you say,
> in this way of yours
> very much cleverness,
> if on purpose these fellows
> like *dēmosioi* you nourish
> on the Pnyx, and then when
> you chance to have no meat on hand,
> whichever of these is fat
> you sacrifice and dine on.
> (Ar. *Eq.* 1131–40)

The scholia offer three possible explanations for the meaning of δημοσίους here: (1) that we should understand cows or bulls or 'some other such sacrificial victim'; (2) that dēmosioi are 'those called pharmakoi, who cleanse the cities with their own blood'; or, simply, (3) that they are 'those fed at public expense' (Schol. Ar. *Eq.* 1136a). Which of these three explanations is correct? Many scholars have accepted the first;[43] but, as Nilsson pointed out, animals kept as sacrificial victims by the state are dēmosia (neuter), not dēmosioi: the latter term should properly refer to people. The third explanation is, of course, correct: dēmosioi were persons supported by the state – public slaves and servants of various sorts.[44] Now, it is not impossible that the term could include pharmakoi: at Massilia pharmakoi were maintained at public expense (see pp. 157–60), and Aristophanes himself says that they were 'used' by Athens (*Ran.* 733). But even if the scholiast is correct, as the term was by no means restricted to pharmakoi I do not see how the audience could have been expected to think of them specifically here. And the identification of dēmosioi with pharmakoi (found only in this scholion) may be no more than an educated guess on the part of the scholiast, who, unable to explain an unfamiliar application of the word, arrived at this definition largely on the basis of *Eq.* 1405, where Demos refers to Paphlagon as a 'pharmakos'. He may also have deduced from *Eq.* 1137–40 that dēmosioi were customarily sacrificed and eaten and, already believing that the Athenians killed their pharmakoi, identified the two.

But of course there is no need to read *Eq.* 1137–40 so closely with the preceding lines: picking up on a joke started by Demos (1127–30) and perhaps playing on two senses of *trephein* (used both of supporting people and feeding animals), the chorus moves rapidly to an implicit comparison of demagogues with animals fattened for consumption. The explicit comparison with dēmosioi has been dropped (although there may be a further pun on dēmosioi and dēmosia). In any case, line 1140 cannot be referred to the treatment of pharmakoi: whether or not they were ever killed, there is no evidence, or reason to believe, that they were sacrificed and eaten.

Another passage from fifth-century comedy sometimes thought to refer to Athenian pharmakos ritual[45] is Eupolis fr. 132 Kassel-Austin: 'who should in the crossroads and among the refuse/as a pollutant of the city be burned, crackling'. The sole reason for seeing an allusion to pharmakos ritual in this piece of comic invective is Tzetzes' contention that the pharmakos was burned on a pyre. But I hope to have shown that Tzetzes' account is suspect for a number of reasons; and in any case it is dubious methodology to interpret a fifth-century fragment using a source from the twelfth century after Christ. The speaker simply wishes an enemy burned among the oxuthumia – clearly a reference to ritual, although we cannot conclude from this that human beings were actually burned at the crossroads at Athens, any more than we can say that the wish of another comic poet that someone be burned on sixteen wooden phalluses (Dio Chrys. 33.63 = *Adespota* fr. 7 Kock) reflects actual practice. Also, the word 'prostropaios' in the Eupolis fragment (rendered 'pollutant' above) is never applied to the pharmakos; rather, it is used of murderers and other serious offenders and of 'polluting visitants'.[46] And surely the humour of both comic fragments lies precisely in the fact that the speakers represent their human enemies as 'pollutants' deserving of a ritual disposal in reality reserved for inanimate waste matter.

There are two references to the pharmakos from the fourth century, in orations attributed to Lysias and Demosthenes:

> Therefore we should think that by punishing and ridding ourselves of Andocides we are cleansing the city and freeing it from pollution and sending away a pharmakos and freeing ourselves from a sinner, as this man is all of these in one.
>
> ([Lys.] 6.53)

> So this is the man who will win his pardon, the pharmakos, the plague, whom anyone would shun at sight as an evil omen rather than be willing to address him. . . .
>
> ([Dem.] 25.80)

Both orators employ religious language to characterize the objects of their attacks: τὴν πόλιν καθαίρειν, ἀποδιοπομπεῖσθαι, ἀλιτήριος, οἰωνίσαιτο, and φαρμακός.[47] In the *Against Andocides' Impiety* attributed to Lysias the verb governing φαρμακόν is ἀποπέμπειν, which indicates that at Athens the pharmakos was sent away or banished from the city. This does not in itself prove that he was not also killed, but it does suggest that the sending of the pharmakos out of the city was an element, and perhaps the essential element, of the Athenian ritual, as it was in other Greek cities (cf. Hippon. fr. 153: p. 144). In a comic but quite similar passage of Dio Chrysostom, Diogenes the Cynic remarks of the athletes at Isthmia: 'Or do you think these men with their big bellies are of any use, whom we should lead around and cleansing all around throw out. . . ?' (Dio Chrys. *Or.* 8.14: οὓς ἐχρῆν περιαγαγόντας καὶ περικαθάραντας ἐκβαλεῖν). It is quite possible that this is an allusion to pharmakos rituals.[48] If so, as with pseudo-Lysias the emphasis is on the expulsion of the offending persons, and again the implication is that the pharmakoi were not killed, especially since Diogenes goes on to say 'but rather' (μᾶλλον δὲ) the athletes should be immolated, cut into pieces, and feasted on, a bit of comic abuse reminiscent of Ar. *Eq.* 1137–40.

The references to the pharmakos in Aristophanes and the two orations suggest that the ritual was still being performed in Athens in the fifth and fourth centuries BC, but they tell us very little about the ceremony itself or of the ultimate fate of the Athenian pharmakoi. It is not until much later antiquity that we hear of them again. The two most important sources are Harpocration's *Words of the Ten Orators* (first or second century after Christ) and Helladius (fourth century), whose *Chrestomathy* is preserved in prose extracts by Photius:

> Pharmakos. Lysias in the *Against Andocides' Impiety*, if the speech is genuine. In Athens they used to lead out two men to be purifications of the city during the Thargelia, one on behalf of the men, the other on behalf of the women. But that Pharmakos is a proper name and that he stole the sacred bowls of Apollo, was caught by the companions of Achilles, and was stoned to death, and that the things performed at the Thargelia are imitations of these events, Istros has said in the first book of the *Manifestations of Apollo*. And although Demosthenes in the *Against Aristogeiton* says 'So this is the man who will win his pardon, the pharmakós', Didymus thinks that the word should be circumflexed on the penultimate; but we have not found such usage anywhere.
>
> (Harp. s.v. Φαρμακός = Istros, *FGrHist* 334 F 50)

> That it was the custom in Athens to lead two pharmakoi, the one on behalf of the men, the other on behalf of the women, led for the sake of purification. And the one representing the men had black figs around his neck, the other white. And *subakchoi*, he says, they were called. This purification was a means of averting pestilential diseases, taking its origin from Androgeos the Cretan, because of

whose unlawful death in Athens the Athenians suffered from a pestilential disease, and the custom persisted always to cleanse the city with the pharmakoi.

(Helladius in Phot. *Bibl.* 279, vol. 8: 182 Henry)

Harpocration cites Istros, the pupil of Callimachus, as his source for the story of Pharmakos and the connection between the myth and the ritual performed at the Thargelia. And it would be natural to assume that Istros was also the source for the details of the Athenian ritual, but for the fact that Helladius, who appears in the beginning to be following the same source (and certainly the same tradition) as Harpocration, gives a different aition for the Athenian ritual, the murder of Androgeos and the ensuing plague. Also, the aition given by Istros is inappropriate to Athens, for the single Pharmakos of the myth does not well suit the pair of pharmakoi used in the ritual, and the role of Achilles is inexplicable with reference to Athens. Scholars, therefore, have felt that this must be an aition for Ionian pharmakos ritual.[49] It is uncertain why Harpocration's note contains information about both Athenian and Ionian forms of the custom. But the information about the Athenian pharmakos seems to have been connected with the speech *Against Andocides' Impiety*, and perhaps Harpocration's immediate source was Didymus, the prolific grammarian of the first century BC. Possibly it was Didymus who was responsible for combining Ionian material from Istros with a description of the Athenian ritual.[50]

The accounts of Harpocration and Helladius, brief as they are, provide us with valuable information about the Athenian ritual. Harpocration tells us that there were two pharmakoi, that they were 'led out' or 'driven out' (the verb here is *exagein*) during the festival of the Thargelia, and that one represented the men, the other the women of the city.[51] Helladius confirms that the pharmakoi were two in number, adding that they wore necklaces of figs, that they were also called 'subakchoi' (if correct, a word not attested elsewhere),[52] and that the ritual was intended to ward off pestilence. Neither writer says that the pharmakoi were killed. It is true that Istros wrote that the things done at the Thargelia were imitations (*apomimēmata*) of the myth of Pharmakos, who was stoned to death for his theft of the sacred vessels of Apollo. This myth, however, must belong to a city other than Athens, and the statement need not mean that the pharmakos in this unknown city was stoned to death. 'Imitations' of these mythological events could easily have involved a ceremonial stoning which resulted only in the expulsion of the pharmakos (as at Abdera), or even pelting with objects less harmful than stones.[53]

In fact, in only a few sources earlier than Tzetzes is it stated that the pharmakoi were killed. As we have seen, one of the explanations of the word 'dēmosioi' given in the old scholia on the *Knights* (Schol. Ar. *Eq.* 1136a) was that they were 'those called pharmakoi, who cleanse the city with their own blood'. The phrase is repeated in the Suda (s.v. φαρμακούς), and other entries in the tenth-century lexicon also seem to derive from scholia on Aristophanes.[54] But besides these scholia there is very little earlier than the Suda. Herodian, writing in the time of Marcus Aurelius, defined pharmakos as 'the man dying for the purification of the city' (Herodian s.v. φαρμακός, in 'Arkadius', p. 51 Barker: ὁ ἐπὶ καθαρμῷ τῆς πόλεως τελευτῶν; cf. Suda s.v. φαρμακός: ὁ ἐπὶ καθαρμῷ πόλεως ἀναιρούμενος), but without naming a particular location. Earlier than Herodian there is a similarly phrased and similarly brief definition in 'Ammonius' (a Byzantine edition of Herrenius Philo, *c.* AD 100): ὁ ἐπὶ καθάρσει τῆς πόλεως ῥιπτόμενος (ps.-Ammonius no. 494). The participle has been taken to mean 'thrown over a cliff',[55] but I do not see how the participle alone can bear this meaning. Possibly a prepositional phrase has been lost; but if so, the reference must be to the ritual performed at Leucas (for which Strabo 10.2.9 has ῥιπτεῖσθαι: see pp. 160–2) or some similar rite, not to Athens. And this raises the interesting possibility that the tradition that the pharmakos was killed originated in a confusion between Athenian and Leucadian ritual. Alternatively, we might construe the phrase to mean 'the one expelled for the purification of the city' (cf. Soph. *Aj.* 830 and *Ph.* 265), though here too we would expect a prepositional phrase. In either case the similarity between the two entries suggests that Herodian's definition derived from Herrenius Philo (or at least from a common source), and that the change from ῥιπτόμενος to τελευτῶν was due to a misunderstanding on the part of Herodian. But as both authors speak of the pharmakos in the singular and do not mention Athens, neither statement can be safely referred to Athenian ritual.

Thus the case that the Athenian pharmakoi were killed rests on brief statements in the scholia on Aristophanes (followed by the Suda) and in Herodian – if the latter is indeed a reference to Athens. Over against this testimony stands the tradition represented by Harpocration and Helladius, who in their more detailed and seemingly more knowledgeable accounts (and the only accounts referred to Athens specifically) say nothing about the death of the two pharmakoi. The origin of the tradition that they were killed is obscure, but it seems possible that details from an aetiological myth attached to the ritual – the myth of Pharmakos or a similar story – were taken as historical by later authors. It is also possible that the tradition attached to Aristophanes and the Attic orators was at some point contaminated with information about rituals from other locations (Abdera, Massilia, or possibly Leucas), discussed below.

EPIMENIDES' PURIFICATION OF ATHENS

Athenaeus reports that according to Neanthes of Cyzicus (late third century BC) 'when Epimenides was purifying Attica with human blood because of some ancient pollution', a beautiful young boy named Cratinus volunteered to die on behalf of his country, and his lover, Aristodemus, committed suicide in his grief (Ath. 13, 602C–D = Neanthes, *FGrHist* 84 F 16 = Tresp no. 123). In another version preserved by Diogenes Laertius (1.110) the 'ancient pollution' is specified as that incurred because of the slaying of the Cylonian conspirators on the Acropolis (in the seventh century), and two youths, Cratinus and Ctesibius, were put to death. The ritual murder performed by Epimenides is often mentioned in connection with pharmakos rituals and, surprisingly, has often been accepted as historical.[56] But there are several reasons to reject these accounts as fictional. The two versions do not agree in the details, and, more importantly, Diogenes first gives another version, which he seems to believe to be the correct one, according to which Epimenides led black and white sheep to the Areopagus and sacrificed them. Also, Polemon, in his *Replies to Neanthes* (Ath. 13, 602E–F) dismissed the whole story of the human sacrifice as a fabrication of Neanthes – with good reason, I think, for the story of the voluntary self-sacrifice of a beautiful youth and the suicide of his lover owes a clear debt to myth and Hellenistic romance.[57]

There are also historical problems with the purification of

Athens by Epimenides. The chief difficulty is that the earliest writer to mention Epimenides, Plato, dates Epimenides' visit to ten years before the Persian Wars, i.e. around 500 BC (*Leg.* 1, 642D–E). But Plato's version conflicts with those who placed Epimenides' purification in the early sixth century, as a response to the pollution resulting from the 'Cylonian sacrilege'.[58] Various solutions have been proposed, but even if we reject Plato's testimony in favour of the prevalent tradition, most writers who follow this tradition, Aristotle among them, say nothing of purification by human blood. And the purification of Athens by Epimenides – by whatever means – is of questionable historicity: Herodotus (5.70–1) and Thucydides (1.126–7) do not mention it in their accounts of the Cylonian conspiracy and its aftermath, and Epimenides is at best a semi-legendary figure, to whom all sorts of wonders were attributed.[59]

It is uncertain how much, if anything, acquaintance with pharmakos rituals contributed to the formation of the legend. The story shows some similarity to the aition given for the Athenian pharmakos ritual by Helladius (see pp. 152–3), and it has been pointed out that just as there were two pharmakoi in Athenian ritual, so are there two victims in the story of Epimenides' purification.[60] But the pair of victims appears only in the passage of Diogenes, which may be no more than an abbreviated version of Neanthes' account, where there was a single victim (his lover then committing suicide from grief). Also, stories of pairs of devoted male lovers are of course quite common in Greek literature (e.g. Harmodius and Aristogeiton); in fact, it is during a discussion of such pairs that Athenaeus tells this story. Thus the story may have had little or nothing to do with pharmakos rituals, although it is interesting that in the first version given by Diogenes, Epimenides 'cleansed the city' of Athens using a black and a white sheep, a detail which recalls the black and white figs hung around the necks of the two human 'scapegoats' at Athens.[61]

ABDERA AND MASSILIA

The evidence for the pharmakos ritual at Abdera, a city on the Thracian coast colonized first by Clazomenae and later by emigrants from Teos, serves as an excellent reminder of how unreliable the surviving evidence for ancient customs can be and how much at the mercy of the 'chance of preservation' we are.

Until the 1930s our only sources for the ritual were a couplet from Ovid's *Ibis* and the scholia *ad loc.*:

> Aut te devoveat certis Abdera diebus
> saxaque devotum grandine plura petant.

> Callimachus says that Abdera is a city in which such is the custom: each year they would purify the whole community publicly, and someone whom they were keeping on that day, devoted on behalf of the lives of all, they would kill with stones.
>
> (Ov. *Ib.* 467–8 and Schol. CFD Ov. *Ib.* 467)

Scholars rightly viewed this as a pharmakos ritual and generally accepted the assertions of the scholiast, who professes familiarity with the passage of Callimachus on which the lines of the *Ibis* were based.[62] But in 1934 papyrus fragments of the *Diegeseis* on Callimachus ('Expositions' containing the arguments of the *Aetia* and other information) were published.[63] The commentator explains Callimachus' line Ἔνθ', Ἄβδηρ', οὗ νῦν .[. . .]λ̣εω φαρμακὸν ἀγινεῖ (fr. 90) as follows:

> In Abdera a bought slave, a purification of the city, standing on a grey block and enjoying a plentiful meal, when he is full is led forth to the gates called the Prourides. Then, outside the wall he goes around in a circle cleansing with it [?] the city all around, and then he is stoned by the Basileus and the others, until he is driven over the borders.
>
> (*Diegeseis* II.29–40 on Callim. fr. 90 Pfeiffer)

The detail of the description (the grey stone, the meal, the name of the gate, the role of the Basileus) attests to the relative trustworthiness of the information: the writer either based his description closely on Callimachus or had independent knowledge of the rites. The ceremony culminated in the stoning of a pharmakos, but the purpose was not to kill but to drive him over the boundaries of the city. But the scholiast on the *Ibis* failed to understand (because of Ovid's use of *devovere*?) the nature of the ritual and its outcome.

A similar situation seems to obtain with the evidence for a purificatory ritual performed at Massilia (Greek Massalia, modern Marseille), for which there are also two sources: Servius, who cites Petronius as his source, and a passage from the collection of scholia (fifth or sixth century) on Statius' *Thebais* which has come down to us under the name of Lactantius Placidus. Servius explains *sacra* in Vergil's phrase *auri sacra fames* (*Aen.* 3.57) as equivalent to *execrabilis*. He then adds implausibly:

> The term moreover is derived from a custom of the Gauls [*ex more Gallorum*]. For whenever the Massilians were suffering from pestilence one of the poor would offer himself to be fed [*alendus*] the entire year [*anno integro*] at public expense [*publicis ‹sumptibus›*] and on especially pure foods [*purioribus cibis*]. Later this man, decorated with branches and sacred vestments, was led around through the whole community [*per totam civitatem*] under curses, that the ills of the whole community fall on him, and so was he cast out. And this can be read in Petronius.
>
> (Serv. Verg. *Aen.* 3.57 = Petron. fr. 1)

This is the version in the scholia on Statius:

> To purify the community with a human victim is a Gallic custom [*Gallicus mos*]. For someone of the most needy was enticed by rewards to sell himself for the purpose. And he was fed [*alebatur*] during the whole year [*anno toto*] at public expense [*publicis sumptibus*] on especially pure foods [*purioribus cibis*]; and finally on a specific and solemn day he was led through the whole community [*per totam civitatem*] out of the city beyond the boundaries, and he was killed with stones by the people.
>
> (Lactantius Placidus, *Comm. in Stat. Theb.* 10.793)

Although the accounts differ significantly in some respects, a marked similarity of detail and vocabulary (as can be seen from the words in brackets above) indicates that they both derived ultimately from the same source, namely Petronius. Both writers attribute the custom to the Gauls, but Servius also says that the Massilienses performed the ritual, which suggests that the custom was not Gallic but Greek. Massilia was a fully Greek city, having been colonized in *c.* 600 BC by Ionian settlers from Phocaea, and the Massilians were renowned for the tenacity with which they maintained their Greek identity, customs, and language well into Roman times. They were, in the words of Valerius Maximus, *prisci moris observantia . . . conspicui* (2.6.7); and later in the first century Silius Italicus will marvel how the Massilians, surrounded by barbaric and hostile peoples, manage to preserve the *antiquae morem patriae cultumque habitumque* (*Pun.* 15.168–72). The Massilienses must therefore be these Greek inhabitants of the city, and as the 'scapegoat' was said to have been supported at public expense, it seems certain that the ritual described in the first century by Petronius was in origin an Ionian, and not a Gallic, custom.[64]

One difference between the two accounts is that Servius states that the ceremony was performed in time of plague, while 'Lactantius' implies that it was an annual ritual performed on a specific day in the sacred calendar (*certo et solemni die*). And on this point the account of 'Lactantius' may be the more reliable, for it is difficult to believe that the Massilians, suffering from pestilence, would put off purifying the city for an entire year.[65] A more important difference is that while Servius says that the Massilian 'scapegoat' was merely cast forth (*proiciebatur*)[66] from the city, according to 'Lactantius' he was killed by stoning (*saxis occidebatur*). Whom are we to believe? A similar discrepancy between two accounts of the ritual at Abdera should give us reason to pause before the assertion of 'Lactantius'. And it is surely more understandable that a rite of expulsion, especially if by stoning, would be mistakenly interpreted as a ritual killing than that a ceremony in which a person was killed would be reinterpreted as a rite of mere banishment. And Servius' description may on the whole be closer to the original, as he cites Petronius as his source.[67] 'Lactantius', on the other hand, may have had the account only through one or more intermediate sources. 'Lactantius' in fact betrays an awareness of the role of expulsion in the ritual with the phrase *ductus ex urbe extra pomeria*, and the expulsion may have been effected by a ceremonial stoning, as at Abdera. It also seems possible that the description preserved in the scholia on the *Thebais* had been contaminated with information about another custom. In fact, there are several similarities of language between the scholia on Ovid's *Ibis* and the account of the Massilian ritual in 'Lactantius': *civitatem . . . lustrabant* (Schol. CFD Ov. *Ib.* 467), cf. *lustrare civitatem* (Lact. Plac.); *lapidibus occidebant* (Schol. CFD Ov. *Ib.* 467), cf. *saxis occidebatur* (Lact. Plac.); *certis diebus* (Ov. *Ib.* 467 and Schol. b Ov. *Ib.* 467), cf. *certo . . . die* (Lact. Plac.). The verbal similarities are slight, but the fact that these three phrases of 'Lactantius' do not appear in Servius' account is noteworthy and suggests that they represent additions by the learned scholiast on Statius. Contamination with Latin sources for the ritual at Abdera is probable.[68]

LEUCAS AND KOURION

Frequently discussed in connection with pharmakos rituals is the yearly leap from Leucates, the cliff on the southern tip of the island of Leucas. The promontory was famed as a 'lovers' leap', from which Sappho, Cephalus, and several others were said to have jumped, some dying from the fall, but others surviving, thereby cured of their love.[69] A fragment of Anacreon (fr. 31 Page) contains the earliest extant reference to leaping from the cliff, but presumably the tradition that Sappho jumped from the rock out of love for Phaon, alluded to by Menander in his *Leucadia*, originated in a reference to the cliff in her poetry (Men. fr. 258 Koerte; Sappho fr. 211 Lobel-Page). Strabo, who preserves the Menander fragment, is also our main source for the ritual, and he appears to owe the information to Demetrius of Scepsis (second century BC):[70]

> It was also the ancestral custom among the Leucadians every year during the sacrifice to Apollo for someone of those under criminal charge to be thrown from the cliff for the sake of averting evil. To him were attached feathers of every sort and birds capable of reducing with their flight the force of the leap, and below many men would wait in a circle in small boats and take him up. And when he had been taken up they would do all they could to remove him safely beyond the borders.
>
> (Strabo 10.2.9)

Other sources add little to this account. In the Roman ritual of the Argei human effigies were thrown into the Tiber, and Ovid compares the earlier form of the rite, when human beings were said to have been used, to the Leucadian custom (Ov. *Fast.* 5.630; cf. *Tr.* 5.2.76). Aelian (*NA* 11.8) describes the sacrifice of an ox 'to the flies' (who would feast on the victim's blood) performed at Leucas shortly before 'they leap the leap for the god'. And Photius (s.v. Λευκάτης) says that the priests (ἱερεῖς; ἐρασταί is a modern conjecture) throw themselves from the cliff. According to Servius each year people would hire themselves out to be thrown from the promontory (Serv. Verg. *Aen.* 3.279). And Ampelius' brief notice (8.4: *in summo monte fanum est, ubi sacra fiunt. Et, cum homo inde desiluit, statim excipitur lintribus*) seems to be merely an abbreviated Latin version of Strabo's description. From these brief references it seems possible that the person was not thrown from the cliff (as Strabo states) but rather jumped, and that the 'leapers' would offer their services for a price, although some of the variations may simply reflect poor acquaintance with the actual details of the rite.

The Leucadian ritual shares certain features with pharmakos rituals: the performance during a festival of Apollo, its expressed apotropaic function, and the expulsion of the person thrown from the cliff beyond the borders. But there are also significant differences: nowhere else is the pharmakos said to be a criminal (although this has been frequently assumed for Athens and other locations), and the throwing of a 'scapegoat' from a promontory into the sea separates this ritual from the rites in Ionia, Athens, Abdera, and Massilia. It would also be an unusual feature if the 'leaper' was killed from the fall. But did the leaper plummet from the promontory to his death? As far as I have been able to determine, a dive of some 40 m (130 ft) would certainly be very dangerous. The celebrated divers' cliff in Acapulco, Mexico, is 87 ft 6 in. in height; the men's world record high dive is 174 ft 8 in., the women's 120 ft. These dives, of course, are performed by professionals, and of 696 people (as of 1986) who have jumped from the Golden Gate Bridge (240 ft), only twelve have survived.[71] It would seem, therefore, that a free fall from 130 ft into the sea would be often, but not always, fatal, and it is arguable that the two possibilities open to unhappy lovers in myth – to die or survive cured of passion – reflect the two possible outcomes of the ritual.

But the 'ritual plunge' from Leucates was not a free fall, for Strabo reports that birds and feathers were attached to the chosen criminal. Nilsson remarked that the birds and feathers could not have done much good, and I would agree that live birds would have been useless.[72] But Strabo states clearly that the birds and feathers were effective in reducing the force of impact, he says nothing about the possibility of death, and he implies that the diver was always (or almost always) taken up into the waiting boats and escorted safely beyond the borders; Ampelius in fewer words implies the same. In 1885, a young woman named Sarah Ann Henley attempted to jump from a bridge into the Avon River:

'Her 250-ft fall was slightly cushioned by her voluminous dress and petticoat acting as a parachute. She landed, bruised and bedraggled, in the mud on the Gloucestershire bank and was carried to a hospital by four policemen.'[73] It does not seem impossible that feathers – if attached to a cloth or some kind of frame – could form an effective 'parachute', which would (like Ms Henley's petticoats) allow the leaper to float safely down into the water. Otherwise – if this is indeed an accurate description of an actual ritual – it is difficult to explain Strabo's implication that he usually survived.

Strabo is also our source for what may have been a comparable ritual performed at Kourion in Cyprus, where there is a 'promontory, from which they throw those who have touched the altar of Apollo' (14.6.3). But here the outcome seems certain: the cliff rises some 100 m above sea level, at its bottom rocks project outward into the water, and I have been assured that no one could survive the fall.[74] The similarity with the ritual performed in Leucas and the connection with the cult of Apollo may suggest that at Kourion people were compelled to touch the altar and then were thrown from the cliff in a regularly repeated ritual. But on the surface, Strabo's statement suggests rather that there was a prohibition against touching the altar, occasionally, if ever, violated by an unknowing outsider. The matter-of-fact manner in which Strabo mentions the action may better suit this explanation also, but the brevity of his reference does not permit a decision between these two possibilities.

Similarly brief and perplexing is Photius' gloss of περίψημα:

> Thus they would say over the youth who was thrown each year into the sea for the release from the oppressing ills: 'May you be our *peripsēma*.' Either deliverance or redemption. And thus they would throw him into the sea, as if paying a sacrifice to Poseidon.
>
> (Phot. s.v. περίψημα)

The location of the ritual is not stated, and of its date we can say (on the basis of the imperfect tenses) only that it was earlier than Photius (ninth century). The passage has often been taken to refer to the rites at Leucas or Kourion, but without good reason. The 'victim' is specified by Photius as a young male (*neanias*), whereas at Leucas criminals (presumably of any age) were used, and at Kourion (again presumably) 'those who touched the altar of

Apollo' could be of any age and of either sex. It is also unclear from Photius' description whether the youth was thrown from a cliff, the shore, or a boat. The word 'peripsēma', usually translated as 'offscourings', was (like 'katharma' and 'perikatharma') used as a term of abuse and in self-deprecatory expressions of humility; it is found chiefly in Christian authors.[75] The similarity in meaning between the word and 'katharma' (the latter applied – at least in late authors – to the pharmakos) has suggested to scholars that the ritual referred to by Photius was a 'scapegoat' ritual of some kind. But Photius' statement that they threw the youth into the sea 'as if paying a sacrifice to Poseidon' cannot be taken as certain evidence that the young man died in the presumed ceremony.

OTHER

Plutarch provides us with a fairly detailed description of a ritual known as the 'driving out of boulimos' (*boulimou exelasis*), which he himself performed while archon of Chaeronea. The ceremony was performed both publicly by the archon at the central hearth of the city and by private citizens, who would strike one of their house slaves with rods of the *agnus castus* and drive him out the door, saying at the same time 'out with famine, in with wealth and health' (*Quaest. Conv.* 6.8.1, 693E–F).[76] Although Plutarch does not say so explicitly, it appears that in the public ritual a slave was driven by the archon out of the city gates. The ritual has a number of points in common with pharmakos rites: the whipping with branches, the driving across a boundary, the use of slaves, and the embodiment of evils (here famine) by these human representatives. But, needless to say, at Chaeronea the numerous house slaves and the presumed public slave who participated in the ritual were not killed.

Finally, an incident from Philostratus' *Life of Apollonius* has frequently been mentioned in connection with the pharmakos.[77] The scene is Ephesus, where Apollonius has been summoned because of a pestilence. Apollonius gathers the Ephesians together in the theatre and there directs them to stone a beggar. The Ephesians are reluctant, but finally, when they see by the beggar's fiery eyes that he is a demon, they do as they are instructed, and beneath the pile of stones with which they have buried him they find a large hound (Philostr. *VA* 4.10). Besides the act of stoning (and perhaps the association with plague) the story has little in common with pharmakos rituals.[78] The true model may rather have been Hecuba, who is transformed into a hound with fiery eyes and (in some versions) stoned to death.[79] Also, I am not sure that I can share Burkert's confidence in the historical accuracy of many of the details of the story.[80] And it may be sheer coincidence that the anecdote was set in Ephesus in Asia Minor, where some six centuries earlier Hipponax had often alluded to pharmakoi in his poems, and where we began our inquiry.

CONCLUSION

For the pharmakos rites performed in Ionia and Athens there is a marked contrast between early, contemporary references and the later statements of lexicographers and scholiasts. The occasional assertions of these latter that the pharmakoi were killed cannot be supported by a single unambiguous reference from the times in which the rituals were in practice; and even among the later sources, in the two most detailed descriptions of the Athenian ceremony (Harpocration and Helladius) nothing is said of the alleged killing. The situation with the sources for the ritual performed at Abdera is instructive: a Latin scholiast claims that the pharmakos was killed by stoning, while an evidently more knowledgeable Greek commentator states that he was merely driven across the borders with stones. A similar discrepancy between two sources for the ritual at Massilia indicates how easily such rituals could be misconstrued in late antiquity.

Many sources speak of the leading, sending, or driving out of the pharmakoi. For both Ionia and Athens we find forms of *agein* (Hippon. fr. 10 West; Harp. s.v. Φαρμακός = Istros, *FGrHist* 334 F 50; Helladius in Phot. *Bibl.* 279, vol. 8: 182 Henry) and *pempein* (Hippon. fr. 153 West; [Lys.] 6.53). For Abdera, Callimachus (fr. 90) speaks of leading a pharmakos (*aginein*), and the author of the *Diegeseis* has *exelaunein*, a verb used also by Plutarch of the rites at Chaeronea (*Dieg.* II.39 on Callim. fr. 90 Pfeiffer; Plut. *Quaest. Conv.* 6.8.1, 693E–F). Dio Chrysostom (*Or.* 8.14) uses *ekballein* in what seems to be an allusion to pharmakos rituals; and at Massilia the 'scapegoat' *proiciebatur* (Serv. Verg. *Aen.* 3.57). These terms occur both in contemporary references and in the more detailed later descriptions: it was the expulsion, not the slaying, of pharmakoi which was essential to the efficacy of the rituals.

Little can be said about the period of time over which any of these rituals was in practice. In the sixth century Hipponax was clearly referring to a contemporary ritual in Ionia, as were, to all appearances, Aristophanes in the fifth century and two anonymous speech-writers in the fourth century in Athens. And if Harpocration was quoting Istros more or less exactly, then the present tense (ἔστιν) suggests that in the third century BC Istros described a ritual performed during the Thargelia of an unknown Ionian city (Harp. s.v. Φαρμακός = Istros, *FGrHist* 334 F 50).[81] In the *Diegeseis* on Callim. fr. 90 Pfeiffer the verbs are also in the present tense, which may suggest that the ritual at Abdera was still performed in Callimachus' time. Strabo (14.6.3) refers to the ritual at Kourion in the present tense, but the leap from Leucates was no longer practised in his day (and possibly was obsolete already in the second century BC).[82] The ritual at Massilia seems to have been enacted in the time of Petronius (Serv. Verg. *Aen.* 3.57 = Petron. fr. 1), and Plutarch (*Quaest. Conv.* 6.8.1, 693E–F) described a contemporary ceremony performed in his native Chaeronea. But for our later sources, the pharmakos had become an item of antiquarian and lexicographical curiosity, the customs having long passed into disuse.

6

Strangers in a strange land: the Locrian maiden tribute

EVIDENCE

One of the strangest chapters in the history of Greek religion is the sending of a tribute of young maidens from Locris to serve in the temple of Athena at Troy.[1] According to tradition, the Locrians were required to send the tribute to atone for Aias' violation of Cassandra in the temple during the sack of Troy, and the tribute was to continue for a period of 1,000 years from its institution. It was also reported that the maidens would be killed upon their arrival by the Trojans, if they were caught before reaching the safety of the temple. I am not certain that the Locrian maidens truly belong in this study, but I have included them, largely because the tribute has often been viewed by scholars as a mitigated form of an original human sacrifice. I shall question this interpretation, but if the maidens were regularly slain by the Trojans, then we are dealing with a ritual killing of some kind.

Sometimes cited as the closest parallel to the Locrian tribute is the mythical tribute of boys and girls sent by the Athenians to the Minotaur at Knossos, in atonement for the murder of Androgeos on Attic soil.[2] But even if there is much mistaken and unhistorical detail in our sources, the Locrian tribute was not mythical, for an inscription has been discovered which records a compact made concerning the charge of the maidens. Still, discrepancies in the sources and gaps in our knowledge have given rise to much debate among scholars, particularly over the history of the tribute: when it began, when it was suspended and when renewed (and with what changes), and when it was finally abolished.

The earliest mention of the tribute is that of Aineias 'the Tactician', who wrote in the 350s BC.[3] Aineias is discussing the transmission of letters during the siege of a city:

> And there is proof that it is difficult to guard against things sent in by design. Indeed the people around Ilion have made such an effort and for so long a time, yet in no way are they able to keep the Locrian women from entering in their midst, despite their great care and vigilance. But a few men, intent upon getting through secretly, over many years succeed in sneaking persons in.
>
> (Aen. Tact. 31.24)

A major source for the tribute is Lycophron, supplemented by the scholia. In the *Alexandra*, Cassandra prophesies grief for the Locrians because of her rape by Aias:

> And for many women hereafter shall I fashion woe,
> who, bereft of their maiden daughters, long bemoaning
> the bed-outraging general, plunderer of the love goddess,
> shall send to a hateful lottery
> their daughters denied the marriage bed.
> Larymna and Spercheius and Boagrius
> and Cynus and Scarpheia and Phalorias,
> and the city of Naryx and Thronian streets
> of the Locrians and Pyronaean vales
> and all the house of Ileus son of Hodoedocus,
> you all because of my impious union
> shall pay penalties to the Gygaean goddess Agrisca,
> for a thousand years' time nursing to old age
> your unwed daughters by arbitration of the lot.
> For them, strangers in a strange land, a woeful tomb,
> funeralless, will be washed away by the sandy wave,
> when burning the limbs with barren plants
> Hephaestus throws out to the sea the ashes
> of her who perished from Traron's peaks.
> But at night others equal to those who will die
> will come to the fields of the daughter of Sithon,
> searching along secret pathways
> until they run into the house of Ampheira,
> suppliants clasping in prayer the knees of Stheneia.
> And they will sweep and tidy the floor of the goddess
> and purify it with dew, having eluded the implacable
> fury of the townsfolk. For every man of Ilion
> will keep watch for the girls, holding in his hands
> a stone or black sword or hard bullslaying axe

or branch from Phalacra, eager to sate
a hand that thirsts for blood.
And with impunity will the people praise the killer,
inscribing in decree the disgraced race.
(Lycoph. *Alex.* 1141–73)[4]

In a scholion on the passage it is explained that a plague befell Locris because of Aias' rape of Cassandra and that the god gave the oracle that maidens were to be sent each year for 1,000 years.[5] But the maidens who were sent would be killed by the Trojans, who would come out to meet them with stones. But if any maidens should elude the Trojans and come to the temple of Athena, they would serve thereafter as priestesses of the goddess. Those who were killed were burned on the wood of fruitless, wild trees, their bones were thrown from the cliff Traron into the sea, and others were sent by the Locrians in their place. The scholiast concludes by saying that 'Callimachus also recounts this history', but it appears that this information, with the exception of the plague and the oracle, was merely extrapolated from the passage of Lycophron (Schol. Lycoph. *Alex.* 1141 = Callim. fr. 35 Pfeiffer).

Tzetzes in his note on the same verse adds that the plague befell Locris three years after the Locrians' arrival home from Troy and that the maidens were two in number and selected by lot. He writes further that the maidens would sweep and besprinkle the temple, but that they could not approach the goddess except at night. Their hair was shorn, and they each wore a single chiton and no shoes. The first two maidens sent were named Periboea and Cleopatra. Later, instead of maidens the Locrians sent one-year-old infants with their nurses. 'But when a thousand years had passed', concludes Tzetzes, 'after the Phocian War they stopped this sort of sacrifice, as says Timaeus of Sicily; Callimachus of Cyrene also recounts the history' (Tzetz. Schol. Lycoph. *Alex.* 1141; Callim. fr. 35 Pfeiffer; Timaeus, *FGrHist* 336 F 146b).

Tzetzes cites both Timaeus and Callimachus, and we know from a scholion on the *Iliad* that Callimachus treated the Locrian maidens in the first book of the *Aetia*: but here it is said only that Athena required the Locrians to send maidens chosen by lot to Ilion for a period of 1,000 years (Schol. *Il.* 13.66; Callim. fr. 35 Pfeiffer). Timaeus may have been a source of both Callimachus and Lycophron,[6] but it is not possible to determine how much, if any, of Timaeus' description is preserved in Tzetzes' scholion. For not only did Tzetzes follow the older scholia, but also he used 'Apollodorus'. The Vatican *Epitome* of Apollodorus (probably compiled by Tzetzes himself)[7] gives the same details in similar language: the plague, the dress of the maidens, Periboea and Cleopatra, the substitution of infants, and the cessation of the tribute after the Phocian War. But there is no authority, Callimachus, Timaeus, or other, cited in the *Epitome* (Apollod. *Epit.* 6.20–2).

Indeed it is likely that Tzetzes, just as he had Callimachus' name from the scholion on *Alexandra* 1141, merely borrowed the name of Timaeus from the brief scholion on *Alex.* 1155,[8] where it is stated, on the authority of Timaeus, that two maidens would serve as slaves in the temple of Athena; if one should die she was replaced by another; but maidens who died were not buried but burned on wild wood, and their ashes were thrown into the sea (Schol. Lycoph. *Alex.* 1155 = Timaeus, *FGrHist* 336 F 146a). In the scholion on *Alex.* 1159 it is said that (at some unspecified time) one of the maidens was killed on Traron. The Locrians buried her but stopped sending maidens, claiming that the period of time had elapsed. Dearth befell Locris, and the Locrians resumed sending the tribute; but now they sent one maiden instead of two, deeming this sufficient punishment. There is a lacuna in the text, but it appears that the oracle declared that the Locrians must again send two maidens, but now for an indeterminate period of time (Schol. Lycoph. *Alex.* 1159; cf. Tzetz. Schol. Lycoph. *Alex.* 1159).

Another important, if problematic, source is Aelian fragment 47, which Hercher reconstructed from several entries in the Suda. Apollo says to the Locrians that their suffering will not be relieved unless they send two maidens every year to Ilion as a poinē of Cassandra, 'until you should appease the goddess'. But those who were sent grew old and died in Troy when no replacements arrived. Women in Locris gave birth to deformed children, and when the oracle at Delphi was consulted, the god in his anger at first refused to receive the Locrians. But finally, when they persisted, they were told that the god's anger was due to their negligence concerning the maidens.[9] The Locrians then appealed to King Antigonus to judge which city was to furnish the tribute, and Antigonus ordained that the matter be determined by lot (Ael. fr. 47 Hercher). Thus Aelian, like the scholiast on *Alex.*

1159, described an interruption in the sending of the tribute and a second consultation of the oracle. But as the two accounts differ in the particulars, I am not sure that the two interruptions can be identified.

Two important – but conflicting – sources for the date of the tribute's institution are Polybius and Strabo. In an interesting passage Polybius contends that Aristotle's account of the founding of Locri in Italy is to be preferred to that of Timaeus. Polybius states that among the so-called 'one hundred houses' which constituted the Locrian nobility, the nobility descended through the maternal line.[10] He then adds:

> And these were the hundred houses which were selected by the Locrians before the colony set out, from whom the Locrians, in accordance with the oracle, were to appoint by lot the maidens who would be sent off to Ilion.
>
> (Polyb. 12.5.7)

Strabo, following Demetrius of Scepsis, wrote that the citizens of Ilion themselves maintained that their city was not totally destroyed by the Achaeans, nor was it ever completely abandoned: 'At any rate the Locrian maidens, beginning a little later, were sent every year.' But Demetrius argued that Homer knew nothing of the rape of Cassandra and contended that in fact the maidens were first sent to Troy when the Persians were already in power. Demetrius then provided further evidence to support his contention that Ilion was totally destroyed (Strabo 13.1.40–1).

Other references to the tribute are less informative. In Plutarch's *De sera numinis vindicta*, Timon quotes three lines of a Hellenistic poem when he remarks that 'it is not much time since the Locrians stopped sending to Troy the maidens,

> who cloakless with naked feet like slaves
> at dawn would sweep around Athena's altar
> without a veil, even if heavy old age should come,

because of the licentiousness of Aias' (Plut. *De sera* 12, 557D).[11] And Servius, explaining a reference to Aias' crime in the *Aeneid* (1.41: *unius ob noxam et furias Aiacis Oilei*), provides the story which lies behind the Vergilian allusion:

> For it is said that Minerva was so little content with the punishment of Ajax alone for the violation of Cassandra in

> her temple that later through an oracle she commanded that every year one noble girl from the kingdom of Ajax was to be sent to her at Ilium for sacrifice, and what is more, that she should be from the tribe from which Ajax had come, as Annaeus Placidus reports.
>
> (Serv. Verg. *Aen.* 1.41)

Finally, brief references by Iamblichus (*VP* 8.42) and Jerome (*Adv. Iovinian.* 1.41) add nothing essential to our information (or misinformation) concerning the tribute.

In addition to the literary evidence, in the late nineteenth century an inscription (*IG* IX² 1, 3, no. 706) was discovered in western Locris which refers to the Locrian maidens.[12] The inscription, which dates to the third century BC, is preserved to twenty-seven partial lines (on side A), but as the stone is broken at the right and bottom, much of the contents – despite some plausible conjectures by editors – is uncertain. The inscription records a compact between the East Locrians as a whole and the Aianteioi and the citizens of Naryx, whereby the latter two groups undertake the charge of the maidens in exchange for certain exemptions and privileges. Ilion is not mentioned in the preserved text, and very little information is given (or preserved) about the maidens themselves. In the first line it is stated that the Aianteioi and the city of the Narykaioi received the maidens from the Locrians, or undertook to do something to the maidens (the stone is broken here, and it is uncertain whether ἀνεδέξαντο τὰς κόρα[ς] was followed by an infinitive or not). Money for board (*tropheia*) will be awarded to the parents of each of the girls (line 9), and fifteen *mnai* are to be provided to each of the girls for their dress and food, until . . . (line 10: the stone, with characteristic perversity, breaks off here). Because of the girls the citizens of Naryx will be exempt from the keeping of horses and the provision of hostages in time of war (line 15). In line 23 there is a reference to legal judgement concerning the two girls (dual) and to the summoning of the two former maidens into court. At the end of the preserved inscription there is mention of the girl (acc. sing.) who was sent or (more likely) the girls (gen. plu.) who were sent (line 27). On the left side of the stele (B) are preserved the names of eighteen of the fifty men (cf. side A, line 26) who swore to the treaty.

HISTORY

Among the sources for the Locrian tribute there is so much that is contradictory and confused that I think it can safely be said that the ancient writers themselves were often ill informed about the ritual and its history. Hence any attempt to resolve all of the differences is bound to fail. Scholars have concentrated on the following questions: (1) when the tribute was instituted; (2) what happened in the latter half of the fourth century and in the third century, for which we have a reference to a cessation after the Phocian War, an appeal to a King Antigonus, and an inscription; and (3) whether there were always two maidens, whether they served for one year only or for life, or if the discrepancies in the sources should be attributed to changes in the custom.

According to several sources the Locrians began sending the tribute to Troy shortly after the end of the Trojan War,[13] but this early dating, implausible enough in itself, has been rendered impossible by the re-excavation of the site of Troy. Troy was reoccupied shortly after the destruction of the city identified with the Homeric Troy (VIIa), but this reoccupation (VIIb) was short-lived, and between the years *c.* 1000 and *c.* 700 there appears to have been no Troy to which one could send a tribute of maidens. In around 700 Troy was again settled, by a colony of Aeolic settlers.[14] Thus the tribute could not have begun much before the beginning of the seventh century BC at the earliest.

The date of the institution of the tribute was debated even in antiquity. Strabo followed Demetrius of Scepsis in arguing that Troy was totally destroyed by the Achaeans and in dating the tribute to the time of the Persian domination in Asia Minor, i.e. to after 547/6 BC. As evidence Demetrius cited Homer's silence about Aias' rape of Cassandra, but in fact in the very passage which Demetrius adduced in support of his case, Aias is said to be particularly hated by Athena (Strabo 13.1.40; *Od.* 4.502). It is clear that the poet of the *Odyssey* knew of some offence by Aias against Athena, but this may not have been the actual rape of Cassandra, for it has been pointed out that the story of the rape would be inconsistent with the tradition, known to the poet of *Odyssey* 11 (421–2), that Cassandra accompanied Agamemnon to Argos: had Cassandra been violated by Aias, she would not have been deemed an acceptable war-prize.[15] Thus the poet of the *Odyssey* may have known or preferred the alternate, 'milder' version, according to which Aias merely dragged Cassandra from the image of Athena.

It has been argued that the story of the rape was an invention of the Hellenistic period,[16] but there is some evidence which suggests that this may not have been the case. Beginning in the early sixth century there are numerous representations on vases and bronze reliefs of Aias' crime, and in these Cassandra is depicted naked or nearly naked. And even if this representation is strangely proleptic, Cassandra's nakedness which is highly exceptional in Archaic art – can only have been meant as a reference to the rape; at least there can be no doubt about Aias' intentions.[17] Also, in the Lesche of the Cnidians at Delphi there was a painting by Polygnotus which depicted Aias swearing an oath 'concerning the outrage against Cassandra' in the presence of Agamemnon and Menelaus (Paus. 10.26.3): it has been plausibly suggested that Aias was swearing that he did not rape Cassandra, which would seem to presuppose a version in which he had actually done so.[18] Finally, in a passage attributed to Libanius, the author states that the rape of Cassandra was told 'by the poets who spoke about the capture of Troy' (Lib. *Ref.* 2.1). Unless 'Libanius' is mistaken, this is a reference to Cyclic poetry; and Davreux has argued that it is a reference to the *Ilioupersis* of Arctinus,[19] although Proclus, in his brief summary of the poem, says only that Aias dragged Cassandra from the image of Athena, upsetting the statue in the process, and that when the Greeks tried to stone Aias he ran as a suppliant to the very goddess he had offended (Procl. *Chr.*, p. 108 Allen). The poet of the *Little Iliad* appears to have omitted the actual rape, and Stesichorus seems to have adopted a milder version.[20] Alcaeus possibly followed the tradition of the actual rape,[21] but in the fifth century as far as we know the tragedians were silent about the rape, again probably because the actual violation of Cassandra was inconsistent with the tradition that she fell as booty to Agamemnon.[22]

It seems probable that the story of the rape of Cassandra (or, if you will, the attempted rape), closely associated with the Locrian tribute, was widely known by the sixth century BC at the latest. But this does not necessarily help us to determine the date of the tribute's institution, for scholars have disagreed whether knowledge of the myth instigated the tribute, or if Locrian ritual inspired or influenced the formation of the myth. Thus we are left with the two conflicting statements from the second century BC.

In contrast to Demetrius of Scepsis, Polybius wrote that the maidens began to be sent before the colony of Locri was founded, i.e. before the close of the eighth century or the first quarter of the seventh. Whom are we to believe, Demetrius or Polybius? Demetrius found a modern champion in Wilamowitz, who argued that he may have had a reliable source for his information. As for Polybius' statement, in Wilamowitz's opinion this indicates only that the Italian Locrians believed in the high antiquity of the tribute.[23] On the other hand, some scholars have felt that Demetrius, in his zeal to prove that Troy had been destroyed and abandoned, dated the institution of the tribute as late as possible – and Xerxes' visit to the temple of Athena Ilias in 480 (Hdt. 7.43.1–2) will have been widely known.[24] In short, it is possible that neither historian had solid grounds for his contention; but the archaeological evidence, pointing to the colonization of Troy in around 700, casts further doubt on Polybius' early dating of the tribute.

If the Locrian tribute was instituted in the Archaic period, there is a notable silence until the 350s BC, when Aineias speaks of the tribute in the present tense, but implying that it has had a long history (Aen. Tact. 31.24). Very soon thereafter the tribute was discontinued: according to Apollod. *Epit.* 6.22 and Tzetz. Schol. Lycoph. *Alex.* 1141, it was stopped following the Phocian War, which ended in 347/6. It is also said that this happened 1,000 years after the institution of the tribute, but no known ancient date for the Fall of Troy can be reconciled with this statement, for these dates, with one negligible exception, all fall in the thirteenth or twelfth century BC.[25] Indeed one might be tempted to follow Leaf and emend μετὰ τὸν Φωκικὸν πόλεμον (Apollod. *Epit.* 6.22; Tzetz. Schol. Lycoph. *Alex.* 1141) to μετὰ τὸν Τρωϊκὸν πόλεμον (and to read the phrase with the preceding genitive absolute – 'when a thousand years had passed after the Trojan War' – rather than with the main verb of the sentence), did not the principle of *lectio difficilior* plead strongly for Φωκικόν.[26] Besides, there is some probability that the damages incurred in the Sacred War – including the destruction of Aias' hometown Naryx in 352 – would have occasioned an interruption in the sending of the tribute.[27]

But as we know from the inscription that the tribute was again being sent in the third century, there is a further difficulty: in the *Epitome* and Tzetzes' scholion it is stated clearly that the Locrians *stopped* sending the maidens after the Phocian War. We might suppose that the source for this information wrote in the interval between the discontinuance and renewal of the tribute,[28] but again we are confronted with the problem that any claim by the Locrians in the 340s that the tribute had now lasted 1,000 years would have been unacceptable. What I suspect has happened, rather, is that two pieces of reliable information were conflated by 'Apollodorus' or his source: an *interruption* after the Phocian War and a *cessation* after it had finally been reckoned that 1,000 years (a figure found in several other sources) had passed.[29] At some point these two distinct events became confused in the tradition, but it is possible that only after the interruption in the fourth century was it ordained that the tribute would have to be resumed until a period of 1,000 years had elapsed since the end of the Trojan War.

Two sources speak of an interruption and renewal of the tribute. According to the Schol. Lycoph. *Alex.* 1159, the Locrians stopped sending the tribute after a maiden was killed on Traron, but this story may have been invented in order to make sense of the obscure and probably corrupt verses in which Lycophron refers to 'her who perished from Traron's peaks' (*Alex.* 1157–9). The other source is Aelian fr. 47, which must be regarded with caution, as it was reconstructed from seven glosses in the Suda: there are gaps in the account, and the attribution of some of the individual fragments to Aelian is uncertain.[30] According to the fragment, at some point the maidens grew old and died at Troy when no replacements arrived. Monstrous births in Locris were the consequence, the oracle was consulted, and finally the decision over which city was to furnish the maidens was placed before a King Antigonus. Despite the mythological colouring, it is possible that this interruption should be identified with the discontinuation after the Phocian War; at least with the mention of Antigonus we appear to be securely in the historical period. But unfortunately it is uncertain which of the three Antigoni is meant: Monophthalmus (who ruled in Asia, 306–301 BC), Gonatas (Macedonian king, 276–239), or Doson (Macedonian king, 227–221). Doson is usually considered too late, but scholarly opinion has been divided between Monophthalmus and Gonatas.[31]

The choice from among the three Antigoni has usually been made in connection with the inscription, but it is very questionable whether the renewal of the tribute upon the decision of

Antigonus and the treaty recorded in the inscription can be referred to one and the same event, although this has often been tacitly assumed. In the earlier period, according to Polybius (12.5.7), the maidens were chosen by lot from among the 'one hundred houses', and Lycophron seems to have referred to this earlier period when he listed several Locrian cities which must provide the maidens (*Alex.* 1146–50). But according to Aelian, after the interruption the Locrians set the matter before King Antigonus, asking which city (singular) should send (πέμπειν: present infinitive) the tribute; and Antigonus decreed that this should be determined (διακριθῆναι: aorist) by lot. The language of the passage can only mean that a single city, chosen by lottery on a single occasion, will henceforth be responsible for supplying the maidens each year.

The inscription, on the other hand, records the assumption of the tribute by the Aianteioi from all of the East Locrians. If this treaty followed upon the decision of Antigonus, then it is remarkable that of all the towns in East Locris the lot fell to Naryx and Aias' reputed descendants. Remarkable, and hardly probable. Furthermore, in the preserved inscription there is no mention of a lottery, nor of a King Antigonus: to all appearances the charge of the maidens was assumed by the Aianteioi and the Narykaioi upon an agreement between these parties and the East Locrians as a whole, without the drawing of lots and without any appeal to a Hellenistic monarch. But if the decree of Antigonus and the compact in the inscription did not occur at the same time, then which was earlier? If Antigonus decreed that one city was to be responsible for the tribute, then it does not appear that the inscription could postdate the decree, for the Aianteioi assumed charge of the tribute from all of the East Locrians. On the other hand, if Antigonus' decision postdated the inscription, then we must posit a second interruption, when the Aianteioi in their turn stopped sending the maidens. And for this there is no evidence.

We seem to have reached something of a cul-de-sac. Perhaps the simplest solution is to read the text of Aelian less strictly, or rather to suppose that he (or the compilers of the Suda) was mistaken.[32] Possibly Antigonus actually decreed that each year a city from East Locris should be chosen by lot to provide the maidens, although this would not appear to mark any change from the method of selecting the maidens in the earlier period.[33] The inscription was dated by Wilhelm to 275–240 BC on the basis of letter style, but others, on historical grounds, have preferred a date before 272.[34] If we accept this latter dating and if the decree of Antigonus did in fact predate the inscription, then the first of the Antigoni, Monophthalmus, is our only choice. The identification is also favoured by the fact that the Troad lay within the kingdom of Monophthalmus at the close of the fourth century.[35]

When the tribute ended for good is again uncertain. Plutarch wrote that 'not much time' had passed from when the Locrians had stopped sending the maidens to Troy (*De sera* 12, 557D). Some scholars have thought that Plutarch simply repeated a statement which he found in his source for the three hexameters, but others have objected that this means giving too little credit to Plutarch.[36] And I do not think we need give very much weight to the words οὐ πολὺς χρόνος: as Plutarch was writing of the period between the Trojan War and his own day, 'not much time' could certainly refer even to several centuries. And if there is any validity to the tradition that the tribute lasted for 1,000 years, then it is likely that it ceased in the third or second century, a millennium after one of the traditional dates for the Fall of Troy, the latest of which is that of Ephorus, 1136/5 BC.[37] The tribute seems to have ended before the time of Demetrius of Scepsis (early second century BC), although Strabo's use of the imperfect tense (13.1.40: ἐπέμποντο) is not in itself decisive.

Two other problems – how many maidens were sent each time and for how long a period they served in the temple – remain to be considered. Servius, on the authority of an unknown Annaeus Placidus, wrote that one maiden was sent every year (Serv. Verg. *Aen.* 1.41), and the scholiast on Lycoph. *Alex.* 1159 spoke of a *period* when the Locrians sent only one. It is possible that at some time only one maiden was sent, but it seems more likely that the scholiast on Lycophron was attempting to reconcile a mistaken tradition, followed by Annaeus Placidus, with the prevailing tradition, confirmed by the duals of the inscription, that the tribute consisted of two maidens.[38] A more important question concerns the duration of the maidens' service. Several sources say that the tribute was sent every year, while others suggest that the maidens remained in Troy for life.[39] It is not likely that both situations obtained simultaneously, for if the Locrians sent two maidens every year and if they all remained in Troy till their death, then this would result in an improbably large number of servants in Athena's temple.[40] Besides, Aelian mentions substitutes for the maidens, and the inscription (our most trustworthy source) refers to 'the former maidens' (see p. 171). Scholars therefore have generally thought that the dual tradition reflects a change in the custom: in the early period the maidens would serve for life (a replacement being sent only upon the death of a maiden), but later, perhaps after the interruption in the fourth century, the service was reduced to a service of a year's time.[41] But the most attractive solution is the recent proposal of Graf, that the tribute was always yearly and that the tradition of service until death is not historical but mythical.[42]

To summarize: the Locrian tribute was instituted at some point in the late seventh or the sixth century, and as far as we know continued without interruption into the fourth century BC. After the Phocian War it was discontinued, and this interruption is perhaps to be identified with the interruption described by Aelian. If so, nearly half a century passed before the Locrians, having consulted the Delphic oracle, appealed to Antigonus Monophthalmus to determine which city should send the tribute: the King decreed that this should be determined by lot, perhaps a yearly lottery (although this is not what is said in the preserved text of Aelian). Soon after, the Locrians came to an agreement with the Aianteioi and Naryx, whereby this family and their city would henceforth be responsible for providing the maidens. The tribute ended only when it was reckoned that it had lasted for 1,000 years, probably in the late third or the second century BC; but it may have been in the late fourth century that the Delphic oracle first placed this term on the duration of the tribute. It is likely that the tribute always consisted of two maidens, who remained in Troy for one year. References to a lifelong service probably belong to the realm of myth, not history.

INTERPRETATION

The Locrian maiden tribute has sometimes been viewed as a human sacrifice in mitigated form,[43] but the interpretation has little to recommend itself. Among the ancient sources, Servius wrote that one maiden was sent each year to Troy *ad sacrificium*, but he does not seem to have had a very clear understanding of the nature of the ritual (Serv. Verg. *Aen*. 1.41); and Tzetzes' characterization of the tribute as a *thusia* is of no significance.[44] Also, the pursuit of the maidens by the male citizens of Troy –

whether a sham ritual or in grim earnest – bears little resemblance to sacrificial ritual. In fact, the Trojans' attempt to prevent the maidens from entering Athena's sanctuary is difficult to explain if the ritual represents a survival of an earlier human sacrifice, for it is precisely to this sanctuary that we should expect the maidens to be led.[45]

It also seems improbable that the maidens were ever killed. For if 'every man jack of Ilion' had vigilantly awaited the arrival of the maidens armed with stones, axes, and swords (Lycoph. *Alex.* 1167–71), then it is difficult to believe that very many maidens, if any, would have eluded the Trojans and succeeded in reaching the safety of the temple from the coast, especially as Ilion was only a very small settlement at this time.[46] Yet our earliest source implies that they always, or almost always, did so, despite the best efforts of the Trojans (Aen. Tact. 31.24). And our most reliable source, the compact recorded in the inscription, refers to the two former maidens and the girls who were sent, and it provides for the maidens' clothing and food: there is not the slightest indication that the girls are being sent off to their death.[47] In this connection scholars have aptly compared the ritual performed during the Agrionia at Orchomenos, where the priest of Dionysus pursued a woman with a drawn sword: if his intention had really been to slay the women, they would not have managed year after year to escape his sword (see pp. 130–3). Similarly, the ritual pursuit of the Locrian maidens seems to have been designedly ineffective, and those maidens who were killed and burned on the wood of fruitless trees were probably only creatures of myth.[48]

Schwenn also disputed the interpretation of the tribute as a mitigated form of human sacrifice, but his own explanation – that the maidens were originally pharmakoi – is no more satisfactory.[49] There are a few superficial similarities: the tribute was yearly, the maidens were two in number (like the pharmakoi in Athens), and they were stoned by the populace. A fourth similarity is the alleged manner of burning the maidens' corpses, but as I argued above, Tzetzes' contention that the pharmakoi were burned on the wood of barren trees does not seem to have been based upon fact (see pp. 141–9). And there are significant dissimilarities as well: there is no good evidence that pharmakoi were ever female,[50] much less of aristocratic family. Also, Schwenn's novelistic reconstruction of the historical development of the tribute is far from convincing. According to Schwenn the Locrians had a custom of expelling two female pharmakoi each year. When the Locrians were required to provide temple servants at Troy, they sent these same pharmakoi, killing, as it were, two birds with one stone. But the Trojans, when they realized that they were receiving impure temple servants from the Locrians, attempted to keep the maidens from entering Athena's temple or confined them to that same temple, cutting them off a second time from the community. But why pharmakoi should be confined in a temple, the religious centre of the community and a place from which every sort of impurity was forbidden,[51] Schwenn did not explain, nor why the Locrians themselves would welcome these pharmakoi back into the community when their service was completed.

Still less probable is the interpretation of A. Reinach, that the rite was a re-enactment of a sacred marriage (*hieros gamos*) between the gods Aias and Cassandra, and I think it will suffice to quote Farnell, who wrote of this interpretation that 'any unprejudiced observer who marked the behaviour and the treatment of the Locrian maidens on their landing might exclaim, like Benedict, "this looks not like a nuptial"'.[52] Reinach also maintained that in the early period the maidens were sacrificed, and that later (after the original meaning of the ritual – i.e. sacred marriage – had been forgotten) they served as pharmakoi, thus uniting three implausible interpretations of the tribute into one.[53]

Perhaps the simplest solution is to take the Locrian tribute at face value – that it served to atone for the sacrilege of Aias in Athena's temple. Few would believe with Leaf and Farnell in an actual offence committed by Locrians during the Trojan War,[54] but still, when Troy had been resettled and when the myth of the sacrilege had become widely known, it is possible that the oracle would demand retribution of the Locrians for Aias' legendary crime. In any case, it is apparent that the tribute owed its continuance into Hellenistic times to a belief that it was still necessary to expiate the sin of Aias the Locrian.

But the simplest solution is not always the best solution; and, as Graf has argued, any interpretation of the maiden tribute must take into account all of the elements of the custom. The tribute was of young virgins; they were pursued by the male populace of Troy, and – at least in myth – they were sometimes killed; they remained secluded in Athena's temple for a year, shoeless, with shorn hair, each wearing a single garment. Graf points out that these features are remarkably similar to features common to various *rites de passage*. In ancient Greece mourners would cut their hair or wear it loose; they often went barefoot and wore a special, dark garment. Hair cutting was also a common feature of the passage of young men and women into adulthood, and of marriage rites. In certain mystery cults the participants went barefoot, as did the Spartan ephebes. And Cretan youths wore only a single garment. In these and other cases collected by Graf, the cutting of hair (or the wearing of it loose), the wearing of a special garment, and the removal of shoes stand in opposition to normal practice and serve to mark off certain people – mourners, initiates into mystery cults, children and adolescents, brides and grooms – from the rest of society, placing them in a temporary condition of 'marginality'. And if the Locrian tribute evolved from a 'rite of passage', the fact that the participants were young virgins suggests that the original ritual was a puberty or prenuptial initiation rite.[55]

In fact, understood thus, the Locrian tribute – which at first sight appeared to be unique in ancient Greek religion – begins to betray numerous similarities with other rituals. At Athens two maidens of noble family, known as Arrhephoroi, would spend a period of time on the Acropolis, separated from their families and from society. At Brauron young girls lived apart from society, performing ritual dances barefoot, with their hair loose and either naked or wearing a short chiton. And at Corinth children, dressed in black and with hair shorn, were confined in the temple of Hera Akraia, ostensibly in atonement for the murder of Medea's children. These customs have all been interpreted as initiation rites in origin.[56] The maiden tribute also resembles a ritual performed in the cult of Artemis Triklaria at Patrae, discussed in a previous chapter: in myth, the first priestess of Artemis had intercourse with her lover in the temple, and Artemis demanded annual human sacrifices to atone for the sacrilege (pp. 86–8). For the Locrian tribute there is no story of an original human sacrifice (this appears only in the mythology of modern scholarship), but the myth that the maidens were at one time killed and the ritual pursuit by armed Trojans will have functioned similarly, reinforcing the symbolism of death which figures prominently in many rites of initiation.[57]

If Graf's interpretation is correct, then the Locrian initiation rite will have existed before the tribute was ever sent to Troy, and the maidens will have been confined in a temple in Locris, possibly the temple of Athena Ilias at Physkos. The ritual may also have contributed to the formation of a cult myth of the desecration of Athena's temple by Aias, only later connected with Cassandra and Troy. Indeed, there is reason to believe that Athena's epithet 'Ilias' did not derive from the town of Ilion but rather is connected with (O)ileus, the name of the father of Locrian Aias.[58] At some point Athena Ilias will have been identified with the patron goddess of Troy, and the Locrian cult myth will have found its way into the Trojan Cycle. And when the myth had become widely known, the Delphic oracle will have demanded that the Locrians atone for the crime of their ancestor by sending the maiden tribute. But the essential features of the ritual will have already been established in the initiation rites of the Locrians.

Admittedly this is a highly speculative reconstruction of the early history of the ritual, but it is not implausible. The tribute could only have been instituted after the colonization of Troy, but its character may well have been determined by earlier Locrian ritual: several features point to an origin in rites of initiation. And when it was required of the Locrians that they send a tribute to Troy, they would have acquiesced more readily if a ritual involving the service of noble maidens already existed in Locris: it should not have been difficult to convince them that the maidens belonged rather in Athena's temple in Ilion. As time passed it began to be believed that the maidens had first been sent shortly after the Fall of Troy; or possibly the tribute, even at the time of its institution, was regarded as a renewal.

CONCLUSION

The discovery of the 'maiden inscription' has raised more questions than it has answered and has inspired some remarkable interpretations. C. Robert, for example, argued that the inscription recorded a compact according to which maidens would be sent, not to Troy, but to West Locris to serve in the temple of Athena Ilias at Physkos.[59] It is true that there is no mention of Ilion in the preserved inscription; and it is possible that the stele was set up in the temple at Physkos.[60] But Robert's interpretation does not accord at all well with the many privileges bestowed upon the Aianteioi and the citizens of Naryx. And although Annaeus Placidus may not always have been possessed of the best information, the detail that the maidens came from 'the tribe from which Ajax had come' (Serv. Verg. *Aen.* 1.41: *de ea tribu de qua Aiax fuerat*) certainly seems to derive from knowledge of the treaty recorded in the inscription.[61] And Annaeus says that the maidens were sent to Troy. Also, Robert failed to suggest any good reason why Naryx and the Aianteioi should be asked to provide an imitation of the real tribute, which in Robert's opinion continued to be sent into the second century BC.

Still less tenable is the suggestion of Leaf that the inscription records the *end* of the tribute.[62] In Leaf's view the Aianteioi agreed to pay for the maintenance of all the former maidens still living, while the two maidens referred to in the inscription were the final pair of maidens, who still resided in Troy. But I can find nothing in the text of the inscription, as obscure as much of it is, which supports this interpretation (and certainly nothing to suggest that before the treaty the Aianteioi had been 'treated as the most despicable outcasts and pariahs, excommunicated and banned').[63] And once again, the interpretation would seem to be contradicted by the testimony of Annaeus Placidus.

But perhaps the strangest interpretation is the more recent proposal of Fontenrose. Like Robert, Fontenrose felt that the maidens of the inscription were to serve in the temple of Athena Ilias at Physkos. But he argued further that there never was a tribute sent to Troy and that the inscription records the institution of a tribute sent to Physkos in *c.* 270 BC. Fontenrose was thus obliged not only to reject the reference to the tribute in Aineias' *Poliorcetica* as an interpolation, but also to discount all of the testimony for the antiquity of the ritual.[64] Could poets and historians of the third and second centuries BC date the origin of the tribute to shortly after the Trojan War, to before the foundation of Locri in Italy, or to the period of Persian domination, if it had actually been instituted only in 270? According to Fontenrose, certain Locrians would play the part of 'Trojans' at Physkos and pursue the maidens in a ritual drama, whereupon 'the report of the dramatized acts was taken by men in distant parts of Greece, who never saw the ritual, to be an account of actual events'. But Fontenrose overlooked the fact that one of these 'men in distant parts of Greece' was Demetrius, who was born in the Troad and who apparently spoke about the tribute with the Trojans themselves.[65] Is it possible that Demetrius and the citizens of Troy could have been so mistaken about a ritual that lived in recent memory (if not still being enacted in their day), in fact so mistaken as to believe that the ritual had been performed in their own city, when it had not been? Fontenrose rightly pointed to the confusion in the testimony, to the seemingly mythical nature of much of it, and to the sudden interest taken in the tribute by writers of the early third century (Timaeus, Callimachus, Lycophron). But his solution was extreme. The literary interest in the tribute in the first half of the third century I would attribute to the fame which must have arisen from the role played by King Antigonus (whether Monophthalmus or Gonatas) in the affair and from the circumstances which eventually led to the compact recorded on the stele. But the concentration of literary references in the third century is not sufficient reason to challenge the authenticity of the passage in the fourth-century work of Aineias.

I have included this short chapter on the Locrian tribute, not only because the ritual has frequently been viewed as a survival of earlier human sacrifices (or of a pharmakos rite), but also because the evidence for the tribute offers a chastening lesson to the student of ancient Greek religion. It is not often that we have such an abundance of testimony for a single Greek ritual, including a lengthy, if imperfectly preserved, inscription. And yet in so many respects we remain in the dark about the tribute and its history. Clearly the ancient sources were often poorly informed themselves, and reliable and unreliable pieces of information lie side by side in the texts. The many difficulties presented by this body of incomplete and conflicting testimony have in turn given rise to a large body of modern scholarship, which rivals – or surpasses – the ancient literature in its lack of concord. The study of the ancient and modern literature on the tribute should serve as a reminder of how much there is that we still do not know about ancient Greek society and its religious institutions.

7

Conclusion

My opinion of the value of most of the evidence, literary and archaeological, for the ritual killing of human victims in ancient Greece should now be quite clear. In the majority of cases, I have expressed scepticism. But I also concluded the preceding chapter on a pessimistic note: given the fragmentary and uncertain nature of the evidence, how much can we now recapture of what was actually done in ancient religious ritual? In this chapter I shall briefly explore some of the implications of this study and discuss what roles human sacrifice may have played in the thought of the Greeks – for, whatever opinion we may form about the extent of the practice in actuality, clearly many of the ancients themselves believed that human sacrifices had been performed on Greek soil in the past, and clearly human sacrifice enjoyed a thriving existence *as an idea* throughout antiquity.

It should be emphasized that in recent years several scholars have expressed similar scepticism, in general or in specific cases: Brelich, Burkert, Graf, and Henrichs, to name some of the most prominent. And that pharmakoi were not killed is becoming the *communis opinio*.[1] Thus, if my evaluation of the evidence is wide of the mark, I am in good company. But it also should be stressed that every alleged case of ritual murder discussed here has at one time or another been accepted as factual, and in the past the prevailing view among historians of Greek religion was that human sacrifice was a common practice in an early (but usually undefined) period in Greek history, which only gradually died out as the culture emerged from its primitive past to the enlightened and refined religion of the Classical Age.[2] In fact, even when no direct ancient testimony exists scholars have often seen 'survivals' and 'memories' of early human sacrifices in some of the more violent myths and rituals of the Greeks, thus creating new aetiological myths of their own.[3] And even now there is hardly scholarly consensus: 'modern myths' of human sacrifice are still sometimes revived;[4] scholars continue to find references to slain pharmakoi in the tattered fragments of Hipponax (pp. 145–8); claims of human sacrifice in Greek literature (including some of the most dubious) still find adherents;[5] and at the very time that the written evidence is being viewed with increasing scepticism by religious historians, new human sacrifices come to light beneath the archaeologist's spade.

Still, some readers may be surprised that one could doubt that the Greeks performed ritual killings of human beings in the face of so much ancient testimony that they did so. But certainly classicists (even if unfamiliar with much of the material studied here) will not be surprised, for they will be aware of how much fanciful and unhistorical material is blithely reported by ancient writers of history and biography. And there is no reason why reports of religious practices should be considered *a priori* more reliable than, for example, Diogenes' lives of the philosophers or much of Diodorus' history – or, for that matter, much of Herodotus'. We smile indulgently when the Father of History asserts that in India the ants are bigger than foxes (Hdt. 3.102.2) and that Indian men have black semen (3.101.2). Should we be any more willing to believe when in this same passage he relates that the Padaei sacrifice and consume their elderly (3.99.2)? Or even when, closer to home, he describes human sacrifices performed at Alos in Thessaly (7.197: pp. 92–6)? I hardly mean to suggest that everything we read in Herodotus and other Greek writers is untrue, but it has long been the historian's task to separate the wheat from the chaff. It should be the religious historian's task also.

But was there not fire where there is so much smoke? How is it possible that so many of the Greeks believed that their own ancestors (or in some cases their contemporaries) practised human sacrifice, if they did not? And how could the very idea of human sacrifice have arisen, without any basis in actual practices? Is it credible that human sacrifice was a purely imaginative creation, existing from the beginning solely on the level of myth? These are certainly valid questions; but if there are to be any satisfactory answers they probably will be related to the practice of animal sacrifice. It is quite unlikely that myths of human sacrifice would have arisen and endured without the existence of a custom of sacrificing animals. Indeed, they may have arisen because of it.

Human sacrifice and animal sacrifice are often closely associated in our sources: animals slaughtered in Greek cult are said to have replaced earlier human victims (pp. 82–6 and 125–7); Empedocles sees animal sacrifice as nothing less than human sacrifice, with fathers unwittingly slaying sons and sons their fathers (fr. 137 Diels-Kranz); and Theophrastus derives the custom of blood sacrifice from the cannibalistic human sacrifices of our early ancestors (fr. 13 Pötscher: pp. 116–17). Animal sacrifice was the central act of Greek cult, and Meuli demonstrated that several puzzling elements of sacrificial ritual reflect an uneasiness and anxiety over the taking of the animal's life (pp. 6–7). Possibly myths of human sacrifice also originated in the ambiguous emotions aroused by sacrificial killing: by viewing their victims as substitutes for human beings, and the slaughter as a mitigated form of a far more terrible act, the worshippers both acknowledged the seriousness of the killing and reduced their responsibility for the animal's death. And as initiation rituals were often accompanied by animal sacrifices,[6] it is not surprising to find myths of human sacrifice (where the identity of the initiate and sacrificial victim is suggested) attached to these also. But opponents of blood sacrifice like Empedocles and Theophrastus can readily turn these conceptions back against practitioners of the traditional religion.

But for the historical Greeks human sacrifice was largely a thing of the remote past. Plato and Theophrastus view existing human sacrifices as survivals;[7] and the custom is particularly associated with non-Greeks, an unholy and unlawful practice explicitly contrasted by the author of the *Minos* with Hellenic customs, although he knows two exceptions from Greece.[8] But most human sacrifices have long been abolished by various civilizers, divine and human: Lycurgus at Sparta (p. 79), Dionysus at Potniae (p. 82), Eurypylus at Patrae (p. 87), and Diphilus in Cyprus (p. 126). Gods and heroes have put an end to the practice among non-Greeks also: the descendants of Orestes upon arrival in Tenedos (p. 134); Aphrodite, who turns the Cypriot Cerastae into bulls for sacrificing humans to Zeus (Ov. *Met.* 10.219–37); and Heracles, who, led to the altar as a victim by the Egyptian king Bousiris, kills Bousiris and his followers, thus putting an end to the savage custom. The scene was popular with vase painters, who often depict the archetypal meat-eater and sacrificer Heracles slaying Bousiris over the altar, thus turning the tables on the Egyptian king and performing a sort of human sacrifice to end all human sacrifices, which symbolizes the triumph of Hellenic culture and sacrificial custom over the barbarian.[9]

In these respects the evidence for human sacrifice closely resembles the ancient testimony for the practice of cannibalism, where we find the same distancing on the temporal and spatial planes.[10] Cannibalism is often attributed to contemporary, barbarian peoples living on the margin of the known world, e.g. the Androphagi ('Maneaters'), who lead a nomadic and lawless existence in the region beyond Scythia (Hdt. 4.106), a mythic tribe reminiscent of Homer's Cyclopes, who know no laws and relish human flesh (*Od.* 9.106–15). Several other examples may be found in Herodotus and later writers, who explicitly or implicitly contrast the uncivilized cultures with their own.[11] Cannibalism was also thought to have been a practice of humanity as a whole at an early stage in its history. 'There was a time when mortals took flesh-eating sustenance from one another,/ and the stronger would feast on the weaker', runs an Orphic fragment quoted by Sextus Empiricus (*Math.* 2.31 = fr. 292 Kern). The same conception is expressed by several other writers, particularly in 'Orphic' and vegetarian contexts.[12] And as with human sacrifice, the abolition of cannibalism is attributed to various divinities and bringers of culture: Zeus, who brings to an end the cannibalistic reign of Kronos; the nymphs called 'Melissai' (Bees); Isis and Osiris; (probably) Orpheus; and (in a comic passage) the cook who first discovers the superiority of roasted animal flesh. Others simply attribute the end of the custom to the passage of time and the progress of the species.[13]

Of course for the Greeks meat-eating was inherently sacrificial, and anthropophagy and (consumed) human sacrifice amount to much the same thing, as can be seen from Theophrastus' theory of the origin of sacrifice, and from a passage of the *Laws*, where Plato writes that 'the practice of human beings sacrificing one another we see still even now remaining among many peoples'; as Plato goes on to discuss peoples who refrain from meat altogether, it is clear that τὸ θύειν ἀνθρώπους ἀλλήλους is a reference to consumed human sacrifices (*Leg.* 6, 782C). It should also be clear that the modern conception of human sacrifice as a primitive practice gradually replaced by more humane customs (such as animal sacrifices) is not really modern at all, but was modelled on views held by the ancients themselves. But few people if any would believe that Greek writings on cannibalism reflect actual conditions of prehistory, or the actual practices of non-Greek peoples. Rather, these passages demonstrate that a custom may indeed exist, removed to a distant past or the spatially distant present, in the world of the imagination alone. Myths of human sacrifice and cannibalism served to answer the needs of the culture which invented them, differentiating the Greeks and their sacrificial and alimentary customs both from the peoples around them and from an imagined past, and having a conceptual value quite independent of the existence of the customs in reality.

But if myths of human sacrifice were originally linked to animal sacrifice and specific cult practices, by the seventh century they had begun to enjoy a new existence, apart from cult, in poetry. The attempted sacrifice and rescue of Iphigeneia (probably a cult myth in origin: pp. 83–5) and the sacrifice of Polyxena (probably inspired by the Iphigeneia legend: p. 62) were told in the Epic Cycle. Presumably a few other stories of human sacrifice connected with the Trojan War and its aftermath (pp. 76–7), as perhaps some myths of the willing self-sacrifice of noble young women and men in time of war (pp. 73–6), also appeared in early epic; and the myth of Lycaon (originally a cult myth also) goes back at least to the sixth century (p. 101). But I do not think it will be inaccurate to say that human sacrifice flourished nowhere in ancient Greece so much as in Athens, upon the tragic stage. In the *Oresteia*, Aeschylus, for obvious dramatic reasons, omits the rescue of Iphigeneia by Artemis; in addition, the murders of Agamemnon, Cassandra, and Clytemnestra are represented as sacrifices, and sacrificial language and imagery pervade the trilogy.[14] Aeschylus also wrote an *Iphigeneia* and several plays on Dionysian subjects, which possibly involved human sacrifice or (like Euripides' *Bacchae*) sacrificial metaphor.[15] If we were to judge solely from his extant plays, the theme of human sacrifice would not seem to have had much appeal for Sophocles; but among his lost tragedies we find two Athamas plays, an *Iphigeneia*, a *Polyxena*, and three tragedies (apparently) on the Thyestes story; and even in the extant tragedies there is occasional sacrificial imagery.[16] But it was Euripides above all who realized the dramatic possibilities of human sacrifice: in the *Electra*, he follows

Aeschylus in the use of sacrificial metaphor, colouring the murders of Clytemnestra and Aegisthus with the language of sacrifice; and sacrificial imagery is found sporadically in many other plays.[17] In several dramas human sacrifice plays a prominent or central role: the two Iphigeneia plays, the *Heracleidae* (Macaria), the *Phoenician Women* (Menoeceus), and the *Trojan Women* and *Hecuba* (Polyxena); and, of plays extant only in fragments, the *Erechtheus* (fr. 39–65 Austin), *Phrixus* (fr. 819–38 Nauck), and *Cretans*, where Pasiphae denounces Minos as a murderous, cannibalistic sacrificer of humans (fr. 82.36–9 Austin).

Beginning in the fourth century, numerous writers collect obscure local myths and cult practices, and it is to such collections that most of our 'historical' human sacrifices, accounts of pharmakos rituals, and information about the Locrian maidens can be traced. New stories of human sacrifice begin to appear in historical writings.[18] And soon after, human sacrifice becomes a favourite theme of the novelists.[19] In Achilles Tatius (3.15–22) there is a pretended sacrifice of Leucippe, staged by friends of Cleitophon (who is not in on the ruse and looks on in horror) in order to rescue the heroine from her captors; in the *Ephesiaca* of Xenophon (2.13) outlaws attempt to sacrifice Anthia to Ares, but at the last minute she is rescued by policemen; in the *Aethiopica* of Heliodorus (10.4–41) Charicleia and Theogenes are on the point of being sacrificed to the Sun and Moon when Charicleia reveals her identity as the King's daughter, and the novel ends with the joyous abolition of human sacrifice among the Aethiopians. And in a fragment of the *Phoenicica* of Lollianus, a boy is slain in a gruesome oath sacrifice performed by bandits, who drink his blood; but possibly this sacrifice was a *Sheintod* also, staged by allies of the victim, as in Achilles Tatius.[20]

This rapid and selective survey of human sacrifice in literature is only indirectly relevant to our study of the practice in Greek cult and history. Certainly few would claim that those who saw the tragedies of Euripides performed in Athens (and who were moved by the nobility of Iphigeneia, Polyxena, and Macaria, or shuddered at the 'sacrificial' deaths of Clytemnestra, Pentheus, and the children of Medea) ever themselves witnessed or participated in a human sacrifice. Human sacrifice is potent dramatic material, perhaps far more potent to the fifth-century Athenians than to us, for sacrifice – animal sacrifice – was very much a part of their religious lives. Indeed Burkert has seen a direct connection between animal sacrifice and the prominence of sacrificial themes and imagery in Classical tragedy, for he traces the tragic genre to performances accompanying goat sacrifices in the cult of Dionysus.[21] Human sacrifice will again be put to good use by the novelists, but when their heroes and heroines are threatened with gruesome sacrificial deaths at the hands of pirates and outlaws, the scenes (though perhaps reflecting dimly initiatory origins) are exploited for obvious melodramatic effects, which do not depend upon the historical accuracy of the descriptions of ritual.[22]

If the practice of human sacrifice gradually decreased and died out under the salutary influence of new religious beliefs and a higher moral sense, over the centuries the evidence for it was gradually accumulating: no human sacrifices in the Homeric poems (if the slaughter of the Trojan captives in the *Iliad* may be excepted), a few then in other early epic; in the fifth century, a sudden burgeoning of human sacrifices on the tragic stage; then, beginning in the fourth, the creation of new human sacrifices by historical writers and the scholarly collection of human sacrifices in local cults – or cult myths – from throughout Greece; and finally, human sacrifice (now little more than the ancient equivalent of tying the heroine to the railroad tracks)[23] as a convenient narrative device in the novel. If anything, the extant literature gives an impression of an increase in human sacrifices in Classical and Hellenistic times; and by the time Plutarch, Pausanias, Clement, Porphyry, and various scholiasts and lexicographers can preserve the testimony for posterity, it is little wonder that the belief that the 'ancients' practised human sacrifice is now firmly entrenched, and that non-fatal (if not quite harmless) scapegoat rituals can now be readily misconstrued. But for these later writers the 'ancients' are as far removed as the Age of Heroes was for the Classical Greeks, and again a distant and largely imaginary past can serve as a backdrop against which present customs and concepts (both pagan and Christian) may be meaningfully contrasted.

But if the gradual accumulation of literary testimony is deceptive, it remains possible that human sacrifice was a practice of the prehistoric Greeks, which died out and was reborn (for various reasons) in the myths and literature of historical times. Indeed, even for the historical period, when (I have argued) our sources are most often unreliable and poorly informed, it is possible that human sacrifices were performed without word ever reaching the study of a Hellenistic scholar, and thereby reaching us: for every false report of human sacrifice, might there not have been an actual human sacrifice which went unrecorded? Possibly; but at this point we must put the ball back in the court of the archaeologists: if human sacrifice was ever an accepted practice anywhere in ancient Greece, then only archaeology can provide us with concrete evidence to identify the periods and places. But I do not think archaeology has yet done so, at least not with sure, unequivocal examples.

In fact, at present very few connections can be made between the written and the archaeological evidence. Most of the archaeological evidence comes from funerary contexts, while there is very little written evidence (when compared to the evidence for human sacrifice in Greek cult) for funerary ritual murder of any kind (a discrepancy perhaps due largely to the greater likelihood of material evidence for ritual killing being preserved in tombs, but which might also be seen to support my contention that the myths and literature of historical Greece do not accurately or fully reflect the realities of prehistory). There is written evidence for the performance of executions and vengeance killings at the graves of important men, and I have tentatively suggested that some of the skeletons found outside of Mycenaean and Cypriot tombs might be the remains of such ritual killings; but if the common interpretation (that they represent servants slain to attend their masters after death) is correct, it receives no support from the written record (pp. 65–9). The excavation of the altar of Zeus Lykaios has been the only opportunity for archaeology to test, in a specific case, the literary evidence; but archaeology failed to confirm the tradition of human sacrifices performed on the Arcadian mountaintop (p. 105). And recent efforts to bridge the gulf between the archaeological and written records have not been successful.[24]

In the past, the written evidence for human sacrifice (and its widespread acceptance by religious historians) seems to have had an influence on archaeologists, who quite naturally expected confirmation to be forthcoming from the soil. But the curious and varied collection of texts studied here – in which human sacrifice, originally a significant symbol on the level of myth, becomes in turn a stirring subject for poets, playwrights, historians, and novelists, and then an object of much misunderstanding for writers of late antiquity – is more a testament to the capacity and breadth of the imagination of the Greeks than a documentary record of their practices. For these we must turn to archaeology for certain answers; and at present the safest course is to regard the literary and archaeological evidence separately, neither seeking support for interpretations of material remains in literature (unless a truly convincing case for a direct connection can be made) nor allowing the dubious nature of the written evidence to affect the objective evaluation of new finds.

Appendix A
Cut marks and mass burials

CUT AND CHOPPED HUMAN BONES

From an EM I–MM IA tholos tomb excavated in southern Crete, the excavators report that 'amongst the few bone fragments recovered . . . we noted at least five which appear to have been chopped at each end. To this observation we may add the small size of the bone fragments here and at other sites surveyed by us in the Kaloi Limenes area, and the discovery at Kaminospilio of a quern-stone on which fragments of bone were "cemented". All of these observations raise the possibility that bones were collected from the tholoi during the period of their use and were chopped, broken, and/or ground, presumably for ritual purposes.'[1]

In a burial in the LM IIIA–B cemetery at Armenoi, the skeleton of a 25-year-old male was found to have cut marks on the bones. In addition, several bones had been completely severed, and stains resembling blood stains were observable on some bones, including the skull. T. McGeorge feels that the blows (ten in all) which resulted in the cuts and fractures were probably made with an axe, and she suggests that the man had been murdered or killed in a fight or duel.[2]

In 1982–3 thirty-eight tombs were excavated in a large Early Helladic cemetery at Manika, located northwest of Chalkis in Euboea. Associated with one group of twenty-one tombs were fifteen pits used as ossuaries (although some contained no bones). Several of the tombs had been looted, and only twenty-two provided skeletal material, most of it fragmentary and poorly preserved, for study.[3] It is reported that on the majority of the bones recovered there are deep cut marks, chop marks, holes, and fractures.[4] A. Sampson, who at first suggested that the cut marks on the human bones may have been due to 'some sort of ritual anthropophagy or human sacrifice before burial',[5] now believes that the marks were made during preparation for burial. Many of the cuts and holes are at places of muscle and tendon attachment, which suggests to Sampson that they resulted from cutting the tendons in order to force the corpse into a contracted position for burial. He further suggests the possibility that the corpses were cut or dismembered in order to disarm them, i.e. to prevent their spirits from returning as 'revenants' to harm the living.[6]

Sampson also announces the recent discovery of an Early Helladic ossuary located across the island at Aulonari (Kyme), which contained the remains of around fifteen persons. These bones are said to have similar cut marks, and it is possible that evidence for a widespread practice will accumulate.[7] Perhaps further study of the bones will help determine what the nature of the practice is: certainly this is not 'human sacrifice', for at Manika the majority of the bones, of both children and adults and from several areas of a large cemetery, had cut marks. It is therefore highly probable that we are dealing with some kind of mortuary practice. If all of the various marks and fractures can be shown to be due to human agency (i.e. not caused by accidental post-mortem damage, or by insects or rodents),[8] then what is most remarkable about the material from Manika is the extremely high frequency of the marks: this may suggest primary rather than secondary burial customs, although defleshing a few weeks or months after death might also result in a high percentage of marked bones.

Among many possible explanations for the presence of cut marks on human bones are: (1) human sacrifice, or other ritual killing; (2) cannibalism, whether ritual cannibalism, 'alimentary cannibalism', or survival cannibalism; (3) wounds sustained in a battle or fight; (4) wounds sustained in a massacre of civilians; (5) murder, which could involve mutilation or dismemberment; (6) execution or torture; (7) accident, e.g. from careless use of tools; (8) surgery, surgical bleeding, trephination, or other medical operation;[9] (9) conceivably, scientific use of corpses as cadavers; (10) preparation for primary burial, possibly involving cutting of the tendons, removal of internal organs, or defleshing; (11) preparation for secondary burial by defleshing of the bones; (12) attempts to render a corpse harmless and incapable of vengeance, by cutting the sinews or dismemberment, as in the practice of *maschalismos*;[10] (13) some use, sacred, magical, or profane, of human bones recovered from burials. No doubt someone with a more macabre imagination could add to this list. To determine with any degree of probability the causes of the alteration of human skeletal remains is not a simple matter, but in most cases it should be possible to rule out many of the explanations listed above, if not to argue persuasively for a single interpretation. Among the factors which might lead to such a determination are the context in which the bones are found; the nature of the marks (how were they made – by cutting, chopping, sawing, scraping? – and with what sort of instrument?); the amount, location, and distribution of the marks on a given skeleton; evidence suggesting that the cuts were made while the person was living (e.g. signs of healing), or on fresh bone ('immediate processing') rather than dry, older bone ('delayed processing');[11] the number of skeletons with cut marks, the sex and age of the person(s) involved, and the existence of close parallels from similar contexts.

SOME UNEXPLAINED MASS BURIALS

Near Old Corinth a well, dating to EH III, was found to contain over twenty human skeletons, along with fragmentary animal bones (ox, dog, fox, bird, lizard, pig, sheep, etc.). The humans ranged in age from adolescent to elderly. From the fact that 'in most cases the mandibles were in proper position with regard to the crania', F. O. Waage concluded that 'bodies, and not skeletons, must have been thrown into the well'. Waage continued:

> Nor is there any evidence whether it was through disease, starvation, earthquake, or human agency that the deceased met their end. Any speculations must take into account two factors, first the abandonment of the well and second, the presence of human bodies in its filling.

Waage proposed two possible explanations:

> a severe drought, resulting in the drying of the well and starvation, or some profanation of the well (and so of the community) leading to its abandonment and the expiatory sacrifice of the offending clan and its possessions.[12]

At Nichoria in Messenia a circular structure containing a number of burials was excavated in the early 1970s.[13] The structure, called the 'Little Circle' by its excavators, was built adjacent to a tholos tomb in the end of LH I or the beginning of LH IIA. A deep pit at the eastern end of the circle held the remains of at least four people. In the eastern and southern areas of the circle were seventeen or more secondary burials. Above the secondary burials at the southern end was the burial of an adult male, and directly above this was a burial of at least eleven persons, men, women, and children, who had been 'laid carelessly on top of one another', with no grave goods.[14] At first it was thought that these persons had died violently, but this possibility was rejected upon examination of the skeletons.[15]

In 1971 a well, dating to early LH IIIC, was excavated at Argos. The well contained about twenty human skeletons, of persons aged from 1 to 80, mixed (as at Corinth) with animal bones. No trace of violence or disease was found on the skeletons. The bodies were unaccompanied by grave goods and appear to have been thrown carelessly into the well. Kritzas listed seven possible reasons for this unusual burial, five of which he quickly rejected. Kritzas felt that epidemic (the conclusion of A. Poulianos, the anthropologist who studied the bones) was a possible explanation, but he argued at some length that the persons had drowned in a flooding of the Argive plain. Among the possibilities dismissed was that the well had served as a sacrificial bothros: Kritzas felt that the absence of grave goods, the lack of any secure parallel, and the fact that there was no cemetery or sanctuary in the vicinity all argue against a 'sacrificial' interpretation.[16]

Finally, a remarkable mass burial was discovered in a well located northeast of the Hephaistion in Athens, excavated in 1938. The filling of the well has now been dated to 'very shortly after 150 B.C.'.[17] In the lower fill of the well were found the bones of about 175 infants ('mostly newborn or full-term fetuses, together with several older infants'); also found were the remains of around 100 dogs and a few other domestic animals, and the bones of one adult human and one child. It is uncertain whether the infants were placed in the well at the same time or over a period of time: T. L. Shear, the excavator, appears to have assumed the latter, but J. L. Angel stated that the burials were made simultaneously.[18] Shear, who identified a herm-like statue found in the well as a statue of Aphrodite Ourania, suggested that the infant burial may have been connected with the cult of the goddess: 'Although infant sacrifice was not practiced in Greece, perhaps infants who died at childbirth were dedicated to the goddess as a symbolic sacrifice and a token survival of the original oriental ritual.' Angel, however, felt that starvation or plague was probably responsible for the mass burial.[19] The burial, unparalleled I believe in any period of Greek history or prehistory, merits further study.

From the brief descriptions, none of these collective burials seems to represent human sacrifice or ritual killing of any kind. But in general there has been a tendency among archaeologists to seek religious explanations for unusual and enigmatic finds; and the suggestions of Waage and Shear are perhaps symptomatic of this tendency. In the case of mass burials, non-ritual explanations, such as (purely secular) massacre and disease, should receive due consideration also. On the other hand, if in the future an archaeologist were to come upon the undisturbed remains of the 914 people who perished during the 'White Night' at Jonestown and to suggest 'cult activity' and a religious cause, the explanation would be – if only by accident and only partially – correct. But if we now have difficulty comprehending this extraordinary event of our own time,[20] then how much more difficult it is to account for mass burials of the third and second millennia BC! It will be, I suppose, impossible in most cases; but any attempt at interpretation – and I am not suggesting that we give up the attempt – must begin with the scientific study of the excavated remains.

Appendix B
Pylos tablet Tn 316

Pylos tablet Tn 316, 'the most important single Mycenaean document to give evidence of cult practices',[1] unfortunately presents so many difficulties of interpretation that the exact nature of the cult practice it records is disputed and, in effect, remains unknown. Still, the general purport of the inscription is clear: Tn 316 contains a list of gold vessels and unnamed women and men dedicated in some way to a number of deities, including Zeus, Hera, Potnia, Hermes (apparently), and one I-pe-me-de-ja.[2] The tablet is inscribed on both sides and divided into four sections, each with the heading PU-RO, 'Pylos' (written in large characters in the left-hand 'margin'), and a brief introductory formula, where most of the crucial problems lie. It is agreed that these introductions supply the names of the sanctuaries or sacred districts where the dedications were made. The do-ra (*dōra*, 'gifts') and po-re-na mentioned together in the formula have been taken by most scholars to refer respectively to the gold vessels and the persons listed below. And the words (apparently verbs) which accompany the two nouns, pe-re and a-ke, have usually been interpreted as forms of *pherein* and *agein*,[3] with the result that Chadwick, for example, translates the introductory formula, 'Pylos *sacrifices* at [name of sanctuary] and brings gifts and leads *victims*', taking PU-RO as the subject of the verbs and indicating with italics words of doubtful meaning.[4]

The content of the four 'paragraphs' which follow the obscure introductions is more certain: the names of goddesses and gods in the dative case, each followed by an ideogram for cup or bowl (qualified by the ideogram GOLD), and, in most cases, the ideogram for woman or man. More often one gold vessel and one human being are assigned to a deity (e.g. 'For Hera: one gold bowl, one woman'), although four gods receive a gold vessel only. In one case no deity is named before the entry 'one gold cup, two women', but the signs which follow may conceal the names of one or two goddesses.[5] With the possible exception of this last case, the sex of the human beings matches that of the corresponding divinities. In all, the tablet lists twelve, perhaps fourteen deities, thirteen gold vessels, eight women, and two men.

Several explanations have been put forward for the role played by the women and men in the ceremony or offering recorded on the tablet: (1) that the ideograms WOMAN and MAN do not represent human beings at all, but rather figurines dedicated to the divinities along with the gold vessels;[6] (2) that the women and men were cupbearers who carried the sacred vessels in a procession;[7] (3) that the women and men were dedicated to serve in some capacity in the sanctuaries;[8] or (4) that they were offered as sacrificial victims.[9] In the first edition of *Documents in Mycenaean Greek*, Ventris and Chadwick, while noting the possibility of human sacrifice, decided in favour of the second of these interpretations.[10] But in the second edition of *Documents* and elsewhere, Chadwick argues for the fourth:

> The revulsion which we feel for human sacrifice must not influence our judgement here. It is clear that the gold vessels would become the property of the god, and we may presume that the owners of the human beings equally divested themselves of ownership. This might be by dedicating the person to the god's service; but the *doeloi* or *doelai* of deities in the tablets appear to be persons of some standing, since they can hold land. The true slaves appear to be owned by persons. Hence the alternative, that these people were committed to divine service by being sacrificed, begins to appear more likely.[11]

In Chadwick's opinion the fact that in some cases gold vessels are listed without ideograms for woman or man invalidates the cupbearer theory and may suggest that these divinities were 'not judged important enough' to receive a human sacrificial offering.[12] Chadwick also notes the appearance of a word po-re-si on Thebes tablet Of 26, where a quantity of wool is assigned to the po-re-si (dative) in what is called 'a religious context'; and 'since sacrificial victims in Greek ritual were frequently decked out with wool, this is some slight confirmation of the meaning of the word', i.e. 'victims', which Chadwick tentatively adopts for po-re-na in his translation of Tn 316.[13] Finally, the unparalleled offering of so many gold vessels and human victims, considered together with the sloppiness and apparent haste with which the tablet was inscribed, suggests to Chadwick (who acknowledges the speculative nature of this) that Tn 316 may have been the product of 'an unusually stormy meeting' and that the offering was made in the face of an extraordinary danger – the impending invasion which would soon destroy Pylos.[14]

In its present state of obscurity the introductory formula is of little use for the interpretation of the role of the women and men in the dedication or ceremony recorded on the tablet. The conjunction of grammatically parallel do-ra and po-re-na in a sentence which introduces a list of vessels and human beings may be deceiving: it is not certain that 'po-re-na' designates the women and men, and Palmer argued that po-re-na were aniconic cult objects.[15] We seem to have forms of the same word in compounds on two other tablets, but po-re-no-tu-te-[ri-ja] (PY Ua 1413) and po-re-no-zo-te-ri-ja (PY Un 443) have also defied certain interpretation.[16] The forms po-re-na of Tn 316 and po-re-si of Thebes Of 26 may not belong to the same word. But if they do, then the word must be a masculine n-stem (po-re-na on Tn 316 in this case representing an accusative plural),[17] and it is thus unlikely to have been a general term for 'victims', including animals, as such words are exclusively neuter in Classical Greek. Therefore, if Chadwick's interpretation is correct, we must conclude that Of 26 records the dispensing of wool to *human* sacrificial victims together with other named human recipients. And if po-re-na were in fact human sacrificial victims, their appearance on the tablet from Thebes (the context of which otherwise seems industrial rather than cultic)[18] is surprising and seems totally inconsistent with a point upon which Chadwick has insisted: that the offering of human sacrifices at Pylos was an extraordinary measure taken in exceptional circumstances.

One aspect of this multiple dedication which should not be overlooked is the evident connection between the gold vessels and the women and men. Why were they listed together on the same tablet? And if the women and men were sacrificial victims, why were the cups and bowls listed first? Were the vessels more important than the human beings, or was the role of the latter related to and in some way dependent upon the dedication of the former? Although the offering recorded on Tn 316 is unique, there is other evidence for gold in the sanctuaries at Pylos. Tablet Ae 303 is a record of fourteen (or more) female 'slaves of the priestess', who were 'for the sake of', 'on account of', or possibly 'in charge of' (e-ne-ka; *heneka*) the sacred gold.[19] The exact significance of Ae 303 is itself obscure, but there is a clear indication of some kind of relationship between human beings (as on Tn 316, unnamed and indicated by ideogram only) and gold in a cultic context. And tablet Ae 303 was found in the same spot as Tn 316.[20] It therefore seems possible that the women and men of Tn 316 also were 'slaves of the priestess' who were responsible for the maintenance of the sacred treasuries.

Without additional evidence, no interpretation of Tn 316 can be argued, or ruled out, with complete confidence. Little is known of the functions of the 'slaves of the priestess' and 'slaves of the god' mentioned in the tablets. They both should probably be distinguished from actual slaves and in fact seem to have been persons of some status.[21] But in a society which appears to have been at once highly stratified and highly religious, there must have been several forms and levels of sacred service possible. In my opinion, the most probable interpretation of Tn 316 is that the women and men served in the sanctuaries of the various gods named on the tablet. From the fact that they were listed together with cups and bowls it is a reasonable inference that their duties were in some way related to the maintenance of precious vessels. The fact that in four cases no human beings are listed with the vessels remains problematic but does not present a serious difficulty for this interpretation (as it does for the theory that the persons were cupbearers): the dedication of the women and men may have been connected with the sacred treasuries without their role being directly tied to these particular vessels. And the fact that the eight women and two men were listed alongside but *after* the cups and bowls also presents, in my opinion, a formidable obstacle for those who would see here inscriptional evidence for human sacrifice in the Late Bronze Age.[22]

Notes

1 SACRIFICE AND RITUAL KILLING: TERMINOLOGY AND TYPES

1 Brelich (1969b) 200 n. 7.

2 Burkert (1979) 37 and (1985) 8. See also Burkert (1983) 22–9, (1981) 91–125, and (1987) 149–62. For a different view of ritual (but not so different as its title might suggest) see Staal (1979) 2–22.

3 Underlying behaviour: Burkert (1979) 35–9; social action: 45–52; stabilizing functions: Burkert (1985) 254–60.

4 Burkert (1981) 105–6, (1983) 25–9, and (1987) 149–62.

5 Cf. Meuli (1975) 1: 325–31, 335–8, and 353–85. Professional mourners in Greece: Garland (1985) 142. When Regulus slays horses, dogs, and pet birds around his son's pyre, Pliny (*Ep.* 4.2) comments wryly: *nec dolor erat ille, sed ostentatio doloris.* I do not mean to suggest that insincerity is an essential feature of ritual, but *ostentatio* is, and where the primary function of actions has been diverted to serve the purpose of display, sincerity is no longer a necessity (cf. Meuli (1975) 1: 336 n. 2 and 365 nn. 9–10).

6 But see Burkert (1983) 54–5, on the role of renunciation in such rituals. For food offerings see Meuli (1975) 2: 911–16; and on basic beliefs concerning the dead, 1: 303–31. Even Burkert will speak of intentionality, e.g. Burkert (1985) 60 (on Hom. *Il.* 23.34): 'when it is related that "about the dead man flowed blood such as could be drawn up in cups", it is clear that the intention was for the blood to reach the dead man in some way, to give him back life and colour . . .'

7 Burkert (1983) 29–34; Kirk (1970) 8–31 and (1974) 223–53; Versnel (1990) 25–90. Kirk is overly disdainful of 'aetiological myths' and far too sceptical and selective, as I believe much of the material discussed here will show. Burkert views myth and ritual as parallel and complementary forms of expression. For the possibility of ritual re-enactment see Kirk (1974) 237 and 249–53.

8 Vengeance killing: see pp. 49–60. Execution (which sometimes has a sacral, if not sacrificial, character): Burkert (1983) 46 n. 46 and Schwenn (1915) 28–31. Even killing in battle often has ritual

features, especially regarding the treatment of the slain enemy (e.g. Hdt. 4.64–5 and 4.103.3).

9 Brelich (1969b) 200 n. 7; see also Schwenn (1915) 9; Henninger (1958) 797–8, with further references; Brelich (1967) 6–14.

10 Sacrificial vocabulary: Stengel (1910), Rudhardt (1958) 213–300, and Casabona (1966). Greek sacrifice: Meuli (1975) 2: 907–1018; Burkert (1966) 102–13 (1983) 1–12 and index, s.v. Sacrifice, and (1985) 55–68 and index, s.v. sacrifices. Recent theoretical approaches: Detienne and Vernant (1989); Rudhardt and Reverdin (1981). Human sacrifice: Schwenn (1915) 1–139 and (1932) 948–56; Henrichs (1981) 195–235; O'Connor-Visser (1987) 211–33.

11 Homeric sacrifice: Stengel (1910) 1–6 and 59–65; Rudhardt (1958) 253–7. Classical *thusia*: Rudhardt (1958) 257–71. The two are usually treated together (e.g. Meuli (1975) 2:935–48; Nilsson, *GGR* 1:142–51; Burkert (1983) 3–7 and (1985) 55–9); but there are some differences, and *thuein* has a restricted sense in Homer, never designating the procedure as a whole: Rudhardt (1958) 253; Casabona (1966) 69–72. *Thuein* and related words: Casabona (1966) 69–154. Homeric terminology: Casabona (1966) 5–7, 18–26, 28–30, 39–58, and 155–9. Sacrifices on lesser occasions: Rudhardt (1958) 158, 264 n. 17, and 265; Burkert (1985) 255.

12 Stengel (1910) 126–45 and index, s.vv. Heroenkult and Totenopfer; Meuli (1975) 2:924–32; Nilsson, *GGR* 1:178–82 and 186–7; Burkert (1983) 48–58. Terminology: Rudhardt (1958) 238–9 and 285; Casabona (1966) 164–74, 204–7, and 226–7.

13 Meuli (1975) 2: 932–4; Rudhardt (1958) 286–7; Burkert (1985) 62–6 (cf. 199–203). The convenient division between consumed sacrifices offered to Olympians and unconsumed sacrifices to chthonic deities and heroes, originating in scholia (Rudhardt (1958) 250–1) and often followed by modern scholars, does not hold up under the evidence. Holocausts are offered to Olympian deities, sacrifices to chthonic gods or heroes are sometimes consumed, and we even find the combination of 'destructive' sacrifices and consumption in the same ceremony (e.g. Paus. 2.10.1, with a single victim offered in both ways): Stengel (1910) 131–3; Meuli (1975) 2: 920 n.1; Burkert (1966) 103–4 n. 36 and (1985) 63–4; Rudhardt (1958) 251–3 and 264–5.

14 Exceptional are the Spartan pre-battle sacrifices to Artemis Agrotera: Burkert (1985) 60 with n. 37. Sacrifice before battle: Pritchett (1974–85) 1: 109–16 (bibliography 109) and 3: 83–90; Lonis (1979) 95–110. There were two sorts of military sacrifice: in one (τὰ ἱερὰ θύεσθαι), animals were slaughtered in camp or in town, primarily for the purpose of divination (by hepatoscopy); in the other (σφάγια, σφαγιάζεσθαι), the victims were slain directly before an encounter (or when crossing a frontier) – but these 'propitiatory sacrifices' could also be interpreted as favourable or unfavourable, apparently from the flow of blood. The terminology is not always consistent: Pritchett (1974–85) 1: 109–15 and 3: 73–90; Casabona (1966) 87–94, 183–4, 189–91, and 317–21.

15 Stengel (1910) 19–21, 78–80, and index, s.v. Schwuropfer; Nilsson,

GGR 1: 139–42; Burkert (1985) 250–4; Gernet (1981) 167–73; Rudhardt (1958) 203; Casabona (1966) 212–25 and 323–6.

16 Purifications: Nilsson, *GGR* 1: 104–7; Burkert (1985) 80–2; Rudhardt (1958) 278–9; Stengel (1910) 92. At Athens: Istros, *FGrHist* 334 F 16, with other sources in Jacoby *ad loc*. Boeotian and other 'dichotomy rites': see pp. 108–9. According to Plutarch (*Rom.* 21.8 and *Quaest. Rom.* 68, 280B) dogs were frequently used in rituals called *periskulakismoi*.

17 Divination: Burkert (1985) 112–13 and Pritchett (1974–85) 3: 47–90. Bloodless sacrifices: Rudhardt (1958) 231–4 and 249; Casabona (1966) 73, Haussleiter (1935) 12–18 and index, s.v. Opfer, unblutige.

18 Stengel (1910) 113–25; Burkert (1985) 56 and 199–200; Rudhardt (1958) 261–2. In sacrifices for the dead, heroes, and chthonic gods the victims may have been beheaded (so Schol. Ap. Rhod. *Argon.* 1.587 and Schol. Thuc. 5.11).

19 Hero-sacrifices clearly developed from sacrifices to the dead, and 'destructive' sacrifices to chthonic deities may also be related (Meuli (1975) 2: 932). There are resemblances between oath sacrifices and the killing of animals for purification, especially 'dichotomy' rituals: see Gernet (1981) 171 and Casabona (1966) 216–19 and 224, who notes that in both cases the animals are employed in 'rites of passage'; for rites of passage see van Gennep (1960). In fact, in most 'destructive' sacrifices the killing seems to operate as an act of demarcation in passage rites: funerals, going into battle and crossing frontiers, swearing oaths, passing through severed bodies for 'purification', and marking off areas with blood. But the distinction between consumed sacrifices and all forms of 'destructive sacrifices', although frequently ignored in monolithic sacrificial theories, is difficult to explain away.

20 Meuli (1975) 2: 907–1018. Meuli's theory has been revived and amplified fruitfully by Burkert (1966) 105–13, (1983) 12–22, and (1987) 164–8.

21 Meuli (1975) 2: 907–9; Burkert (1985) 57 and (1983) 7–8.

22 Burkert (1983) 4; Burkert (1966) 106–7, 109, and 118; Meuli (1975) 2: 995–6. For the Bouphonia and a similar rite on Tenedos see pp. 85–6.

23 See Burkert (1983) 13–14 and (1987) 166–8; for other criticisms see e.g. Nilsson, *GGR* 1: 145 n. 2 and Kirk (1981) 70–2.

24 Meuli (1975) 1: 333–51 and 2: 887–91 and 924–31.

25 For 'suttee' see also pp. 43–7 and 60–5. 'Suttee' might be explained as the ritualized version of suicide from grief. But the belief that one will rejoin one's spouse in an afterlife will also play a role, if not in the institution then in the continuation of this practice.

26 Rudhardt (1958) 251–3 and 264 with n. 2; Casabona (1966) 84–5.

27 θύουσι; but also ἀποσφάζουσι, a word used according to Casabona (1966: 167–8) only with human objects and mostly of non-sacrificial killings; but for later Greek cf. Ael. *VH* 8.3 and Lucian *Sacr.* 15, of animal sacrifices.

28 Cf. Casabona (1966) 228, who prefers to translate 'il accomplit sur eux les (*rites appelés*) ἔντομα'.

29 Casabona (1966) 155–67.

30 Just as 'sacrificial' words used with human objects carry a sense 'to kill like an animal', so too the use of *phonos* and *phoneuein* to characterize animal sacrifice (found most often in vegetarian and antisacrificial contexts) implies that the animals are murdered like human beings: Emp. fr. 136.1 Diels-Kranz; Plut. *De esu carnium* 1, 996B; Lucian *Sacr.* 15; Iamb. *VP* 186; Porph. *Abst.* 2.22.1, 2.22.2, 2.26.5, 2.29.5 (= Theophr. fr. 12.21, 12.30–1, 13.13, 18.18 Pötscher), and 3.20.6.

31 See p. 109 (a mythical case) and 155–6 (Epimenides' purification of Athens, discussed for convenience with pharmakos rites). See also pp. 92–6 on the sacrifice of the descendants of Athamas (Hdt. 7.197), where Herodotus employs the verb *thuein* throughout but in recounting the myth of Athamas says that the Achaeans were 'making Athamas a purification'.

2 ARCHAEOLOGICAL EVIDENCE

1 Brief announcements: *Ergon* 1979: 31–2; *AR* 1979–80: 50–1; *AR* 1980–1: 42; *BCH* 104 (1980) 673–5. Detailed preliminary report: Sakellarakis and Sakellaraki (1979) 347–92, upon which I have largely based my description here. Unreliable but most accessible to the reader of English is Sakellarakis and Sakellaraki (1981) 205–22.

2 Sakellarakis and Sakellaraki (1981) 213. A tiny exception is the skeleton of a human foetus found in the destruction layer of a Middle Minoan building at Knossos: Popham (1974b) 186. The Knossos children's bones were discovered in the same season; and in the same area parts of two skeletons were found near the preserved tops of some MM walls in 1981: Warren (1980–1) 20. For other partial human skeletons from non-funerary contexts in Crete see Wall *et al.* (1986) 387.

3 The corridor is termed a 'prothalamos' (Sakellarakis and Sakellaraki (1979) 351, etc.), an identification which depends upon the contention that the building was entered from the north. That the wider east entrance was the main entrance is denied on the grounds that the slope of the hill is very steep at this point (349). But it is questionable if the three doorways to the north were entrances *into* the building at all (see below, n. 11).

4 Sakellarakis and Sakellaraki (1979) 369–72. Finds in the corridor: 352–60.

5 East room: Sakellarakis and Sakellaraki (1979) 372–81. The earth and stones are said to have been exceptionally burnt in the area where the clay feet were found, possibly suggesting the presence of wood (369).

6 Sakellarakis and Sakellaraki (1979) 382–8.

7 ibid., 387; but 'the right heel' in Sakellarakis and Sakellaraki (1981)

207 and 222. From the photograph (207), it appears that the uppermost (and left) leg is the leg in question.

8 Coloration: Sakellarakis and Sakellaraki (1981) 219; Sakellarakis and Sakellaraki (1979) 387; blade: 387.

9 Sakellarakis and Sakellaraki (1979) 389 90; Sakellarakis and Sakellaraki (1981) 218–19. It is also suggested (222) that the person who perished in the corridor was in the process of taking the bull vase, filled with blood from the human sacrifice, to the idol in the central room. The vase's height is not provided, but a comparison of the photographs of the vase and of the 'altar' (212–13 and 207) shows that it would be extremely awkward, if not impossible, to collect blood from a victim (human or animal) lying on the platform.

10 Rhytons: Sakellarakis and Sakellaraki (1979) 354–5; offering tables: 354 and 381; bull vase: 360, 369–72, 389, and pl. 181; horns of consecration: 347 and 351; clay feet: 368–9 and pl. 180α–β.

11 Certainly not a 'tripartite shrine', as the excavators originally identified the building (*AR* 1979–80: 50); for tripartite shrines see Shaw (1978) 429–48. That there was more to the building than has been preserved or excavated is indicated by walls which extend from the building to the north and east (Sakellarakis and Sakellaraki (1979) 390–2 and 348 fig. 1). The walls extending to the north correspond (as in a mirror image) to the walls separating the three excavated rooms, and it seems likely that across the corridor from these rooms was a corresponding set of rooms.

12 Bull sacrifices: Sakellarakis and Sakellaraki (1979) 389. The width is not provided, but from the scale (348 fig. 1) the entrance does not appear to be much more than a metre wide; see now Marinatos (1986) 19, who also notes that the small 'altar' would hardly be adequate for bull sacrifices. Many of the finds suggest to Marinatos that the area was used for storage of food and cooking utensils and perhaps also for cooking.

13 Sakellarakis (1970) 165; see also 172 and 194, and Marinatos (1986) 14–22. The presence of trees (particularly the date-palm) on sacrificial seals strongly suggests an outdoor setting.

14 Altarlike structure: Sakellarakis and Sakellaraki (1979) 389; altar: Sakellarakis and Sakellaraki (1981) 218, etc. That the platform is very low can be seen from the photograph, (1981) 207.

15 Marinatos (1986) 14–15; Sakellarakis (1968) pls 43–7 and (1970) 168–92. The best-known example is the altar on the Agia Triada sarcophagus, pictured in Sakellarakis and Sakellaraki (1981) 207, on the same page as the 'altar' from Anemospilia – and where (despite the assertion, 218) the contrast between the two could not be more apparent. The brownish colour of the table depicted on the sarcophagus is also suggestive of wood: Marinatos (1986) 15.

16 That there was an upper story is suggested by the thickness of the walls (especially the west wall: Sakellarakis and Sakellaraki (1979) 391 and 348 fig. 1), by the great amount of bricks, stones, and burnt earth in the destruction layer (351–2, 361, 373, 376, 382), and by fragments of pottery found widely scattered over the floor or on a

level above the floor (357–8, 361, 363, 366, 368, 374, 384). The excavators argue repeatedly that this pottery fell from shelves or from the roof (358, 363–4, 368, 374, 383–4) and that the bricks had been used in the construction of the walls, roof, or shelves (361, 373, 382). But there was also a staircase leading upward from the southwest corner of the corridor (383 and 391).

17 Sakellarakis and Sakellaraki (1979) 389 (τελετουργικὸ μαχαίρι); Sakellarakis and Sakellaraki (1981) 218.

18 See the blades classified as spearheads by Branigan (1974) 17–19 and pls 9 and 27. The largest of these, however, is 33.5 cm long, most considerably shorter. The closest parallel comes from the Late Minoan period, but the blade is 'clearly derived from a Middle Bronze Age type': Hood and de Jong (1952) 261 and 262 fig. 8. The blade is 0.38 m long, has two slots in the same position as those on the blade from Anemospilia, and is decorated on each side with an incised spiral. For a convincing depiction of how such blades were mounted on the shaft see Childe (1957) 53 fig. 26.

19 By A. Koutselinis, assistant professor of criminology at the University of Athens (Sakellarakis and Sakellaraki (1981) 222).

20 Sakellarakis and Sakellaraki (1979: 387) report that the legs (plural) were bent so that the left heel nearly touched the thigh, thus implying that the other leg was not so sharply bent. In the photograph in Sakellarakis and Sakellaraki (1981) 207, to the right of the left foreleg are what appear to be other bones: if these are the tibia and fibula of the right leg, then it was not nearly so sharply bent as the left one.

21 Sakellarakis and Sakellaraki (1981) 219; and (1979) 387.

22 Ubelaker (1978) 34. I owe this information to personal communications with Dr Paul W. Sciulli of the Ohio State University Department of Anthropology.

23 Sakellarakis and Sakellaraki (1979) 387.

24 It is also said that 'the two other skeletons close by showed uniform coloration': Sakellarakis and Sakellaraki (1981) 219 (caption beneath photographs). But unless the photograph, 221, is misleading, it seems that while most of the priest's skeleton had been 'smoked' by the fire, the front surfaces of the bones of his right leg (the closest of his limbs to the youth on the platform) were white.

25 Brief announcements in *AR* 1979–80: 49 and *AR* 1981–2: 52. Detailed preliminary reports: Warren (1980–1) 18–21, (1981a) 79–92, (1981b) 155–66, and (1984) 48–55. For the skeletal remains and their find-spots these reports are now superseded by Wall *et al.* (1986) 333–88.

26 Warren (1981a) 80–5; a few more loomweights were recovered in 1981 (*AR* 1981–2: 52). Pithos: Warren (1981a) 83; Wall *et al.* (1986) 345; jug: 345.

27 Wall *et al.* (1986) 335–45.

28 ibid., 348 and table 1; cut vertebra: 340–1 and pl. 37a-b.

29 Warren (1981a) 91 and (1981b) 159; Wall *et al.* (1986) 344–5.

30 Skulls: Wall *et al.* (1986) 341–2, 349 (nos 1–3), 367–8 figs 6–7,

378–82, and pls 27–9 and 31a. Leg bones: 342 and 376–7.

31 Warren (1981a) 91; Wall *et al.* (1986) 365–73 and 386.

32 Wall *et al.* (1986) 365–73; Warren (1981b: 159) suggests that the instrument was a 'thin, sharp-edged blade such as one of obsidian'.

33 Warren (1981a) 91.

34 Wall *et al.* (1986) 345–6, 363–5, and 375 table 3.

35 ibid., 346 and 365.

36 Warren (1981a) 92; see also Warren (1981b) 159–65, (1984) 48–53; Wall *et al.* (1986) 386–8. But to conclude from the children's *apparent* good health that they had been 'deliberately killed' (Warren (1984) 53) requires quite a leap of the imagination. 'Many diseases do not, of course, involve changes in the skeleton': Brothwell (1981) 127; cf. Janssens (1970) 114–19 and Wells (1964) 85–92.

37 Warren (1984) 53 and (1981a) 92; Wall *et al.* (1986) 345. It is now suggested that 'inedible or otherwise unrequired parts' were discarded in the vessel. But is it possible that the snails were simply intrusive?

38 See Appendix A (pp. 194–6) for references.

39 So Tumasonis (1983) 305–7.

40 Warren (1981b) 159 and (1981a) 91.

41 Wall *et al.* (1986) 342.

42 ibid., 376–7. The possibility of disintegration is considered, but 'the absence of certain other bones, such as the greater part of skull C, and the missing limb bone shafts, is more likely attributable to their absence from the bone assemblage at the time of deposition' (377).

43 Ubelaker (1974) 33–7 and (1978) 30–3.

44 Reconstructed skeleton: Wall *et al.* (1986) 366 fig. 5; chart: 374 table 2; children's bones from elsewhere in the house: 375 table 3. Percentages: 333 n. 2. Rates of decomposition can vary widely: Ubelaker (1978) 33. See also 76–7 figs 101–2, for photographs of bones from an American Indian site in Virginia, with cut marks ('probably produced during intentional disarticulation or defleshing of the body') which bear a striking resemblance to many of the marks under discussion here.

45 Wall *et al.* (1986) 373 and 386.

46 ibid., 373 and 375. Removal of internal organs need not imply consumption; Egyptian embalmers removed the brain (with an iron hook) and internal organs (with a sharp stone tool): Hdt. 2.86.3–4.

47 Warren (1981a) 92 and (1984) 48; Wall *et al.* (1986) 386.

48 Cf. the ovicaprid teeth and skull fragments found in an LM II chamber tomb at Knossos: Hood and de Jong (1952) 49. For animal bones in LM tombs see also Pini (1968) 68; there are many more cases from the Early and Middle Minoan periods (27).

49 Wall *et al.* (1986) pl. 37a-b.

50 Reburial in ossuaries is a feature of the Early and Middle Minoan periods, but secondary burials continued to be made in the Late Minoan period in pits and larnakes (Pini (1968) 17–19 and 59–60).

51 For the Early Helladic period see Appendix A. For modern Greece see Lawson's graphic eyewitness account of the cleaning of

exhumed human skeletons in the Peloponnesus in the late nineteenth century: Lawson (1910) 540–1, quoted by Tumasonis (1983) 307. For secondary burial among native Americans (and some equally graphic descriptions) see Ubelaker (1974) 8–14 and (1978) 19–20. For secondary burial at Çatal Hüyük see Macqueen (1978) 226–39, and for possible affinities between this Neolithic culture and the Minoan, Dietrich (1974) 94–126.

52 Sakellarakis has suggested that Phourni Building 4 functioned under the 'priesthood', and the building certainly had some connection with funerary rites, for it was located within a cemetery: *Ergon* 1974: 105–7; *Ergon* 1977: 169–74; *AR* 1978–9: 37–8; Sakellarakis (1974) 207–12; Hiller (1977) 190. I note in passing that forty-seven loomweights were found in Building 4, possibly indicating the presence of a loom on the upper floor (for the weaving of shrouds?: cf. Hom. *Od*. 2.96–102 and Popham (1974b) 214). I do not mean to imply any connection between this LM I building and the Knossos finds, as Building 4 was located within a cemetery and as no human bones were found within it. I mention this unique structure only as a reminder of how little is known about Minoan burial customs and the tendance of the dead, and because its discovery suggests that 'undertaking' was a specialized and possibly sacred activity in the Late Minoan period, as in Egypt.

53 Wall *et al*. (1986) 346.

54 Some of the bones associated with the pithos had cut marks; but possibly the pithos was used repeatedly to move skeletons to and from a cemetery. And conceivably the cutting was not done in the house at all: no cutting tools are reported among the finds. Burial in pithoi was common in the Middle Minoan period, but there are also a few examples from LM I and later (Pini (1968) 11–13, 55–6, and 58; Hiller (1977) 178).

55 Russell (1987) 381–97, who compared the Krapina material with bones from a fourteenth-century ossuary at Juntunen, Michigan, and with bones of butchered reindeer from the Combe Grenal rock shelter in France. Several features observed on both the Krapina and Juntunen skeletons and associated by Russell with defleshing for secondary burial also appear on the Knossos bones. Cut marks were often found in 'repetitive ladder-rung series' and frequently on curved and complexly shaped bones; the bones showing the most marks were the claviculae, scapulae, and femora; and multiple cut marks were particularly frequent on the femoral necks (393–4; cf. Wall *et al*. (1986) 366 fig. 5, 370–2 figs 9–11, and pls 32–5). The Krapina and Juntunen cut marks were also 'fine, delicate, shallow incisions, in contrast to the coarser, V-shaped Combe Grenal butchery marks which appear to bite deeply into the bone surface' (Russell (1987) 392). And while butchery marks were found on less than 10 per cent of the reindeer bones, the percentage of cut human bones was much higher (Krapina, 48 of 128; Juntunen, 104 of 310: 384 table 4) and more or less comparable to the percentages for Knossos: 21.7 to 35.7 per cent of the bones from the Room of the

Children's Bones, 16 per cent of children's bones found elsewhere (Wall *et al.* (1986) 333 n. 2 and 375 table 3). But the amount of marks resulting from defleshing for reburial will in any given case depend upon how much tissue remains clinging to the bone.

56 Arens (1979), cited in this connection by Tumasonis (1983) 305–7. For the controversy see Tumasonis (1983) 309 n. 12, the generally unfavourable review of Brady (1982) 595–611, and Sahlins's scathing reply in Arens and Sahlins (1979) 46–7. And cannibalism continues to be proposed to account for cut and broken bones (e.g. Villa *et al.* (1986) 431–7).

57 Arens (1979) 119–35; Brothwell (1961) 304–7; Wells (1964) 138–40; Janssens (1970) 18, 20–1, 64, and 140–1; Binford (1981) 11–13 and 291–2; Brothwell (1981) 174; Zivanović (1982) 192–7.

58 For the suggestion that clay figurines of humans and human body parts found in peak sanctuaries represent a survival of earlier human sacrifices see Verbruggen (1981) 115–17. Concentrating on the figurines from Petsofa, Verbruggen follows Nilsson (1950: 74–6) in rejecting the interpretation of the figurines as votives offered to a healing deity, on the grounds that the complaints represented would have been too uniform. But Verbruggen ignores the discovery and excavation of any peak sanctuaries beyond the early twentieth century (Dietrich (1974) 290–307; Peatfield (1983) 273 n. 2; Burkert (1985) 26–8; Rutkowski (1986) 73–98); and the discovery of figurines representing deformity or disease, and pregnant women and women giving birth (Rutkowski (1986) 87–8, 86 figs 109–10, and 245 nn. 70–1), would appear to confirm that such figures, like similar votives offered in healing sanctuaries in later Greece, were offered either in hope of or in gratitude for a cure. But the healing function of the deity or deities worshipped on the mountaintops will have been one of several, as there are many more figurines of healthy individuals (very often in an attitude of supplication); and figurines of animals, chiefly domestic, form the largest class (85–8). But there is no good reason to question the accepted opinion that all of the figurines were votives, even if the nature of the ceremonies during which they were offered is imperfectly known.

59 Warren (1972) 81–3 and 342.

60 Warren (1984) 53; Papapostolou (1977) 78–80.

61 Papapostolou (1977) 79. The end appears pointed in pl. 42, but this may be illusory: cf. pls 4γ and 43. Nor do the two rounded objects on the upper end resemble the hilt and handle of a sword. N. Marinatos suggests *per litteras* that the object is more likely a standard of some kind than a mallet but agrees that the figure is holding the object in her hand.

62 Furtwängler (1900) 1: pl. II fig. 6 and 2: 8. That the central figure's hands are free does not argue for the suggestion that he is a prisoner. For combat scenes see e.g. 1: pl. II fig. 2, and Vermeule (1964) pl. XIX fig. H. The latter seal also has three figures, one upside-down (and thus apparently dead) and wearing a similar triangular helmet.

63 Nilsson (1950) 229–30; Sakellarakis (1968) 242–4 and pls 41–7 and (1970) 166–88 and 169 fig. 8; Marinatos (1986) 11–25, with figs 1–5, 11, and 15.

64 Persson (1931) 8–70; skeletal material: Fürst (1930) 78–82. See also Pelon (1976) 178–80 and Mylonas (1966) 127–30. Persson's designations 'west pit', 'east pit', etc., used throughout the publication and followed by Mylonas, are incorrect: the dromos extends approximately west from the tomb, not south, as it would according to Persson's designations (autopsy; rightly Pelon (1976) 179). Hence I employ the Roman numerals I-IV from Persson (1931) 28 fig. 22.

65 Persson (1931) 18. Finds from pit IV: 40–1. Pit II: 39.

66 Persson (1931) 27, 31, 39, 41, and 66 fig. 46. The concentration of sherds on the floor near and above pit I suggests that the vase stood originally in this area (31 with 28 fig. 22).

67 Pit III: Persson (1931) 13–14 and 39–40. Pit I: 14–17, 31–9, 43–54, 56–8, 60–5.

68 ibid., 12, 29–31, and 28 fig. 22. Two of the skeletons are 4FD and 5FD (Fürst (1930) 81–2), identified as belonging to males (their sex, remarked Fürst, 'gut mit der Auffassung von Professor Axel Persson übereinstimmt, dass nämlich diese Schädel den Sklaven angehört haben'). Together with these were a few bones of a third adult of undetermined sex (82), apparently the remains found in quadrant Z5 above pit I: see Persson (1931) 28 fig. 22, and cf. the *Errata* following the List of Plates (viii).

69 Persson (1931) 68–70.

70 Mylonas (1966) 128–9; cf. Pelon (1976) 364–5.

71 Persson (1931) 31 and 28 fig. 22.

72 Cf. Mylonas (1966) 128–30. Stirrup jar: above, n. 66; jug: Persson (1931) 27, 31, 39, 41; small finds on the floor: 29–31. Reconstruction of funeral ceremony: 70.

73 Persson (1931) 69.

74 Mylonas (1966) 128–9; Persson (1931) 43–9 and 67. The bull cup Persson felt was contemporary with or a little older than the octopus cup (50–2); the silver goblet with the hunting scene he dated to *c.* 1500 (52–4).

75 Furumark (1972) 1: 610 (type 164.2) and 2: 53. Absolute chronology: Warren and Hankey (1989) 146–8 and 169 table 3.1.

76 Hurwit (1979) 413–14 n. 6. For the correspondence of LC IIA to LH IIIA1 see Warren and Hankey (1989) 117–18.

77 Hurwit (1979) 413–26. For the King's swords see Sandars (1963) 119–20, 125, and 144–5; according to Sandars the various sword types date to the latter half of the fifteenth century but continue into the following century.

78 Persson (1931) 67. Lest it be thought that I have forgotten the 'little Princess', I note that in Persson's view she had been buried at some time prior to the burial of the King and Queen (68). The complete absence in her burial pit of fragments of the otherwise nearly ubiquitous stirrup jar and jug with the beaked spout suggests that

she was not buried at the time of the digging of pits I, II, and IV (and perhaps more likely earlier).

79 Persson (1931) 68. The ostrich egg, however, was found at about 0.75 m below floor level, i.e. about halfway down and just beneath the covering slabs (14). The lamp and necklace seem to have lain on the floor of the pit (16).

80 Though conceivably sherds from the same vases could find their way into the pit during a later extension. The pit's floor was coated with plaster (Persson (1931) 16 and 17–18); but as Persson speaks of individual beds of plaster it appears that these were not contiguous. And no difference in the consistency of the fill is reported.

81 See Pelon (1976) 362–3 for a few minor exceptions. The closest parallel is pit A in Pylos Tholos IV, 9 m long and like Dendra pit I shaped in a curve along the tomb wall; but as the pit had been thoroughly plundered, it is uncertain how many burials it contained and how often it was used (361 and 192–4).

82 Protonotariou-Deïlaki (1968) 236–8, (1969a) 104–5, and (1969b) 3–6; Pelon (1976) 181–2.

83 Protonotariou-Deïlaki (1969b) 3–4: two men and one woman; but the sexes seem to have been determined by grave goods only.

84 ibid., 3: 'εὑρέθησαν . . . εἰς θέσιν γονυκλινῆ'. How the skeletons were supported in this remarkable position is not stated. In Protonotariou-Deïlaki (1969a) 105, it is reported only that the remains (λείψανα) of two human skeletons were found on the floor.

85 Protonotariou-Deïlaki (1969b) 3 and 6. In support of her interpretation, Deïlaki compared the Dendra tholos and wrote that human sacrifice had 'evidently' (προφανῶς) taken place in Shaft Grave Gamma of Grave Circle B at Mycenae. For the grave see Mylonas (1972–3) 1: 43–50 and (1966) 100 and 104. The skull of one skeleton had undergone trephination; another lay with knees wide apart, which suggests that the legs were trussed in a raised position at the time of burial. But I see no evidence whatsoever pointing to human sacrifice.

86 Earlier burials were also swept to the side of the chamber or reinterred in pits within the tomb: Mylonas (1948) 69–71 and (1966) 113; Blegen (1937) 1: 234–5 and 247–8; Wace (1932) 129–30.

87 Wace (1932) 15; Frödin and Persson (1938) 158–9 and 356 (cf. 160 and 191–2: post-Mycenaean burials within chamber); Persson (1931) 10–11 figs 5–6.

88 Tsountas (1888) 130–1; Tsountas and Manatt (1897) 151. For the contents of the tomb see Tsountas (1888) 142. These tombs are said to have contained more than one, and up to five or six, skeletons, but mostly in such poor condition that Tsountas did not give totals for the individual tombs (135).

89 Vollgraff (1904) 370.

90 The only bones found were a small skull fragment and some teeth in a niche in the wall (Vollgraff (1904) 391). Shattered vases: 375. The many finds in the tomb (375–87) indicate that it had been used

often for successive burials; and walls in the west corner of the chamber contained fragments of gold and pottery, clearly from funeral gifts (373 and 397).

91 Wace (1932) 12–15.

92 ibid., 145 and 129.

93 Andronikos (1968) 82: 'Wace endeckte Reste dreier Skelette im Zugang zu Grab 505; ein Schädel und ein paar verstreute Knocken davon befanden sich vor dem Grabeingang.' The skull and bones are clearly Wace's no. I (Wace (1932) 12: 'a skull, no. I, with a few scattered bones'), and the three skeletons are apparently nos I–III (cf. Andronikos (1968) 82 n. 625). Mylonas (1948:72) wrote only of the skeleton 'of a man found buried in tomb 505 of the Kalkani [*sic*] Cemetery'.

94 Wace (1932) 129–30; cf. 13 fig. 7. Wace distinguished the skeletons buried under 'special circumstances' from nos I–III and X–XIII. This leaves IV–IX and XIV–XV. I would be tempted to think that he meant the latter two; but he clearly considered these to belong to burials made after the chamber was no longer in use (15), and they were not found directly before the door.

95 Wace (1932) 15.

96 Blegen (1937) 1: 156–7; see also 235–6.

97 ibid., 158–9; cf. 250–2. The bones and skull fragments found in the burnt layer Blegen considered the remains of prior burials. There was also a pit in the floor containing unburnt remains of earlier burials (159).

98 Blegen (1937) 249; Wace (1932) 15, 50, 88, and 108; Frödin and Persson (1938) 188; Mylonas (1966) 118; Cavanagh (1978) 171–2. Mylonas suggested that some tombs were used as cenotaphs and no longer employed for burials, Cavanagh that the tombs were entered to perform some kind of secondary burial practice on the most recent interment. Total disintegration of the last burial is of course a possibility, but unlikely in cases where numerous disturbed skeletons have survived.

99 Frödin and Persson (1938) 356.

100 Mylonas (1948) 72 and (1966) 116–17; cf. Tsountas and Manatt (1897) 97 and 151. The skeletons were shown by Wace to belong to burials from the Middle Helladic cemetery: Wace (1932) 146 n. 1; Mylonas (1948) 72. Tsountas had also suggested that a woman buried beneath the dromos of 'Clytemnestra's Tomb' was a sacrificed slave (Tsountas and Manatt (1897) 151–2), but without good reason (Pelon (1976) 295–6 and 364 n. 1).

101 Enkomi Tomb 11A was a burial, called by Sjöqvist a 'servant's tomb', made in the dromos of Tomb 11: 'Possibly the servant had been sacrificed in connection with the last funeral ceremonies' (*SCE* 1: 515). But the burials in the chamber date to Late Cypriot II, while the burial in the dromos probably belongs to Late Cypriot III (524–5). And there are other Late Cypriot III shaft graves in the cemetery (507 and 575).

102 Hill (1940) 66; *SCE* 4.2: 433 (Gjerstad); Karageorghis (1965b) 309;

Andronikos (1968) 84; Hood (1973) 40–1.

103 Absolute chronology: Cypro-Geometric I, II, III = 1050–950, 950–850, 850–700; Cypro-Archaic I, II = 700–600, 600–475; Cypro-Classic I, II = 475–400, 400–325 BC (*SCE* 4.2: 427). But the Swedish chronology requires revision: see Birmingham (1963) 15–42, who shows that adjustment of the absolute dates will not resolve the problems and that revision of the pottery sequence itself is needed.

104 *SCE* 1: 216–18. 'Chavara' is 'a calcareous tufa containing small pebbles, which is employed as gravel' (xvii).

105 That the chamber was used for at least one burial is indicated by the presence of pottery (*SCE* 1: 217 fig. 77.5). Although Gjerstad considered the skeletons to be *in situ*, it appears from fig. 77.4 that several bones were missing and a few out of place. It therefore seems possible that at least one of the skeletons (and perhaps all three) had been moved here from the tomb.

106 Tomb 428: *SCE* 1: 256–62; Tomb 407: 201–4; Tomb 408: 204–8; Tomb 410: 210–13.

107 *SCE* 1: 226–33.

108 ibid., 228.

109 ibid., 228. Pottery from earlier burials sometimes was thrown into the dromos: 243, 249, 257–8.

110 ibid., 234–40.

111 ibid., 236.

112 ibid., 241–6, 242 figs 88–9, and 247 fig. 94.3–4.

113 ibid., 244; for the blocks see also 247 fig. 94.3 and 243 fig. 90 (the larger) and 244 fig. 92 (the smaller). In the text, Gjerstad, who had been speaking of a single block, suddenly wrote, 'At the place where the blocks were found' – only to revert in mid-sentence to a discussion of the one (larger) block. The larger block measured 1.18 m in length, 0.51 m in width, and 0.34 m in height, and the hole, 0.23 m × 0.12 m. The dimensions of the smaller block are not provided.

114 *SCE* 1: 243 and 247 fig. 94.6.

115 ibid., 242–3. Tomb 426 had been looted (252–4).

116 Pieridou (1965) 75; cf. 74 fig. 1.

117 ibid., 76. The third burial described apparently was undisturbed, and it seems possible that this skeleton represented the final burial, although Pieridou seems to have had reasons for not considering it so.

118 Karageorghis (1963b) 373–80, (1963c) 549–50, (1965b) 305–13, (1967) 6–24, and (1969) 28–32 and 49–50.

119 Karageorghis (1967) 9–10 and (1969) 31–2. Scattered remains of horses or asses from the first burial period were also found in the dromos. For horse burials in Cyprus and elsewhere in the Mediterranean see Karageorghis (1965a) 282–90, (1963d) 294–7, and (1967) 117–18; Andronikos (1968) 85–7; Sakellarakis (1970) 199–205; Garland (1985) 35 and 144.

120 Karageorghis (1967) 9. Dikaios (1963: 143 n. 13) felt that these

bones represented later burials, like the apparent pit burials in the dromos of Salamis Tomb 1 (below, n. 122). But in his reply Karageorghis (1965b: 311) emphasized the homogeneity of the surrounding earth and excluded 'beyond the shadow of a doubt' the possibility that the skeleton represented a later burial.

121 Karageorghis (1967) 121 and (1969) 31. The skull and other bones are said to have belonged to two additional skeletons: Karageorghis (1963b) 378, (1963c) 549, and (1965b) 308 (but cf. (1965b) 312 n. 16: 'nos deux "esclaves" trouvés dans la tombe de Salamine').

122 Masson (1964) 213–21; cf. Karageorghis (1969) 27 and 31. Masson also thought this interpretation probable for skeletons found in the dromos of Salamis Tomb 1, for which see Dikaios (1963) 143 and 164–5. Dikaios, the excavator, interpreted these burials as later pit burials, but 'the evidence was obscured owing to the disturbance which must have taken place in recent times' (164).

123 Karageorghis (1970) 123–6 and (1969) 130 and 132.

124 Karageorghis (1970) 124, 208, 232, and 234.

125 ibid., 208. Here the ring is said to be bronze, but cf. 125 (no. 3): 'iron finger ring'.

126 *SCE* 3: 322. Chronology (of Tombs 7 and 11): 315 and 324.

127 ibid., 311; *SCE* 4.2: 42.

128 Persson (1931) 68 with n. 1.

129 Frödin and Persson (1938) 122 and 342 (skeletal material in Fürst (1930) 24–6). The tomb dates to MH III, and the reference to a 'burial of L.H. II times' (Persson (1931) 68) must be an error.

130 Blegen (1930–1) 64 and 62 fig. 11.

131 Blegen (1928) 55–7 and figs 46b and 47. Adult–child burials are not uncommon: for the Middle Helladic period see Dietz (1980) 75 and 25–6 (woman and infant); Blegen (1937) 1: 48 (woman and infant) and 43–4 (adult and child, but probably not simultaneous); Dimakopoulou and Consola (1975) 52–3 (adult and infant). The most reasonable explanation for simultaneous woman–child burials is death from the same illness; but see the references in Maringer (1942–3) 12 n. 8.

132 Blackburn (1970). The figure 9 per cent (291), i.e. twenty or twenty-one graves, must include Graves 90, 91, 92, and 120, which contained minimal and presumably intrusive skeletal material; there were scattered bones from earlier burials above Grave 22 (42).

133 Consecutive: Graves 25, 36, 69, 84, 224; probably consecutive: Graves 124 and 193. Probably simultaneous: Graves 22, 62, 152, 206; possibly simultaneous: 27, 57, 145, and 154. Grave 83 may have been used for a dual burial and then later reused for a third burial (Blackburn (1970) 80–1).

134 Male and female: Graves 57 and 62. Five skeletons: Grave 22. Dual burials of males: Graves 27 (simultaneous?), 84 (probably consecutive), 124 (consecutive?), and 152 (simultaneous). In the latter two cases a family resemblance between the skeletons is reported (Blackburn (1970) 107 and 124).

135 So Blackburn (1970) 291.

136 Frödin and Persson (1938) 116–28 (Tomb MH 90 contained a child's skeleton and some bones of an 'older individual': 125); Blegen (1930–1) 62–4. From the MH graves excavated at Asine more recently, four dual burials are reported: a woman-child burial (Dietz (1980) 75 and 25–6), a grave of a male skeleton with an infant buried on the capstone (75–7 and 63–4), and two burials in pithoi, one containing the 'scanty remains' of an adult man and woman (79, 58, 63).

137 Blackburn (1970) 291. At Kirrha the percentage was considerably higher: fifteen of fifty-nine graves held more than one burial (Dor *et al.* (1960) 116–24). In some cases the burials appear to have been simultaneous (55), and sometimes sex is identified, although it is unclear on what basis. In two cases skeletons were found outside of the tombs, lying against the covering slabs (122); but the possibility of 'sacrifices humains' is rejected (55–6).

138 The findings from Lerna and other MH cemeteries may be contrasted with those from a Celtic cemetery at Thuizy, where twenty-eight of fifty-six graves contained skeletons of a man and a woman, all buried in identical positions (four other graves contained one adult and two adolescents): Fourdrignier (1880) 319–23; Maringer (1942–3) 31 n. 96.

139 Cf. Maringer (1942–3) 16–19, 24, 31, 47, 56, and 60.

140 Mylonas (1966) 89–110 and (1972–3) 1: *passim*. Schliemann's contention (1879: 336–7) that all of the burials in Grave Circle A were simultaneous resulted from his zeal to prove that the graves contained the slain Agamemnon and his retinue. This, of course, we now know could not have been the case, and it is probable despite Schliemann's arguments that the shaft graves were used for successive burials as they were in Grave Circle B.

141 Hood and de Jong (1952) 248 n. 17.

142 Hood *et al.* (1958–9) 197 (Tombs X and XVIII: 210–12 and 220–4).

143 Hood (1973) 40–1. There is no evidence that the two cremations in Tomb 40 of the Kaloriziki cemetery (41) were simultaneous. And although the Lapithos tombs frequently held more than one skeleton, there is no certain evidence of simultaneous burial.

144 This can often be determined by careful excavation and observation: Blackburn (1970) 18; Dor *et al.* (1960) 55; Maringer (1942–3) 11.

145 Maringer (1942–3) 11.

146 ibid., 19, 20, 31, 32–3, and 52.

147 Popham *et al.* (1982) 173. Woman: 172 and pl. XXIIa. Male: 172–3, though the reasons for the sex-identification are not specifically stated. There was also a clay chest against the nearby crosswall, holding ash and small bone fragments, 'seemingly the remains of the pyre collected up after the cremation' (173).

148 At first glance we might be inclined to consider the burial of the richly adorned woman the principal burial in the grave. But how then are we to explain the cremation of the man (if the amphora held the cremation of a man, as the grave goods suggest)? The horse burials might further suggest that the cremation was of a male and

that the funeral was held chiefly in his honour. For horse burials accompanying possible cases of 'suttee' see Maringer (1942–3) 14–15, 17, 18, 24, and 32.

149 For Indian 'suttee' see Maringer (1942–3) 60–3. For the combination of cremation and inhumation, which Maringer includes among factors indicating 'ritual character', see 11, 31, 33–4, 39, 41–2, 43, and 50: in the last three cases it was the woman who was cremated.

150 It remains to be seen if evidence of violence can be found on the woman's skeleton; but it seems possible that she was bound. If this is a case of 'suttee', then clearly we are dealing with an *Adelssitte*, and I know of no other evidence for the practice in the area. For burial practices at Lefkandi see Popham *et al.* (1980) 209–16. One double inhumation and two dual cremations are reported (159 and 431); but identification of the sexes was not possible.

3 FUNERARY RITUAL KILLING IN GREEK LITERATURE AND HISTORY

1 Murray (1924) 130–2; Bowra (1962) 68; Schwenn (1915) 110–11. Homer does not mention – or is not aware of (so Schol. *Il.* 9.145) – the sacrifice of Iphigeneia; in fact, Agamemnon has a living daughter Iphianassa (*Il.* 9.145 = 9.287; cf. *Cypria* fr. 15 Allen). Pausanias (1.22.6) commends Homer for not mentioning the sacrifice of Polyxena.

2 Imitated by Vergil (*Aen.* 10.517–20; 11.81–2) and Nonnus (*Dion.* 37.47–9). For artistic representations see Kossatz-Diessmann (1981) 118–19, 121, and 131; the scene appealed particularly to the Etruscans: Camporeale (1981) 205–6 and 211; Touchefeu (1981a) 323–4.

3 Pl. *Resp.* 3, 391B; Proclus (*in R.*, vol. 1: pp. 151–3 Kroll) responds with a lengthy justification of Achilles' actions. For modern expressions of shock see e.g. Murray (1924) 141; and for the view that Homer disapproved of Achilles' actions see below, nn. 21 and 24. Readers may confirm for themselves how little attention the incident has received in literary studies of the poem.

4 Rohde (1925) 12–17; Murray (1924) 141; Andronikos (1968) 27–9, although he cites Schwenn and Nilsson (below, n. 5) with approval; Fink (1978) 303. As Schwenn (1915: 62 n. 2) noted, 'die Meisten sprechen einfach von einem "Opfer"', and one could add substantially to his short list of references. Ducrey (1968: 205), while calling the act 'le sacrifice suprême', in effect combines the three interpretations into one. In antiquity, Vergil in his imitation represented the killing as 'sacrificial' (*Aen.* 10.519: *inferias quos immolet umbris*; 11.81–2: *quos mitteret umbris/inferias*); and a scholiast on the *Iliad* understood it as a sacrifice (below, n. 17). The word used by Plato, *sphagai* (*Resp.* 3, 391B), was by his time used not only of sacrificial slaughter but also of any brutal or unjustified killing (Casabona (1966) 174–8).

5 Stengel (1910) 158 and (1920) 128; Schwenn (1915) 62; Persson (1931) 69; Wilamowitz (1931–2) 1: 307; Nilsson (1932) 117 and *GGR* 1: 178 and 376.

6 Fritze (1893) 73; Lawson (1910) 529 n. 3; Bassett (1933) 57; Kurtz and Boardman (1971) 186 ('more a matter of sheer revenge and anger than ritual'); Mylonas (1948) 60–1 and (1962) 480. Mylonas also suggested that the Trojans were to serve as Patroclus' escorts on his journey to Hades, citing as support Deiphobus' boast over the body of Hypsenor that Asius does not lie unavenged, 'for though on his way to the house of Hades . . . he will rejoice at heart, since I have provided him with a *pompos*' (*Il.* 13.414–16). But Deiphobus may mean simply that Asius will be happy to know that an enemy has followed him to Hades (so Andronikos (1968) 28), although the literal (but jocular) sense is that he will be glad of the company or guidance on the journey down. In any case, this statement – an example of the familiar taunting language of the battlefield – cannot be taken as evidence of serious religious belief, any more than Polydamas' similar taunt that Prothoenor will have the spear which killed him to use as a staff on his way to Hades (14.456–7).

7 Rohde (1925) 13 and 45 n. 12.

8 ibid., 12–17.

9 Andronikos (1968) 26. Schnapp-Gourbeillon (1982: 81) sees an indication of the sacrificial character in the words ἔδερόν τε καὶ ἄμφεπον (*Il.* 23.167), a formula found also in a sacrifice scene (*Il.* 24.622; cf. *Il.* 7.316; *Od.* 8.61 and 19.421). But I would hesitate to read very much into a similarity such as this in formulaic poetry. The poet wants the animals flayed and uses a phrase at his disposal: it is not surprising that this should be supplied from sacrificial scenes. But the similarity ends with the flaying, for the dead animals are employed in wholly different ways.

10 Fritze (1893) 72; Mylonas (1948) 59 and (1962) 480; Lowenstam (1981) 152 (with Hittite and Indic parallels n. 71).

11 Schnapp-Gourbeillon (1982) 82–3.

12 Stengel (1910) 158; Mylonas (1948) 59; Andronikos (1968) 26–7. The idea that the dead could enjoy possessions and pets is also inconsistent with the Homeric picture of the afterlife, but we should not expect consistency or logic here or in funerary practices in general: see Andronikos (1968) 26–7, and Vermeule (1979) 56–61. For archaeological evidence for the killing of horses at funerals see ch. 2 n. 119; and for dogs, Day (1984) 21–32.

13 There are several formal similarities between sacrificial ritual and funeral rites: see Burkert (1983) 49–53. Both Lowenstam (1981: 150–9) and Furley (1981: 29–30) view Patroclus' funeral itself as a kind of sacrifice. But slight similarities of language, such as that noted by Furley, 29, do not count for much, especially in formulaic poetry. And similarity does not mean identity: Vernant (1989) 39–41.

14 Rather, I think, than 'behead' specifically (although this might well

be a consequence). The word seems to be equivalent to *sphazein* (*Od.* 11.35 and 45); and the force of the prefix is that in words such as *apokteinein* and the post-Homeric *aposphazein* (for which see Casabona (1966) 167–8). But the use in the *Theogony*, with 'head' as direct object, requires a rendering 'cut from the neck' or 'cut off'.

15 Casabona (1966) 155–9.

16 *Il.* 17.566; cf. *Il.* 8.534, 11.153, 12.227, 16.650, and *Od.* 4.226. But 23.176 may be an interpolation (below, n. 24).

17 *Il.* 6.93, 6.274, 6.308; *Od.* 8.59 and 13.181–2; Germain (1954) 18. Sacrifice of twelve victims in Greek cult: 47; Stengel (1920) 119; *LSJ* and *LSJ* Suppl. s.vv. δυωδεκαΐς and δωδεκαΐς. The connection between the twelve captives and the *duōdekaïs* was made already by the Schol. *Il.* 21.27.

18 Germain (1954) 17–18, 35–6, 99 and 101.

19 See Maringer (1942–3) 102–7 and below, n. 73.

20 *Poinē*: cf. *Il.* 3.290, 5.266, 9.633–6, 13.659, 14.483, 16.398, 17.207, 18.498; *Od.* 23.312. For vengeance and compensation in Homer and in early Greek society see Glotz (1904) 47–134 and Gagarin (1981) 4–18.

21 Rohde (1925) 14; Murray (1924) 141.

22 Segal (1971).

23 Bowra (1972) 49: 'This is a tremendous occasion, and Homer not only treats it fully but in the case of the young men gives notice in advance.'

24 Murray (1924) 141; Ducrey (1968) 205 and 314 n. 2; Andronikos (1968) 28; Segal (1971) 13 (with references n. 1); so already Schol. *Il.* 23.174–6 and Eust., *Il.* 23.166–76. *Contra*: Bassett (1933) 44–6; Griffin (1980) 85 n. 9. Bassett examined the phrases κακὰ ἔργα and ἀεικέα ἔργα thoroughly and concluded that although they may occasionally convey moral disapproval (and his only examples are from the *Odyssey*), in the great majority of cases it is the 'harm done to the object of the action' which is suggested (e.g. *Il.* 7.478, 8.458, and 16.783). But 23.176 may be a post-Homeric interpolation: so Ameis and Hentze (1906) *ad loc.* Hentze found the phrase κακὰ . . . ἔργα 'ganz ungehörig' here and pointed to the fact that we should expect not δηϊόων but the aorist participle, corresponding to δειροτομήσας in 174. And the formula χαλκῷ δηϊόων, borrowed from the battlefield (above, n. 16), is unnecessary, as δειροτομήσας could easily govern υἱέας as well. Finally, we would expect μήδετο to refer forward to a future action, and not to the act which Achilles has just completed (cf. *Il.* 2.38, 7.478, 21.19, 22.395; *Od.* 3.132 and 14.243). These objections, perhaps slight in themselves, may carry some weight cumulatively, although it is difficult to distinguish between a later interpolation and a formula awkwardly or inappropriately applied by the original poet. But if 23.176 is post-Homeric, it is likely that the interpolator inserted the verse (fashioned from *Il.* 17.566 and 21.19?) in order to voice disapproval of Achilles' actions here (so Ameis and Hentze (1906) *ad loc.*).

25 Mylonas (1948) 60: 'on the same level as the killing of any warrior in revenge of a friend lost'. Bassett (1933: 57) compared the slaying of Cleobulus (*Il.* 16.330–4), who 'like the twelve youths, was captured alive'. But the similarity ends there, for Aias kills Cleobulus immediately.

26 Andronikos (1968) 27–8; Fink (1978) 303.

27 Definitions of Burkert (1979) 37.

28 For the reintegrating functions of funeral customs see Versnel (1980) 581–7. For vengeance killing at the grave in other cultures see Maringer (1942–3) 86–8.

29 Meuli (1975) 2: 924; see also ch. 1 n. 24. Cf. Burkert (1983) 53 and (1985) 192–3; Versnel (1980) 579–80.

30 Cf. Meuli (1975) 2: 888–91.

31 In tragedy, vengeance killings are often described in sacrificial language (see pp. 189–90); and in Eur. *Hec.* 262–6, Hecuba wonders if vengeance may be a motive for the sacrifice of Polyxena. And in the seventh century Ashurbanipal represents the punishment of his grandfather's killers as a funerary sacrifice: Pritchard (1955) 288; Dhorme (1933) 115. In his discussion of vengeance killing at the grave ('Strafopfer') Maringer (1942–3: 86–7) wrote: 'In dieser Strafart steckt . . . zweifellos noch ein tieferer, glabensmässiger Sinn: Es gunügte nicht allein, dass der Mörder Leben mit Leben bezahlte, sondern er sollte durch das Begrabenwerden mit seinem Opfer dessen Sklave im Jenseits werden.' Possibly; but *zweifellos*? In any case, there is no indication of such beliefs in Homer, nor in any of the historical cases I shall discuss here.

32 For Schnapp-Gourbeillon (1982: 77–88) the killing is a sacrifice, perverse and monstrous because sacrifice is appropriate to the gods, not to mortals. But the sacrifice is pure fiction, as human sacrifice 'est historiquement inexistant en Grèce' (81). But if human sacrifice was nonexistent in Greece, the later historical instances (pp. 56–60) show that execution or vengeance killing at funerals was not; and some of the dromos burials from Cyprus (pp. 35–42) seem to present evidence of funerary ritual killing of some kind.

33 In fact, Diodorus' statement does not preclude execution at the funeral, for the first clause (τοὺς φονεῖς . . . τιμωρίας ἠξίωσε) may be taken to refer only to the trial and sentencing. Hammond (1978: 339) suggested that some of the convicted were put to death immediately after the trial, while the execution of others was deferred until the time of the burial. For Diodorus' abridgement of his source see Hammond (1983) 28–9. The source according to Hammond was Diyllus (32–5), while Justinus' account derived from Cleitarchus (94–5).

34 Keramopoulos (1923) 1–110; Gernet (1981) 252–76.

35 *POxy.* 1798 fr. 1 = *FGrHist* 148 F 1; Grenfell and Hunt (1922) 125 and 131; Wilcken (1923) 151–4; Hammond (1978) 343–9. The object of ἀπετυπαν[ι/σαν] (lines 7–8) appears to have been singular and is generally thought to have been Pausanias, the actual assassin, although according to Diod. Sic. 16.94.4 he was killed on the spot.

But there may have been two versions (so Wilcken (1923) 152–3). And the tradition followed in the papyrus may be reflected by Justinus' reference to Pausanias' hanging *in cruce* (*Epit.* 9.7.10), though possibly only his corpse was crucified. Wilcken suggested that his accomplices may also have been executed by apotympanismos at the tomb.

36 Schwenn (1915) 65 n. 5; see also Meuli (1975) 2: 888 and Versnel (1980) 579 n. 175.

37 Callim. fr. 588 Pfeiffer, with other sources *ad loc.* Simus is not mentioned in the extant fragment of Aristotle (fr. 166 Rose), but surely Aristotle substantiated his assertion that the custom was still practised in Thessaly with this very example. For the identification of this Simus with the tyrant of Larissa (which has been doubted) see Sordi (1958) 366–7. According to the preserved text of Porphyry (*Quaestiones Homericae*, p. 268 Schrader), Simus was the *first* to practise the custom and thus by implication predated Achilles. But Aristotle referred to a contemporary practice (καὶ νῦν), and the appearance of Simus of Larissa and Eurydamas son of Meidius together in [Dem.] 59.108 secures the identification.

38 Alexander is said to have dragged the governor of Gaza alive around the city, in imitation of Achilles (Curtius 4.6.29; Dion. Hal. *Comp.* 18 = Hegesias, *FGrHist* 142 F 5); but the incident, not found in other sources, is of questionable historicity (Tarn (1948) 2: 265–70).

39 Walbank (1957–79) 2: 221–2; Errington (1969) 236–7.

40 Glotz (1904) 74–6; Hirzel (1909) 228; Knoch (1960) 80.

41 Tarn (1948) 2: index, s.v. Achilles; but most of Alexander's imitations of Achilles (e.g. above, n. 38) are not historical.

42 Rohde (1925) 529. For the heroic honours accorded Philopoemen see Errington (1969) 193–4; when annual sacrifices were ordained in his honour, they were of oxen (Diod. Sic. 29.18). Schwenn (1915) 65: 'Ob man sich freilich der ursprünglichen Bedeutung der Handlung noch bewusst gewesen ist, lässt sich nicht sagen.' For the 'ursprüngliche Bedeutung' see Schwenn (1915) 62.

43 Plut. *Pel.* 21.4; *De superst.* 13, 171B–E; *De def. or.* 14, 417C–D.

44 Apotympanismos: above, n. 34. Stoning: Hirzel (1909) 223–66; Fehling (1974) 59–82, with further references 59 n. 241. Stoning seems to have been seldom or never an official method of execution in Greece (60–1); rather, it was the resort of *Lynchjustiz* or mob violence, often provoked by religious offences. And although stoning played a role in some religious rituals (Burkert (1983) 5 n. 16), most notably in the expulsion of pharmakoi (ch. 5), it was not a method of sacrificial killing. In Pl. *Leg.* 9, 872B-C, if the flogging did not result in death, the means of execution is not specified (merely θανατωσάτω).

45 Nilsson (1932) 118; Rohde (1914) 119–20 n. 1; Hirzel (1908) 78; Persson (1931) 68; Picard (1933) 145–6; Fontinoy (1950) 390–1. *Contra*: Wilamowitz (1931–2) 1: 308 n. 1; Schwenn (1915) 64. Cf. Collard (1975) 2:354, who notes that 'older scholars were naturally

drawn to the Hindu analogy', with references.

46 Schwenn (1915) 64; Collard (1975) 1: 7. Willing death in Euripides: Schmitt (1921) *passim* (75–6 on Evadne); Loraux (1987) index, s.v. Euripides; Collard (1975) 2: 354–5. Evadne in later literature: 436–7.

47 The principal reference would seem to be to suicide, but Plato may also allude to those who died willingly in other ways after their lovers' deaths (such as Achilles) or even to those who tried like Orpheus to retrieve their lovers from Hades: cf. Pl. *Symp.* 179B-180B. For suicide in antiquity see Hirzel (1908) *passim.*

48 Nilsson (1932) 117.

49 Paus. 4.2.7 (= *Cypria* fr. 17 Allen), where three women (Marpessa, Cleopatra, Polydora), representing three generations of the same family, are said to have taken their own lives upon the deaths of their husbands. The suicide of Polydora/Laodameia may have been known to Homer (*Il.* 2.698–702), although possibly this allusion to Protesilaus' grieving wife inspired the story. Later versions: Schmitt (1921) 76–7 and Sarkissian (1983) 42–4.

50 The existence of a Hellenistic model has been long suspected (e.g. Rohde (1914) 142–6), for Vergil's obscure allusion (*G.* 3.258–63) presupposes familiarity with the tale. A fragment of what may be this model has now been found: Lloyd-Jones and Parsons (1983) no. 951.

51 Another suicide of a male lover in [Plut.] *Amat. Narr.* 1, 772C. Parthenius also tells of the suicides of Oinone, Cleite, and Argathone, who starves herself to death after the death of Rhesus (*Amat. Narr.* 4.72, 8.2, 36.5).

52 See Engster (1970) 1–8, and 116–53 on such suicide as a topos in Germanic literature.

53 Persson (1931) 69; Nilsson, *GGR* 1: 178. *Contra*: Wilamowitz (1931–2) 1: 308 n. 1; Schwenn (1915) 62–4.

54 Procl. *Chr.*, p. 108, 6–8 Allen. Similarly, nothing is known of the treatments of Ibycus (fr. 26 Page) and Simonides (fr. 52 Page), nothing certain of the version of Stesichorus (fr. 28 Page: the *Tabula Iliaca*), and very little of Sophocles' *Polyxena* (fr. 522–8 Radt). For later versions see Apollod. *Ep.* 5.23 and the references in Frazer (1921) *ad loc.* For Polyxena in art see Paus. 1.22.6 (Polygnotus); Wüst (1952) 1845–50; Fontinoy (1950) 393–4; Henrichs (1981) 199 n. 2; Prag (1985) 61–3 and index, s.v. Polyxena.

55 Eur. *Tro.* 628: προσφαγμάτων (cf. Eur. *Hec.* 41 and 265). For the technical sense of *prosphazein* and *prosphagma* see Casabona (1966) 170–4.

56 So Schwenn (1915) 63 (cf. Schmitt (1921) 99–100), who also felt that Achilles' slaughter of the twelve captives had had an influence. This I find less likely, although the appearance of Patroclus' ghost in *Il.* 23.65–92 may have inspired the appearance of Achilles' ghost before the Greek army, a detail probably already in the *Ilioupersis.*

57 Schol. Eur. *Hec.* 41 = *Cypria* fr. 26 Allen = Glauchus Rheginus, *FHG* 4 fr. 6a. Schwenn (1915: 63) argued that since the story could only have been alluded to in passing in the *Cypria* it is more likely

that the allusion was to the original and more familiar version; but it has been doubted that the *Kypriaka* of the scholion is the *Cypria* of the Trojan Cycle: see Jouan (1966) 368–9, with references to earlier scholarship.

58 Jouan (1966) 370; Wüst (1952) 1843; Fontinoy (1950) 384–90; King (1987) 184–201.

59 Schwenn (1915) 64. *Totenhochzeit*: Schrader (1904) 33–4; Fontinoy (1950) 390–6. The wedding motif receives full-blown treatment in Seneca's *Troades*. For what I believe to be the correct interpretation of Eur. *Hec.* 612 (sometimes viewed as a reference to a funerary wedding) see Loraux (1987) 36–41. Lycoph. *Alex.* 323–4 may also be a case of wedding imagery rather than a reference to an actual marriage in Hades (King (1987) 188).

60 See Caster (1937) 275–83, with references to earlier scholarship 275 n. 1, 277 n. 4, and 279 n. 8.

61 I find no mention in Schwenn, Andronikos, Nilsson, and others. Chudzinski (1907) cited the *De luctu* frequently (27 n. 3, 46 n. 2, 48 n. 1, 50 n. 3, 59 n. 2) but did not mention *Luct.* 14 in his discussion of *Menschenopfer* (53–4). Andronikos (1968: 27) cited the passage, but only as evidence for the burning of clothing and ornaments with the dead; and Nilsson of course knew the diatribe (*GGR* 2: 546–7). Thus it seems possible that these scholars simply assumed what I shall take pains to argue here.

62 Stengel (1910) 158; Bruck (1926) 33–4; Stommel (1954) 206: 'Mitverbrannt werden die Grabbeigaben, darunter in alter Zeit auch Menschen (Il. 23.175f; Luc. luct. 14).'

63 Rohde (1925) 524–5 with 550 n. 2.

64 Kurtz and Boardman (1971) 215.

65 Parth. *Amat. Narr.* 10.4 and 31.2; [Plut.] *Amat. Narr.* 1, 772C; Paus. 4.2.7; Ach. Tat. 3.16.2; cf. Paus. 4.13.4 (a father's suicide) and Hdt. 1.45 (Adrastus' suicide at the tomb of Atys).

66 Strabo 15.1.30 (= Onesicritus, *FGrHist* 134 F 21) and 15.1.62 (= Aristoboulus, *FGrHist* 139 F 42); Diod. Sic. 17.91.3 and 19.33–34.1–6; further references in Heckel and Yardley (1981) 305–11. Lucian had read Onesicritus (*Peregr.* 25).

67 For an indication of Lucian's familiarity with and interest in the historian see Bompaire (1958) index, s.v. Hérodote. That he particularly associated Herodotus with ethnography is suggested by his parody of Herodotean language in the *De Syria dea*: Oden (1977) 20–2.

68 See e.g. Caes. *BGall.* 6.19 on Gallic funerals. The practice of burning or burying clothing and other belongings with the dead is of course common to many peoples, including the Greeks and Romans (cf. Lucian *Nigr.* 30 and *Philops.* 27).

69 Andronikos (1968) 135.

70 ibid., 37–135.

71 Tsountas (1888) 131; Tsountas and Manatt (1897) 151; Persson (1931) 69; Wace (1932) 145–6; Karageorghis (1963a) 34, (1965b) 310, (1967) 121, and (1969) 31.

72 There were thirty-nine 'burial groups' in the Lapithos tombs, but many more individual burials (*SCE* 1: 264). The dromos burials in Tombs 417 and 420 date to early Cypro-Geometric I, while those in 422 date to later Cypro-Geometric III (233, 240, and 246).

73 Cf. Alexandrescu and Eftimie (1959) 160: 'Or, partout où les vestiges de tels rites sanglants ont été découverts par les recherches archéologiques, dans les tumulus des steppes du nord de la mer Noire ou dans les Kourganes de Moyen-Dnieper, de la Crimée du Kouban, ils révèlent une conception toute differente sur le sens du sacrifice funeraire. Dans ces tombes les individus sacrifiés étaient déposés dans une position rituelle identique à celle du personnage principal. Ils étaient luxueusement vêtus et avaient auprès d'eux certains objets et instruments dont ils se servaient pendant leur vie . . .' In the royal tombs at Ur, the women wore elaborate headdresses, musicians were buried with their harps and lyres, etc.; and there was no sign of violent death: Woolley (1934) 33–134. For a striking recent instance see Alva (1988) 510–49. At Ur the attendants were buried in a separate 'death-pit', but there were also servants buried within the chamber.

74 Alexandrescu and Eftimie (1959) 143–64; Alexandrescu (1965) 336–9 (further references 339 nn. 1–2).

75 Coldstream (1972) 20–2 and (1977) 349–50; followed by Luce (1975) 97–9. For Homeric parallels in Cyprus see also Karageorghis (1963a) 31–9 and Dikaios (1963) 172–4.

76 But Coldstream's statement (1977: 349) that 'the body of Patroclus was conveyed on his chariot to the place of burial' is unfounded: Patroclus, still on his bier (*Il.* 18.233, 18.352, 23.25, 23.171), is carried to the pyre, either in the midst of the foot soldiers or between these and the warriors in chariots (23.134; the language is ambiguous).

77 Coldstream (1977) 349.

78 ibid., 349–50.

79 Lapithos Tombs 412, 417, 420 (Cypro-Geometric I), and P. 74 (Cypro-Geometric II); absolute chronology: ch. 2 n. 103. The dromos burial of Tomb 422 dates to later Cypro-Geometric III, i.e. to the eighth century, and thus very possibly to pre-Homeric Cyprus also. This is acknowledged by Coldstream (1977: 357 n. 22): 'The Lapithos tombs . . . offer precedents for human sacrifice, but one hopes that this was never a normal practice at any time.'

80 Coldstream (1977) 350 (italics Coldstream's).

81 Karageorghis (1963a) 36 n. 19.

82 ibid., 33 n. 6; Karageorghis (1967) 10–11. Luce's statement (1975: 99) that 'cremation is the rule in the Salamis interments' (implicit in Coldstream (1972) 20 and (1977) 349–50) is incorrect: see Karageorghis (1967) 119–21.

83 Coldstream (1972) 21.

84 Bowra (1972) 49.

4 HUMAN SACRIFICE IN GREEK MYTH, CULT, AND HISTORY

1 Wachsmuth (1846) 2: 551. Cf. Pearson (1913) 847; Frazer (1921) 2: 119 n. 1; Parke and Wormell (1956) 1: 296; Nilsson, *GGR* 1: 23. Farnell (*CGS* 4: 209), in a discussion of human sacrifices prescribed by Delphi, wrote as follows: 'The instances quoted above are myths, it is true: but for the purpose of our investigation into prehistoric thought and practice, myths are facts.'

2 Schwenn (1915) 132. More recently: Brelich (1969b) 195; Henrichs (1981) 195.

3 Cf. Veyne (1988) *passim*.

4 Daughters of Erechtheus: Lycurg. *Leoc.* 98–101, with a lengthy excerpt from Euripides' *Erechtheus* (= fr. 50 Austin); Phanodemus, *FGrHist* 325 F 4; Apollod. *Bibl.* 3.15.4, with other sources in Frazer (1921) *ad loc.*; Parke–Wormell no. 195; Fontenrose (1978) no. L32. Aglaurus: Philochorus, *FGrHist* 328 F 105. On the chronological difficulty of having a daughter of Cecrops sacrificed during the reign of Erechtheus see Jacoby's commentary *ad loc.*

5 Apollod. *Bibl.* 3.15.8; further references in Frazer (1921) *ad loc.* Identified with daughters of Erechtheus: Eur. fr. 65.73–4 Austin; Dem. 60.27; Phanodemus, *FGrHist* 325 F 4.

6 Dem. 60.29; Ael. *VH* 12.28; Paus. 1.5.2; further references in Frazer (1921) 2: 118–19 n. 1; Parke–Wormell no. 209; Fontenrose (1978) no. L44.

7 Eur. *Heracl.* 406–629; Paus. 1.32.6; Schol. Pl. *Hp. Ma.* 293A.

8 Paus. 9.17.1; Schachter (1981–6) 1: 35.

9 Ant. Lib. *Met.* 25 (= Corinna fr. 3 Page); Ov. *Met.* 13.65–99; Schachter (1981–6) 2: 116–17; Dowden (1989) 168.

10 Cf. Diod. Sic. 8.8 (= Myron, *FGrHist* 106 F 9–10); Parke–Wormell nos 361–2; Fontenrose (1978) no. Q14; Dowden (1989) 24. Messenian Wars: Pearson (1962) 397–426.

11 Eur. *Phoen.* 903–1094; Paus. 9.25.1; Apollod. *Bibl.* 3.6.7, with further references Frazer (1921) *ad loc.* For Euripides' apparent invention of the incident see O'Connor-Visser (1987) 74 and 83–5 and Foley (1985) 107–8, with references 108 n. 7.

12 Plut. *Thes.* 32.4 (= Dicaearchus fr. 66 Wehrli); the story appears only here, and elsewhere the eponymous hero is named Marathon.

13 Schol. and Tzetz. Schol. Lycoph. *Alex.* 160, explaining the obscure reference in *Alex.* 159–60. Cook, *Zeus* 3.1: 525–6, argued for actual human sacrifices in the cult of Zeus Ombrios (cf. Farnell, *CGS* 1: 42).

14 References in Burkert (1979) 169–70 n. 13; Latin quotation: Hor. *Carm.* 3.19.2.

15 Burkert (1979) 62.

16 See Halliday (1928) 76.

17 Parke and Wormell (1956) 1: 296; Fontenrose (1978) 25 (Topic Ic).

18 Burkert (1979) 22–6.

19 Burkert (1983) 66 with n. 33 and (1985) 439 n. 13. In Orchomenos, *koroi* and *korai* made yearly offerings to Metioche and Menippe (Ant. Lib. *Met.* 25), which may suggest an association with initiations of both sexes.

20 Cf. Graf (1984) 245–54.

21 Burkert (1983) 64.

22 Cf. Loraux (1987) 31–48.

23 Parke–Wormell no. 532; Fontenrose (1978) no. L128.

24 [Plut.] *De fluviis* 9.1 = Timolaus, *FGrHist* 798 F 1, and Agathocles, *FGrHist* 799 F 1; cf. the alternate version in *De fluviis* 9.2 and a similar dive by Aegyptus (upon sacrificing his daughter) in 16.1. Jephthah's vow: *Judges* 11.29–40. For the motif of sacrificing the first thing one meets cf. Callim. fr. 200b Pfeiffer; see also Frazer (1921) 2: 394–404 and Thompson (1955–8) 5: 317, no. S241, and 6: index, s.v. First.

25 Lack of favourable winds prompts the sacrifice of Polyxena (see pp. 61–2), while a storm at sea leads to Idomeneus' sacrifice of his son. And Sinon pretends that he was chosen to be sacrificed to placate the winds (Verg. *Aen.* 2.108–44; cf. Quint. Smyrn. 12.375–86). The sacrifice of Iphigeneia before the Greeks' departure for Troy seems to have inspired tales of human sacrifices required before their return (Schwenn (1915) 122–3), and the connection is made explicitly in Sinon's fictitious oracle (*Aen.* 2.116–19).

26 Plut. *Conv. sept. sap.* 20, 163A–D, and *De sollertia animalium* 36, 984E (= Myrsilus, *FGrHist* 477 F 14); cf. Ath. 11.15, 466C-781C (= Anticleides, *FGrHist* 140 F 4), where the maiden is sacrificed to Poseidon.

27 Bacchyl. 17; Hellanicus, *FGrHist* 323a F 14; Eur. *Heracl.* 1326–8; Diod. Sic. 4.60.1–61.4; Plut. *Thes.* 15–19; Apollod. *Bibl.* 3.15.8 and *Epit.* 1.7–9, with further references in Frazer (1921) *ad loc.*; Schwenn (1915) 106 n. 2; Parke–Wormell no. 210; Fontenrose (1978) no. L45.

28 Hesione: Hellanicus, *FGrHist* 4 F 26b and 108; Diod. Sic. 4.42; Philostr. Jun. *Imag.* 12 (ecphrasis); Apollod. *Bibl.* 2.5.9, with further references in Frazer (1921) *ad loc.*; Schwenn (1915) 135 n. 3. Andromeda: Soph. fr. 126–36 Radt; Eur. fr. 114–56 Nauck; Apollod. *Bibl.* 2.4.3, with further references Frazer (1921) *ad loc.*; Schwenn (1915) 135 n. 4; ecphrases in Philostr. *Imag.* 1.29 and Ach. Tat. 3.6–7.

29 See also Callim. fr. 98–9 Pfeiffer and Bremmer (1983a) 106–7. This is often called a 'sacrifice', and it would be natural to assume that the maiden would not return from her conjugal visit. But Strabo (6.1.6) mentions only a tribute (*dasmos*), and the *Diegeseis* on Callim. fr. 98 now make the nature of the tribute clear: a bed and a young girl were left for the Hero; the next morning her parents would return to escort their daughter – a virgin no longer – home.

30 Eusebius (*Praep. Evang.* 5.18.5) says that the Athenian youths were sent to Crete to be sacrificed (τυθησομένους); and human sacrifice is mentioned in Soph. fr. 126 Radt, but not in direct reference to the exposure of Andromeda. And there is occasional

sacrificial colouring: Alcyoneus is led by a priest to the cave crowned with *stemmata* (Ant. Lib. *Met.* 8.4–6; cf. Hdt. 2.45.1 and 7.197.2; Eur. *IA* 1080, 1478, 1567; Eur. *Heracl.* 529; Callim. fr. 481 Pfeiffer). It is perhaps unnecessary to dwell on the non-sacrificial character of these exposures; but often they are called 'human sacrifices' and have been taken as evidence for actual practices, e.g. by Frazer (1921) 1: 208 n. 2 (of Andromeda and Hesione): 'Both tales may have originated in a custom of sacrificing maidens to be brides of the Sea.'

31 See e.g. Kirk (1970) 31–41. For similar stories in the folk literature of other cultures see Thompson (1955–8) 5: 319 (no. S262) and Burkert (1983) 64 n. 25.

32 E.g. Jeanmaire (1939) 227–383; Calame (1977) 1: 228–9.

33 Cf. Philostr. *VA* 6.20; Serv. Verg. *Aen.* 2.116; Hyg. *Fab.* 261; ps.-Acro Schol. Hor. *Carm.* 1.7.10.

34 Cic. *Tusc.* 2.14, 34; Plut. *Apophthegmata Laconica* 40, 239C–D; Paus. 3.16.10–11; Philostr. *VA* 6.20; Lucian *Anach.* 38–9; Sext. Emp. *Pyr.* 3.208. Of these writers Cicero, Plutarch, and Lucian report that the youths frequently died under the blows; but in *VA* 6.20 Apollonius states that they do not die.

35 See n. 34. For the historical relationship between the two rituals see Tigerstedt (1965–78) 2: 453–4 nn. 49–50 and Graf (1985) 88 n. 86. The late date of the myth of human sacrifice is also indicated by the role of the four Spartan *obai* in the story, a detail which seems to reflect conditions only of Hellenistic times (Graf (1985) 87 n. 81).

36 Frazer (1898) 3: 341–2; Farnell, *CGS* 2: 439; Jeanmaire (1939) 511; Brelich (1969a) 133–6 and (1969b) 203 (with references n. 12); Calame (1977) 1: 278–81; Bremmer (forthcoming) ch. 3; further references in Graf (1985) 86 n. 79.

37 See Frazer (1898) 3: 342; van Gennep (1960) 78–9 and 174–5; Brelich (1969a) index, s.v. fustigazione; Bremmer (1978) 10–13 (further references 11 n. 44); for ritual flagellation in Greek cult see Graf (1985) 140 n. 21.

38 Brelich (1969b) 203–7. Symbolic death: Eliade (1965) 13–20; van Gennep (1960) 75; Brelich (1969a) index, s.vv. morte rituale and sacrifici umani nel mito; Burkert (1985) 260–1; Graf (1985) 414 with n. 49. For a striking instance from antiquity see Diod. Sic. 4.24.4–6: in what was clearly a rite of passage attached to the cult of Iolaus at Agyrium, boys left their hair uncut from birth until they performed certain sacrifices; those failing to do so were rendered speechless and 'like the dead', until they pledged to make the sacrifices (for silence and symbolic death cf. Brelich (1969a) 80 n. 84).

39 Paus. 9.16.7–9; Graf (1979) 33–41.

40 Lloyd-Jones (1983) 96–7; Dowden (1989) 33–4; Graf (1985) 414–15. Graf cites what may be the closest parallel from antiquity, a ritual of the Luperci in which two noble youths are touched on the forehead with a knife bloody from a goat sacrifice (Plut. *Rom.* 21.4–5).

41 Brelich (1969a) index, s.v. Artemis; Jeanmaire (1939) 257–64 and 511; Kahil (1977) 89 n. 28; Dowden (1989) name index, s.v.

Artemis. A close connection between Brauron and Halai is supported by the presence at Halai of krateriskoi (fragments of which have been found in abundance in the sanctuary at Brauron): Dowden (1989) 88 and 95–6.

42 Parke–Wormell no. 551; Fontenrose (1978) nos 174–5; Farnell, *CGS* 5: 168; Schwenn (1915) 126–7; Schachter (1981–6) 1: 182; Brelich (1969a) 362 and (1969b) 197–8.

43 [Plut.] *Parall.* 35, 314C = Aristodemus, *FGrHist* 22 F 1a; Lydus *Mens.* 4.147 = Aristodemus, *FGrHist* 22 F 1b; Parke–Wormell no. 530; Fontenrose (1978) no. L126.

44 Schwenn (1915) 126.

45 Further references in Frazer (1921) *ad loc.*; Burkert (1983) 114 n. 27; Radt (1977) 99–100; Piccaluga (1968) 191–210.

46 Procl. *Chr.*, p. 104 Allen; cf. Apollod. *Epit.* 3.21–3, with further references Frazer (1921) *ad loc.* For the few artistic representations see Prag (1985) 61–7.

47 Mounychia: Suda s.v. Ἔμβαρός εἰμι; other sources in Brelich (1969a) 248–9 n. 44 and Sale (1975) 275–7. Brauron: Schol. Ar. *Lys.* 645 and Suda s.v. Ἄρκτος ἢ Βραυρωνίοις; texts in Brelich (1969a) 248–9 n. 44. For these myths and their relationship to the Iphigeneia story see Brelich (1969a) 246–89; Sale (1975) 265–84; Montepaone (1979a) 343–64 and (1979b) 65–76; Henrichs (1981) 199–208; Lloyd-Jones (1983) 87–102; Dowden (1989) 9–47. The Arcadian myth of Callisto also seems related: Henrichs (1981) 201–3; Dowden (1989) 182–91.

48 In addition to the references in n. 47, see the fundamental articles of Kahil (1965) 20–33 and (1977) 86–98, both with references to excavation reports; see also Parke (1977) 137–41; Burkert (1985) 263; Cole (1984) 238–44; Osborne (1985) 154–72; Garland (1987) 113–14 and 208 (Mounychia); extensive bibliography in Perlman (1989) 131–3.

49 Foundation of cult: Eur. *IT* 1462–7; Paus. 1.33.1. Iphigeneia's tomb/heröon: Eur. *IT* 1464; Kahil (1965) 20 n. 2; Osborne (1985) 156 and 249 n. 6. Iphigeneia sacrificed at Brauron: Schol. Ar. *Lys.* 645 (= Euphorion fr. 91 Powell); Phanodemus, *FGrHist* 325 F 14.

50 Osborne (1985) 164 and 250 n. 19.

51 The plot has thickened considerably with the appearance of a goddess I-pe-me-de-ja on a Linear B tablet: see Appendix B. Iphigeneia is often thought to have been a goddess (or a hypostasis of Artemis) in origin: e.g. Clement (1934) 395–7; Schachter (1981–6) 1: 96; Lloyd-Jones (1983) 95–6. But see Dowden (1989) 45–6.

52 See Dowden (1989) 23–5. Inscriptions from Demetrias and Larissa in Thessaly provide evidence for a practice *nebeuein*, possibly related to *nebros* ('fawn') and parallel to *arkteuein*, 'play the bear' (41–2; Clement (1934) 401–9). Cf. Schachter (1981–6) 1: 94–8, who entertains the possibility that Iphigeneia was worshipped at Aulis before her appearance in the Trojan Cycle but concedes that 'we cannot overlook the possibility that it was the epic tradition which

gave rise to a "reconstruction" of the sanctuary in conformity with it'. Activity on the site at Brauron goes back to the Geometric period, and Iphigeneia's shrine originates in the sixth century (Osborne (1985) 156 with 249 nn. 5–6).

53 See Henrichs (1981) 203 n. 3, and to his references add Solmsen (1981) 357.

54 Henrichs (1981) 198–9 n. 2; Aesch. *Ag*. 104–247, 1525–9, 1555–9; Pind. *Pyth*. 11.22–3.

55 Solmsen (1981) 353–8.

56 Farnell, *CGS* 4: 274. Ancient sources: Schol. Eur. *Phoen*. 1408; Zen. 4.29; further references in Nilsson (1906) 169 n. 1.

57 Borthwick (1972) 17–21.

58 Prott (1897) 203; Cook, *Zeus* 1: 659: 'We must suppose that originally a child, not a calf, was struck by the axe.' For the assertion of Euelpis that human sacrifices were offered to Dionysus on Tenedos (possibly a remnant of a myth attached to this rite) see pp. 127–8.

59 Meuli (1975) 2: 1007–8. See also Burkert (1983) 165 and 183; Graf (1985) 76–7.

60 Porph. *Abst*. 2.29–30 = Theophr. fr. 18 Pötscher; other sources in Bouffartigue and Patillon (1977–9) 2: 51–2. For the Bouphonia see 51–8, with bibliography 52 n. 1; Meuli (1975) 2: 1004–6; Burkert (1983) 136–43 and (1985) 230–1; Durand (1986) *passim*.

61 Prott (1897) 187–204; answered by Stengel (1897) 399–411 and (1910) 215–18.

62 Herbillon (1929) 43; cf. the story of Coresus and Callirhoe, also involving human sacrifice, which soon follows (Paus. 7.21.1–5).

63 Farnell, *CGS* 2: 455, followed by Frazer (1898) 4: 146. Nilsson (1906) 216–17 and 294–7. Herbillon (1929) 37–54.

64 Massenzio (1968) 101–32, with full discussion of other interpretations, 107–111; see also Brelich (1969a) 366–77; Furley (1981) 114–51, esp. 116–28; Dowden (1989) 169–73.

65 See van Gennep (1960) index, s.v. Baptism; Eliade (1965) index, s.vv. Baptism and Baths, Ritual. For ritual bathing in Greek cult see Ginouvès (1962) 235–428.

66 Furley (1981) 126 and 140–1. Initiation into a particular cult and into adulthood are by no means mutually exclusive; in ancient Greece the two are often inseparable, participation in religious life serving to define age divisions and social status.

67 See Dowden (1989) 172–3 for interpretation.

68 Drunkenness and murder: Paus. 9.8.2 (see p. 82); murder of Icarius: Burkert (1983) 223 n. 37. Child-slaying: Burkert (1983) 168–79. Resistance myths: Dodds (1960) xxv–xxvii; Coche de la Ferté (1980) 174–9. See also Coche de la Ferté (1980) 148–9 for a fragment of a late poem (Page (1942) no. 134), in which an enemy of Dionysus is dressed in a deerskin to be torn apart and eaten by his fellows. Death of Dionysus: Coche de la Ferté (1980) 179–85; West (1983) 74 and 160–1; Detienne (1979) 68–94. For more violent stories connected with Dionysus see below, n. 150.

69 Dodds (1951) 278 and (1960) xviii-xix; Rohde (1925) 283–5; Farnell, *CGS* 5: 164–72; Coche de la Ferté (1980) 135–74 and 230–1. For Dionysiac cannibalism imputed to the Thracian Bassaroi see Porph. *Abst.* 2.8.3 (= Theophr. fr. 3.19–25 Pötscher), and for sparagmos of human victims among the Celts, Strabo 4.4.6.

70 West (1983) 160 n. 69; Henrichs (1978) 121–60 and (1982) 137–60, esp. 143–7. See also Bremmer (1984) 267–86 and, for the development of the modern conception of the god, Henrichs (1984) 205–40.

71 Henrichs (1978) 147–52 and (1982) 143–4. For the sole inscriptional evidence for omophagy, of disputed significance, see Henrichs (1982) 149–52 and Coche de la Ferté (1980) 134–5.

72 Oppermann (1934) 34. Other etymologies: 34–5.

73 England (1886) xx; Platnauer (1938) 117–18 (on *IT* 1459). More recently, Muth (1988: 97 n. 215) writes of 'ein Alibi'.

74 E.g. Paus. 8.53.2–3 (Artemis' pursuit of Leimon re-enacted in ritual); Paus. 2.3.6–7 (yearly sacrifices at Corinth grounded in the murder of Medea's children); Paus. 2.32.2 (festival of the Lithobolia at Troezen traced to the stoning of maidens during *stasis*); Paus. 8.23.6–7 (similar aition of the Hanged Artemis); Plut. *Quaest. Graec.* 12, 293D-F (Delphic ritual grounded in story of Charila's suicide); Schol. Pind. *Ol.* 13.56 (aition for the Hellotia, involving the murder of Eurytione and Hellotis and the resultant plague). Many more examples could be adduced; my point is that human sacrifice is a prominent but hardly essential element in myths which follow the pattern violation-plague-oracle-institution of ritual, and that only the last of these elements may safely be regarded as historical.

75 Brelich (1969b) 197–8; Henrichs (1981) 205; cf. Burkert (1985) 65–6. For the equivalence of human and animal victim cf. Porph. *Abst.* 2.55.1.

76 There are brief allusions also in [Pl.] *Minos* 315C (see p. 115) and Schol. Ap. Rhod. *Argon.* 2.653, where, however, it is said only that it is the custom for the descendants of Phrixus to enter the prytany building and sacrifice (active) to Zeus Laphystios, presumably an error or case of textual corruption (cf. Cook, *Zeus* 2.2: 904 n. 1).

77 The phrase bracketed in my translation seems to be a gloss. The main difficulties lie in 197.2, where there is an abrupt change from plural to singular with ὡς θύεται. In the previous clause the MSS give either ἐσελθόντες or ἐστέλλοντο; most editors print the latter, and I follow them in my translation. But I am inclined to favour ἐσελθόντες (cf. Schol. Ap. Rhod. *Argon.* 2.653: εἰσιέναι εἰς τὸ πρυτανεῖον), although there must then be a lacuna after πρυτανήιον: so Legrand *ad loc.*, who would also like to place ὡς θύεται . . . ἐξαχθείς after θύσεσθαι μέλλῃ. This drastic measure removes the sudden change of number; but the lacuna remains.

78 So Burkert (1983) 115

79 ibid., 115; Harrison (1922) 109–10; Fontenrose (1948) 161 n. 89.

80 *Mellein* is also found in the myth of Phrixus: Paus. 9.34.5; Schol.

Ap. Rhod. *Argon.* 2.653; Schol. Ar. *Nub.* 257.

81 Certainly not a pharmakos rite, as Schwenn (1915: 43–5) argued (cf. Harrison (1922) 110). It is true that the sacrificial victim is said to have been led out in a procession (Hdt. 7.197.2: σὺν πομπῇ ἐξαχθείς; for *agein* and compounds used of pharmakos rituals see p. 164). But Herodotus uses forms of *thuein* throughout the passage, and his description of the human sacrifice is strikingly reminiscent of his account of the attempted sacrifice of Heracles, whom the Egyptians crowned and led out for sacrifice to Zeus (2.45.1: στέψαντες οἱ Αἰγύπτιοι ὑπὸ πομπῆς ἐξῆγον ὡς θύσοντες τῷ Διί). In 7.197.3 the Achaeans were 'making Athamas a purification', which suggests that this was a 'purification sacrifice' (cf. ch. 1 n. 16), closer to Epimenides' purification of Attica with human blood (pp. 155–6) than to pharmakos rites. And other details, especially the return of the young man after his exile, do not accord with what is known of pharmakos ritual (see ch. 5).

82 Cf. Fehling (1971) 106–7 and 132–3.

83 Paus. 8.32.2; Schol. Ap. Rhod. *Argon.* 1.599. Zeus Lykaios also had cults in Megalopolis (Paus. 8.30.2), Tegea (Paus. 8.53.11), and possibly Sparta (see below, n. 85). And outside of Cyrene there was a hill of Zeus Lykaios (Hdt. 4.203.2; Cook, *Zeus* 1: 89–92).

84 Every four years: Fougères (1904) 1433 (others have argued that the festival was trieteric, or that it was held every nine years, the time of the werewolves' tenure in the wild). Among the oldest in Greece: see Immerwahr (1891) 3 for references. For the cult see 1–24; Nilsson (1906) 8–10 and *GGR* 1: 397–401; Cook, *Zeus* 1: 63–99; Schwenn (1915) 20–5; Eckels (1937) 49–63; more recently: Piccaluga (1968) 15–28; Burkert (1983) 84–93; Mainoldi (1984) 11–18; Jost (1985) 180–5 and 249–69; Buxton (1987) 67–74. Testimonia for the sanctuary, cult, and games in Immerwahr (1891) 1–24; for inscriptions see also Burkert (1983) 92 n. 39 and Jost (1985) 183–5.

85 While in Sparta: Alcman fr. 24 Page. Wide (1893: 11–12) placed a cult of Zeus Lykaios in Sparta, but 'nicht ohne Bedenken'. Possibly Alcman composed the hymns for nearby Tegea, where there was an altar of Lycaean Zeus on the road leading to Sparta (Paus. 8.53.11).

86 Theophrastus has τοῖς Λυκαίοις, which Cook (*Zeus* 1: 76 n. 3), unwilling to accept periodic sacrifices in the cult, took either for a 'loose expression for "in the rites of Zeus *Lýkaios*"' or for an error on the part of Porphyry. In the *Minos* ἐν τῇ Λυκαίᾳ probably = ἐν τῇ Λυκαίᾳ ἑορτῇ (Burkert (1983) 85: 'at the "Lykaia festival"').

87 = *FGrHist* 320 F 1 and Scopas, *FGrHist* 413 F 1. The text bristles with cruces. Euanthes is otherwise unknown, and possibly the fragment should be assigned to Neanthes: Müller, *FHG* 3: 11; Jacoby, *FGrHist* 3B, Komm. (Noten), 54 n. 5; Neanthes, *FGrHist* 84 F 41. For the author of the *Olympionikai* the MSS give *ita copas* or *acopas*, and Scopas and other names have been proposed. After *senio*, the MSS have *id quoque fabius*; but the mention of a Latin author

Fabius at this point does not accord with the content of the following sentence, and I thus accept the emendation *fabulosius* for my translation. Demaenetus and Damarchus are certainly one and the same boxer, although Jost (1985: 259) treats them as two distinct persons.

88 Burkert (1983) 88; Cook (*Zeus* 1: 73) also suggested a historical change. For other solutions see Mainoldi (1984) 31 n. 11 and Jost (1985) 260–1.

89 Hyde (1903) no. 74; Moretti (1957) no. 359. Hyde placed Damarchus' victory either before Ol. 75 (480 BC) or shortly after Ol. 83 (448). Burkert (1983: 85) accepts Moretti's date of *c.* 400. The dates are based on the style of the epigram quoted by Pausanias and the fact that the statues described by Pausanias before he comes to Damarchus' belong (with one exception) to the fifth century, while those which follow belong to the fifth or the early fourth century.

90 Jost (1985) 260–1.

91 References in Frazer (1921) 1: 390–1 n. 1 and Piccaluga (1968) 27 n. 43. For the myth see Piccaluga (1968) 31–146; Eckels (1937) 55–8; Halliday (1928) 169–70; Burkert (1983) 86–7; Buxton (1987) 72–4.

92 In Achaeus fr. 2 Snell-Kannicht (*Azanes*), it appears that the chorus pleads with Lycaon to stop the human sacrifice. Xenocles (fr. 1 Snell-Kannicht) and Astydamas (fr. 4a Snell-Kannicht) each wrote a *Lycaon*. For Tantalus, Thyestes, and similar stories see Burkert (1983) 99–105 and Piccaluga (1968) 156–90 and 210–13.

93 Roscher (1892) 701–9; Halliday (1928) 172–3; Jacoby, *FGrHist* 3B, Komm. (Text), 65–6; Jost (1985) 255–8.

94 Frazer (1921) 1: 394–5 n. 2; Burkert (1983) 87 n. 18; Henrichs (1987) 254–67; see also above, n. 47.

95 Immerwahr (1891) 16–18; Cook, *Zeus* 1: 63–8; Nilsson *GGR* 1: 398; Jost (1985) 250–1.

96 Müller (1851) 22–38 and (1857–69) 2: 78–108; Mannhardt (1905) 2: 336–44; Immerwahr (1891) 22–4.

97 Cook, *Zeus* 1: 63–81; Nilsson (1906) 9–10 and *GGR* 1: 400–1.

98 Gernet (1981) 126–7; Jeanmaire (1939) 555–9; Frazer (1898) 4: 189–90; Burkert (1983) 88–9.

99 Burkert (1983) 84–93, followed by Buxton (1987) 69–72.

100 See the brief but excellent discussion of Burkert (1985) 260–4; see also Jeanmaire (1939) *passim*; Brelich (1969a) *passim*; Versnel (1990) 44–59.

101 See Piccaluga (1968) 42–6 and Burkert (1983) 86–7, who notes that in the Hesiodic version Zeus brings Arcas back to life, perhaps another indication of the initiatory character of the Arcadian myth–ritual complex. 'Death' of the initiate: above, n. 38. For a brighter picture of the education of Arcadian youth see Polyb. 4.20–1.

102 Bremmer (1978) 18; Dowden (1989) subject index, s.v. selectivity; cf. the ritual performed at Alos (pp. 92–6).

103 For Jeanmaire (1939: 55–9) the priesthood was a survival of a

society of *loups-garous*. For Burkert (1983: 89–92) the ritual was originally an initiation into the adult warrior society. There is no indication that the boxer Damarchus became a priest of Zeus Lykaios; but in the (historically later?) ritual described by Euanthes possibly the member of the family of Anthus who underwent the 'transformation' was thus initiated into the priesthood.

104 Burkert (1983) 127–30; Halliday (1928) 66–71; Jeanmaire (1939) 387–401; Brelich (1969a) 387–438.

105 Gernet (1981) 128–9.

106 Hes. fr. 163 Merkelbach-West; Apollod. *Bibl.* 3.8.1; further references in Piccaluga (1968) 49 n. 8. Thyestes and Tereus also upset tables: 49–52; Guépin (1968) 52–4; Burkert (1983) 129.

107 Kourouniotis (1904) 153–214, esp. 163–70; further references in Burkert (1983) 85 n. 10, Cook, *Zeus* 1: 81–8, and Jost (1985) 180–3.

108 Kourouniotis (1904) 167–8.

109 Coche de la Ferté (1980) 150; Mainoldi (1984) 11–18; Jost (1985) 258–67. Jost (1985: 254) also sees a human sacrifice in a passage of Nicolaus Damascenus (*FGrHist* 90 F 31), which describes the Spartans' murder of Cresphontes and their attempts to eradicate his offspring: the Spartans desired to kill Cresphontes' sons, 'whom at that time their grandfather had taken to Trapezous together with his pregnant daughter, intending to sacrifice to Zeus Akraios' (οὓς τότε ὁ μητροπάτωρ ἅμα τῇ θυγατρὶ κυούσῃ θύειν μέλλων Διὶ Ἀκραίῳ εἰς Τραπεζοῦντα μετεπέμψατο). Although it is of course possible to construe the relative pronoun as the object of θύειν as well as μετεπέμψατο, θύειν is clearly intransitive here (as often); for a grandfather's duties in this regard cf. Isae. 8.15–16. By deceiving the grandfather (Cypselus), the Spartans succeed in killing the two boys but not the newborn Aegyptus. There is no reason why Cypselus should wish to sacrifice his grandchildren, and had he really intended to do so, then obviously the Spartans could have achieved their aim simply by leaving well enough alone.

110 E.g. Eckels (1937) 51–4 and 58–9; Burkert (1983) 90; Buxton (1987) 68–9. Already in the nineteenth century Mannhardt wrote of 'das wirkliche oder symbolische Opfer eines Kindes', questioning the reality of the human sacrifice at least for the time of Plato; and even for earlier times he felt that Zeus's anger and punishment of Lycaon were inconsistent with the actual offering of a human victim to this same deity (Mannhardt (1905) 2: 340–2).

111 Burkert (1983) 90.

112 Cf. Buxton (1987) 72.

113 Plin. *NH* 8.34: *Euanthes . . . tradit Arcadas scribere*. Mayhoff's tentative suggestion *scribit Arcadas tradere*, though often accepted, is 'sicher falsch': Jacoby, *FGrHist* 3B, Komm. (Noten), 54 n. 5.

114 Kourouniotis (1904) 178–84.

115 ibid., 164–8; Dow (1937) 120–6.

116 Roman period: Jost (1985) 182–3 and 185. Inscriptions: *IG* V, 2, nos 515Bb.31 and 463.7, from Lycosura and Megalopolis respectively.

Fougères (1904: 1435) suggested that the games had been transferred to Megalopolis. Jost (1985: 185) is inclined to believe that Lykaion was still the site of the Lykaia in the second century. But it is difficult to explain away Pausanias' explicit statement about the hippodrome and stadium that 'in antiquity [τὸ δὲ ἀρχαῖον] they would hold the contest of the Lykaia here' (8.38.5). And surely if the games were still held the victors would continue to set up statues.

117 But if Phylarchus, *FGrHist* 81 F 69, is any indication of his readiness to report fictional human sacrifices as historical, it may give us some idea of the context: instructed by an oracle to sacrifice yearly a noble maiden selected by lot, King Demophon of Elaeusa withholds his daughters from the lottery; when this privilege is challenged by one Mastusius, Demophon sacrifices his daughter; Mastusius retaliates by killing the King's daughters and serving him wine mixed with their blood; and Demophon has Mastusius and the mixing bowl thrown into the sea (see Burkert (1983) 245–6).

118 See ch. 1 n. 14.

119 Eitrem (1938) 20–3; cf. Nilsson (1906) 405–6 and Stengel (1910) 93. Human sacrifice at Salamis: pp. 111–15; Messenian War: p. 74.

120 Hittites: Masson (1950a) 5–9; Kümmel (1967) 150–68. Persians: Hdt. 7.39.3–40.1; Masson (1950a) 13–15. For 'dichotomy rites' in these and other cultures see Masson (1950a) 10–17; Nilsson (1906) 404–6; Casabona (1966) 216–19 and 224; Mainoldi (1984) 52–4; Pritchett (1974–85) 3: 196–202; Versnel (1975) 104–8.

121 Nilsson (1913) 314 and *GGR* 1: 106–7; so also Schwenn (1915) 80–1.

122 Hittites and Persians: above, n. 120. Punishment: see Versnel (1975) 107–8. Hippolyta: 108; Pind. *Nem.* 4.57; Schol. Ar. *Nub.* 1063a; Schol. Ap. Rhod. *Argon.* 5.224.

123 So Frazer (1921) 2: 72–3 n. 1. In Pherecydes, *FGrHist* 3 F 62, Peleus plunders Iolcus together with Jason and the Tyndaridae, details found also in the *Bibliotheca*.

124 References in Burkert (1979) 174 n. 13. See also Fontenrose (1978) 145–8 and Schachter (1981–6) 2: 122.

125 So Schwenn (1915) 120.

126 But see now Cartledge (1987) 212 and 291, who traces Agesilaus' undying hatred of the Thebans to this very incident.

127 Henrichs (1981) 213–17.

128 *POxy.* 2165 = Alcaeus fr. 129.9 Lobel-Page. For the relevance of the fragment here see Henrichs (1981) 222–3 and Graf (1985) 76. Omestes has now shown up, again in a Lesbian context, on another papyrus: below, n. 150.

129 Pritchett (1974–85) 3: 175–8. Themistocles built a temple of Artemis Aristoboule in thanks for the victory: Plut. *De Herodoti malignitate* 37, 869C–D, and *Them.* 22.1–2; Frost (1980) 184–5.

130 Bodin (1917) 122; Henrichs (1981) 210 n. 2.

131 Vermeule (1979) 96, without explanation.

132 Ion of Chios, *FGrHist* 392 F 7, with Jacoby's commentary *ad loc.*

133 E.g. Harrison (1922) 487–8; Green (1970) 185; Podlecki (1975) 104; Frost (1980) 150; Henrichs (1981) 208–24; Graf (1985) 76. On the other hand Cook (*Zeus* 1: 656–7 n. 1) wrote, 'It is only too probable that the Persian youths met their fate as described by Plutarch'; and Schwenn (1915: 75–6) did not rule out the historicity of the incident; see also Stengel (1910) 93–4 and 99; Eitrem (1938) 20; Baelen (1961) 159–61, who, while noting the difficulty presented by the inclusion of Psyttaleia, accepted the account as factual; Nilsson (1906) 406 n. 1 and *GGR* 1: 133; Brelich (1969b) 200 n. 7; Guépin (1968) 163 ('a historical fact'); Vermeule (1979) 96; Coche de la Ferté (1980) 158–9. Further references in Graf (1985) 76 n. 19 and Henrichs (1981) 211 nn. 1–3 and 212 nn. 1–2. As Graf and Henrichs note, until recently the dividing line has been between historians proper and historians of religion. Harrison and Baelen are notable exceptions.

134 So Bodin (1917) 119–20, who felt that the source was Ephorus. But on the dangers of attributing everything in this section (Books 11–15) to Ephorus see Frost (1980) 32.

135 Cf. the remarks of Henrichs (1981: 242) following his paper. Phainias fr. 26 and 28 Wehrli (= Plut. *Them.* 27 and 29.7; cf. fr. 27) concern Themistocles' stay in the Persian court, but, surprisingly, Plutarch says nothing about his having to answer for the human sacrifice. Presumably Phainias did. Another possible influence on the genesis of the story is Hdt. 7.180, where Persians sacrifice a Greek named Leon, who, like the Persian victims at Salamis, is *kallistos* (cf. Henrichs (1981) 217 n. 2).

136 Henrichs (1981) 215 n. 1; Frost (1980) 150.

137 Green (1970) 185. I borrow the final phrase from Henrichs (1981: 215 n. 1), although Henrichs does not feel that the story originated with a hostile source.

138 Tresp (1914) 1–39.

139 Reading ἀρθμίου for ἀριθμείου of the MSS (Bouffartigue and Patillon (1977–9) 2: 210 n. 3); others read ἀνθρωπείου.

140 Bernays (1866) 116–18. Wilamowitz and Meuli took the second clause to refer to Arcadian ritual also, but to a symbolic blood-letting rather than actual human sacrifices (Wilamowitz (1931–2) 1: 294 n. 2; Meuli (1975) 2: 1009). But I do not see how this is possible, for Theophrastus has already written that they perform human sacrifices in Arcadia, in the present tense (ἀνθρωποθυτοῦσιν). I intend to discuss this problem in more detail elsewhere.

141 For a fifth-century example of the metaphor (similar to our own use of the word 'sacrifice', but surprisingly uncommon in Greek) see Pind. fr. 78 Snell-Maehler. Herodotus does not use sacrificial imagery to characterize the death of Leonidas (7.119.1 and 7.224.1).

142 The identification has been doubted, but see Tigerstedt (1953) 8–13 and (1965–78) 1: 62. For Pherecydes' death see now Schibli (1990) 6–10.

143 Paus. 3.11.11; Diog. Laert. 1.115 = Sosibius, *FGrHist* 595 F 15 (where the Spartans preserve his body κατά τι λόγιον, a phrase

found also in Plut. *Pel.* 21.2, of Pherecydes). Epimenides' skin: Epimenides, *FGrHist* 457 T 5. For a mythical human sacrifice and preservation of the victim's skin (in a Euhemeristic version of the Phrixus story) see Diod. Sic. 4.47.5.

144 Tigerstedt (1965–78) 1: 61–2.

145 Farnell, *CGS* 1: 42: 'We seem to have a tradition of it [human sacrifice] in the cult of Zeus Ithomatas, to whom Aristomenes sacrificed five hundred [*sic*] prisoners of war.' Nilsson (1906) 32: 'Eine Spur von Menschenopfer darf vielleicht gesehen werden in der Erzählung bei Clem. Alex. . . . wonach Aristomenes dem Zeus Ithomaios 300 spartanische Gefangene nebst dem König abgeschlachtet hat' (followed by Cook, *Zeus* 2.2: 890–1 n. 6).

146 A similar misunderstanding seems to underlie a confused and corrupt passage of Fulgentius, who imputes human hekatomphonia (to Ares) to the Athenians and Cretans: Fulg. *serm. ant.* 5 = Diophantus Lacedaemonius, *FHG* 4 fr. 1, and Sosicrates, *FHG* 4 fr. 9 (cf. Jacoby, *FGrHist* 3B, Komm. (Text), 337); Tresp no. 134. For the passage see Pizzani (1969) 77–87 and Huxley (1973) 124–6.

147 So Schwenn (1915) 79; cf. Cook, *Zeus* 1: 652–3. A possible obstacle is the fact that in Serv. Verg. *Aen.* 11.264 Idomeneus vows a sacrifice to Neptune (from the edition of Daniel; not in Serv. Verg. *Aen.* 3.121), certainly the expected recipient (for the offering of a maiden to Poseidon in Anticleides see above, n. 26). Still, we cannot be certain that Idomeneus vowed the sacrifice to Poseidon in Anticleides' version; or in assigning the human sacrifices to Zeus Clement may simply have been mistaken (as often).

148 Ath. 9, 375F–376A = Agathocles, *FGrHist* 472 F 1. See Cook, *Zeus* 1: 653–4, who felt that the secret sacrifices on Dikte were human sacrifices.

149 Cf. Henrichs (1981) 222–3 n. 6: 'The alleged practice of human sacrifice is a mere inference from the god's savage and vaguely cannibalistic epithets . . . or from maenadic myth.' See now more fully Graf (1985) 74–80.

150 *POxy.* 3711, col. ii: see Haslam (1986) 116–17 and 121–4. In another Lesbian story the two sons of a priest of Dionysus play at sacrifice, and one slays the other on the altar of the god (Ael. *VH* 13.2; Graf (1985) 78–9 n. 32).

151 Citation questioned by Hiller (1886) 127–30; but see also Graf (1985) 410–11. The human sacrifice was accepted as historical by Schwenn (1915: 76–7; cf. Oppermann (1934) 37; Farnell, *CGS* 2: 440–1), who interpreted it as a pharmakos rite, later incorporated into the cult of Artemis. There was a pharmakos ritual practised in the Phocaean colony Massilia, but the human 'scapegoat' was not killed (see pp. 157–60); and the practice of burning the corpse of the pharmakos is known only from a late and unreliable source (pp. 141–9). For the alleged human sacrifices in Phocaea see now the detailed discussion of Graf (1985) 410–17.

152 Hiller (1886) 126–31.

153 Pohlenz (1922) 1997–8; Schwenn (1915) 80 n. 1; Farnell, *CGS* 1:

28–9; Versnel (1987) 128–9 and 134. The myth of Kronos' efforts to kill his offspring contributed to the association, and Diod. Sic. 20.14.7 explicitly connects the Carthaginian human sacrifices with Kronos' swallowing of his children.

154 Deubner (1932) 186; so also Nilsson (1906) 38 and *GGR* 1: 512.

155 Plut. *De curiositate* 6, 518B; Lloyd-Jones (1981) 28.

156 Sanctuary: see also above, n. 129. There was a Rhodian fraternity of Aristobouliastai: *IG* XII, 1, no. 163.

157 So Bouffartigue and Patillon (1977–9) 2: 225 n. 7 and 226 n. 8. For the Cypriot kingships see Hill (1940) 113–16 and, for their demise, 158–72, and Strabo 14.6.6. Hill (1940: 65 n. 1) suggested that our Seleucus may have been the Alexandrian grammarian and that the title of Basileus had been preserved as a religious or ceremonial title in Cyprus after the abolition of the kingships; but he acknowledged the weakness of the hypothesis, which lacks epigraphical corroboration. Jacoby (*FGrHist* 3B, Komm. (Text), 92–3) felt that our Seleucus was the author of the *Περὶ θεῶν*, wrongly attributed by the Suda to the grammarian from Alexandria. Both Hill and Jacoby assumed that Seleucus was Porphyry's source for the information about the Cypriot human sacrifice, and admittedly it is peculiar to date a king by a *theologos*; but this would also be an unparalleled way for Porphyry to acknowledge a source. Possibly Seleucus played some role (such as that of advisor) in the story. And if Seleucus was a contemporary of an actual Cypriot king, then he cannot have been Porphyry's *immediate* source, for the mention of the month Aphrodisios indicates that the account was written after *c.* 15 BC (see below, n. 171).

158 Schwenn (1915) 70–1.

159 So Furley (1981) 115–16. A spear is used in human sacrifices imputed to the Albanians (Strabo 11.4.7), and the Getae send messengers to Salmoxis by tossing them onto upturned spears (Hdt. 4.94.2–3); but I am not aware of any use of spears in Greek sacrificial rites. For ephebic participation in sacrifices see Rudhardt (1958) 261 and Burkert (1985) 263 with 449 n. 30; and for running around the altar in what may be an initiation rite on Delos see Callim. *Del.* 321–4 with the schol. *ad loc.* and Hesych. s.v. Δηλιακὸς βωμός.

160 So Nilsson (1906) 306 and Graf (1985) 77. Nilsson and Graf (1985: 79) also cite Aen. Tact. 17.5, a short description of the Chian Dionysia, where there is no mention of human sacrifice.

161 See now Graf (1985) 76–7.

162 Schwenn (1915) 77–8. Artemis Agrotera: Burkert (1985) 60 with n. 37; Henrichs (1981) 219 n. 3; Wide (1893) 101. Sacrifices to Ares: Plut. *Instituta Laconica* 25, 238F, and *Ages.* 33.4; dog sacrifices: Paus. 3.14.9 and 3.20.2; Plut. *Quaest. Rom.* 111, 290D. For Ares-Enyalius see also Wide (1893) 147–52.

163 Jacoby, *FGrHist* 3B, Suppl. 1 (Text), 651, with references in Suppl. 2 (Notes), 519 nn. 1–2; Bouffartigue and Patillon (1977–9) 2: 227 n. 10. See also Schwenn (1915) 79–80 and Versnel (1987) 129. For τὸ

παλαιόν cf. Plut. *De def. or.* 14, 417C (τὰς πάλαι ποιουμένας ἀνθρωποθυσίας) and *Pel.* 21.2 (τῶν . . . παλαιῶν), both clear references to heroic times. The assertion of Athanasius (*Contra gentes* 25) that the 'Phoenicians and Cretans used to propitiate Kronos in child sacrifices of their own children' is based upon this passage (*via* Euseb. *Praep. Evang.* 4.16.6–7).

164 E.g. Cook, *Zeus* 2.1: 549.

165 Burkert (1985) 261–2; West (1983) 167; Graf (1985) 416–17.

166 So Hill (1940) 65 n. 1; Seel (1949) 239–41; Turcan (1975) 39–41, with further references.

167 Schwenn (1915) 187; Bouffartigue and Patillon (1977–9) 2: 227–8 n. 11; further references in Turcan (1975) 40.

168 Seel (1949) 240. For Roman edicts see Schwenn (1915) 186–7.

169 Jupiter Latiaris: Schwenn (1915) 180–1. I note as a curiosity that Hadrian himself was rumoured to have performed a human sacrifice (of Antinous!): Cass. Dio 69.11.2–3.

170 Turcan (1975: 41) attributes the information about Laodicea to Pallas; and the γάρ (*Abst.* 2.56.4) certainly suggests that Porphyry continues to quote or paraphrase Pallas in the following sentence(s). Elsewhere it is Gelon who is said to have abolished the Carthaginian practice (Schwenn (1915) 118 n. 4). The goddess at Laodicea was identified with Artemis, not Athena (Farnell, *CGS* 2: 441–2); and Seleucus I was said to have brought the image of Artemis from Brauron to Laodicea (Paus. 3.16.8). Thus the Syrians seem to have adopted a version of the Iphigeneia myth along with the statue. Seleucus I was credited with human sacrifices of his own (in a clearly legendary context), performed at the founding of Antioch and Laodicea (Pausanias Damascenus, *FGrHist* 854 F 10, 4 and 9).

171 But, curiously, Porphyry gives the Cypriot month-name Aphrodisios, from the Augustan calendar which replaced the Egyptian at Paphos and elsewhere (but not at Salamis) in *c.* 15 BC, while for Rhodes he gives Metageitnion, the Attic and Ionian equivalent of Rhodian Karneios: see Samuel (1972) 183–6 (Cyprus), 107–10 (Rhodes), and index, s.v. Metageitnion. Similarly, in Ath. 8, 360 B–C, we find Attic Boedromion in a quotation of Theognis (*FGrHist* 526 F 1) on Rhodian ritual, while the Rhodian form is Badromios. Alternatively, it is possible that Metageitnion was mistakenly substituted for the Rhodian month Pedageitnyos, its linguistic, but not calendric, equivalent (cf. Nilsson, *GGR* 1: 512 n. 2).

172 Above, n. 170. Turcan (1975: 41) suggests that Pallas was Syrian; and he may have discussed human sacrifices (and perhaps compiled a list of them) in order to defend Mithraism against charges of the practice.

173 Halliday (1928) 165; so also Nilsson (1906) 273; Wilhelm (1911) 178; Farnell, *CGS* 5: 169–70; further references in Schwenn (1915) 56 n. 3.

174 For the text see Halliday (1928) 167–8 and Schachter (1981–6) 1: 180–1. Daughters of Minyas: Burkert (1983) 174.

175 Although we cannot be certain how recently the event had taken place. And the details of the divine vengeance upon Zoilus and the citizens of Orchomenos may be fictional in part: cf. Hom. *Il.* 6.138–40, where Lycurgus is struck blind for his pursuit of Dionysus' nurses. The legend-making process may have already been at work (Fontenrose (1948) 162–3).

176 Cf. Meuli (1975) 2: 1007: 'eine solche Verbindung von zwei unmittelbar aufeinanderfolgenden Opfern, wobei der Opfernde nach Darbringung seines Opfers nun selbst geopfert worden wäre, ist im gesampten griechischen Kultus unerhört und schon darum ganz unwahrscheinlich'.

177 Plut. *Quaest. Rom.* 112, 291A, and *Is. et Os.* 35, 364F; Burkert (1983) 41; Halliday (1928) 167.

178 Pausanias does not say how the ritual ended, but surely he would have had some comment had it ended in death. Of the ritual Schwenn (1915: 54 n. 3) noted that 'die meisten denken an ein altes Menschenopfer', with references (to which add Farnell, *CGS* 4: 151, and Jost (1985) 399).

179 Meuli (1975) 2: 1007: 'Entweder war dies ein unglücklicher Zufall oder die Tat eines archaisierenden Zeloten; so blutig ernst war das Zeremoniell ganz sicher nicht gemeint.' Burkert (1983) 175: 'With the fanaticism of a zealot, Zoilus apparently failed to recognize the theatrical, playacting nature of the ritual and thus pursued it *ad absurdum.*' But as the priest of Dionysus performed the ritual every other year, it seems improbable that Zoilus' fanaticism or his failure to understand the harmless nature of the ritual was the cause. Even if this was the first time he performed the ritual himself, he certainly would have witnessed it many times before. Thus I think accident the more likely explanation.

180 Halliday (1928) 166–7.

181 Meuli (1975) 2: 1006–8 and 1018–21; Graf (1985) 77–80 and index, s.v. Ausnahmeritual; Dowden (1989) 82–5. For the abnormal nature of Dionysiac sparagmos and omophagy see Detienne (1979) 62–4.

182 = Chavane and Yon (1978) no. 39.

183 Porph. *Abst.* 2.54.3–55.1 = Chavane and Yon (1978) no. 41. In Nilsson's opinion (1906: 402; cf. 33) Lactantius 'nach aller Wahrscheinlichkeit' referred to the same human sacrifices as Porphyry; so more recently Yon (1980) 86–7. But the only certain point in common is the location in Salamis; the two sacrifices belong to different cults, and the details of both their foundations and abolitions differ.

184 Ath. 4, 174A = Hegisander, *FHG* 4 fr. 30; Cook, *Zeus* 1: 654 n. 4 and 3.1: 652–3 (n. 1). There was also a Zeus Epikoinios at Salamis: Hesych. s.v. Ἐπικοίνιος = Chavane and Yon (1978) no. 38.

185 Omestes and Omadios refer to sacrifices involving uncooked meat (Henrichs (1981) 222 n. 5; Graf (1985) 80 n. 44); Splanchnotomos is clearly related to sacrificial procedure also. Anthroporrhaistes is more difficult to explain, but it does not seem to have a *sacrificial*

reference; at least I am unaware of any uses of *rhaiein* ('shatter') in sacrificial contexts.

186 Cook, *Zeus* 1: 675; rejected as unhistorical by Schwenn (1915) 78.

187 See Burkert (1983) 196–9. For the various versions of the myth see 178 n. 42, and Apollod. *Bibl.* 3.4.3 with references Frazer (1921) *ad loc.*

188 But see Schachter (1981–6) 2: 49 n. 4a.

189 Philochorus, *FGrHist* 328 F 100–1; Plut. *Quaest. Graec.* 21, 296B, and *Mulierum virtutes* 8, 247A–E (image of Artemis). For the passage of Herodotus and its relation to Hecataeus (Hdt. 6.137.1 = Hecataeus, *FGrHist* 1 F 127) see Jacoby, *FGrHist* 3B, Suppl. 1 (Text), 405–20.

190 Nilsson, *GGR* 1: 833–6, and Garland (1987) 118–22, 209, and 231–3, both with bibliography. Great Goddess = Bendis: references in Kassel-Austin on Ar. fr. 384. Association with Artemis: Garland (1987) 118; Cratinus fr. 85 Kassel–Austin; Hesych. s.v. Βενδῖς; Schol. Pl. *Resp.* 1, 327A; Procl. *in R.*, vol. 1: p. 18 Kroll; Palaeph. *De incredibilibus* 32. The Thracian 'Artemis' of Hdt. 4.33.5 and 5.7 must be Bendis also; and it is not by chance that the Bendideion was located near the sanctuary of Artemis Mounychia in the Piraeus (Xen. *Hell.* 2.4.11; Garland (1987) 121).

191 Ar. fr. 372–91 Kassel–Austin. Bendis: fr. 381 and 384. 'Playing the bear': fr. 386 = Harp. s.v. ἀρκτεῦσαι (= Eur. fr. 767 Nauck; there must also have been an allusion to Brauronian ritual in the *Hypsipyle*). Thoas: fr. 373; identified with Thoas king of the Tauri: V. Fl. 2.300–3 and 8.208; Hyg. *Fab.* 15.1 and 120.1. These are late sources preserving a variant tradition; but in fr. 373 (on the Lemnian king) Aristophanes pokes fun at Euripides' etymologizing at *IT* 32–3 (on the Taurian king), which, even if Aristophanes did not himself identify the two, suggests that conditions were already ripe for the identification. For the story of the Lemnian women see Burkert (1983) 190–6.

192 I would not go so far as to conclude with Farnell (*CGS* 2: 452) that the arkteia was practised on Lemnos also. On the other hand, Jacoby may have erred to the opposite extreme when he held that the choice of Brauron as the site of the rape was more or less arbitrary, although possibly influenced by the fact that Brauron was Miltiades' home (*FGrHist* 3B, Suppl. 2 (Notes), 311 n. 22).

193 See Henrichs (1970) 18–35 and (1972) 33–7. The ultimate model may be Hdt. 3.11.2–3, where Greek and Carian mercenaries slaughter boys and drink wine mixed with their blood.

194 Fontenrose (1978) 128; Pliny *HN* 8.34.

5 THE PHARMAKOS AND RELATED RITES

1 Gebhard (1926), with bibliography of previous scholarship v-viii; more recently: Bremmer (1983b) 299–320, Burkert (1979) 59–77 and (1985) 82–4; Parker (1983) 24–6 and 257–80.

2 Mannhardt (1884) 129–38; Frazer (1913) 252–74 (but these 'embodiments of vegetation' later served chiefly as 'public scapegoats': 273); Deubner (1932) 193–8. For discussion of these and other interpretations see Gebhard (1926) 49–60 and (1934) 1301–2; Burkert (1979) 68–9.

3 Burkert (1979) 70–2 and (1985) 83–4; cf. Girard (1977) 94–8.

4 Scapegoat (*Leviticus* 16.20–2): Bremmer (1983b) 299. Hittites: Burkert (1979) 60–1, with references 169 n. 6; Bremmer (1983b) 305–6. Tibet: 317–18. Abundant comparative material in Frazer (1913) *passim*.

5 Thersites: Murray (1924) 212–15; Parker (1983) 260–1; Gebhard (1926) 58–60. Aesop: Bremmer (1983b) 308 n. 51. Codrus: Burkert (1979) 62–3. Pentheus: e.g. Dodds (1960) on Eur. *Bacch.* 963–5 and 1096–8; Coche de la Ferté (1980) 166–73. Oedipus: Vernant (1981) 100–7, after a suggestion of Gernet; Girard (1977) 94–6; Guépin (1968) 89–90. Ostracism: Vernant (1981) 105–7; Burkert (1985) 83 and (1979) 70–1; but cf. the cautions of Parker (1983) 269–71.

6 Thargelia: Gebhard (1934) 1287–90; Deubner (1932) 179–98; Parke (1977) 146–7; Bremmer (1983b) 318–20. *Eiresiōnē*: 318–19; not a feature of the Thargelia according to Deubner (1932: 191–2), but see Parker (1983) 25 n. 31.

7 Nilsson (1906) 113–15; Deubner (1932) 192; but cf. Parker (1983) 25–6.

8 Below, n. 47.

9 Etymology: Gebhard (1934) 1290; Schwenn (1915) 38–9 with n. 4; Nilsson, *GGR* 1: 108 with n. 6. Association of Apollo with purification and disease: Nilsson, *GGR* 1: 538–44; Burkert (1985) 145–7; Parker (1983) 25, 275–6, and 332–51.

10 For the text and the line numbers of the *Chiliades* I follow the edition of Leone (1968). For fragments of Hipponax I use the numbering of West (1971–2) 1: 109–71, who follows Masson (1962). In a few cases I depart from West's readings, and Degani's text (1983), with an exhaustive apparatus, should also be consulted.

11 Thargelia are attested for Miletus: Nilsson (1906) 109–10; Gebhard (1934) 1288. Probably the ritual was performed during the Thargelia in several Ionian cities. Hipponax was born in Ephesus, but later lived in Clazomenae (Suda s.v. Ἱππῶναξ). Mimnermus, who played the tune which accompanied the expulsion of pharmakoi ([Plut.] *De musica* 8, 1133F-1134A = Hippon. fr. 153 West) was probably from Smyrna, not Colophon as is sometimes reported in the tradition (West (1974) 72).

12 Reading θυμῶι in fr. 10: see Degani (1983) on his fr. 30; cf. Bremmer (1983b) 300 n. 8, who feels that this was not a feature of actual ritual, attributing the detail instead to the 'malicious imagination' of Hipponax.

13 Also unsupported is the claim that the pharmakos was the 'ugliest of all', repeated elsewhere by Tzetzes (*Chil.* 8.906; Schol. Ar. *Plut.* 454b; Schol. Ar. *Ran.* 733a) and, with some embellishment, in scholia (Schol. Ar. *Plut.* 454; Schol. Ar. *Ran.* 730; Schol. Aesch.

Sept. 680; Schol. Tzetz. *Epistulae* 104) which are later than, and apparently dependent upon, Tzetzes (below, n. 15).

14 So Harrison (1922) 99 and Pfister (1929) 96–7.

15 Gebhard (1926) 3–5 and 47–8, followed by Deubner (1932: 184–5), with a few minor adjustments. But Gebhard's argument that Tzetzes misconstrued the meaning of the word *thusia* (in later antiquity used generally of any ritual) is not convincing, for this word does not appear anywhere in the extant earlier tradition. And both Gebhard and Deubner erred in believing that Tzetzes' claims were based on scholia which mention the sacrifice (employing forms of *thuein*) of pharmakoi, for these are all later than Tzetzes: Koster (1962) on Tzetz. Schol. Ar. *Ran.* 733a.

16 Gebhard (1934) 1294. Criticism: Pfister (1929) 96–7; Delcourt (1944) 32–3; Masson (1949) 317; Nilsson, *GGR* 1: 109 n. 3.

17 Tzetz. *Chil.* 5.728, 8.905, 13.333–4; Tzetz. Schol. Ar. *Plut.* 454b and Schol. Ar. *Ran.* 733a–b. The words are also identified in the Schol. Vet. Ar. *Ran.* 733 (see Koster (1962) on Tzetz. Schol. Ar. *Ran.* 733a), in the Suda (s.vv. κάθαρμα, φαρμακός, and πονηροῖς), and by Tzetzes' contemporary Eustathius (on *Od.* 1.260 and 22.481).

18 Parker (1983) 221 n. 75; Bremmer (1983b) 308–13. See esp. Phryn. *PS*, p. 15.12–13 de Borries (τὰ τερατώδη τὴν φύσιν ἐπ' ἀγρίοις ἔκαιον ξύλοις), and cf. Tzetz. *Chil.* 5.737 (κατέκαιον ἐν ξύλοις τοῖς ἀγρίοις).

19 Harp. s.v. ὀξυθύμια (= Autocleides, *FGrHist* 353 F 2) and Phot. s.v. ὀξυθύμια, both citing Eupolis fr. 132 Kassel–Austin; *Etym. Magn.* s.v. ὀξυθύμια; Poll. *Onom.* 2.231 and 5.163. Katharmata: *LSJ*, s.v. κάθαρμα.

20 They are used similarly as terms of abuse (below, n. 42). But even in the fifth century after Christ Hesychius can define 'katharma' as the pig used in public purifications at Athens, not as a synonym for pharmakos (Hesych. s.v. κάθαρμα; so also Schol. Ar. *Ach.* 44; this definition appears s.v. καθάρσιον in Harpocration and Photius, but both words are given in the Schol. Aeschin. 1.23; cf. Ar. *Ach.* 44, where the area so purified is called the 'katharma'). The identification of katharma and pharmakos seems to originate in the scholia on Aristophanes (above, n. 17) and probably derives from their similar use as *Schimpfwörter* in comic poetry.

21 So Nilsson (1906) 106; Bremmer (1983b) 301. The scholia cited by Deubner (1932: 184), where it is said that pharmakoi were used during plagues and famine, all postdate Tzetzes (above, n. 15). The Athenian ritual was a 'means of averting pestilential diseases' which had its origin in the plague following the murder of Androgeos (Helladius in Phot. *Bibl.* 279, vol. 8: 182 Henry). But Helladius adds that thereafter it was the custom to cleanse the city always with pharmakoi, which implies a regularly repeated ritual.

22 Above, n. 12.

23 Gebhard (1926) 8–9; West (1974) 145–6; Degani (1983) on fr. 107.

24 Stengel (1920) 131 with n. 12; Rohde (1925) 321 n. 87; Pearson

(1913) 848; cf. Nilsson (1906) 107. *Contra*: Gebhard (1926) 9; Deubner (1932) 182.

25 *Thuein* and *thusia* are first used of the ritual by Tzetzes (*Chil*. 5. 731, 733, 759; Schol. Ar. *Plut*. 454b) and then by later scholiasts (above, n. 15).

26 Deubner (1932) 182. West (1974: 146) suggests 'before the φαρμακός event'.

27 Nilsson (1906) 107; but cf. Gebhard (1926) 36.

28 Masson (1949) 312–14 and (1962) 169. So also Rodriguez Adrados (1959) on fr. 135; Medeiros (1961) on fr. 121; Farina (1963) on fr. 70; West (1974) 148; and Degani (1983) on fr. 126.4, with further references. On the fragment see also Hirzel (1909) 229–30, 238 n. 6, and 244.

29 Degani (1983) on Hippon. fr. 126.3. For ψηφῖδι κακῇ cf. Callim. fr. 85.8 and fr. 193.13 Pfeiffer. The supplement is now favoured by Medeiros (1969) 58 and Degani (1983) on fr. 126.3. *Contra*: Masson (1949) 313.

30 Ch. 3 n. 44.

31 Masson (1949) 317; Medeiros (1961) on fr. 54; Degani (1983) on fr. 46 ('ft. recte' of Masson's suggestion).

32 Masson (1949) 311–12 and 318–19. Of the fragment Lobel wrote that 'it might be tempting to suppose that the greater part of this fragment relates to the treatment of the φαρμακός', but rightly adding that 'much of the detail does not exactly agree with what is elsewhere recorded' (Lobel *et al*. (1941) 95–6). Masson is followed by Rodriguez Adrados (1959: fr. 118), Medeiros (1961: fr. 114), and Degani (1983: fr. 130). So now after some hesitation Slings in Bremer *et al*. (1987) 89–92. *Contra*: Latte (1948) 44 n. 1; Moulinier (1952) 99 n. 3.

33 I follow the text and line numbers of Slings in Bremer *et al*. (1987) 72–3.

34 Bremer *et al*. (1987) 80 and 92.

35 Three (by our reckoning, two) days was the customary period between death and the *ekphora* of the corpse: Rohde (1925) 190–1 n. 50; Degani (1983) on fr. 130; Slings in Bremer *et al*. (1987) 81. The verb *ekballein* (Hippon. fr. 118E.4 and 17), on the other hand, is often used of casting out corpses without burial (Pl. *Leg*. 9, 873B, and 10, 909C; Soph. *Aj*. 1388).

36 Similarly unjustified is the interpretation of fr. 24 West, which describes something 'sodden and rotting' as a reference to a dead pharmakos (so Medeiros (1961) on his fr. 33). West (1974: 146) suggests that the words refer to rotting clothing, but Degani (1983: fr. 9) cites several later parallels which suggest that the reference is indeed to a dead body. But a corpse does not a pharmakos make, and once again there is nothing in Tzetzes' account to suggest that the body was left to rot for any length of time before cremation.

37 Masson (1949) 317–19.

38 Koster (1962) on Tzetzes Schol. Ar. *Ran*. 733a. Fr. 65 West refers to people who are pouring something into the sea from the stern of a

ship. Medeiros (1961: fr. 32), Masson (1962: 139 and 112), and Degani (1983: fr. 31) feel that Hipponax probably described here the scattering of a pharmakos' ashes. But nowhere does Tzetzes say that the ashes were taken on board a ship; and, more importantly, it is Tzetzes himself who preserves fr. 65, in a discussion of pouring *liquids* into the sea (Tzetz. *Exegesis Il.* 1.314; text in West (1971–2) and Degani (1983) *ad loc.*).

39 Hippon. fr. 153 West. In Athens murderers were not allowed into the agora (e.g. Dem. 20.158 and Antiphon 5.10), and it is a reasonable inference that (in Athens and elsewhere) ritual murder was forbidden there also.

40 Leone (1968) *indices scriptorum*, s.v. Lucianus.

41 Geographical detail: *Chil.* 1.865 (Naxos a city of Euboea); *Chil.* 1.622 (Simonides a *son* of Amorgos). Tzetzes' scholia on Aristophanes were written after the *Chiliades* (Koster (1962) on Tzetz. Schol. Ar. *Ran.* 733a), but the repetition of information from the earlier descriptions, including details culled from Hipponax, indicates that he took no care to distinguish between the Ionian and Athenian rituals.

42 Gebhard (1926) 22–4. Pharmakos: Ar. *Eq.* 1405, *Ran.* 733, and fr. 655 Kassel–Austin. Katharma: Ar. *Plut.* 454; Eupolis fr. 384.8 Kassel–Austin; later uses: Gebhard (1926) 23–4.

43 See Gebhard (1926) 13, who himself favoured this explanation but later (1934: 1291) followed others in seeing a reference to pharmakoi here.

44 Nilsson (1906) 106 n. 1; *LSJ* Suppl., s.v. δημόσιος (III.2c) and *LSJ*, s.v. δημόσιος (IIa). In Ar. *Lys.* 436 the word is used of an archer in the service of the Magistrate. See also Lysias 30.2 and 30.5.

45 Rohde (1925) 296 and 321 n. 87; Pfister (1929) 97. *Contra*: Gebhard (1926) 15; Deubner (1932) 184 n. 1.

46 Hatch (1908) 180–6; Moulinier (1952) 219–20 and 267–70; Parker (1983) 108 with n. 13.

47 τὴν πόλιν καθαίρειν (a phrase often used of pharmakos rituals): Hippon. fr. 5 (West); Schol. Ar. *Eq.* 1136a; Helladius in Phot. *Bibl.* 279, vol. 8: 182 Henry; Diog. Laert. 2.44; cf. Hesych. s.vv. φαρμακοί and φαρμακή ('the pot which they would prepare for those cleansing the cities'); *Dieg.* II.36–7 on Callim. fr. 90 Pfeiffer. ἀποδιοπομπεῖσθαι: Nilsson, *GGR* 1: 110–12. ἀλιτήριος: Hatch (1908) 157–62; Parker (1983) 109, 268, and 270; Halliday (1928) 126–8. οἰωνίσαιτο: *LSJ*, s.v. οἰωνίζομαι.

48 So Bremmer (1983b) 314. This is clearly ritual language, but it also seems possible that the allusion is to purifications using animal victims. For *perikathairein* of pharmakos ritual see the *Diegeseis* on Callim. fr. 90 Pfeiffer and Hesych. s.v. φαρμακοί; but see also Dio Chrys. *Or.* 48.17 ('cleansing the city all round, not with squill or water, but with a much purer thing, reason'). For περιαγαγόντας, cf. Serv. Verg. *Aen.* 3.57 = Petron. fr. 1, *circumducebatur* (see p. 158), but also Ath. 14, 626F (rephrasing

Polyb. 4.21.9), σφάγια περιαγαγόντες κύκλῳ (of purification with animal victims).

49 Farnell, *CGS* 4: 281; Gebhard (1926) 17–18 and (1934) 1294; Deubner (1932) 181.

50 Deubner (1932: 181) suggested that Istros was Harpocration's source for the Athenian material also, but that this was fully separated from the myth of Pharmakos in his more detailed discussion. Jacoby felt that Didymus was probably Harpocration's source for the excerpt of Istros, but that for the description of the Athenian ceremony 'the most likely source is a book *Περὶ ἑορτῶν*, e.g. that of Philochoros quoted twice in Harpokration, though an *Atthis* would also be possible' (*FGrHist* 3B, Suppl. 1 (Text), 653).

51 The statement of Hesych. s.v. φαρμακοί that the pharmakoi were a man and a woman probably represents a misunderstanding or abbreviation of the information in Harpocration and Helladius.

52 See Gebhard (1926) 93–100 and (1932) 999–1002; and Masson (1950b) 449–54, who prefers to read σύμβακχοι.

53 Cf. Plut. *Quaest. Graec.* 12, 293C, where the ritual performed during the Delphic Septerion is called a *mimēma* and *apomimēsis* of Apollo's slaying of Python and his purification; but here as elsewhere the 'imitation' is not very close to the myth. There is a marked tendency for Greek myths to be exaggerated and more gruesome than the rituals they served to explain: Bremmer (1984) 272–3. For Abdera see pp. 156–7. Very possibly Istros, who will have been familiar with Callimachus' lines on the pharmakos (fr. 90 Pfeiffer), wrote in his *Manifestations of Apollo* about the Thargelia at Abdera.

54 Suda s.vv. φαρμακός and πονηροῖς. The only addition is that the pharmakos was ἐστολισμένος (s.v. κάθαρμα); cf. Serv. Verg. *Aen.* 3.57 (= Petron. fr. 1): *ornatus verbenis et vestibus sacris.*

55 Höfer (1897–1909) 2282; Gebhard (1926) 24 and (1934) 1297.

56 Diels (1969) 40–1 n. 4; Demoulin (1901) 67–8; Pearson (1913) 848; Schwenn (1915) 58; Stengel (1920) 130; Weber (1925) 246. *Contra*: Gebhard (1926) 20–1; Parker (1983) 259.

57 As Parker notes (1983: 259 n. 16), Polemon's dismissal of the story is 'a fact often neglected in modern works'. Willing self-sacrifice in myth: see pp. 73–6; suicide upon the death of a loved one (a favourite theme in Hellenistic erotic literature): pp. 60–1.

58 Arist. *Ath. Pol.* 1; Plut. *Sol.* 12; Cic. *Leg.* 2.11, 28; Suda s.v. Ἐπιμενίδης. Diels (1969) 36–52; Demoulin (1901) 106–14; Moulinier (1952) 50–8; Jacoby, *FGrHist* 3B, Komm. (Text) 310–11; Rhodes (1981) 79–84.

59 Diog. Laert. 1.109–15; Epimenides, *FGrHist* 457 T 1–11; Demoulin (1901) *passim*.

60 Schwenn (1915) 58; Weber (1925) 246.

61 Helladius in Phot. *Bibl.* 279, vol. 8: 182 Henry. For 'cleansing the city' see above, n. 47.

62 An exception is Deubner (1932) 185–6, who expressed doubt

shortly before the publication of the *Diegeseis*. Geffcken (1890: 95) questioned the citation of Callimachus – but, as it turns out, wrongly.

63 Deubner (1934) 185–92; Gebhard (1938) 1841–2.

64 Colonization: Clerc (1927–9) 1: 115–40; conservation of ancestral custom: ibid., 458–70; government: ibid., 424–49. For Clerc's argument that Petronius' description was based on myth (ibid., 454–7) see Deubner (1932) 187 and Moulinier (1952) 96 n. 1. The attribution of the custom to the Gauls may have been influenced by the Gauls' reputation for performing human sacrifices (Nilsson (1906) 109).

65 Nilsson (1906) 109; Farnell, *CGS* 4: 279; Deubner (1932) 186–7. But if the phrase *certo . . . die* derived from a description of the ritual at Abdera, as I think probable, then he may have been correct only, as it were, accidentally.

66 Stephanus' reading *praecipitabatur*, sometimes accepted, has no manuscript authority: Bremmer (1983b) 316 n. 89.

67 Petronius is also associated with Massilia in the obscure allusion of Sid. Apoll. *Carm.* 23.155–7 = Petron. fr. 4. The significance of this reference is uncertain, but it seems not unlikely (1) that Petronius visited Massilia and (2) that a lost portion (perhaps the opening) of the *Satyricon* was set there: Clerc (1927–9) 2: 259–61; Sullivan (1968) 40–2. Curiously, Petronius (*Sat.* 107.5) is also the sole extant Latin writer to use the word *pharmacus*.

68 'Lactantius' also says that a poor person would sell himself for the purpose, a detail reminiscent of the bought slave of *Dieg.* II.30–1 on Callim. fr. 90 Pfeiffer (cf. Schol. Conr. Ov. *Ib.* 467: *unum emptum*).

69 Cic. *Tusc.* 4.18, 41 (general, cf. *Tusc.* 4.34, 72–3); Strabo 10.2.9 (Sappho and Cephalus); Ov. *Her.* 15.161–220 (Sappho) and 15.167–70 (Deucalion, who survived the fall); Serv. Verg. *Aen.* 3.274 (Sappho) and 279 (an unnamed woman in love with Phaon and the eponymous Leucates, who leaps to escape Apollo's advances); Serv. Verg. *Ecl.* 8.59 (those 'who desired to find their parents or who longed to be loved by those whom they loved'); Ath. 14, 619D-E = Aristoxenus, *FHG* 2 fr. 72 = Stesichorus fr. 100 Page (spurious: Calyce); Phot. s.v. Λευκάτης (Sappho, either the poetess or the hetaira; cf. Ael. *VH* 12.18); Ptolemaeus Chennus in Phot. *Bibl.* 190, vol. 3: 70–2 Henry (Aphrodite and eight others, several surviving the fall).

70 The information that Cephalus was the first to leap from Leucates seems to derive from Demetrius (so Lasseure (1971) *ad loc.*); it thus seems likely that he was the source for the description of the ritual also.

71 McWhirter and McWhirter (1986) 305 (s.v. Diving, High). The height of the cliff is given as 40 m by Maull (1925) 2224. For Apollo's sanctuary see Dörpfeld (1927) 1: 271–4 and 325, with photographs of the cliff, ibid., 2: pls 12–13.

72 Nilsson (1906) 111.

73 McWhirter and McWhirter (1986) 305.

74 V. Karageorghis and D. Buitron, personal communications. The figure 100 m marks the point of the cliff nearest the sanctuary (Buitron). For the excavations of Apollo's sanctuary, which uncovered a large, circular altar, see Buitron and Soren (1981) 99–116 and Soren (1987), with photographs of the cliffs 54–5 figs 27–8. Traces of ancient construction on the edge of the cliff are also reported (Soren (1987) 303 n. 10).

75 *LSJ*, s.v. περίψημα; further references in Bremmer (1983b) 304 n. 35.

76 See Rotolo (1980) 1947–61.

77 Höfer (1897–1909) 2280–1; Gebhard (1926) 35 and 46 and (1934) 1295; Pfister (1929) 97; Burkert (1979) 70; Bremmer (1983b) 316–17.

78 For Burkert (1979: 70) the expulsion of pharmakoi is a ritualized form of communal aggression in times of crisis, and this incident an instance of the 'underlying unritualized behaviour'. But Burkert condenses the story to the point of distortion when he writes that the beggar was 'immediately stoned'. When Apollonius commands the Ephesians to stone the beggar, they are appalled, deeming it a terrible thing (*deinon*) to murder an impoverished stranger. Only after Apollonius' repeated entreaties do *some* of the Ephesians throw stones, and only when at last the beggar shows himself to be a demon (and therefore inhuman), do they all stone him in grim earnest. Thus the story is not the best example one could find to demonstrate how 'confronted with the impalpable terror of a plague, masses may explode into aggression against a "scapegoat"' (ibid.).

79 Roscher (1897) 30–8; Frazer (1921) on Apollod. *Ep*. 5.23; Mainoldi (1984) 47–8, with references 85 n. 112.

80 Burkert (1979) 70 and 173 n. 22; *contra*: Bremmer (1983b) 316–7, with references.

81 Gebhard (1926:32 n. 6) felt that Istros had reproduced the present tense of a still earlier source; but possibly the city was Abdera and the source Callimachus (above, n. 53).

82 'It *was* the custom', wrote Strabo (10.2.9); and if Strabo is repeating the words of Demetrius (above, n. 70), then the custom was already obsolete in the second century BC. The present tenses found in later sources (pp. 160–1) may safely be discounted.

6 STRANGERS IN A STRANGE LAND THE LOCRIAN MAIDEN TRIBUTE

1 See especially Graf (1978) 61–79, with bibliography 61 n. 1.

2 Schwenn (1915) 52 n. 1; Farnell (1921) 300.

3 For the date see Dain and Bon (1967) vi–ix: 357/6 or 356/5 BC. Hercher (1870) and other early editors bracketed the passage as an interpolation, chiefly on the grounds that the exemplum is inappropriate to the context. But the example is perfectly apt: if the Trojans are unable to keep people from being smuggled in, how

much more difficult is it to prevent letters from being passed into a besieged city. See Schwartz (1894) 1020 ('die Stelle ist mit Unrecht verdächtigt'); Behrendt (1910) 17–18; and Dain and Bon (1967) lii–liii, generally on Hercher's misguided penchant for athetizing. But Fontenrose (1978: 134) revived the old view. There are some problems in the text: see Graf (1978) 66 n. 30.

4 There are textual problems, and sense is uncertain in places. The chief difficulties lie in vv. 1157–9, for which see Wilamowitz (1920) 387 and Corssen (1913) 240–1. In the final verse (1173) I follow Corssen (1913: 244) in taking γένος (rather than τὸν κτάνοντα) as the object of χαράξας, though most editors print a comma after γένος. But in neither case would I see this as a reference to an actual inscription in Ilion.

5 Parke–Wormell no. 332; Fontenrose (1978) no. L157.

6 Jacoby, *FGrHist* 3B, Komm. (Noten), 346 n. 564.

7 Frazer (1921) xxxvi; Wilhelm (1911) 182.

8 Wilamowitz (1920) 385: 'Wer da behauptet, Tzetzes hätte den Timaios in der Bibliothek gefunden, kannt sie beide nicht.'

9 Parke–Wormell no. 331; Fontenrose (1978) no. Q232.

10 Pembroke (1970) 1250–5.

11 The author and date of the hexameters are unknown. The common attribution of the lines to Euphorion (e.g. Euphorion fr. 53 Powell) is 'sine iusta causa': Pfeiffer (1949–53) on Callim. fr. 35. 'Per mirum errorem', Leaf (1912: 395) attributed the hexameters to Callimachus, who treated the tribute in the *Aetia*; but the *Aetia* are in elegiacs (same error in Reinach (1914) 28).

12 *Editio princeps*: Wilhelm (1911) 163–256. Improved texts: Klaffenbach (1968) no. 706 and Schmitt (1969) no. 472.

13 Implicit in Schol. Lycoph. *Alex.* 1141; three years after the Locrians' return: Apollod. *Epit.* 6.20 and Tzetz. Schol. Lycoph. *Alex.* 1141. Serv. Verg. *Aen.* 1.41 has *postea*. The Trojans themselves believed that the tribute had started shortly after the Fall of Troy (Strabo 13.1.40), and the first segment of Ael. fr. 47 Hercher probably refers to this period also.

14 Blegen *et al.* (1958) 147 and 249–50. But colonization may have taken place somewhat earlier: Cook (1973) 101.

15 Davreux (1942) 14.

16 Corssen (1913) 236–9; Robert (1923) 1267; further references in Davreux (1942) 52 nn. 3 and 5.

17 Davreux (1942) 12 and 140–1, with references (and convincing objections) to other interpretations; so also Graf (1978) 75. Artistic representations: Davreux (1942) 139–90; Touchefeu (1981b) 336–49.

18 Davreux (1942) 12–13. Robert (1923: 1269) suggested that Aias is swearing to send the maiden tribute; so more recently Rösler (1987) 5 and (1989) 127 n. 1. But not only is this not what Pausanias himself understood (Davreux (1942) 13), but also according to the tradition (above, n. 13) the tribute was demanded – by an oracle – three years after the Locrians' return from Troy – and after Aias was dead (*Od.* 4.499–511).

19 Davreux (1942) 13–14 (text of 'Libanius': 72–5). For the incident in the *Ilioupersis* see now Rösler (1987) 1–8.

20 Stesichorus fr. 28 Page (the *Tabula Iliaca*); Davreux (1942) 15–16, 18, and 189. The two traditions seem to be reflected in the iconography: 15 and 139–40.

21 Alcaeus fr. 298 Lobel–Page, now supplemented by the Cologne papyrus: Graf (1978) 75 n. 91; van Erp Taalman Kip in Bremer *et al.* (1987) 95–127, with bibliography 127.

22 Eur. *Tro.* 69–71; Davreux (1942) 42. It is not clear which version was followed by Sophocles: Davreux (1942) 32–3; Soph. fr. 10a–18 Radt.

23 Wilamowitz (1920) 391–3; so also Bethe (1927) 128; Lérat (1952) 2: 22 n. 1; Graf (1978) 74.

24 Leaf (1912) 135 and (1923) 192–3; Farnell (1921) 295–6; Huxley (1966) 153; see also Coldstream (1977) 348.

25 Jacoby (1904) 146–7; Forsdyke (1956) 62–3 (with a discussion of the tribute, 63–7). The exception is the date of Douris, 1334/3 (Douris, *FGrHist* 76 F 41a), which, calculated as it is from the year of Alexander's crossing into Asia, would not seem to be relevant here.

26 Vidal-Naquet (1986) 193–4; Leaf (1912) 132.

27 Wilhelm (1911) 183. Manni (1963: 167–72) argued that the Phocian War mentioned here was the Gallic attack on Delphi in 278/7. But there is no evidence that this attack was ever called 'the Phocian War' (Vidal-Naquet (1986) 201 n. 27).

28 Momigliano (1945) 49–53.

29 One thousand years: Lycoph. *Alex.* 1153; Schol. and Tzetz. Schol. Lycoph. *Alex.* 1141; Apollod. *Epit.* 6.20; Iamb. *VP* 8.42; Hieron. *Adv. Iovinian.* 1.41; Schol. *Il.* 13.66 (= Callim. fr. 35 Pfeiffer). Vidal-Naquet (1986: 201 n. 27) suggested that Jerome may have written *per annos circiter mille* because he found something chronologically suspect in the tradition.

30 Hercher (1866) 205–6. Of the individual entries in the Suda, Aelian is named in the first, fifth, and sixth; the second clearly concerns the maidens, but does not necessarily follow directly upon the first, which seems to concern the institution of the tribute. The seventh fragment follows upon the sixth, which is attributed to Aelian. But the third and fourth fragments cannot be assigned to Aelian with certainty, and even their applicability to the maiden tribute might be questioned.

31 Monophthalmus: Leaf (1912) 131; Corssen (1913) 191; Reinach (1914) 22, 35 n. 1, and 41; Schmitt (1969) 122; Vidal-Naquet (1986) 194. Gonatas: Wilamowitz (1920) 384; Robert (1923) 1272; Momigliano (1945) 53 n. 1; Walbank (1957–79) 2: 335; Manni (1963) 174; Graf (1978) 63–4. Huxley (1966: 152) favoured Monophthalmus but did not rule out even Doson (160); and others (e.g. Wilhelm (1911) 186–7; Schwenn (1915) 47) left the question open.

32 So Corssen (1913) 192.

33 Although possibly the 'one hundred houses' were now no longer responsible for the tribute. For evidence of these families in the fifth

century see Walbank (1957–79) 2: 334 and Pembroke (1970) 1253 n. 3.

34 Wilhelm (1911) 249–56. Before 272: Klaffenbach (1968) 83; Schmitt (1969) 125; but cf. Momigliano (1945) 53.

35 Leaf (1912) 131; Huxley (1966) 152; Vidal-Naquet (1986) 194. *Contra*: Momigliano (1945) 53 n. 1.

36 Wilamowitz (1920) 384; Walbank (1957–79) 2: 335; Schmitt (1969) 123; little credit to Plutarch: Huxley (1966) 152; Graf (1978) 79 n. 119.

37 See above, n. 25.

38 Vidal-Naquet (1986) 196. For the statement in Apollod. *Epit.* 6.22 and Tzetz. Schol. Lycoph. *Alex.* 1141 that the Locrians at one point sent infants with their nurses see Graf (1978) 63, with references n. 10.

39 Every year: Schol. Lycoph. *Alex.* 1141 (but here it is also said that the maidens remained in Troy for life); Strabo 13.1.40; Ael. fr. 47 Hercher; Serv. Verg. *Aen.* 1.41. Lifelong service: Schol. Lycoph. *Alex.* 1141; Lycoph. *Alex.* 1154; Plut. *De sera* 12, 557D; implicit in Apollod. *Epit.* 6.21–2.

40 So Huxley (1966) 150; Graf (1978) 64. For Leaf (1912: 130) a collection of 100 or so maidens in Troy was 'not *a priori* incredible'; but for the small size of Troy at this time see below, n. 46.

41 Vürtheim (1907) 107–9; Wilhelm (1911) 219–20; Reinach (1914) 37–42; Wilamowitz (1920) 391. Corssen (1913: 198–9) argued for the opposite, that an original year's stay was altered in the third century to a lifelong service.

42 Graf (1978) 65–6.

43 Wilhelm (1911) 178–80; Vürtheim (1907) 122–3; Reinach (1914) 37–8; Bethe (1927) 129 n. 10 and 130; further references in Robert (1923) 1272 n. 2.

44 Tzetz. Schol. Lycoph. *Alex.* 1141. When Tzetzes wrote that 'after the Phocian War they stopped sending such a sacrifice', it was his own addition to the version of the *Epitome*, where it was said merely that they stopped 'sending the suppliants' (Apollod. *Epit.* 6.22). Tzetzes also uses *thusia* of pharmakos ritual (ch. 5 n. 25); for the word used of rituals other than sacrifices in later antiquity see Gebhard (1926) 47–8.

45 Schwenn (1915) 50.

46 Forsdyke (1956) 66; Bethe (1927) 129; Bremmer (1987) 110, who stresses the small size of Troy, citing Cook (1973) 100. *Contra*: Leaf (1912) 129 n. 1; Farnell (1921) 297.

47 The interpretation of the hostages (*IG* IX^2 1, 3, no. 706.15–17) put forward by Reinach (1914) 19–20 and Leaf (1914–16) 154 was based on a misreading of the text.

48 Vürtheim (1907) 109; Wilhelm (1911) 178; Reinach (1914) 45; Schwenn (1915) 55; Graf (1978) 66–7.

49 Schwenn (1915) 49–52. For pharmakoi see ch. 5.

50 Hesychius seems to have been mistaken in claiming that one of the Athenian pharmakoi was a woman: ch. 5 n. 51.

51 See Parker (1983) index, s.v. Temples.
52 Reinach (1914) 43–53; Farnell (1921) 299 (quoting Benedick in *Much Ado about Nothing* IV.i.68).
53 Reinach (1914) 37–8 and 46–9.
54 Leaf (1923) 192; Farnell (1921) 300–1.
55 Graf (1978) 67–71, with references to ancient texts.
56 See ibid., 71–2, for references.
57 Patrae: Graf (1978) 75; symbolic death: 77, and ch. 4 n. 38.
58 Graf (1978) 74–9.
59 Robert (1923) 1274.
60 As has been generally maintained since Wilhelm's suggestion (1911: 163; most recently Graf (1978) 75–6). But as the inscription was found some 15 km south of the site of ancient Physkos, this cannot be taken as an established fact (Lérat (1952) 2: 157).
61 Graf (1978) 65.
62 Leaf (1914–16) 148–54.
63 ibid., 150. Here as elsewhere Leaf seems to have followed Reinach (1914: 20).
64 Fontenrose (1978) 131–7. Interpolation: see above, n. 3.
65 ibid. 135. Fontenrose, of course, was aware that Strabo was following Demetrius here (133). He was therefore obliged to attribute the statement about the maidens to Strabo and to maintain that Strabo had placed this argument for the continuity of the city in the mouths of the Trojans, although 'Strabo himself did not accept it' (135 n. 14). This is contorted and quite implausible; and it is virtually certain that this entire passage derived from Demetrius.

7 CONCLUSION

1 Brelich (1969b) 195–207 (although, strangely, he accepted Themistocles' human sacrifice at Salamis as historical: 200 n. 7); Burkert (1983) 89–90 (Zeus Lykaios) and 114–15 (Hdt. 7.197; elsewhere Burkert is quite cautious: (1983) index, s.v. human sacrifice, (1985) index, s.v. human sacrifice, and (1981) 105–6); Graf (1978) 66–7 and (1985) 74–80 and 410–17; Henrichs (1981) 195–235; Bremmer (1983b) 315–18 (pharmakos).
2 See ch. 4 n. 1; see also Cook, *Zeus* 1: 656, 658 n. 3, and 659; 2.1: 668; 2.2: 890 n. 6, 924 (n. 5) and 1021; 3.1: 525; Farnell, *CGS* 1: 28, 41–2, and 203–4; 4: 26, 151; 5: 168–71 and 404–5; Murray (1924) 11–15, 21, and 131–8.
3 See ch. 4 nn. 58, 61, and 178. Other examples: Gruppe (1906) 1: 65 (human sacrifices to Nauplius); Schwenn (1915) 70 with n. 2 (Diomedes); Farnell, *CGS* 1: 42 (Zeus Idaios) and 4: 274 (Apollo at Megara); Cook, *Zeus* 2.1: 549 (Kronos), 2.2: 924 n. 5 (Zeus on Rhodes) and 1021–2 (a storm-god Thyestes, after Müller (1857–69) 2: 154–8); Nilsson (1906) 467 and Halliday (1928) 72 (Delphic ritual of hanged doll a substitute for prior human sacrifices).
4 Muth (1988) 103 n. 236 (with references: Cycnus), and 125 n. 323

(Kronos); Jost (1985) 398–9 (Artemis at Stymphalus, apparently following Nilsson (1906) 228).

5 E.g. Jost (1985) 254, 258–9, 264–7, and 588; Muth (1988) 40, 40–2 n. 61 and index, s.v. Menschenopfer; Coche de la Ferté (1980) 135–65; O'Connor-Visser (1987) 211–32 (largely just a catalogue, but uncritical). And popular and non-specialist writers reflect outdated views, e.g. Davies (1981) 52–9.

6 Burkert (1983) 40 and 46. See esp. pp. 125–7 on the ox sacrifice at Salamis; other cases of 'animal substitution' (e.g. at Potniae, where a sacrificed *pais* is replaced by a goat: p. 82) may also have been connected with initiations.

7 Pl. *Leg.* 6, 782C: ἔτι καὶ νῦν παραμένον; Theophr. fr. 13.22 Pötscher: μέχρι τοῦ νῦν; cf. Cic. *Font.* 14, 31 (of the Gauls): *Quis enim ignorat eos usque ad hanc diem retinere illam immanem ac barbaram consuetudinem hominum immolandorum*?

8 [Pl.] *Minos* 315B-C; cf. Eur. *IT* 463–6; Isoc. *Bus.* 5 and 32; Sext. Emp. *Pyr.* 1.149 and 3.208. See also ch. 3 n. 43; Schwenn (1915) 112–18; Stengel (1920) 131–2.

9 Piccaluga (1968) 149–55; Laurens (1986) 147–52; Durand (1986) 107–32. What is suggested in the vase paintings is stated explicitly by Plutarch, who writes that Heracles, wont to inflict on his enemies the fate which they had devised for him, thus sacrificed (ἔθυσεν) Bousiris (*Thes.* 11.1). For Bousiris as cannibal see below, n. 11. Heracles will also abolish human sacrifices at Rome: Schwenn (1915) 152–3 n. 2.

10 Festugière (1972) 145–9; Detienne (1979) 53–67 and index, s.v. Cannibals; Haussleiter (1935) index, s.v. Anthropophagie; Versnel (1980) 591 n. 209; Henrichs (1972) 70 n. 78. When I first began this study, like Henrichs (1981: 234–5 n. 2) I was struck by the resemblances between the Greek evidence, both for cannibalism and human sacrifice, and the more recent cases studied by Arens (1979).

11 Hdt. 1.216.2–3, 3.38.3–4, 3.99, 4.26.1; Porph. *Abst.* 2.8.3 (= Theophr. fr. 3.19–25 Pötscher); Strabo 4.5.4 and 7.39 (= Ephorus, *FGrHist* 70 F 42); Sext. Emp. *Pyr.* 3.207 and 3.225; further references in Festugière (1972) 146–7 and Detienne (1979) 58. That Bousiris ate his victims was claimed by Polycrates (Isoc. *Bus.* 5, 7, and 31–2).

12 Haussleiter (1935) 65–71 and 77; Festugière (1972) 145; Detienne (1979) 55–62.

13 Zeus: Euhemerus, *FGrHist* 63 F 22; Melissai: Mnasaeas Patrensis, *FHG* 3 fr. 5; Isis and Osiris: Festugière (1972) 145 and 147–8 n. 36; Orpheus: Festugière (1972) 147–8 n. 36 and Haussleiter (1935) 77–8; the first cook: Athenion fr. 1 Kassel-Austin; human progress: Theophr. fr. 13 Pötscher and Moschion fr. 6 Snell-Kannicht.

14 Zeitlin (1965) 463–508 and (1966) 645–53; Guépin (1968) 2; Burkert (1966) 119–21; Vidal-Naquet (1981) 150–74.

15 Aesch. fr. 94 Radt (*Iphigeneia*). Dionysian subjects: fr. 23–5 (*Bassarai* or *Bassarides*), 57–67 (*Edonoi*), 124–6 (*Lycurgus*), and 146–9 (*Neaniskoi*), comprising a tetralogy; fr. 22 (*Bacchae*) and fr. 183 (*Pentheus*).

16 Soph. fr. 1–10, 305–12, 522–8, and 247–69 Radt. Sacrificial imagery: Guépin (1968) 2–4; Burkert (1966) 117.

17 *Electra*: Burkert (1966) 116 n. 66; Guépin (1968) 2; Zeitlin (1970) 651–9. Other plays: Burkert (1966) 116–19; Guépin (1968) 2–4; Foley (1985) 152–62 and 205–58.

18 E.g. Phainias: pp. 111–15; Phylarchus: ch. 4 n. 117; see also p. 74 (Messenian Wars) and pp. 109–11 (fourth-century human sacrifices enjoined but not carried out).

19 Winkler (1980) 166–71. This is also a period of free invention in the retelling of old legends, and Philostratus has Achilles slaughter the last surviving daughter of Priam (*Her.* 19.18).

20 *Scheintod*: Winkler (1980) 173–5. Text and commentary: Henrichs (1972) 82–129.

21 Burkert (1966) 87–121; cf. Foley (1985) 17–64.

22 Henrichs (1970: 29–35; 1972: 28–79) argued that the scene in Lollianus' novel was based upon actual cannibalistic practices of the Egyptian Boukoloi; but Winkler (1980: 155–81) shows that Lollianus was following a traditional narrative theme rather than recording an actual cult practice.

23 Cf. Winkler (1980) 168.

24 E.g. Huxley's improbable suggestion (1966: 157) that a 'place of burning' in Troy VIII containing half-burnt human and animal bones was used by the Trojans to burn 'the body of any unfortunate Locrian maiden they had caught' (but Vidal-Naquet's criticism (1986: 200 n. 8) was unfair: Huxley did not claim that these were the maidens' bones, but only that their bodies would be cremated here). Sakellarakis and Sakellaraki (1981: 218; 1979: 389) support their interpretation of the finds from Anemospilia by appealing to some of the most questionable cases from literature. And Warren (1981b: 161–5 and 1984: 53–5) suggests that the children whose bones were found at Knossos had been sacrificed and ritually consumed in the cult of Zagreus, who in myth is cut up and consumed by Titans. Warren assumes that Zagreus is a pre-Greek name and in origin a Minoan deity (deduced from Eur. *Cretans* fr. 79 Austin); but see West (1983) 153 (Zagreus connected with Greek *zagrē*, a pitfall for trapping animals; other derivations: 153 n. 39) and 153–4 (on Eur. fr. 79: 'It would be unsafe to infer from this passage that Zagreus played a part in Cretan cult; the inference should be rather that he played a part in mysteries which claimed a Cretan origin'). Most questionable of all is the assumption that the myth of Zagreus' dismemberment reflects actual practices of any place or period. I note as a (final) curiosity the Archaic-Classical altar at Ephesus, which contained over 2,000 bones, three of which were human (Bammer *et al.* (1978) 107–8 and 149–50). The human bones appear to be intrusive, like the bones of certain animals not attested as sacrificial victims; Bammer suggests that they came from a makeshift soldier's burial (149) but then (149 n. 134) rather mysteriously cites Schwenn (1915).

APPENDIX A CUT MARKS AND MASS BURIALS

1 Blackman and Branigan (1982) 53–4.
2 McGeorge (1984) 12–16.
3 Sampson (1985) 153–242, ossuaries: 208–10 and 182 plan 51; English summary: 383–7; skeletal material: 393–458. For eight more tombs excavated at Manika (and some acerbic criticisms of Sampson) see Sapouna-Sakellarakis (1987) 233–64; no cut marks on these bones are reported.
4 Sampson (1985) 234–6 and 422–54. Marked and burnt animal bones are also reported (452).
5 Sampson (1983) 73.
6 Sampson (1985) 234–6 and 386–7. It is also suggested that some bodies may have been placed in the tombs only in pieces: 218–19, 234, and 386. For the location and nature of the marks see 422–48 and 454.
7 Sampson (1985) 219, 234, 366, and 386. Bones with cut marks from Neolithic Argissa are also mentioned (234 and 386), but without reference (unpublished?).
8 Cf. Binford (1981) 35–86 and Ubelaker (1978) 75.
9 The art of trephination was known in the Argolid in the Middle Bronze Age (Mylonas (1972–3) 1: 380), and there is now possible evidence from Crete (Wall *et al.* (1986) 341).
10 Rohde (1925) 582–6; Frazer (1921) 1: 328–9 n. 1; Vermeule (1979) 236 n. 30.
11 Villa *et al.* (1986: 435 and 437 n. 27) report the development of methods to distinguish between cuts made shortly after death and cuts made a year or more later.
12 Waage (1949) 416 and 421–2.
13 McDonald (1972) 240–2; Shay (1975) 73–5; Rapp and Aschenbrenner (1978) 116–17.
14 Rapp and Aschenbrenner (1978) 117.
15 McDonald (1972) 242; Shay (1975) 75.
16 Kritzas (1976–8) 173–80; Poulianos (1976–8) 319.
17 Rotroff (1976) 132.
18 Shear (1939) 238–9; Angel (1945) 330.
19 Shear (1939) 239; Angel (1945) 311 and 330.
20 Smith (1982) 102–20.

APPENDIX B PYLOS TABLET TN 316

1 Hooker (1980) 157. For the tablet see 157–62; Palmer (1963) 261–8; Heubeck (1966) 100–3; Chadwick and Ventris (1973) 284–9 and 458–64; Chadwick (1976) 89–96; further bibliography in Baumbach (1968) 280 and (1986) 391 and the tablet indices in the subsequent volumes of *Studies*.
2 The presence of Hermes here and elsewhere in the tablets is questioned by Gérard-Rousseau (1968) 85–8.

3 So Lejeune (1964) 92; Heubeck (1966) 102; Chadwick and Ventris (1973) 460–1 and 285. But Palmer long maintained that a-ke is a form (probably aorist passive) of a verb related to *hagnos* and *hazesthai*: Palmer (1963) 266 and (1983) 288–90.

4 Chadwick and Ventris (1973) 463.

5 ibid., 463 (cf. 288); Chadwick (1976) 95; cf. Palmer (1983) 286.

6 The suggestion of E. Bennett, Jr: Chadwick and Ventris (1973) 284 (cf. 460). But such use of the ideograms MAN and WOMAN is unparalleled and we would expect an ideogram indicating the material of the statues, unless the ideogram GOLD might be taken to apply to both vessels and figurines.

7 Chadwick and Ventris (1973) 128 and 284 (= the same pages of the first edition); Gérard-Rousseau (1968) 177; Tritsch (1958) 419–20.

8 Guthrie (1959) 43–4; Lejeune (1964) 93; Vermeule (1974) 67. This seems to be the most common interpretation, although many scholars (e.g. Hooker (1980) 161; Heubeck (1966) 102) leave the question open.

9 Carratelli (1957) 352–4; Chadwick and Ventris (1973) 460; Chadwick (1976) 91–2; now somewhat more tentatively in Chadwick (1987) 42–3; Gérard-Rousseau (1971) 144 with n. 28, after conversations with Chadwick; Baumbach (1983) 33–4.

10 Above, n. 7.

11 Chadwick and Ventris (1973) 460; see also above, n. 9.

12 Chadwick and Ventris (1973) 461 and 464.

13 Chadwick (1976) 92. For Of 26 see Spyropoulos and Chadwick (1975) 94, 99, and 104–5; Hooker (1977) 176–8.

14 Chadwick (1976) 90 and 92; Chadwick and Ventris (1973) 460; see also Baumbach (1983) 33–4; Gérard-Rousseau (1971) 143–4. For the unusual layout of the tablet see now Palaima (1988) 108–10, who concludes: 'The correct conclusion from the epigraphical details of Tn 316 is that its tentative and irregular features do not indicate haste or scribal inexperience as much as difficulty with unwieldy and involved information. The crowding of information in the second section of the verso might imply that the scribe was copying information from other preliminary documents.' This last statement raises the possibility that the tablet does not record a multiple offering made on a single occasion but rather lists separate dedications made over a period of time – which perhaps would remove or lessen the difficulty presented by the vessels listed without a human being.

15 Palmer (1983) 288–90. Previously Palmer (1963: 267 and 466) had interpreted po-re-na as 'pollutions' or 'defilements'. In the first line of the reverse side of the tablet the phrase 'a-ke wa-tu' is inserted into the introductory formula. Wa-tu has been understood to mean 'city' (Greek *astu*), which would seem to be nonsensical either as the object or subject of a verb 'to lead'. And Palmer (1963: 266; 1983: 288–9) rightly insisted that this a-ke must be the same as the a-ke which governs po-re-na. Thus it seems that a meaning other than 'lead' should be sought for a-ke, and the possibility that po-re-na

(apparently subject to the same action as the inanimate wa-tu) does not refer to the human beings should be seriously considered.

16 Chadwick and Ventris (1973) glossary, s.vv.; Palmer (1963) 260 and (1983) 289–90; Lejeune (1964) 93–4; Baumbach (1968) 216 and (1986) 349–50.

17 Chadwick and Ventris (1973) glossary, s.v. po-re-na; Palmer (1983) 290.

18 Palmer (1983) 290.

19 Chadwick and Ventris (1973) 166; Palmer (1963) 127 and 278; Hooker (1980) 104–5; Tritsch (1958) 408 with n. 4 and 409 n. 6 (who suggests a connection between Ae 303 and Tn 316).

20 Tritsch (1958) 408 n. 4. The tablet numbers are the original inventory numbers; thus 303 and 316 were found quite close together (cf. Blegen and Kourouniotis (1939) 564 fig. 7).

21 Guthrie (1959) 43–4; Lejeune (1959) 129–44; Deroy and Gérard (1965) 111–43; Chadwick and Ventris (1973) index, s.vv. 'slaves of the god' and slaves; Hooker (1980) 105; and the subject indices of Baumbach (1968) s.vv. slaves and temple slavery and (1986) s.vv. slaves and slavery and 'slaves of the god' as landholders.

22 Human sacrifice would be more convincingly suggested for a tablet listing human beings with animals (or even human beings alone) and the names of gods in the dative case. PY An 1281 is a list of men who are assigned to other men (religious functionaries or priests?) and, it appears, to a goddess or goddesses: see Palmer (1963) 226–7 and Chadwick and Ventris (1973) 483. But Chadwick acknowledges that 'the twelve named men assigned to deities or religious functionaries on . . . An 1281 can hardly have been sacrificed' (460).

Bibliography

AA	*Archäologischer Anzeiger*
AAA	*Athens Annals of Archaeology* (*᾿Αρχαιολογικὰ ᾿Ανάλεκτα ἐξ ᾿Αθηνῶν*)
AJA	*American Journal of Archaeology*
AJP	*American Journal of Philology*
AntCl	*L'Antiquité classique*
AntK	*Antike Kunst*
AR	(*Journal of Hellenic Studies*) *Archaeological Reports*
ArchEph	*᾿Αρχαιολογικὴ ᾿Εφημερίς*
ArchRW	*Archiv für Religionswissenschaft*
BAAH	Bibliothēkē tēs en Athēnais Archaiologikēs Hetaireias
BCH	*Bulletin de correspondance hellénique*
BICS	*Bulletin of the Institute of Classical Studies of the University of London*
BSA	*Annual of the British School at Athens*
CP	*Classical Philology*
CQ	*Classical Quarterly*
DarSag	Daremberg-Saglio, *Dictionnaire des antiquités grecques et romaines*
Deltion	*᾿Αρχαιολογικὸν Δελτίον*
EPRO	Etudes préliminaires aux religions orientales dans l'empire romain
ERE	Hastings, *Encyclopaedia of Religion and Ethics*
GRBS	*Greek, Roman and Byzantine Studies*
HSCP	*Harvard Studies in Classical Philology*
JHS	*Journal of Hellenic Studies*
LIMC	*Lexicon Iconographicum Mythologiae Classicae*
MMS	*Metropolitan Museum Studies*
MNIR	*Mededelingen van het Nederlandsch historisch Instituut te Rome*
NJbb	*Neue Jahrbücher für das klassische Altertum Geschichte und deutsche Literatur* (*Neue Jahrbücher für Philologie und Pädagogik*)
ÖJ	*Jahreshefte des österreichischen archäologischen Institutes*
PP	*La Parola del Passato*
Praktika	*Πρακτικὰ τῆς ἐν ᾿Αθήναις ᾿Αρχαιολογικῆς ῾Εταιρείας*

RCGO	*Recherches sur les cultes grecs et l'Occident*
RDAC	*Report of the Department of Antiquities, Cyprus*
RE	Pauly-Wissowa, *Real-Encyclopädie der classischen Altertumswissenschaft*
REG	*Revue des études grecques*
RGVV	Religionsgeschichtliche Versuche und Vorarbeiten
RhM	*Rheinisches Museum für Philologie*
RHR	*Revue de l'histoire des religions*
RML	Roscher, *Ausführliches Lexicon der griechischen und römischen Mythologie*
SMEA	*Studi micenei ed egeo-anatolici*
SMSR	*Studi e materiali di storia delle religioni*
SSR	*Studi storico-religiosi*
StItal	*Studi italiani di filologia classica*
TAPA	*Transactions of the American Philological Association*
ZPE	*Zeitschrift für Papyrologie und Epigraphik*

Alexandrescu, P. (1965) 'Les Rapports entre indigènes et Grecs à la lumière des fouilles de la nécropole d'Histria', in *Le Rayonnement des civilisations grecque et romaine sur les cultures périphériques*, Paris, 336–9.

Alexandrescu, P., and Eftimie, V. (1959) 'Tombes thraces d'époque archaïque dans la nécropole tumulaire d'Histria', *Dacia*, n.s., 3: 143–64.

Allen, T. W. (ed.) (1912) *Homeri Opera*, vol. 5, *Hymnos Cyclum Fragmenta Margiten Batrachomyomachiam Vitas Continens*, Oxford.

Alva, W. (1988) 'Discovering the New World's Richest Unlooted Tomb', *National Geographic* 174.4: 510–49.

Ameis, K. F., and Hentze, D. (eds) (1906) *Homers Ilias*, vol. 2, part 4, 4th edn: Leipzig and Berlin.

Andronikos, M. (1968) *Totenkult*, Archaeologia Homerica 3 W, Göttingen.

Angel, J. L. (1945) 'Skeletal Material from Attica', *Hesperia* 14: 279–331.

Arens, W. (1979) *The Man-Eating Myth. Anthropology and Anthropophagy*, New York.

Arens, W., and Sahlins, M. (1979) 'Cannibalism: An Exchange', *New York Review of Books* 26.4: 45–7.

Austin, C. (ed.) (1968) *Nova Fragmenta Euripidea in Papyris Reperta*, Kleine Texte für Vorlesungen und Übungen 187, Berlin.

Baelen, J. (1961) *L'An 480. Salamine*, Paris.

Bammer, A., Brein, F., and Wolff, P. (1978) 'Das Tieropfer am Artemisaltar von Ephesos', in S. Şahin, E. Schwertheim, and J. Wagner (eds), *Studien zur Religion und Kultur Kleinasiens. Festschrift für Friedrich Karl Dörner*, vol. 1, EPRO 66.1, Leiden, 107–57.

Barber, E. A. (1968) *Greek–English Lexicon. A Supplement*, Oxford.

Barker, E. H. (ed.) (1820) *Ἀρκαδίου Περὶ τόνων*, Leipzig.

Bassett, S. E. (1933) 'Achilles' Treatment of Hector's Body', *TAPA* 64: 41–65.

Baumbach, L. (1968) *Studies in Mycenaean Inscriptions and Dialect 1953–1964*, Incunabula Graeca 20, Rome.

—— (1983) 'An Examination of the Evidence for a State of Emergency at Pylos c. 1200 B.C. from the Linear B Tablets', in A. Heubeck and G.

Neumann (eds), *Res Mycenaeae*, Göttingen, 28–40.
—— (1986) *Studies in Mycenaean Inscriptions and Dialect 1965–1978*, Incunabula Graeca 86, Rome.
Behrendt, C. (1910) *De Aeneae Tactici Commentario Poliorcetico Quaestiones Selectae*, Diss.: Königsberg.
Bernays, J. (1866) *Theophrastos' Schrift ueber Frömmigkeit*, Breslau.
Bethe, E. (1927) *Homer. Dichtung und Sage*, vol. 3, *Die Sage von troischen Kriege*, Leipzig and Berlin.
Binford, L. R. (1981) *Bones. Ancient Men and Modern Myths*, New York.
Birmingham, J. (1963) 'The Chronology of Some Early and Middle Iron Age Cypriot Sites', *AJA* 67: 15–42.
Blackburn, E. T. (1970) 'Middle Helladic Graves and Burial Customs with Special Reference to Lerna in the Argolid', Diss.: Cincinnati.
Blackman, D., and Branigan, K. (1982) 'The Excavation of an Early Minoan Tholos Tomb at Ayia Kyriaki, Ayiofarango, Southern Crete', *BSA* 77: 1–57.
Blegen, C. W. (1928) *Zygouries. A Prehistoric Settlement in the Valley of Cleonae*, Cambridge, Mass.
—— (1930–1) 'Goniá', *MMS* 3: 55–80.
—— (1937) *Prosymna. The Helladic Settlement Preceding the Argive Heraeum*, 2 vols, Cambridge.
Blegen, C. W., and Kourouniotis, K. (1939) 'Excavations at Pylos 1939', *AJA* 43: 557–76.
Blegen, C. W., Boulter, C. G., Caskey, J. L., and Rawson, M. (1958) *Troy*, vol. 4, *Settlements VIIa, VIIb, and VIII*, Princeton.
Bodin, L. (1917) 'Histoire et biographie: Phanias d'Erèse', *REG* 30: 117–57.
Bompaire, J. (1958) *Lucien écrivain. Imitation et création*, Bibliothèque des Ecoles françaises d'Athènes et de Rome 190, Paris.
Borries, I. de (ed.) (1911) *Phrynichi Sophistae Praeparatio Sophistica*, Leipzig.
Borthwick, E. K. (1972) 'Two Scenes of Conflict in Euripides', *JHS* 90: 15–21.
Bouffartigue, J., and Patillon, M. (eds) (1977–9) *Porphyre. De l'abstinence*, 2 vols, Paris.
Bowra, [C.] M. (1962) 'Composition', in A. J. B. Wace and F. H. Stubbings (eds), *A Companion to Homer*, London, 38–74.
—— (1972) *Homer*, London.
Brady, I. (1982) 'The Myth-Eating Man', *American Anthropologist* 84: 595–611.
Branigan, K. (1974) *Aegean Metalwork of the Early and Middle Bronze Age*, Oxford.
Brelich, A. (1967) *Presupposti del sacrificio umano*, Rome.
—— (1969a) *Paides e parthenoi*, Incunabula Graeca 36, Rome.
—— (1969b) 'Symbol of a Symbol', in J. M. Kitigawa and C. H. Long (eds), *Myths and Symbols. Studies in Honor of Mircea Eliade*, Chicago, 195–207.
Bremer, J. M., Erp Taalman Kip, A. M. van, and Slings, S. R. (1987) *Some Recently Found Greek Poems*, Mnemosyne Supplement 99, Leiden.

Bremmer, J. N. (1978) 'Heroes, Rituals and the Trojan War', *SSR* 2.1: 5–38.
—— (1983a) *The Early Greek Concept of the Soul*, Princeton.
—— (1983b) 'Scapegoat Rituals in Ancient Greece', *HSCP* 87: 299–320.
—— (1984) 'Greek Maenadism Reconsidered', *ZPE* 55: 267–86.
—— (1987) 'Slow Cybele's Arrival', in J. N. Bremmer and N. M. Horsfall (eds), *Roman Myth and Mythography*, BICS Supplement 52, London, 105–11.
—— (forthcoming) *Birth, Maturity, and Death in Ancient Greece*, London.
Brothwell, D. R. (1961) 'Cannibalism in Early Britain', *Antiquity* 35: 304–7.
—— (1981) *Digging Up Bones. The Excavation, Treatment and Study of Human Skeletal Remains*, 3rd edn: Oxford.
Bruck, E. F. (1926) *Totenteil und Seelgerät im griechischen Recht*, Münchener Beiträge zur Papyrusforschung und antiken Rechtsgeschichte 9, Munich.
Buitron, D., and Soren, D. (1981) 'Excavations in the Sanctuary of Apollo Hylates at Kourion, 1979 and 1980', in J. C. Biers and D. Soren (eds), *Studies in Cypriote Archaeology*, Institute of Archaeology, University of California, Los Angeles, Monograph 18, Los Angeles, 99–116.
Burkert, W. (1966) 'Greek Tragedy and Sacrificial Ritual', *GRBS* 7: 87–121.
—— (1979) *Structure and History in Greek Mythology and Ritual*, Sather Classical Lectures 47, Berkeley.
—— (1981) 'Glaube und Verhalten: Zeichengehalt und Wirkungsmacht von Opferritualen', in J. Rudhardt and O. Reverdin (eds), *Le Sacrifice dans l'antiquité*, Entretiens sur l'antiquité classique 27, Geneva, 91–125.
—— (1983) *Homo Necans. The Anthropology of Ancient Greek Sacrificial Ritual and Myth*, trans. P. Bing, Berkeley.
—— (1985) *Greek Religion. Archaic and Classical*, trans. R. Raffan, London.
—— (1987) 'The Problem of Ritual Killing', in R. G. Hamerton-Kelly (ed.), *Violent Origins. Walter Burkert, René Girard, and Jonathan Z. Smith on Ritual Killing and Cultural Formation*, Stanford, 149–76.
Buxton, R. (1987) 'Wolves and Werewolves in Greek Thought', in J. Bremmer (ed.), *Interpretations of Greek Mythology*, London and Sydney, 60–79.
Calame, C. (1977) *Les Choeurs de jeunes filles en Grèce archaïque*, 2 vols, Filologia e critica 20–1, Rome.
Camporeale, G. (1981) s.v. Achle, *LIMC* 1.1: 200–14.
Carratelli, G. P. (1957) '*Vanaso* in Pilo', *PP* 12: 352–4.
Cartledge, P. (1987) *Agesilaos and the Crisis of Sparta*, London.
Casabona, J. (1966) *Recherches sur le vocabulaire des sacrifices en Grec des origines à la fin de l'époque classique*, Publications des annales de la Faculté des lettres, Aix-en-Provence, n.s., 56, Aix-en-Provence.
Caster, M. (1937) *Lucien et la pensée religieuse de son temps*, Paris.
Cavanagh, W. G. (1978) 'A Mycenaean Second Burial Custom?', *BICS* 25: 171–2.

Chadwick, J. (1976) *The Mycenaean World*, Cambridge.
—— (1987) *Linear B and Related Scripts*, Berkeley and Los Angeles.
Chadwick, J., and Ventris, M. (1973) *Documents in Mycenaean Greek*, 2nd edn: Cambridge.
Chavane, M.-J., and Yon, M. (eds) (1978) *Salamine de Chypre X. Testimonia Salaminia*, fasc. 1, Paris.
Childe, V. G. (1957) *The Dawn of European Civilization*, 6th edn: London.
Chudzinski, A. (1907) *Tod und Totenkultus bei den alten Griechen*, Gymnasial-Bibliothek 44, Gütersloh.
Clement, P. (1934) 'New Evidence for the Origin of the Iphigeneia Legend', *AntCl* 3: 393–409.
Clerc, M. (1927–9) *Massalia. Histoire de Marseille dans l'antiquité des origins à la fin de l'empire romain d'Occident (476 après J.-C.)*, 2 vols, Marseille.
Coche de la Ferté, E. (1980) 'Penthée et Dionysos. Nouvel essai d'interpretation des "Bacchantes" d'Euripide', in R. Bloch (ed.), *Recherches sur les religions de l'antiquité classique*, Hautes études du monde gréco-romain 10, Geneva and Rome, 105–257.
Coldstream, J. N. (1972) 'Cypro-Aegean Exchanges in the 9th and 8th Centuries B.C.', in V. Karageorghis and A. Christodoulos (eds), *Praktika tou Prōtou Diethnous Kupriologikou Sunedriou*, vol. 1, *Archaion Tmēma*, Nicosia, 15–22.
—— (1977) *Geometric Greece*, London.
Cole, S. G. (1984) 'The Social Function of Rituals of Maturation: the Koureion and the Arkteia', *ZPE* 55: 233–44.
Collard, C. (ed.) (1975) *Euripides Supplices*, 2 vols, Groningen.
Cook, A. B. (1914–40) *Zeus. A Study in Ancient Religion*, 3 vols in 5, Cambridge.
Cook, J. M. (1973) *The Troad. An Archaeological and Topographical Study*, Oxford.
Corssen, P. (1913) 'Die Sendung der Lokrerinnen und die Gründung von Neu Ilion', *Sokrates*, n.s., 1: 188–202 and 235–52.
Dain, A., and Bon, A.-M. (eds) (1967) *Enée le tacticien Poliorcétique*, Paris.
Davies, N. (1981) *Human Sacrifice in History and Today*, New York.
Davreux, J. (1942) *La Légende de la prophetesse Cassandre d'après les textes et les monuments*, Paris.
Day, L. P. (1984) 'Dog Burials in the Greek World', *AJA* 88: 21–32.
Degani, H. (ed.) (1983) *Hipponactis Testimonia et Fragmenta*, Leipzig.
Delcourt, M. (1944) *Oedipe ou la légende du conquérant*, Bibliothèque de la Faculté de philosophie et lettres de l'Université de Liège 104, Liège and Paris.
Demoulin, H. (1901) *Epiménide de Crète*, Bibliothèque de la Faculté de philosophie et lettres de l'Université de Liège 12, Brussels.
Deroy, L., and Gérard, M. (1965) *Cadastre mycénien de Pylos*, Incunabula Graeca 10, Rome.
Detienne, M. (1979) *Dionysos Slain*, trans. M. Muellner and L. Muellner, Baltimore and London.
Detienne, M., and Vernant, J.-P. (1989) *The Cuisine of Sacrifice among the Greeks*, trans. P. Wissing, Chicago and London.

Deubner, L. (1932) *Attische Feste*, Berlin.
—— (1934) 'Der Pharmakos von Abdera', *StItal*, n.s., 11: 185–92.
Dhorme, E. (1933) 'Le Sacrifice accadien à propos d'un ouvrage récent', *RHR* 107: 107–25.
Diels, H. (1969) 'Über Epimenides von Kreta', in H. Diels, *Kleine Schriften zur Geschichte der antiken Philosophie*, ed. W. Burkert, Darmstadt, 36–52.
Diels, H., and Kranz, W. (eds) (1951–2) *Die Fragmente der Vorsokratiker*, 3 vols, 6th edn: Berlin.
Dietrich, B. C. (1974) *The Origins of Greek Religion*, Berlin and New York.
Dietz, S. (1980) *Asine II. Results of the Excavations East of the Acropolis 1970–1974*, fasc. 2, *The Middle Helladic Cemetery, the Middle Helladic and Early Mycenaean Deposits*, Skrifter Utgivna av Svenska Institutet i Athen, 4°, 24.2, Stockholm.
Dikaios, P. (1963) 'A "Royal" Tomb at Salamis, Cyprus', *AA* 1963: 126–98.
Dimakopoulou, K., and Consola, D. (1975) 'Λείψανα πρωτοελλαδικοῦ, μεσοελλαδικοῦ, καὶ ὑστεροελλαδικοῦ οἰκισμοῦ στὴ Θήβα', *Deltion* 30, 1, *Meletai*, 44–89.
Dodds, E. R. (1951) *The Greeks and the Irrational*, Sather Classical Lectures 25, Berkeley.
—— (ed.) (1960) *Euripides Bacchae*, 2nd edn: Oxford.
Dor, L., Jannoray, J., Effenterre, H. van, and Effenterre, M. van (1960) *Kirrha. Etude de préhistoire phocidienne*, Paris.
Dörpfeld, W. (1927) *Alt-Ithaka. Ein Beitrag zur Homer-Frage*, 2 vols, Munich.
Dow, S. (1937) 'Athenian Decrees of 216–212 B.C.', *HSCP* 48: 105–26.
Dowden, K. (1989) *Death and the Maiden. Girls' Initiation Rites in Greek Mythology*, London.
Ducrey, P. (1968) *Le Traitement des prisonniers de guerre dans la Grèce antique des origines à la conquête romaine*, Paris.
Durand, J.-L. (1986) *Sacrifice et labour en Grèce ancienne. Essai d'anthropologie religieuse*, Images à l'appui 1, Paris and Rome.
Eckels, R. P. (1937) *Greek Wolf-Lore*, Philadelphia.
Eitrem, S. (1938) 'Mantis und Σφάγια', *Symbolae Osloenses* 18: 9–30.
Eliade, M. (1965) *Rites and Symbols of Initiation. The Mysteries of Birth and Rebirth*, trans. W. R. Trask, New York.
England, E. B. (ed.) (1886) *The Iphigeneia among the Tauri of Euripides*, London.
Engster, H. (1970) *Das Problem des Witwenselbstmordes bei den Germanen*, Diss.: Göttingen.
Errington, R. M. (1969) *Philopoemen*, Oxford.
Farina, A. (ed.), *Ipponatte*, Collana di studi greci 41, Naples, 1963.
Farnell, L. R. (1896–1909) *The Cults of the Greek States*, 5 vols, Oxford.
—— (1921) *Greek Hero Cults and the Idea of Immortality*, Oxford.
Fehling, D. (1971) *Die Quellenangaben bei Herodot. Studien zur Erzählkunst Herodots*, Untersuchungen zur antiken Literatur und Geschichte 9, Berlin and New York.

—— (1974) *Ethologische Überlegungen auf dem Gebiet der Altertumskunde*, Zetemata 61, Munich.

Festugière, A. J. (1972) 'A propos des arétalogies d'Isis', in A. J. Festugière, *Etudes de religion grecque et hellenistique*, Paris, 138–63.

Fink, J. (1978) 'Vorstellungen und Bräuche an Gräbern', in S. Şahin, E. Schwertheim, and J. Wagner (eds), *Studien zur Religion und Kultur Kleinasiens. Festschrift für Friedrich Karl Dörner zum 65. Geburtstag*, vol. 1, EPRO 66.1, Leiden, 295–323.

Foley, H. P. (1985) *Ritual Irony. Poetry and Sacrifice in Euripides*, Ithaca and London.

Fontenrose, J. (1948) 'The Sorrows of Ino and of Procne', *TAPA* 79: 125–67.

—— (1978) *The Delphic Oracle. Its Responses and Operations*, Berkeley.

Fontinoy, C. (1950) 'Le Sacrifice nuptial de Polyxène', *AntCl* 19: 383–96.

Forsdyke, J. (1956) *Greece before Homer. Ancient Chronology and Mythology*, London.

Fougères, G. (1904) s.v. Lykaia, *DarSag* 3.2: 1432–7.

Fourdrignier, E. (1880) 'Sur les sépultures doubles de Thuizy (Marne) (époque gauloise)', *Bulletin de la Société d'anthropologie de Paris*, 3rd ser., 3: 315–23.

Frazer, J. G. (1898) *Pausanias's Description of Greece*, 6 vols, London and New York.

—— (1913) *The Golden Bough. A Study in Magic and Religion*, part 6, *The Scapegoat*, 3rd edn: London.

—— (ed.) (1921) *Apollodorus. The Library*, 2 vols, Cambridge, Mass., and London.

Fritze, J. von (1893) *De Libatione Veterum Graecorum*, Diss.: Berlin.

Frödin, O., and Persson, A. W. (1938) *Asine. Results of the Swedish Excavations 1922–1930*, Stockholm.

Frost, F. J. (1980) *Plutarch's Themistocles. A Historical Commentary*, Princeton.

Furley, W. D. (1981) *Studies in the Use of Fire in Ancient Greek Religion*, New York.

Fürst, C. M. (1930) *Zur Anthropologie der prähistorischen Griechen in Argolis nebst Beschreibungen einiger älteren Schädel aus historischer Zeit*, Lunds Universitets Årsskrift, n.s., 26, no. 8, Lund.

Furtwängler, A. (1900) *Die antiken Gemmen. Geschichte der Steinschneidenkunst in klassischen Altertum*, 3 vols, Leipzig and Berlin.

Furumark, A. (1972) *Mycenaean Pottery*, 2 vols, Skrifter Utgivna av Svenska Institutet i Athen, 4°, 20.1–2, Stockholm.

Gagarin, M. (1981) *Drakon and Early Athenian Homicide Law*, New Haven and London.

Garland, R. (1985) *The Greek Way of Death*, Ithaca.

—— (1987) *The Piraeus from the Fifth to the First Century B.C.*, Ithaca.

Gebhard, V. (1926) *Die Pharmakoi in Ionien und die Sybakchoi in Athen*, Diss.: Munich.

—— (1932) s.v. Sybakchoi, *RE* 4A: 999–1002.

—— (1934) s.v. Thargelia (1), *RE* 5A: 1287–304.

—— (1938) s.v. Pharmakos, *RE* 19: 1841–2.

Geffcken, J. (1890) 'Die Kallimachoscitate der Ibisscholien', *Hermes* 25: 91–6.

Gennep, A. van (1960) *The Rites of Passage*, trans. M. B. Vizedom and G. L. Caffee, Chicago.

Gérard-Rousseau, M. (1968) *Les Mentions religieuses dans les tablettes mycéniennes*, Incunabula Graeca 29, Rome.

—— (1971) 'Les Sacrifices à Pylos', Incunabula Graeca 46, *SMEA* 13: 139–46.

Germain, G. (1954) *Homère et la mystique des nombres*, Paris.

Gernet, L. (1981) *The Anthropology of Ancient Greece*, trans. J. Hamilton and B. Nagy, Baltimore and London.

Ginouvès, R. (1962) *Balaneutikè. Recherches sur la bain dans l'antiquité grecque*, Bibliothèque des Ecoles françaises d'Athènes et de Rome 200, Paris.

Girard, R. (1977) *Violence and the Sacred*, trans. P. Gregory, Baltimore and London.

Gjerstad, E. (1948) *The Swedish Cyprus Expedition*, vol. 4, part 2, *The Cypro-Geometric, Cypro-Archaic and Cypro-Classical Periods*, Stockholm.

Gjerstad, E., Lindros, J., Sjöqvist, E., and Westholm, A. (1934–7) *The Swedish Cyprus Expedition. Finds and Results of the Excavations in Cyprus 1927–1931*, 3 vols, Stockholm.

Glotz, G. (1904) *La Solidarité de la famille dans le droit criminel en Grèce*, Paris.

Graf, F. (1978) 'Die lokrischen Mädchen', *SSR* 2.1: 61–79.

—— (1979) 'Das Götterbild aus dem Taurerland', *Antike Welt* 10.4: 33–41.

—— (1984) 'Women, War, and Warlike Divinities', *ZPE* 55: 245–54.

—— (1985) *Nordionische Kulte. Religionsgeschichtliche und epigraphische Untersuchungen zu den Kulten von Chios, Erythrai, Klazomenai und Phokaia*, Rome.

Green, P. (1970) *The Year of Salamis*, London.

Grenfell, B. P., and Hunt, A. S. (eds) (1922) *The Oxyrhynchus Papyri* 15, London.

Griffin, J. (1980) *Homer on Life and Death*, Oxford.

Gruppe, O. (1906) *Griechische Mythologie und Religionsgeschichte*, 2 vols, Handbuch der klassischen Altertumswissenschaft 5.2, Munich.

Guépin, J.-P. (1968) *The Tragic Paradox. Myth and Ritual in Greek Tragedy*, Amsterdam.

Guthrie, W. K. C. (1959) 'Early Greek Religion in the Light of the Decipherment of Linear B', *BICS* 6: 35–46.

Halliday, W. R. (ed.) (1928) *The Greek Questions of Plutarch*, Oxford.

Hammond, N. G. L. (1978) '"Philip's Tomb" in Historical Context', *GRBS* 19: 331–50.

—— (1983) *Three Historians of Alexander the Great*, Cambridge.

Harrison, J. E. (1922) *Prolegomena to the Study of Greek Religion*, 3rd edn: Cambridge.

Haslam, M. W. (ed.) (1986) *The Oxyrhynchus Papyri* 53, London.

Hatch, W. H. P. (1908) 'The Use of ἀλιτήριος, ἀλιτρός, ἀραῖος, ἐναγής, ἐνθύμιος, παλαμναῖος, and προστρόπαιος: a Study in Greek

Lexicography', *HSCP* 19: 157–86.
Haussleiter, J. (1935) *Der Vegetarismus in der Antike*, RGVV 24, Berlin.
Heckel, W., and Yardley, J. C. (1981) 'Roman Writers and the Indian Practice of Suttee', *Philologus* 125: 305–11.
Henninger, J. (1958) 'Menschenopfer bei den Arabern', *Anthropos* 53: 721–805.
Henrichs, A. (1970) 'Pagan Ritual and the Alleged Crimes of the Early Christians: A Reconsideration', in P. Granfield and J. A. Jungmann (eds), *Kyriakon. Festschrift Johannes Quasten*, vol. 2, Münster, 18–35.
—— (1972) *Die Phoinikika des Lollianos. Fragmente eines neuen griechischen Romans*, Papyrologische Texte und Abhandlungen 14, Bonn.
—— (1978) 'Greek Maenadism from Olympias to Messalina', *HSCP* 82: 121–60.
—— (1981) 'Human Sacrifice in Greek Religion: Three Case Studies', in J. Rudhardt and O. Reverdin (eds), *Le Sacrifice dans l'antiquité*, Entretiens sur l'antiquité classique 27, Geneva, 195–235.
—— (1982) 'Changing Dionysiac Identities', in B. F. Meyer and E. P. Sanders (eds), *Jewish and Christian Self-Definition*, vol. 3, *Self-Definition in the Graeco-Roman World*, London, 137–60.
—— (1984) 'Loss of Self, Suffering, Violence: the Modern View of Dionysus from Nietzsche to Girard', *HSCP* 88: 205–40.
—— (1987) 'Three Approaches to Greek Mythography', in J. Bremmer (ed.), *Interpretations of Greek Mythology*, London and Sydney, 242–77.
Henry, R. (ed.) (1959–77) *Photius Bibliothèque*, 8 vols, Paris.
Herbillon, J. (1929) *Les Cultes de Patras*, Baltimore and London.
Hercher, R. (ed.) (1866) *Claudii Aeliani Varia Historia, Epistolae, Fragmenta*, Leipzig.
—— (ed.) (1870) *Aeneas Commentarius Poliorceticus*, Berlin.
Heubeck, A. (1966) *Aus der Welt der frühgriechischen Lineartafeln*, Göttingen.
Hill, G. (1940) *A History of Cyprus*, vol. 1, *To the Conquest by Richard Lion Heart*, Cambridge.
Hiller, E. (1886) 'Zur Quellenkritik des Clemens Alexandrinus', *Hermes* 21: 126–33.
Hiller, S. (1977) *Das minoische Kreta nach den Ausgrabungen des letzten Jahrzehnts*, Mykenische Studien 5, Vienna.
Hirzel, R. (1908) 'Der Selbstmord', *ArchRW* 11: 75–104, 243–84, and 417–76.
—— (1909) *Die Strafe der Steinigung*, Abhandlungen der philologisch-historischen Klasse der königlich sächsischen Gesellschaft der Wissenschaften 27, no. 7: 223–66 [1–44].
Höfer, O. (1897–1909) s.v. Pharmakos, *RML* 3.2: 2276–85.
Hood, M. S. F., and de Jong, P. (1952) 'Late Minoan Warrior-Graves from Agios Ioannis and the New Hospital Site at Knossos', *BSA* 47: 243–77.
Hood, S. (1973) 'Mycenaean Settlement in Cyprus and the Coming of the Greeks', in *Acts of the International Archaeological Symposium 'The Mycenaeans in the Eastern Mediterranean'*, Nicosia, 40–50.
Hood, S., Huxley, G., and Sandars, N. (1958–9) 'A Minoan Cemetery

on Upper Gypsades (Knossos Survey 156)', *BSA* 53–4: 194–261.
Hooker, J. T. (1977) 'The Language of the Thebes Of Tablets', *Minos* 16: 174–8.
—— (1980) *Linear B. An Introduction*, Bristol.
Hurwit, J. (1979) 'The Dendra Octopus Cup and the Problem of Style in the Fifteenth Century Aegean', *AJA* 83: 413–26.
Huxley, G. L. (1966) 'Troy VIII and the Locrian Maidens', in *Ancient Societies and Institutions. Studies Presented to Victor Ehrenberg on his 75th Birthday*, Oxford, 147–64.
—— (1973) 'Fulgentius on the Cretan Hecatomphonia', *CP* 68: 124–6.
Hyde, W. (1903) *De Olympionicarum Statuis a Pausania Commemoratis*, Halle.
Immerwahr, W. (1891) *Die Kulte und Mythen Arkadiens*, vol. 1, *Die arkadischen Kulte*, Leipzig.
Jacoby, F. (ed.) (1904) *Das Marmor Parium*, Berlin.
—— (ed.) (1923–58) *Die Fragmente der griechischen Historiker*, 3 parts, Berlin and Leipzig.
Janssens, P. A. (1970) *Palaeopathology. Diseases and Injuries of Prehistoric Man*, trans. I. Dequeecker, London.
Jeanmaire, H. (1939) *Couroi et Courètes*, Lille.
Jost, M. (1985) *Sanctuaires et cultes d'Arcadie*, Ecole française d'Athènes, Etudes Péloponnésiennes 9, Paris.
Jouan, F. (1966) *Euripide et les légendes des Chants cypriens. Des origines de la guerre de Troie à l'Iliade*, Paris.
Kahil, L. (1965) 'Autour de l'Artémis attique', *AntK* 8: 20–33.
—— (1977) 'L'Artémis de Brauron: rites et mystère', *AntK* 20: 86–98.
Karageorghis, V. (1963a) ''Αρχαιολογικαὶ παρατηρήσεις ἐπί τινων ὁμηρικῶν ἐθίμων ταφῆς', *Stasinos* 1: 31–9.
—— (1963b) 'Chronique des fouilles et découvertes archéologiques à Chypre en 1962', *BCH* 87: 325–87.
—— (1963c) 'Ten Years of Archaeology in Cyprus 1953–1962', *AA* 1963: 498–601.
—— (1963d) 'Une tombe de guerrier à Palaepaphos', *BCH* 87: 265–300.
—— (1965a) 'Horse Burials in the Island of Cyprus', *Archaeology* 18: 282–90.
—— (1965b) 'Nouvelles découvertes dans la nécropole royale de Salamine de Chypre', in *Le Rayonnement des civilisations grecque et romaine sur les cultures périphériques*, Paris, 305–12.
—— (1967) *Excavations in the Necropolis of Salamis I*, Salamis vol. 3, Nicosia.
—— (1969) *Salamis in Cyprus. Homeric, Hellenistic and Roman*, London.
—— (1970) *Excavations in the Necropolis of Salamis II*, Salamis vol. 4, Nicosia.
Kassel, R., and Austin, C. (eds) (1984–6) *Poetae Comici Graeci*, vols 3.2, 4, and 5, Berlin and New York.
Keramopoulos, A. D. (1923) *Ὁ ἀποτυμπανισμός. Συμβολὴ ἀρχαιολογικὴ εἰς τὴν ἱστορίαν τοῦ ποινικοῦ δικαίου καὶ τὴν λαογραφίαν*, BAAH 48, Athens.
Kern, O. (ed.) (1922) *Orphicorum Fragmenta*, 2nd edn: Berlin.

King, K. C. (1987) *Achilles. Paradigms of the War Hero from Homer to the Middle Ages*, Berkeley, Los Angeles, and London.

Kirk, G. S. (1970) *Myth. Its Meaning and Function in Ancient and Other Cultures*, Sather Classical Lectures 40, Berkeley and Los Angeles.

—— (1974) *The Nature of Greek Myths*, Harmondsworth.

—— (1981) 'Some Methodological Pitfalls in the Study of Ancient Greek Sacrifice (in Particular)', in J. Rudhardt and O. Reverdin (eds), *Le Sacrifice dans l'antiquité*, Entretiens sur l'antiquité classique 27, Geneva, 41–80.

Klaffenbach, G. (ed.) (1968) *Inscriptiones Graecae*, vol. 9, part 1, fasc. 3, *Inscriptiones Locridis Occidentalis*, 2nd edn: Berlin.

Knoch, W. (1960) *Die Strafbestimmungen in Platons Nomoi*, Klassisch-philologische Studien 23, Wiesbaden.

Kock, T. (ed.) (1880–8) *Comicorum Atticorum Fragmenta*, 3 vols, Leipzig.

Koerte, A. (ed.) (1938–53) *Menandri Quae Supersunt*, 2 vols, Leipzig.

Kossatz-Diessmann, A. (1981) s.v. Achilleus, *LIMC* 1.1: 37–200.

Koster, W. J. W. (ed.) (1962) *Scholia in Aristophanem*, part 4, *Jo. Tzetzae Commentarii in Aristophanem*, fasc. 3, *Continens Commentarium in Ranas et in Aves, Argumentum Equitum*, Groningen and Amsterdam.

Kourouniotis, K. (1904) 'Ἀνασκαφαὶ Λυκαίου', *ArchEph* 1904: 153–214.

Kritzas, Ch. B. (1976–8) 'Μυκηναϊκὸ πηγάδι μὲ σκελετοὺς στὸ Ἄργος', in *Praktika tou Prōtou Diethnous Sunedriou Peloponnēsiakōn Spoudōn*, vol. 2, Peloponnesiaca Supplement 6, Athens, 173–80.

Kroll, W. (ed.) (1899–1901) *Procli Diadochi in Platonis Rem Publicam Commentarii*, 2 vols, Leipzig.

Kümmel, H. M. (1967) *Ersatzrituale für den hethitischen König*, Studien zu den Bolğazköy-Texten 3, Wiesbaden.

Kurtz, D. C., and Boardman, J. (1971) *Greek Burial Customs*, London.

Lasseure, F. (ed.) (1971) *Strabon Géographie*, vol. 7 (*Livre X*), Paris.

Latte, K. (1948) 'De nonnullis papyris oxyrrhynchiis', *Philologus* 97: 37–47.

Laurens, A.-F. (1986) s.v. Bousiris, *LIMC* 3.1: 147–52.

Lawson, J. C. (1910) *Modern Greek Folklore and Ancient Greek Religion*, Cambridge.

Leaf, W. (1912) *Troy. A Study in Homeric Geography*, London.

—— (1914–16) 'The Lokrian Maidens', *BSA* 21: 148–54.

—— (ed.) (1923) *Strabo on the Troad, Book XIII, CAP. I*, Cambridge.

Legrand, Ph.-E. (ed.) (1951) *Herodote Histoires, Livre VII, Polymnie*, Paris.

Lejeune, M. (1959) 'Textes mycéniens relatifs aux esclaves', *Historia* 8: 129–44.

—— (1964) 'Sur le vocabulaire économique mycénien', in E. L. Bennett, Jr. (ed.), *Mycenaean Studies*, Madison, 77–109.

Leone, P. A. M. (ed.) (1968) *Ioannis Tzetzae Historiae*, Pubblicazioni dell' Instituto di filologia classica, Università degli studi di Napoli 1, Naples.

Lérat, L. (1952) *Les Locriens de l'Ouest*, 2 vols, Bibliothèque des Ecoles françaises d'Athènes et de Rome 176, Paris.

Liddell, H. G., Scott, R., and Jones, H. S. (1940) *A Greek–English*

Lexicon, 9th edn: Oxford.
Lloyd-Jones, H. (1981) 'A Fragment of Achaeus?', *ZPE* 41: 27–8.
—— (1983) 'Artemis and Iphigeneia', *JHS* 103: 87–102.
Lloyd-Jones, H., and Parsons, P. (eds) (1983) *Supplementum Hellenisticum*, Texte und Kommentare 11, Berlin and New York.
Lobel, E., and Page, D. (eds) (1963) *Poetarum Lesbiorum Fragmenta*, Oxford.
Lobel, E., Roberts, C. H., and Wegener, E. P. (eds) (1941) *The Oxyrhynchus Papyri* 18, London.
Lonis, R. (1979) *Guerre et religion en Grèce à l'époque classique*, Paris.
Loraux, N. (1987) *Tragic Ways of Killing a Woman*, trans. A. Forster, Cambridge, Mass., and London.
Lowenstam, S. (1981) *The Death of Patroklos. A Study in Typology*, Beiträge zur klassischen Philologie 133, Königstein.
Luce, J. V. (1975) *Homer and the Heroic Age*, London.
McDonald, W. A. (1972) 'Excavations at Nichoria in Messenia: 1969–71', *Hesperia* 41: 218–73.
McGeorge, T. (1984) ''Έγκλημα στὴν ὑστερομινωϊκὴ III περίοδο', *Archaiologia* 11: 12–16.
Macqueen, J. G. (1978) 'Secondary Burial at Çatal Hüyük', *Numen* 25: 226–39.
McWhirter, N., and McWhirter, R. (eds) (1986) *Guinness Book of World Records*, 24th US edn: New York.
Mainoldi, C. (1984) *L'Image du loup et du chien dans la Grèce ancienne d'Homère à Platon*, Paris.
Mannhardt, W. (1884) *Mythologische Forschungen*, Quellen und Forschungen zur Sprach- und Culturgeschichte der germanischen Völker 51, Strasbourg and London.
—— (1905) *Wald- und Feldkulte*, 2 vols, 2nd edn: Berlin.
Manni, E. (1963) 'Le Locridi nella letteratura del III sec. a. C.', in *Miscellanea di studi alessandrini in memoria di Augusto Rostagni*, Turin, 166–79.
Marinatos, N. (1986) *Minoan Sacrificial Ritual*, Skrifter Utgivna av Svenska Institutet i Athen, 8°, 9, Stockholm.
Maringer, J. (1942–3) 'Menschenopfer im Bestattungsbrauch Alteuropas. Eine Untersuchung über die Doppel- und Mehrbestattungen im vor- und frühgeschichtlichen Europa, insbesondere Mittleuropa', *Anthropos* 37–8: 1–112.
Massenzio, M. (1968) 'La festa di Artemis Triklaria e Dionysos Aisymnetes a Patrai', *SMSR* 39.1: 101–32.
Masson, O. (1949) 'Sur un papyrus contenant des fragments d'Hipponax (P.Oxy. XVIII.2176)', *REG* 62: 300–19.
—— (1950a) 'A propos d'un rituel hittite pour la lustration d'une armée', *RHR* 137: 5–25.
—— (1950b) 'Le Nom des "pharmakoi" athéniens: Σύβακχοι ou Σύμβακχοι?', in *Mélanges Henri Gregoire*, vol. 2, Annuaire de l'Institut de philologie et d'histoire orientales et slaves 10, Brussels, 449–54
—— (ed.) (1962) *Les Fragments du poète Hipponax*, Etudes et commentaires 43, Paris.

—— (1964) 'Kypriaka I. Recherches sur les antiquités de Tamassos', *BCH* 88: 199–238.

Maull, O. (1925) s.v. Leukas, Leukadia (1) IV, *RE* 12: 2219–29.

Medeiros, W. de Sousa (ed.) (1961) *Hipónax de Efeso*, vol. 1, *Fragmentos dos Iambos*, Coimbra.

—— (1969) *Hipponactea. Subsídios para uma nova edição crítica do iambógrafo de Efeso*, Coimbra.

Merkelbach, R., and West, M. L. (eds) (1967) *Fragmenta Hesiodea*, Oxford.

Meuli, K. (1975) *Gesammelte Schriften*, ed. T. Gelzer, 2 vols, Basel and Stuttgart.

Momigliano, A. (1945) 'The Locrian Maidens and the Date of Lycophron's *Alexandra*', *CQ* 39: 49–53.

Montepaone, C. (1979a) 'L'ἀρκτεία a Brauron', *SSR* 3.2: 343–64.

—— (1979b) 'Il mito di fondazione del rituale munichio in onore di Artemis', *RCGO* 1: 65–76.

Moretti, L. (1957) *Olympionikai. I vincitori negli antichi agoni olimpici*, Atti della Accademia nazionale dei Lincei, memorie, ser. 8, 8.2, Rome.

Moulinier, L. (1952) *Le Pur et l'impur dans la pensée des Grecs d'Homère à Aristote*, Etudes et commentaires 11, Paris.

Müller, H. D. (1851) *Über den Zeus Lykaios*, Göttingen.

—— (1857–69) *Mythologie der griechischen Stämme*, 2 vols, Göttingen.

Müller, K. (ed.) (1841–70) *Fragmenta Historicorum Graecorum*, 5 vols, Paris.

Murray, G. (1924) *The Rise of the Greek Epic*, 3rd edn: Oxford.

Muth, R. (1988) *Einführung in die griechische und römische Religion*, Darmstadt.

Mylonas, G. E. (1948) 'Homeric and Mycenaean Burial Customs', *AJA* 52: 56–81.

—— (1962) 'Burial Customs', in A. J. B. Wace and F. H. Stubbings (eds), *A Companion to Homer*, London, 478–88.

—— (1966) *Mycenae and the Mycenaean Age*, Princeton.

—— (1972–3) *Ὁ ταφικὸς κύκλος Β τῶν Μυκηνῶν*, BAAH 73, Athens.

Nauck, A. (ed.) (1889) *Tragicorum Graecorum Fragmenta*, 2nd edn: Leipzig.

Nilsson, M. P. (1906) *Griechische Feste von religiöser Bedeutung*, Leipzig.

—— (1913) 'Lustration des Heeres', *ArchRW* 16: 314.

—— (1932) *The Mycenaean Origin of Greek Mythology*, Sather Classical Lectures 8, Berkeley.

—— (1950) *The Minoan–Mycenaean Religion and its Survival in Greek Religion*, 2nd edn: Lund.

—— (1967–74) *Geschichte der griechischen Religion*, 2 vols, Handbuch der Altertumswissenschaft 5.2, 3rd edn: Munich.

O'Connor-Visser, E. A. M. E. (1987) *Aspects of Human Sacrifice in the Tragedies of Euripides*, Diss.: Amsterdam.

Oden, R. A. (1977) *Studies in Lucian's De Syria Dea*, Harvard Semitic Monographs 15, Missoula, Montana.

Oppermann, H. (1934) s.v. Tauropolos, *RE* 5A: 34–8.

Osborne, R. (1985) *Demos. The Discovery of Classical Attika*, Cambridge.

Page, D. L. (ed.) (1942) *Greek Literary Papyri*, vol. 1, Cambridge, Mass., and London.

—— (ed.) (1962) *Poetae Melici Graeci*, Oxford.

Palaima, T. G. (1988) *The Scribes of Pylos*, Incunabula Graeca 87, Rome.

Palmer, L. R. (1963) *The Interpretation of Mycenaean Greek Texts*, Oxford.

—— (1983) 'Studies in Mycenaean Religion', in P. Händel and W. Meid (eds), *Festschrift für Robert Muth*, Innsbrucker Beiträge zur Kulturwissenschaft 22, Innsbruck, 283–96.

Papapostolou, I. A. (1977) *Τὰ σφραγίσματα τῶν Χανιῶν. Συμβολὴ στὴ μελέτη τῆς μινωϊκῆς σφραγιδογλυφίας*, BAAH 87, Athens.

Parke, H. W. (1977) *Festivals of the Athenians*, Ithaca.

Parke, H. W., and Wormell, D. E. W. (1956) *The Delphic Oracle*, 2 vols, Oxford.

Parker, R. (1983) *Miasma. Pollution and Purification in Early Greek Religion*, Oxford.

Pearson, A. C. (1913) s.v. Human Sacrifice (Greek), *ERE* 6: 847–9.

Pearson, L. (1962) 'The Pseudo-History of Messenia and its Authors', *Historia* 11: 397–426.

Peatfield, A. A. A. (1983) 'The Topography of Minoan Peak Sanctuaries', *BSA* 78: 273–9.

Pelon, O. (1976) *Tholoi, tumuli et cercles funéraires. Recherches sur les monuments funéraires de plan circulaire dans l'Egée de l'âge du bronze (III*[e] *et II*[e] *millenaires av. J.-C.)*, Bibliothèque des Ecoles françaises d'Athènes et de Rome 229, Athens.

Pembroke, S. (1970) 'Locres et Tarente: le rôle des femmes dans la fondation de deux colonies grecques', *Annales Economies, Sociétés, Civilisations* 25: 1240–70.

Perlman, P. (1989) 'Acting the She-bear for Artemis', *Arethusa* 22: 111–33.

Persson, A. W. (1931) *The Royal Tombs at Dendra near Midea*, Skrifter Utgivna av Kungl. Humanistiska Vetenskapssamfundet i Lund 15, Lund.

Pfeiffer, R. (ed.) (1949–53) *Callimachus*, 2 vols, Oxford.

Pfister, F. (1929) review of V. Gebhard, *Die Pharmakoi in Ionien und die Sybakchoi in Athen*, *Gnomon* 5: 94–8.

Picard, C. (1933) 'Les Bûchers sacrés d'Eleusis', *RHR* 107: 137–54.

Piccaluga, G. (1968) *Lykaon. Un tema mitico*, Quaderni SMSR 5, Rome.

Pieridou, A. (1965) 'An Early Cypro-Geometric Tomb at Lapethos', *RDAC* 1965: 75–111.

Pini, I. (1968) *Beiträge zur minoischen Gräberkunde*, Wiesbaden.

Pizzani, U. (ed.) (1969) *Fabio Planciade Fulgenzio Definizione di parole antiche*, Scriptores Latini 9, Rome.

Platnauer, M. (ed.) (1938) *Euripides Iphigenia in Tauris*, Oxford.

Podlecki, A. J. (1975) *The Life of Themistocles. A Critical Survey of the Literary and Archaeological Evidence*, Montreal and London.

Pohlenz, M. (1922) s.v. Kronos, *RE* 11: 1982–2018.

Popham, M. R. (1974a) 'Sellopoulo Tombs 3 and 4, Two Late Minoan Graves near Knossos', *BSA* 69: 195–257.

—— (1974b) 'Trial KV (1969), a Middle Minoan Building at Knossos', *BSA* 69: 181–94.

Popham, M. R., Sackett, L. H., and Themelis, P. G. (eds) (1980) *Lefkandi I. The Iron Age. The Settlement and the Cemeteries*, The British School of Archaeology at Athens supplementary vol. 11, London.

Popham, M. [R.], Touloupa, E., and Sackett, L. H. (1982) 'The Hero of Lefkandi', *Antiquity* 56: 169–74.

Pötscher, W. (ed.) (1964) *Theophrastos' Περὶ Εὐσεβείας*, Philosophia Antiqua 11, Leiden.

Poulianos, A. (1976–8) ''Ομαδικὸς τάφος στὸ Ἄργος', in *Praktika tou Prōtou Diethnous Sunedriou Peloponnēsiakōn Spoudōn*, vol. 2, Peloponnesiaca Supplement 6, Athens, 313–19.

Powell, J. U. (1925) *Collectanea Alexandrina*, Oxford.

Prag, A. J. N. W. (1985) *The Oresteia. Iconographic and Narrative Tradition*, Warminster and Chicago.

Pritchard, J. B. (ed.) (1955) *Ancient Near Eastern Texts Relating to the Old Testament*, 2nd edn: Princeton.

Pritchett, W. K. (1974–85) *The Greek State at War*, 4 parts, Berkeley, Los Angeles, and London.

Protonotariou-Deïlaki, E. (1968) 'Θολωτὸς τάφος Καζάρμας', *AAA* 1: 236–8.

—— (1969a) ''Ανασκαφὴ θολωτοῦ μυκηναϊκοῦ τάφου', *Deltion* 24, 2, *Chronika* 1: 104–5.

—— (1969b) 'Θολωτὸς τάφος Καζάρμας', *AAA* 2: 3–6.

Prott, H. von (1897) 'Buphonien', *RhM*, ser. 3, 52: 187–204.

Radt, S. (ed.) (1977) *Tragicorum Graecorum Fragmenta*, vol. 4, *Sophocles*, Göttingen.

—— (ed.) (1985) *Tragicorum Graecorum Fragmenta*, vol. 3, *Aeschylus*, Göttingen.

Rapp, G., and Aschenbrenner, S. E. (eds) (1978) *Excavations at Nichoria in Southwest Greece*, vol. 1, *Site, Environs, and Techniques*, Minneapolis.

Reinach, A. (1914) 'L'Origine de deux légendes homériques', *RHR* 69: 12–53.

Rhodes, P. J. (1981) *A Commentary on the Aristotelian Athenaion Politeia*, Oxford.

Robert, C. (1923) *Die griechische Heldensage*, book 3, part 2.1, *Der troische Kreis bis zu Ilions Zerstörung*, 4th edn of L. Preller, *Griechische Mythologie*, vol. 2.3, Berlin.

Rodriguez Adrados, F. (ed.) (1959) *Líricos griegos. Elegiacos y yambógrafos arcaicos (siglos VII-V a. C.)*, vol. 2, Barcelona.

Rohde, E. (1914) *Der griechische Roman und seine Vorläufer*, 3rd edn: Leipzig.

—— (1925) *Psyche. The Cult of Souls and Belief in Immortality among the Greeks*, trans. G. B. Hillis, London and New York.

Roscher, W. H. (1892) 'Die Schattenlosigheit des Zeus-abatons auf dem Lykaion', *NJbb* 145: 701–9.

—— (1897) *Das von der 'Kynanthropie' handelnde Fragment des Marcellus von Side*, Abhandlungen der philologisch-historischen Classe der königlich sächsischen Gesellschaft der Wissenschaften 17, no. 3: 1–92.

Rose, V. (ed.) (1886) *Aristotelis Qui Ferebantur Librorum Fragmenta*, Leipzig.

Rösler, W. (1987) 'Der Frevel des Aias in der "Iliupersis"', *ZPE* 69: 1–8.
—— (1989) 'Formes narratives d'un mythe dans la poésie épique, la poésie lyrique et les arts plastiques: Ajax de Locres et les Achéens', in C. Calame (ed.), *Métamorphoses du mythe en Grèce antique*, Geneva, 123–8.
Rotolo, V. (1980) 'Il rito della ΒΟΥΛΙΜΟΥ ΕΞΕΛΑΣΙΣ', in *Miscellanea di studi classici in honore di Eugenio Manni*, vol. 6, Rome, 1947–61.
Rotroff, S. I. (1976) 'Megarian Bowls in the Athenian Agora', Diss.: Princeton.
Rudhardt, J. (1958) *Notions fondamentales de la pensée religieuse et actes constitutifs du culte dans la Grèce classique*, Geneva.
Rudhardt, J., and Reverdin, O. (eds) (1981) *Le Sacrifice dans l'antiquité*, Entretiens sur l'antiquité classique 27, Geneva.
Russell, M. D. (1987) 'Mortuary Practices at the Krapina Neandertal Site', *American Journal of Physical Anthropology* 72: 381–97.
Rutkowski, B. (1986) *Cult Places of the Aegean*, New Haven and London.
Sakellarakis, I. [= Y.] A. (1968) 'Παρατηρήσεις ἐπὶ τῆς σημειωθείσης εἰς Ἀρχάνας ΥΜ ΙΙΙ θυσίας ταύρου', in *Pepragmena tou Deuterou Diethnous Krētologikou Sunedriou*, vol. 1, Athens, 238–46.
—— (1970) 'Das Kuppelgrab A von Archanes und das kretisch-mykenische Tieropferritual', *Praehistorische Zeitschrift* 45: 135–219.
—— (1974) 'Ἀνασκαφὴ Ἀρχανῶν', *Praktika* 1974: 207–12.
Sakellarakis, Y., and Sakellaraki, E. (1979) 'Ἀνασκαφὴ Ἀρχανῶν', *Praktika* 1979: 331–92.
—— (1981) 'Drama of Death in a Minoan Temple', *National Geographic* 159.2: 204–22.
Sale, W. (1975) 'The Temple-Legends of the Arkteia', *RhM*, ser. 3, 118: 265–84.
Sampson, A. (1983) 'Ὁ πρωτοελλαδικὸς οἰκισμὸς καὶ τὸ νεκροταφεῖο τῆς Μάνικας Χαλκίδας', *Archaiologia* 6: 69–76.
—— (1985) *Μάνικα. Μία πρωτοελλαδικὴ πόλη στὴ Χαλκίδα*, vol. 1, Chalkis.
Samuel, A. E. (1972) *Greek and Roman Chronology. Calendars and Years in Classical Antiquity*, Handbuch der Altertumswissenschaft 1.7, Munich.
Sandars, N. K. (1963) 'Later Aegean Bronze Swords', *AJA* 67: 117–53.
Sapouna-Sakellarakis, E. (1987) 'New Evidence from the Early Bronze Age Cemetery at Manika, Chalkis', *BSA* 82: 233–64.
Sarkissian, J. (1983) *Catullus 68. An Interpretation*, Mnemosyne Supplement 76, Leiden.
Schachter, A. (1981–6) *Cults of Boiotia*, 2 vols, BICS Supplement 38.1–2, London.
Schibli, H. S. (1990) *Pherekydes of Syros*, Oxford.
Schliemann, H. (1879) *Mycenae. A Narrative of Researches and Discoveries at Mycenae and Tiryns*, New York.
Schmitt, H. H. (1969) *Die Staatsverträge des Altertums*, vol. 3, *Die Verträge der griechisch-römischen Welt von 338 bis 200 v. Chr.*, Munich.
Schmitt, J. (1921) *Freiwilliger Opfertod bei Euripides. Ein Beitrag zur seiner dramatischen Technik*, RGVV 17.2, Giessen.

Schnapp-Gourbeillon, A. (1982) 'Les Funérailles de Patrocle', in G. Gnoli and J.-P. Vernant (eds), *La Mort, les morts dans les sociétés anciennes*, Cambridge, 77–88.

Schrader, H. (ed.) (1880) *Porphyrii Quaestionum Homericarum ad Iliadem Pertinentium Reliquiae*, Leipzig.

Schrader, O. (1904) *Totenhochzeit*, Jena.

Schwartz, E. (1894) s.v. Aineias (3), *RE* 1: 1019–21.

Schwenn, F. (1915) *Die Menschenopfer bei den Griechen und Römern*, RGVV 15.3, Giessen.

—— (1932) s.v. Menschenopfer, *RE* 15: 948–56.

Seel, O. (1949) s.v. Pallas (2), *RE* 18.3: 239–44.

Segal, C. (1971) *The Theme of the Mutilation of the Corpse in the Iliad*, Mnemosyne Supplement 17, Leiden.

Shaw, J. W. (1978) 'Evidence for the Minoan Tripartite Shrine', *AJA* 82: 429–48.

Shay, C. T. (1975) 'The Little Circle', in W. A. McDonald, 'Excavations at Nichoria in Messenia: 1972–1973', *Hesperia* 44: 73–5 (69–141).

Shear, T. L. (1939) 'The Campaign of 1938', *Hesperia* 8: 201–46.

Smith, J. Z. (1982) *Imagining Religion. From Babylon to Jonestown*, Chicago and London.

Snell, B., and Kannicht, R. (eds) (1986) *Tragicorum Graecorum Fragmenta*, vol. 1, *Didascaliae Tragicae, Catalogi Tragicorum et Tragoediarum, Testimonia et Fragmenta Tragicorum Minorum*, 2nd edn: Göttingen.

Snell, B., and Maehler, H. (eds) (1987) *Pindari Carmina cum Fragmentis*, part 2, 8th edn: Leipzig.

Solmsen, F. (1981) 'The Sacrifice of Agamemnon's Daughter in Hesiod's *Ehoeae*', *AJP* 102: 353–8.

Sordi, M. (1958) *La lega tessala fino ad Alessandro Magno*, Studi pubblicati dall' Instituto italiano per la storia antica 15, Rome.

Soren, D. (ed.) (1987) *The Sanctuary of Apollo Hylates at Kourion, Cyprus*, Tuscon.

Spyropoulos, T. G., and Chadwick, J. (1975) *The Thebes Tablets II*, Minos Supplement 4, Salamanca.

Staal, F. (1979) 'The Meaninglessness of Ritual', *Numen* 26: 2–22.

Stengel, P. (1897) 'Buphonien', *RhM*, ser. 3, 52: 399–411.

—— (1910) *Opferbräuche der Griechen*, Leipzig and Berlin.

—— (1920) *Die griechischen Kultusaltertümer*, Handbuch der klassischen Altertumswissenschaft 5.3, 3rd edn: Munich.

Stommel, E. (1954) s.v. Bestattung. A II. Griechisch-römisch, *Reallexicon für Antike und Christentum* 2: 200–7.

Sullivan, J. P. (1968) *The Satyricon of Petronius. A Literary Study*, Bloomington, Ind., and London.

Tarn, W. W. (1948) *Alexander the Great*, 2 vols, Cambridge.

Thompson, S. (1955–8) *Motif-Index of Folk Literature*, 6 vols, 2nd edn: Bloomington, Ind., and Copenhagen.

Tigerstedt, E. N. (1953) 'Pherecydes in Sparta', *Eranos* 51: 8–13.

—— (1965–78) *The Legend of Sparta in Classical Antiquity*, 3 vols, Uppsala.

Touchefeu, O. (1981a) s.v. Aias I, *LIMC* 1.1: 312–36.

—— (1981b) s.v. Aias II, *LIMC* 1.1: 336–51.

Tresp, A. (ed.) (1914) *Die Fragmente der griechischen Kultschriftsteller*, RGVV 15.1, Giessen.

Tritsch, F. J. (1958) 'The Women of Pylos', in E. Grumach (ed.), *Minoica. Festschrift zum 80. Geburtstag von Johannes Sundwall*, Berlin, 406–45.

Tsountas, Ch. D. (1888) ''Ανασκαφαὶ τάφων ἐν Μυκήναις', *ArchEph* 1888: 119–80.

Tsountas, Ch. [D.], and Manatt, J. I. (1897) *The Mycenaean Age. A Study of the Monuments and Culture of Pre-Homeric Greece*, London.

Tumasonis, D. (1983) 'Some Aspects of Minoan Society. A View from Social Anthropology', in O. Kryzyszkowska and L. Nixon (eds), *Minoan Society. Proceedings of the Cambridge Colloquium 1981*, Bristol, 303–10.

Turcan, R. (1975) *Mithras Platonicus. Recherches sur l'hellénisation philosophique de Mithra*, EPRO 47, Leiden.

Ubelaker, D. H. (1974) *Reconstruction of Demographic Profiles from Ossuary Skeletal Samples. A Case Study from the Tidewater Potomac*, Smithsonian Contributions to Anthropology 18, Washington, DC.

—— (1978) *Human Skeletal Remains. Excavation, Analysis, Interpretation*, Manuals of Archaeology 2, Washington, DC.

Verbruggen, H. (1981) *Le Zeus crétois*, Paris.

Vermeule, E. (1964) *Greece in the Bronze Age*, Chicago and London.

—— (1974) *Götterkult*, Archaeologia Homerica 3 V, Göttingen.

—— (1979) *Aspects of Death in Early Greek Art and Poetry*, Sather Classical Lectures 46, Berkeley.

Vernant, J.-P. (1981) 'Ambiguity and Reversal. On the Enigmatic Structure of *Oedipus Rex*', in J.-P. Vernant and P. Vidal-Naquet, *Tragedy and Myth in Ancient Greece*, trans. J. Lloyd, Sussex and Atlantic Highlands, N.J., 87–119.

—— (1989) 'At Man's Table: Hesiod's Foundation Myth of Sacrifice', in M. Detienne and J.-P. Vernant, *The Cuisine of Sacrifice among the Greeks*, trans. P. Wissing, Chicago and London, 21–86.

Versnel, H. S. (1975) 'Sacrificium Lustrale: The Death of Mettius Fufetius (Livy I, 28), Studies in Roman Lustration Ritual I', *MNIR* 37: 97–115.

—— (1980) 'Destruction, *Devotio* and Despair in a Situation of Anomy: the Mourning for Germanicus in Triple Perspective', in *Perennitas. Studi in onore di Angelo Brelich*, Rome, 541–618.

—— (1987) 'Greek Myth and Ritual: The Case of Kronos', in J. Bremmer (ed.), *Interpretations of Greek Mythology*, London and Sydney, 121–52.

—— (1990) 'What's Sauce for the Goose is Sauce for the Gander: Myth and Ritual, Old and New', in L. Edmunds (ed.), *Approaches to Greek Myth*, Baltimore and London, 25–90.

Veyne, P. (1988) *Did the Greeks Believe in Their Myths? An Essay on the Constitutive Imagination*, trans. P. Wissing, Chicago and London.

Vidal-Naquet, P. (1981) 'Hunting and Sacrifice in Aeschylus' *Oresteia*', in J.-P. Vernant and P. Vidal-Naquet, *Tragedy and Myth in Ancient Greece*, trans. J. Lloyd, Sussex and Atlantic Highlands, N.J., 150–74.

—— (1986) 'The Immortal Slave-Women of Athena Ilias', in P. Vidal-Naquet, *The Black Hunter. Forms of Thought and Forms of Society in the Greek World*, trans. A. Szegedy-Maszak, Baltimore and London, 189–204.

Villa, P., Bouville, C., Courtin, J., Helmer, D., Mahieu, E., Shipman, P., Belluomini, G., and Branca, M. (1986) 'Cannibalism in the Neolithic', *Science* 233: 431–7.

Vollgraff, W. (1904) 'Fouilles d'Argos', *BCH* 28: 364–99.

Vürtheim, J. (1907) *De Aiacis Origine, Cultu, Patria*, Leiden.

Waage, F. O. (1949) 'An Early Helladic Well near Old Corinth', in *Commemorative Studies in Honor of Theodore Leslie Shear*, Hesperia Supplement 8, Athens, 415–22.

Wace, A. J. B. (1932) *Chamber Tombs at Mycenae*, Archaeologia 82, Oxford.

Wachsmuth, W. (1846) *Hellenische Altertumskunde*, 2 vols, 2nd edn: Halle.

Walbank, F. W. (1957–79) *A Historical Commentary on Polybius*, 3 vols, Oxford.

Wall, S. M., Musgrave, J. H., and Warren, P. M. (1986) 'Human Bones from a Late Minoan IB House at Knossos', *BSA* 81: 333–88.

Warren, P. (1972) *Myrtos. An Early Bronze Age Settlement in Crete*, British School of Archaeology at Athens supplementary vol. 7, London.

—— (1980–1) 'Knossos: Stratigraphical Museum Site', *The British School at Athens. Annual Report of the Managing Committee* 1980–1: 18–21.

—— (1981a) 'Knossos: Stratigraphical Museum Excavations 1978–1980, Part 1', *AR* 1981: 73–92.

—— (1981b) 'Minoan Crete and Ecstatic Religion: Preliminary Observations on the 1979 Excavations at Knossos', in R. Hägg and N. Marinatos (eds), *Sanctuaries and Cults in the Aegean Bronze Age*, Skrifter Utgivna av Svenska Institutet i Athen, 4°, 28, Stockholm, 155–66.

—— (1984) 'Knossos: New Excavations and Discoveries', *Archaeology* 37.4: 48–55.

Warren, P., and Hankey, V. (1989) *Aegean Bronze Age Chronology*, Bristol.

Weber, L. (1925) 'Androgeos', *ArchRW* 23: 34–44 and 229–51.

Wehrli, F. (ed.) (1967–9) *Die Schule des Aristoteles. Texte und Kommentar*, 10 vols, 2nd edn: Basel and Stuttgart.

Wells, C. (1964) *Bones, Bodies and Disease. Evidence of Disease and Abnormality in Early Man*, London.

West, M. L. (ed.) (1971–2) *Iambi et Elegi Graeci ante Alexandrem Cantati*, 2 vols, Oxford.

—— (1974) *Studies in Greek Elegy and Iambus*, Untersuchungen zu antiken Literatur und Geschichte 14, Berlin and New York.

—— (1983) *The Orphic Poems*, Oxford.

Wide, S. (1893) *Lakonische Kulte*, Leipzig.

Wilamowitz-Moellendorff, U. von (1920) *Die Ilias und Homer*, 2nd edn: Berlin.

—— (1931–2) *Der Glaube der Hellenen*, 2 vols, Berlin.

Wilcken, U. (1923) 'Alexander der Grosse und die indischen Gymnosophisten', *Sitzungsberichte der Preussischen Akademie der Wissen-*

schaften, philosophisch-historische Klasse 1923: 150–83.
Wilhelm, A. (1911) 'Die lokrische Mädcheninschrift', *ÖJ* 14: 163–256.
Winkler, J. (1980) 'Lollianos and the Desperadoes', *JHS* 100: 155–81.
Woolley, C. L. (1934) *Ur Excavations*, vol. 2, *The Royal Cemetery. A Report on the Predynastic and Sargonid Graves Excavated between 1926 and 1931*, London.
Wüst, E. (1952) s.v. Polyxena (1), *RE* 21: 1840–50.
Yon, M. (1980) 'Zeus de Salamine', in R. Bloch (ed.), *Recherches sur les religions de l'antiquité classique*, Hautes études du monde gréco-romain 10, Geneva and Rome, 85–103.
Zeitlin, F. I. (1965) 'The Motif of the Corrupted Sacrifice in Aeschylus' *Oresteia*', *TAPA* 96: 463–508.
—— (1966) 'Postscript to the Sacrificial Imagery in the *Oresteia* (*Ag.* 1235–37)', *TAPA* 97: 645–53.
—— (1970) 'The Argive Festival of Hera and Euripides' *Electra*', *TAPA* 101: 645–69.
Zivanović, S. (1982) *Ancient Diseases. The Elements of Palaeopathology*, trans. L. F. Edwards, London.

Index locorum

Square brackets around authors and works indicate false or doubtful attribution.

Subject index

For ancient authors and works see also the Index locorum.